ALL GLORY TO ŚRĪ GURU AND GAURĀṄGA

ŚRĪMAD BHĀGAVATAM

of

KṚṢṆA-DVAIPĀYANA VYĀSA

नैवोद्विजे पर दुरत्ययवैतरण्या-
स्त्वद्वीर्यगायनमहामृतमग्नचित्तः ।
शोचे ततो विमुखचेतस इन्द्रियार्थ-
मायासुखाय भरमुद्वहतो विमूढान् ॥

naivodvije para duratyaya-vaitaraṇyās
tvad-vīrya-gāyana-mahāmṛta-magna-cittaḥ
śoce tato vimukha-cetasa indriyārtha-
māyā-sukhāya bharam udvahato vimūḍhān

(p. 257)

BOOKS by
His Divine Grace A. C. Bhaktivedanta Swami Prabhupāda

Bhagavad-gītā As It Is
Śrīmad-Bhāgavatam, Cantos 1-7 (21 Vols.)
Śrī Caitanya-caritāmṛta (17 Vols.)
Teachings of Lord Caitanya
The Nectar of Devotion
The Nectar of Instruction
Śrī Īśopaniṣad
Easy Journey to Other Planets
Kṛṣṇa Consciousness: The Topmost Yoga System
Kṛṣṇa, the Supreme Personality of Godhead (3 Vols.)
Perfect Questions, Perfect Answers
Transcendental Teachings of Prāhlad Mahārāja
Kṛṣṇa, the Reservoir of Pleasure
Life Comes from Life
The Perfection of Yoga
Beyond Birth and Death
On the Way to Kṛṣṇa
Rāja-vidyā: The King of Knowledge
Elevation to Kṛṣṇa Consciousness
Kṛṣṇa Consciousness: The Matchless Gift
Back to Godhead Magazine (Founder)

A complete catalogue is available upon request

The Bhaktivedanta Book Trust
3764 Watseka Avenue
Los Angeles, California 90034

ŚRĪMAD BHĀGAVATAM

Seventh Canto
"The Science of God"

(Part Two—Chapters 6–10)

With the Original Sanskrit Text,
Its Roman Transliteration, Synonyms,
Translation and Elaborate Purports

by

His Divine Grace
A.C. Bhaktivedanta Swami Prabhupāda
Founder-*Ācārya* of the International Society for Krishna Consciousness

THE BHAKTIVEDANTA BOOK TRUST
New York · Los Angeles · London · Bombay

Readers interested in the subject matter of this book
are invited by the International Society for Krishna Consciousness
to correspond with its Secretary.

International Society for Krishna Consciousness
3764 Watseka Avenue
Los Angeles, California 90034

Library of Congress Catalogue Card Number: 73-169353
International Standard Book Number: 0-912776-87-0

First printing, 1976: 20,000 copies

Printed in the United States of America

Table of Contents

Preface

We must know the present need of human society. And what is that need? Human society is no longer bounded by geographical limits to particular countries or communities. Human society is broader than in the Middle Ages, and the world tendency is toward one state or one human society. The ideals of spiritual communism, according to *Śrīmad-Bhāgavatam*, are based more or less on the oneness of the entire human society, nay, on the entire energy of living beings. The need is felt by great thinkers to make this a successful ideology. *Śrīmad-Bhāgavatam* will fill this need in human society. It begins, therefore, with the aphorism of Vedānta philosophy (*janmādy asya yataḥ*) to establish the ideal of a common cause.

Human society, at the present moment, is not in the darkness of oblivion. It has made rapid progress in the field of material comforts, education and economic development throughout the entire world. But there is a pinprick somewhere in the social body at large, and therefore there are large-scale quarrels, even over less important issues. There is need of a clue as to how humanity can become one in peace, friendship and prosperity with a common cause. *Śrīmad-Bhāgavatam* will fill this need, for it is a cultural presentation for the re-spiritualization of the entire human society.

Śrīmad-Bhāgavatam should be introduced also in the schools and colleges, for it is recommended by the great student devotee Prahlāda Mahārāja in order to change the demonic face of society.

kaumāra ācaret prājño
dharmān bhāgavatān iha
durlabhaṁ mānuṣaṁ janma
tad apy adhruvam arthadam
(*Bhāg.* 7.6.1)

Disparity in human society is due to lack of principles in a godless civilization. There is God, or the Almighty One, from whom everything emanates, by whom everything is maintained and in whom everything is merged to rest. Material science has tried to find the ultimate source of creation very insufficiently, but it is a fact that there is one ultimate source of everything that be. This ultimate source is explained rationally and authoritatively in the beautiful *Bhāgavatam* or *Śrīmad-Bhāgavatam.*

Śrīmad-Bhāgavatam is the transcendental science not only for knowing the ultimate source of everything but also for knowing our relation with Him and our duty towards perfection of the human society on the basis of this perfect knowledge. It is powerful reading matter in the Sanskrit language, and it is now rendered into English elaborately so that simply by a careful reading one will know God perfectly well, so much so that the reader will be sufficiently educated to defend himself from the onslaught of atheists. Over and above this, the reader will be able to convert others to accept God as a concrete principle.

Śrīmad-Bhāgavatam begins with the definition of the ultimate source. It is a bona fide commentary on the *Vedānta-sūtra* by the same author, Śrīla Vyāsadeva, and gradually it develops into nine cantos up to the highest state of God realization. The only qualification one needs to study this great book of transcendental knowledge is to proceed step by step cautiously and not jump forward haphazardly as with an ordinary book. It should be gone through chapter by chapter, one after another. The reading matter is so arranged with its original Sanskrit text, its English transliteration, synonyms, translation and purports so that one is sure to become a God realized soul at the end of finishing the first nine cantos.

The Tenth Canto is distinct from the first nine cantos, because it deals directly with the transcendental activities of the Personality of Godhead Śrī Kṛṣṇa. One will be unable to capture the effects of the Tenth Canto without going through the first nine cantos. The book is complete in twelve cantos, each independent, but it is good for all to read them in small installments one after another.

I must admit my frailties in presenting *Śrīmad-Bhāgavatam,* but still I am hopeful of its good reception by the thinkers and leaders of society on the strength of the following statement of *Śrīmad-Bhāgavatam.*

tad-vāg-visargo janatāgha-viplavo
yasmin pratiślokam abaddhavaty api

nāmāny anantasya yaśo 'ṅkitāni yac
chṛṇvanti gāyanti gṛṇanti sādhavaḥ
(*Bhāg.* 1.5.11)

"On the other hand, that literature which is full with descriptions of the transcendental glories of the name, fame, form and pastimes of the unlimited Supreme Lord is a transcendental creation meant to bring about a revolution in the impious life of a misdirected civilization. Such transcendental literatures, even though irregularly composed, are heard, sung and accepted by purified men who are thoroughly honest."

Oṁ tat sat

A. C. Bhaktivedanta Swami

Introduction

"This *Bhāgavata Purāṇa* is as brilliant as the sun, and it has arisen just after the departure of Lord Kṛṣṇa to His own abode, accompanied by religion, knowledge, etc. Persons who have lost their vision due to the dense darkness of ignorance in the age of Kali shall get light from this *Purāṇa.*" (*Śrīmad-Bhāgavatam* 1.3.43)

The timeless wisdom of India is expressed in the *Vedas,* ancient Sanskrit texts that touch upon all fields of human knowledge. Originally preserved through oral tradition, the *Vedas* were first put into writing five thousand years ago by Śrīla Vyāsadeva, the "literary incarnation of God." After compiling the *Vedas,* Vyāsadeva set forth their essence in the aphorisms known as *Vedānta-sūtras. Śrīmad-Bhāgavatam* is Vyāsadeva's commentary on his own *Vedānta-sūtras.* It was written in the maturity of his spiritual life under the direction of Nārada Muni, his spiritual master. Referred to as "the ripened fruit of the tree of Vedic literature," *Śrīmad-Bhāgavatam* is the most complete and authoritative exposition of Vedic knowledge.

After compiling the *Bhāgavatam,* Vyāsa impressed the synopsis of it upon his son, the sage Śukadeva Gosvāmī. Śukadeva Gosvāmī subsequently recited the entire *Bhāgavatam* to Mahārāja Parīkṣit in an assembly of learned saints on the bank of the Ganges at Hastināpura (now Delhi). Mahārāja Parīkṣit was the emperor of the world and was a great *rājarṣi* (saintly king). Having received a warning that he would die within a week, he renounced his entire kingdom and retired to the bank of the Ganges to fast until death and receive spiritual enlightenment. The *Bhāgavatam* begins with Emperor Parīkṣit's sober inquiry to Śukadeva Gosvāmī:

> "You are the spiritual master of great saints and devotees. I am therefore begging you to show the way of perfection for all persons, and especially for one who is about to die. Please let me know what a man should hear, chant, remember and worship, and also what he should not do. Please explain all this to me."

Śukadeva Gosvāmī's answer to this question, and numerous other questions posed by Mahārāja Parīkṣit, concerning everything from the nature of the self to the origin of the universe, held the assembled sages in rapt attention continuously for the seven days leading to the King's death. The sage Sūta Gosvāmī, who was present on the bank of the Ganges when Śukadeva Gosvāmī first recited *Śrīmad-Bhāgavatam*, later repeated the *Bhāgavatam* before a gathering of sages in the forest of Naimiṣāraṇya. Those sages, concerned about the spiritual welfare of the people in general, had gathered to perform a long, continuous chain of sacrifices to counteract the degrading influence of the incipient age of Kali. In response to the sages' request that he speak the essence of Vedic wisdom, Sūta Gosvāmī repeated from memory the entire eighteen thousand verses of *Śrīmad-Bhāgavatam*, as spoken by Śukadeva Gosvāmī to Mahārāja Parīkṣit.

The reader of *Śrīmad-Bhāgavatam* hears Sūta Gosvāmī relate the questions of Mahārāja Parīkṣit and the answers of Śukadeva Gosvāmī. Also, Sūta Gosvāmī sometimes responds directly to questions put by Śaunaka Ṛṣi, the spokesman for the sages gathered at Naimiṣāraṇya. One therefore simultaneously hears two dialogues: one between Mahārāja Parīkṣit and Śukadeva Gosvāmī on the bank of the Ganges, and another at Naimiṣāraṇya between Sūta Gosvāmī and the sages at Naimiṣāraṇya Forest, headed by Śaunaka Ṛṣi. Furthermore, while instructing King Parīkṣit, Śukadeva Gosvāmī often relates historical episodes and gives accounts of lengthy philosophical discussions between such great souls as the saint Maitreya and his disciple Vidura. With this understanding of the history of the *Bhāgavatam*, the reader will easily be able to follow its intermingling of dialogues and events from various sources. Since philosophical wisdom, not chronological order, is most important in the text, one need only be attentive to the subject matter of *Śrīmad-Bhāgavatam* to appreciate fully its profound message.

The translator of this edition compares the *Bhāgavatam* to sugar candy—wherever you taste it, you will find it equally sweet and relishable. Therefore, to taste the sweetness of the *Bhāgavatam*, one may begin by reading any of its volumes. After such an introductory taste, however, the serious reader is best advised to go back to Volume One of the First Canto and then proceed through the *Bhāgavatam*, volume after volume, in its natural order.

This edition of the *Bhāgavatam* is the first complete English translation of this important text with an elaborate commentary, and it is the first widely available to the English-speaking public. It is the product of the scholarly and devotional effort of His Divine Grace A. C. Bhaktivedanta Swami Prabhupāda, the world's most distinguished teacher of Indian religious and philosophical thought. His consummate Sanskrit scholarship and intimate familiarity with Vedic culture and thought as well as the modern way of life combine to reveal to the West a magnificent exposition of this important classic.

Readers will find this work of value for many reasons. For those interested in the classical roots of Indian civilization, it serves as a vast reservoir of detailed information on virtually every one of its aspects. For students of comparative philosophy and religion, the *Bhāgavatam* offers a penetrating view into the meaning of India's profound spiritual heritage. To sociologists and anthropologists, the *Bhāgavatam* reveals the practical workings of a peaceful and scientifically organized Vedic culture, whose institutions were integrated on the basis of a highly developed spiritual world view. Students of literature will discover the *Bhāgavatam* to be a masterpiece of majestic poetry. For students of psychology, the text provides important perspectives on the nature of consciousness, human behavior and the philosophical study of identity. Finally, to those seeking spiritual insight, the *Bhāgavatam* offers simple and practical guidance for attainment of the highest self-knowledge and realization of the Absolute Truth. The entire multivolume text, presented by the Bhaktivedanta Book Trust, promises to occupy a significant place in the intellectual, cultural and spiritual life of modern man for a long time to come.

—The Publishers

His Divine Grace
A. C. Bhaktivedanta Swami Prabhupāda
Founder-Ācārya of the International Society for Krishna Consciousness

PLATE ONE

When Hiraṇyakaśipu, the King of the demons, went to Mandarācala mountain to execute severe austerities, in his absence the demigods, headed by King Indra, made a great attempt to subdue all the demons in warfare. When the leaders of the demons, who were being killed one after another, saw the unprecedented exertion of the demigods in fighting, they began to flee, scattering themselves in all directions. Simply to protect their lives, they hastily fled from their homes, wives, children, animals and household paraphernalia. The victorious demigods plundered the palace of Hiraṇyakaśipu and destroyed everything within it. Then Indra, King of heaven, arrested Prahlāda's mother. As she was being led away, crying in fear like a small bird captured by a vulture, the great sage Nārada appeared on the scene and saw her in that condition. Nārada Muni said, "O Indra, King of the demigods, this woman is certainly sinless. You should not drag her off in this merciless way. You must immediately release her." King Indra said, "In the womb of this woman, the wife of the demon Hiraṇyakaśipu, is the seed of that great demon. Therefore, let her remain in our custody until her child is delivered, and then we shall release her." Nārada Muni replied, "The child within this woman's womb is faultless and sinless. Indeed, he is a great devotee, a powerful servant of the Supreme Personality of Godhead. Therefore you will not be able to kill him." *(pp. 43–48)*

PLATE TWO

Lord Kṛṣṇa, who is known as Govinda, is the supreme controller. He has an eternal, blissful, spiritual body. He is the origin of all. He has no other origin, for He is the prime cause of all causes. In this material world, to render service to the lotus feet of Govinda, and to see Him everywhere, is the only goal of life. *(pp. 114–115)*

PLATE THREE

Wanting his son Prahlāda to be trained as a ruthless diplomatic ruler, King Hiraṇyakaśipu sent him to school along with the sons of other demons. Prahlāda's teachers tried systematically and unceasingly to teach him about politics, economic development, sense gratification and other mundane topics, but the great devotee Prahlāda did not like such instructions, for they were based on the duality of worldly affairs. Whenever the teachers went home to attend to their household affairs, Prahlāda Mahārāja, who was the supremely learned person, would very kindly teach his class friends about the uselessness of the materialistic way of life. He explained the transcendental science of knowing the Supreme Personality of Godhead, Kṛṣṇa, and requested his friends to engage in the Lord's devotional service, especially by chanting His holy names. All the sons of the demons appreciated Prahlāda's transcendental instructions and took them very seriously. They rejected the materialistic instructions given by their teachers. *(pp. 1–119)*

PLATE FOUR

When Prahlāda's teachers observed that all the students were becoming advanced in Kṛṣṇa consciousness, they approached King Hiraṇyakaśipu and described the situation. The King became extremely angry and decided to kill his son Prahlāda. Cursing him again and again, Hiraṇyakaśipu took up his sword and with great anger struct his fist against a nearby column. Then from within the pillar came a fearful sound, which appeared to crack the covering of the universe. At that time the Supreme Personality of Godhead, exhibiting the wonderful, fearsome form of Lord Nṛsiṁhadeva, emerged from the pillar. Lord Nṛsiṁhadeva was half man and half lion. His angry eyes resembled molten gold, His teeth were deadly, His nostrils and gaping mouth appeared like caves of a mountain, His jaws parted fearfully and His entire body touched the sky. His neck was very short and thick, His chest broad, His waist thin, and the hairs on His body as white as the rays of the moon. His arms, spread in all directions, carried His conchshell, disc, club, lotus and other weapons. The demon Hiraṇyakaśipu attacked Nṛsiṁhadeva with great force, but the Lord captured him and placed him on His lap, supporting him with His thighs. Then, in the doorway of the assembly hall, the Lord very easily tore the demon to pieces with the nails of His hand. Lord Nṛsiṁhadeva's mouth and mane were sprinkled with drops of blood, and his fierce eyes, full of anger, were impossible to look at. Licking the edge of His mouth with His tongue, the Supreme Personality of Godhead, Nṛsiṁhadeva, decorated with a garland of intestines taken from Hiraṇyakaśipu's abdomen, resembled a lion that has just killed an elephant. *(pp. 120–150)*

PLATE FIVE

After He had killed the great demon Hiraṇyakaśipu, the Supreme Personality of Godhead Lord Nṛsiṁhadeva, who had many, many arms, threw the demon's body aside and turned toward his soldiers. These soldiers had come in thousands to battle Lord Nṛsiṁhadeva with raised weapons and were very faithful followers of Hiraṇyakaśipu, but the Lord killed all of them merely with the ends of His nails. The hair on Nṛsiṁhadeva's head shook the clouds and scattered them here and there, His glaring eyes stole the effulgence of the luminaries of the sky, and His breathing agitated the seas and oceans. Because of His roaring, all the elephants in the world began to cry in fear. Airplanes were thrown into outer space and the upper planetary system by the hair on Nṛsiṁhadeva's head. Because of the pressure of the Lord's lotus feet, the earth appeared to slip from its position, and all the hills and mountains sprang up because of His intolerable force. Because of the Lord's bodily effulgence, both the sky and all directions diminished in their natural illumination. Manifesting a full effulgence and a fearsome countenance, Lord Nṛsiṁhadeva exhibited His great anger, power and opulence. *(pp. 151–154)*

PLATE SIX

After killing the soldiers of the demon Hiraṇyakaśipu, the Supreme Lord Nṛsiṁhadeva sat down in the assembly hall on the excellent throne of the King. Lord Nṛsiṁhadeva appeared in such a fearsome form, however, that none of the demigods could directly approach Him. Lord Brahmā then requested Prahlāda Mahārāja, who was standing very near him: "My dear son, Lord Nṛsiṁhadeva is extremely angry at your demoniac father. Please go forward and appease the Lord." Although the exalted devotee Prahlāda was only a little boy, he accepted Lord Brahmā's words. He gradually proceeded toward Lord Nṛsiṁhadeva and fell down to offer his respectful obeisances with folded hands. When Lord Nṛsiṁhadeva saw the small boy Prahlāda Mahārāja prostrated at the soles of His lotus feet, He became most ecstatic in affection toward His devotee. Raising Prahlāda, the Lord placed His lotus hand upon the boy's head. By the touch of Lord Nṛsiṁhadeva's hand on his head, Prahlāda was completely freed of all material contaminations and desires, as if he had been thoroughly cleansed. Therefore he at one became transcendentally situated, and all the symptoms of ecstasy became manifest in his body. His heart filled with love, and his eyes with tears, and thus he was able to completely capture the lotus feet of the Lord within the core of his heart. Prahlāda Mahārāja fixed his mind and sight upon Lord Nṛsiṁhadeva with full attention in complete trance. With a fixed mind, he began to offer prayers. *(pp. 154–191)*

PLATE SEVEN

Lord Nṛsiṁhadeva, the Supreme Personality of Godhead, was greatly pleased by the pure devotion of Prahlāda Mahārāja, and ordered him to take charge of his father's kingdom. Thereafter, the inauguration of Prahlāda Mahārāja was performed by Lord Brahmā in the presence of other saintly persons and demigods. Thus, as ordered by the Supreme Personality of Godhead, Prahlāda Mahārāja was made the King of all the demons and giants in the universe. Prahlāda Mahārāja was the most exalted devotee of the Lord, and never desired any kind of material opulence. Nonetheless, the Supreme Lord allowed him to enjoy the kingdom created by his father. Whenever and wherever there are peaceful, equipoised devotees who are well behaved and decorated with all good qualities, that place and the dynasties there, even if condemned, are purified. Those who follow Prahlāda's example will naturally become pure devotees of the Lord. He is the best example of a devotee, and others should follow in his footsteps. *(pp. 295–316)*

CHAPTER SIX

Prahlāda Instructs His Demoniac Schoolmates

This chapter describes Prahlāda Mahārāja's instructions to his class friends. In speaking to his friends, who were all sons of demons, Prahlāda Mahārāja stressed that every living entity, especially in human society, must be interested in spiritual realization from the very beginning of life. When human beings are children, they should be taught that the Supreme Personality of Godhead is the worshipable Deity for everyone. One should not be very much interested in material enjoyment; instead, one should be satisfied with whatever material profits are easily obtainable, and because the duration of one's life is very short, one should utilize every moment for spiritual advancement. One may wrongly think, "In the beginning of our lives let us enjoy material facilities, and in old age we may become Kṛṣṇa conscious." Such materialistic thoughts are always useless because in old age one cannot be trained in the spiritual way of life. Therefore, from the very beginning of life, one should engage in devotional service (*śravaṇaṁ kīrtanaṁ viṣṇoḥ*). This is the duty of all living entities. Material education is infected by the three modes of nature, but spiritual education, for which there is a great need in human society, is transcendental. Prahlāda Mahārāja disclosed the secret of how he had received instructions from Nārada Muni. By accepting the lotus feet of Prahlāda Mahārāja, who is in the *paramparā* succession, one will be able to understand the mode of spiritual life. In accepting this mode of activity, there is no need for material qualifications.

After Prahlāda Mahārāja's class friends had listened to Prahlāda Mahārāja, they inquired how he had become so learned and advanced. In this way the chapter ends.

TEXT 1

श्रीप्रह्राद उवाच

कौमार आचरेत्प्राज्ञो धर्मान् भागवतानिह ।
दुर्लभं मानुषं जन्म तदप्यध्रुवमर्थदम् ॥ १ ॥

śrī-prahrāda uvāca
kaumāra ācaret prājño
dharmān bhāgavatān iha
durlabhaṁ mānuṣaṁ janma
tad apy adhruvam arthadam

śrī-prahrādaḥ uvāca—Prahlāda Mahārāja said; *kaumāraḥ*—in the tender age of childhood; *ācaret*—should practice; *prājñaḥ*—one who is intelligent; *dharmān*—occupational duties; *bhāgavatān*—which are devotional service to the Supreme Personality of Godhead; *iha*—in this life; *durlabham*—very rarely obtained; *mānuṣam*—human; *janma*—birth; *tat*—that; *api*—even; *adhruvam*—impermanent, temporary; *artha-dam*—full of meaning.

TRANSLATION

Prahlāda Mahārāja said: One who is sufficiently intelligent should use the human form of body from the very beginning of life—in other words, from the tender age of childhood—to practice the activities of devotional service, giving up all other engagements. The human body is most rarely achieved, and although temporary like other bodies, it is meaningful because in human life one can perform devotional service. Even a slight amount of sincere devotional service can give one complete perfection.

PURPORT

The whole purpose of Vedic civilization and of reading the *Vedas* is to attain the perfect stage of devotional service in the human form of life. According to the Vedic system, therefore, from the very beginning of life the *brahmacarya* system is introduced so that from one's very childhood—from the age of five years—one can practice modifying one's human activities so as to engage perfectly in devotional service. As confirmed in *Bhagavad-gītā* (2.40), *svalpam apy asya dharmasya trāyate mahato bhayāt:* "Even a little advancement on this path can protect one from the most dangerous type of fear." Modern civilization, not referring to the verdicts of Vedic literature, is so cruel to the members of human society that instead of teaching children to become *brahmacārīs,* it teaches mothers to kill their children even in the womb, on the plea of curbing the increase of population. And if by chance a child is saved, he is educated only for sense gratification. Gradually, throughout the entire world, human society is losing interest in the perfection of life. Indeed, men are living like cats and dogs, spoiling the duration of their human lives by actually preparing to transmigrate again to the degraded species among the 8,400,000 forms of life. The Kṛṣṇa consciousness movement is anxious to serve human society by teaching people to perform devotional service, which can save a human being from being degraded again to animal life. As already stated by Prahlāda Mahārāja, *bhāgavata-dharma* consists of *śravaṇaṁ kīrtanaṁ viṣṇoḥ smaraṇaṁ pāda-sevanam/ arcanaṁ vandanaṁ dāsyaṁ sakhyam ātma-nivedanam.* In all the schools, colleges and universities, and at home, all children and youths should be taught to hear about the Supreme Personality of Godhead. In other words, they should be taught to hear the instructions of *Bhagavad-gītā*, to put them into practice in their lives, and thus to become strong in devotional service, free from fear of being degraded to animal life. Following *bhāgavata-dharma* has been made extremely easy in this age of Kali. The *śāstra* says:

harer nāma harer nāma
harer nāmaiva kevalam
kalau nāsty eva nāsty eva
nāsty eva gatir anyathā

One need only chant the Hare Kṛṣṇa *mahā-mantra.* Everyone engaged in the practice of chanting the Hare Kṛṣṇa *mahā-mantra* will be completely cleansed, from the core of his heart, and be saved from the cycle of birth and death.

TEXT 2

यथा हि पुरुषस्येह विष्णोः पादोपसर्पणम् ।
यदेष सर्वभूतानां प्रिय आत्मेश्वरः सुहृत् ॥ २ ॥

yathā hi puruṣasyeha
viṣṇoḥ pādopasarpaṇam

yad eṣa sarva-bhūtānāṁ
priya ātmeśvaraḥ suhṛt

yathā—in order that; *hi*—indeed; *puruṣasya*—of a living entity; *iha*—here; *viṣṇoḥ*—of Lord Viṣṇu, the Supreme Personality of Godhead; *pāda-upasarpaṇam*—approaching the lotus feet; *yat*—because; *eṣaḥ*—this; *sarva-bhūtānām*—of all living entities; *priyaḥ*—the dear one; *ātma-īśvaraḥ*—the master of the soul, the Supersoul; *suhṛt*—the best well-wisher and friend.

TRANSLATION

The human form of life affords one a chance to return home, back to Godhead. Therefore every living entity, especially in the human form of life, must engage in devotional service to the lotus feet of Lord Viṣṇu. This devotional service is natural because Lord Viṣṇu, the Supreme Personality of Godhead, is the most beloved, the master of the soul, and the well-wisher of all other living beings.

PURPORT

The Lord says in *Bhagavad-gītā* (5.29):

bhoktāraṁ yajña-tapasāṁ
sarva-loka-maheśvaram
suhṛdaṁ sarva-bhūtānāṁ
jñātvā māṁ śāntim ṛcchati

"The sages, knowing Me as the ultimate purpose of all sacrifices and austerities, the Supreme Lord of all planets and demigods and the benefactor and well-wisher of all living entities, attain peace from the pangs of material miseries." Simply by understanding these three facts—that the Supreme Lord, Viṣṇu, is the proprietor of the entire creation, that He is the best well-wishing friend of all living entities, and that He is the supreme enjoyer of everything—one becomes peaceful and happy. For this transcendental happiness, the living entity has wandered throughout the universe in different forms of life and different planetary systems, but because he has forgotten his intimate relationship with Viṣṇu, he has merely suffered, life after life. Therefore, the educational system in the human form of life should be so perfect that one will understand his intimate relationship with God, or Viṣṇu. Every living entity has an intimate relationship with God. One should therefore glorify the Lord in the adoration of *śānta-rasa* or revive his eternal relationship with Viṣṇu as a servant in *dāsya-rasa*, a friend in *sakhya-rasa*, a parent in *vātsalya-rasa* or a conjugal lover in *mādhurya-rasa*. All these relationships are on the platform of love. Viṣṇu is the center of love for everyone, and therefore the duty of everyone is to engage in the loving service of the Lord. As stated by the Supreme Personality of Godhead (*Bhāg.* 3.25.38), *yeṣām ahaṁ priya ātmā sutaś ca sakhā guruḥ suhṛdo daivam iṣṭam.* In any form of life, we are related with Viṣṇu, who is the most beloved, the Supersoul, son, friend and *guru.* Our eternal relationship with God can be revived in the human form of life, and that should be the goal of education. Indeed, that is the perfection of life and the perfection of education.

TEXT 3

सुखमैन्द्रियकं दैत्या देहयोगेन देहिनाम् ।
सर्वत्र लभ्यते दैवाद्यथा दुःखमयत्नतः ॥ ३ ॥

sukham aindriyakaṁ daityā
deha-yogena dehinām
sarvatra labhyate daivād
yathā duḥkham ayatnataḥ

sukham—happiness; *aindriyakam*—with reference to the material senses; *daityāḥ*—O my dear friends born in demoniac families; *deha-yogena*—because of possessing a particular type of material body; *dehinām*—of all embodied living entities; *sarvatra*—everywhere (in any form of life); *labhyate*—is obtainable; *daivāt*—by a superior arrangement; *yathā*—just as; *duḥkham*—unhappiness; *ayatnataḥ*—without endeavor.

TRANSLATION

Prahlāda Mahārāja continued: My dear friends born of demoniac families, the happiness perceived with reference to the

sense objects by contact with the body can be obtained in any form of life, according to one's past fruitive activities. Such happiness is automatically obtained without endeavor, just as we obtain distress.

PURPORT

In the material world, in any form of life, there is some so-called happiness and so-called distress. No one invites distress in order to suffer, but still it comes. Similarly, even if we do not endeavor to obtain the advantages of material happiness, we shall obtain them automatically. This happiness and distress are obtainable in any form of life, without endeavor. Thus there is no need to waste time and energy fighting against distress or working very hard for happiness. Our only business in the human form of life should be to revive our relationship with the Supreme Personality of Godhead and thus become qualified to return home, back to Godhead. Material happiness and distress come as soon as we accept a material body, regardless of what form. We cannot avoid such happiness and distress under any circumstances. The best use of human life, therefore, lies in reviving our relationship with the Supreme Lord, Viṣṇu.

TEXT 4

तत्प्रयासो न कर्तव्यो यत आयुर्व्ययः परम् ।
न तथा विन्दते क्षेमं मुकुन्दचरणाम्बुजम् ॥ ४ ॥

tat-prayāso na kartavyo
yata āyur-vyayaḥ param
na tathā vindate kṣemaṁ
mukunda-caraṇāmbujam

tat—for that (sense gratification and economic development); *prayāsaḥ*—endeavor; *na*—not; *kartavyaḥ*—to be done; *yataḥ*—from which; *āyuḥ-vyayaḥ*—waste of the duration of life; *param*—only or ultimately; *na*—nor; *tathā*—in that way; *vindate*—enjoys; *kṣemam*—the ultimate goal of life; *mukunda*—of the Supreme Personality of Godhead, who can deliver one from the material clutches; *caraṇa-ambu-jam*—the lotus feet.

TRANSLATION

Endeavors merely for sense gratification or material happiness through economic development are not to be performed, for they result only in a loss of time and energy, with no actual profit. If one's endeavors are directed toward Kṛṣṇa consciousness, one can surely attain the spiritual platform of self-realization. There is no such benefit from engaging oneself in economic development.

PURPORT

We see materialistic persons busily engaged in economic development all day and all night, trying to increase their material opulence, but even if we suppose that they get some benefit from such endeavors, that does not solve the real problem of their lives. Nor do they know what the real problem of life is. This is due to a lack of spiritual education. Especially in the present age, every man is in darkness, in the bodily conception of life, not knowing anything of the spirit soul and its needs. Misguided by the blind leaders of society, people consider the body to be everything, and they are engaged in trying to keep the body materially comfortable. Such a civilization is condemned because it does not lead humanity toward knowing the real goal of life. People are simply wasting time and the valuable gift of the human form because a human being who does not cultivate spiritual life but dies like the cats and dogs is degraded in his next life. From human life, such a person is put into the cycle of continuous birth and death. Thus one loses the true benefit of human life, which is to become Kṛṣṇa conscious and solve life's problems.

TEXT 5

ततो यतेत कुशलः क्षेमाय भवमाश्रितः ।
शरीरं पौरुषं यावन्न विपद्येत पुष्कलम् ॥ ५ ॥

tato yateta kuśalaḥ
kṣemāya bhavam āśritaḥ

śarīraṁ pauruṣaṁ yāvan
na vipadyeta puṣkalam

tataḥ—therefore; *yateta*—should endeavor; *kuśalaḥ*—an intelligent man interested in the ultimate goal of life; *kṣemāya*—for the real benefit of life, or for liberation from material bondage; *bhavam āśritaḥ*—who is in material existence; *śarīram*—the body; *pauruṣam*—human; *yāvat*—as long as; *na*—not; *vipadyeta*—fails; *puṣkalam*—stout and strong.

TRANSLATION

Therefore, while in material existence [bhavam āśritaḥ], a person fully competent to distinguish wrong from right must endeavor to achieve the highest goal of life as long as the body is stout and strong and is not embarrassed by dwindling.

PURPORT

As stated by Prahlāda Mahārāja at the beginning of this chapter, *kaumāra ācaret prājñaḥ.* The word *prājña* refers to one who is experienced and who can distinguish right from wrong. Such a person should not waste his energy and valuable human lifetime simply working like a cat or dog to develop his economic condition.

For one word in this verse there are two readings—*bhavam āśritaḥ* and *bhayam āśritaḥ*—but accepting the meaning of either of them will bring one to the same conclusion. *Bhayam āśritaḥ* indicates that the materialistic way of life is always fearful because at every step there is danger. Materialistic life is full of anxieties and fear (*bhayam*). Similarly, accepting the reading *bhavam āśritaḥ*, the word *bhavam* refers to unnecessary trouble and problems. For want of Kṛṣṇa consciousness, one is put into *bhavam,* being perpetually embarrassed by birth, death, old age and disease. Thus one is surely full of anxieties.

Human society should be divided into a social system of *brāhmaṇas, kṣatriyas, vaiśyas* and *śūdras,* but everyone can engage in devotional service. If one wants to live without devotional service, his status as a *brāhmaṇa, kṣatriya, vaiśya* or *śūdra* certainly has no meaning. It is said, *sthānād bhraṣṭāḥ patanty adhaḥ:* whether one is in a higher or lower division, one certainly falls down for want of Kṛṣṇa consciousness. A sane man, therefore, is always fearful of falling from his position. This is a regulative principle. One should not fall from his exalted position. The highest goal of life can be achieved as long as one's body is stout and strong. We should therefore live in such a way that we keep ourselves always healthy and strong in mind and intelligence so that we can distinguish the goal of life from a life full of problems. A thoughtful man must act in this way, learning to distinguish right from wrong, and thus attain the goal of life.

TEXT 6

पुंसो वर्षशतं ह्यायुस्तदर्धं चाजितात्मनः ।
निष्फलं यदसौ रात्र्यां शेतेऽन्धं प्रापितस्तमः ॥ ६ ॥

puṁso varṣa-śataṁ hy āyus
tad-ardhaṁ cājitātmanaḥ
niṣphalaṁ yad asau rātryāṁ
śete 'ndhaṁ prāpitas tamaḥ

puṁsaḥ—of every human being; *varṣa-śatam*—one hundred years; *hi*—indeed; *āyuḥ*—duration of life; *tat*—of that; *ardham*—half; *ca*—and; *ajita-ātmanaḥ*—of a person who is a servant of his senses; *niṣphalam*—without profit, without meaning; *yat*—because; *asau*—that person; *rātryām*—at night; *śete*—sleeps; *andham*—ignorance (forgetting his body and soul); *prāpitaḥ*—being completely possessed of; *tamaḥ*—darkness.

TRANSLATION

Every human being has a maximum duration of life of one hundred years, but for one who cannot control his senses, half of those years are completely lost because at night he sleeps twelve hours, being covered by ignorance. Therefore such a person has a lifetime of only fifty years.

PURPORT

Lord Brahmā, a human being and an ant all live for one hundred years, but their lifetimes of one hundred years are different from one another. This world is a relative world, and its relative moments of time are different. Thus the one hundred years of Brahmā are not the same as the one hundred years of a human being. From *Bhagavad-gītā* we understand that Brahmā's daytime of twelve hours equals 4,300,000 times 1,000 years (*sahasra-yuga-paryantam ahar yad brahmaṇo viduḥ*). Thus the *varṣa-śatam*, or one hundred years, are relatively different according to time, person and circumstances. As far as human beings are concerned, the calculation given here is right for the general public. Although one has a maximum of one hundred years of life, by sleeping one loses fifty years. Eating, sleeping, sex life and fear are the four bodily necessities, but to utilize the full duration of life a person desiring to advance in spiritual consciousness must reduce these activities. That will give him an opportunity to fully use his lifetime.

TEXT 7

मुग्धस्य बाल्ये कैशोरे क्रीडतो याति विंशतिः ।
जरया ग्रस्तदेहस्य यात्यकल्पस्य विंशतिः ॥ ७ ॥

mugdhasya bālye kaiśore
krīḍato yāti viṁśatiḥ
jarayā grasta-dehasya
yāty akalpasya viṁśatiḥ

mugdhasya—of a person bewildered or not in perfect knowledge; *bālye*—in childhood; *kaiśore*—in boyhood; *krīḍataḥ*—playing; *yāti*—passes; *viṁśatiḥ*—twenty years; *jarayā*—by invalidity; *grasta-dehasya*—of a person overcome; *yāti*—passes; *akalpasya*—without determination, being unable to execute even material activities; *viṁśatiḥ*—another twenty years.

TRANSLATION

In the tender age of childhood, when everyone is bewildered, one passes ten years. Similarly, in boyhood, engaged in sporting and playing, one passes another ten years. In this way, twenty years are wasted. Similarly, in old age, when one is an invalid, unable to

perform even material activities, one passes another twenty years wastefully.

PURPORT

Without Kṛṣṇa consciousness, one wastes twenty years in childhood and boyhood and another twenty years in old age, when one cannot perform any material activities and is full of anxiety about what is to be done by his sons and grandsons and how one's estate should be protected. Half of these years are spent in sleep. Furthermore, one wastes another thirty years sleeping at night during the rest of his life. Thus seventy out of one hundred years are wasted by a person who does not know the aim of life and how to utilize this human form.

TEXT 8

दुरापूरेण कामेन मोहेन च बलीयसा ।
शेषं गृहेषु सक्तस्य प्रमत्तस्यापयाति हि ॥ ८ ॥

durāpūreṇa kāmena
mohena ca balīyasā
śeṣaṁ gṛheṣu saktasya
pramattasyāpayāti hi

durāpūreṇa—which is never fulfilled; *kāmena*—by a strong aspiration to enjoy the material world; *mohena*—by bewilderment; *ca*—also; *balīyasā*—which is strong and formidable; *śeṣam*—the remaining years of life; *gṛheṣu*—to family life; *saktasya*—of one who is too attached; *pramattasya*—mad; *apayāti*—wastefully pass; *hi*—indeed.

TRANSLATION

One whose mind and senses are uncontrolled becomes increasingly attached to family life because of insatiable lusty desires and very strong illusion. In such a madman's life, the remaining years are also wasted because even during those years he cannot engage himself in devotional service.

PURPORT

This is the account of one hundred years of life. Although in this age a lifetime of one hundred years is generally not possible, even if one has one hundred years, the calculation is that fifty years are wasted in sleeping, twenty years in childhood and boyhood, and twenty years in invalidity (*jarā-vyādhi*). This leaves only a few more years, but because of too much attachment to household life, those years are also spent with no purpose, without God consciousness. Therefore, one should be trained to be a perfect *brahmacārī* in the beginning of life and then to be perfect in sense control, following the regulative principles, if one becomes a householder. From household life one is ordered to accept *vānaprastha* life and go to the forest and then accept *sannyāsa.* That is the perfection of life. From the very beginning of life, those who are *ajitendriya,* who cannot control their senses, are educated only for sense gratification, as we have seen in the Western countries. Thus the entire duration of a life of even one hundred years is wasted and misused, and at the time of death one transmigrates to another body, which may not be human. At the end of one hundred years, one who has not acted as a human being in a life of *tapasya* (austerity and penance) must certainly be embodied again in a body like those of cats, dogs and hogs. Therefore this life of lusty desires and sense gratification is extremely risky.

TEXT 9

को गृहेषु पुमान्सक्तमात्मानमजितेन्द्रियः ।
स्नेहपाशैर्दृढैर्बद्धमुत्सहेत विमोचितुम् ॥ ९ ॥

ko gṛheṣu pumān saktam
ātmānam ajitendriyaḥ
sneha-pāśair dṛḍhair baddham
utsaheta vimocitum

kaḥ—what; *gṛheṣu*—to household life; *pumān*—man; *saktam*—very much attached; *ātmānam*—his own self, the soul; *ajita-indriyaḥ*—who has not conquered the senses; *sneha-pāśaiḥ*—by the ropes of affection; *dṛḍhaiḥ*—very strong; *baddham*—bound hand and foot; *utsaheta*—is able; *vimocitum*—to liberate from material bondage.

TRANSLATION

What person too attached to household life due to being unable to control his senses can liberate himself? An attached householder is bound very strongly by ropes of affection for his family [wife, children and other relatives].

PURPORT

Prahlāda Mahārāja's first proposal was *kaumāra ācaret prājño dharmān bhāgavatān iha:* "One who is sufficiently intelligent should use the human form of body from the very beginning of life—in other words, from the tender age of childhood—to practice the activities of devotional service, giving up all other engagements." *Dharmān bhāgavatān* means the religious principle of reviving our relationship with the Supreme Personality of Godhead. For this purpose Kṛṣṇa personally advises, *sarva-dharmān parityajya mām ekaṁ śaraṇaṁ vraja:* "Give up all other duties and surrender unto Me." While in the material world we manufacture so many duties in the name of so many isms, but our actual duty is to free ourselves from the cycle of birth, death, old age and disease. For this purpose, one must first be liberated from material bondage, and especially from household life. Household life is actually a kind of license for a materially attached person by which to enjoy sense gratification under regulative principles. Otherwise there is no need of entering household life.

Before entering household life, one should be trained as a *brahmacārī*, living under the care of the *guru*, whose place is known as the *guru-kula. Brahmacārī guru-kule vasan dānto guror hitam* (*Bhāg.* 7.12.1). From the very beginning, a *brahmacārī* is trained to sacrifice everything for the benefit of the *guru.* A *brahmacārī* is advised to go begging alms door to door, addressing all women as mother, and whatever he collects goes to the benefit of the *guru.* In this way he learns how to control his senses and sacrifice everything for the *guru.* When he is fully trained, if he likes he is allowed to marry. Thus he is not an ordinary *gṛhastha* who has learned only how to satisfy his senses. A trained *gṛhastha* can gradually give up household life and go to the forest to become increasingly enlightened in spiritual life and at last take *sannyāsa.* Prahlāda Mahārāja explained to his father that to be freed from all material anxieties one should go to the forest. *Hitvātma-pātaṁ gṛham andha-kūpam.* One should give up his household, which is a place for going further and further down into the darkest regions of material existence. The first advice, therefore, is that one must give up household life (*gṛham andha-kūpam*). However, if one prefers to remain in the dark well of household life because of uncontrolled senses, he becomes increasingly entangled by ropes of affection for his wife, children, servants, house, money and so on. Such a person cannot attain liberation from material bondage. Therefore children should be taught from the very beginning of life to be first-class *brahmacārīs.* Then it will be possible for them to give up household life in the future.

To return home, back to Godhead, one must be completely free from material attachment. Therefore, *bhakti-yoga* means *vairāgya-vidyā,* the art that can help one develop a distaste for material enjoyment.

vāsudeve bhagavati
bhakti-yogaḥ prayojitaḥ
janayaty āśu vairāgyaṁ
jñānaṁ ca yad ahaitukam

"By rendering devotional service unto the Personality of Godhead, Śrī Kṛṣṇa, one immediately acquires causeless knowledge and detachment from the world." (*Bhāg.* 1.2.7) If one engages in devotional service from the beginning of life, he easily attains *vairāgya-vidyā,* or *asakti,* detachment, and becomes *jitendriya,* the controller of his senses. One who perfectly engages in devotional service is therefore called *gosvāmī* or *svāmī,* master of the senses. Unless one is master of the senses, he should not accept the renounced order of life, *sannyāsa.* A strong inclination for sense enjoyment is the cause of the material body. Without full knowledge one cannot be unattached to material enjoyment, but as long as one is not in that position one is not fit to return home, back to Godhead.

TEXT 10

को न्वर्थतृष्णां विसृजेत् प्राणेभ्योऽपि य ईप्सितः ।
यं क्रीणात्यसुभिः प्रेष्ठैस्तस्करः सेवको वणिक् ॥१०॥

ko nv artha-tṛṣṇāṁ visṛjet
prāṇebhyo 'pi ya īpsitaḥ
yaṁ krīṇāty asubhiḥ preṣṭhais
taskaraḥ sevako vaṇik

kaḥ—who; *nu*—indeed; *artha-tṛṣṇām*—a strong desire to acquire money; *visṛjet*—can give up; *prāṇebhyaḥ*—than life; *api*—indeed; *yaḥ*—which; *īpsitaḥ*—more desired; *yam*—which; *krīṇāti*—tries to acquire; *asubhiḥ*—with his own life; *preṣṭhaiḥ*—very dear; *taskaraḥ*—a thief; *sevakaḥ*—a professional servant; *vaṇik*—a merchant.

TRANSLATION

Money is so dear that one conceives of money as being sweeter than honey. Therefore, who can give up the desire to accumulate money, especially in household life? Thieves, professional servants [soldiers] and merchants try to acquire money even by risking their very dear lives.

PURPORT

How money can be dearer than life is indicated in this verse. Thieves may enter the house of a rich man to steal money at the risk of their lives. Because of trespassing, they may be killed by guns or attacked by watchdogs, but still they try to commit burglary. Why do they risk their lives? Only to get some money. Similarly, a professional soldier is recruited into the army, and he accepts such service, with the risk of dying on the battlefield, only for the sake of money. In the same way, merchants go from one country to another on boats at the risk of their lives, or they dive into the water of the sea to collect pearls and valuable gems. Thus it is practically proved—and everyone will admit—that money is sweeter than honey. One may risk everything to acquire money, and this is especially true of rich men who are too attached to household life. Formerly, of course, the members of the higher castes—the *brāhmaṇas, kṣatriyas* and *vaiśyas* (everyone but the *śūdras*)—were trained in the *guru-kula* to adhere to a life of renunciation and sense control by practicing *brahmacarya* and mystic *yoga*. Then they were allowed to enter household life. There have consequently been many instances in which great kings and emperors have given up household life. Although they were extremely opulent and were the masters of kingdoms, they could give up all their possessions because they were trained early as *brahmacārīs*. Prahlāda Mahārāja's advice is therefore very appropriate:

kaumāra ācaret prājño
dharmān bhāgavatān iha
durlabhaṁ mānuṣaṁ janma
tad apy adhruvam arthadam

"One who is sufficiently intelligent should use the human form of body from the very beginning of life—in other words, from the tender age of childhood—to practice the activities of devotional service, giving up all other engagements. The human body is most rarely achieved, and although temporary like other bodies, it is meaningful because in human life one can perform devotional service. Even a slight amount of sincere devotional service can give one complete perfection." Human society should take advantage of this instruction.

TEXTS 11–13

कथं प्रियाया अनुकम्पितायाः
सङ्गं रहस्यं रुचिरांश्च मन्त्रान् ।
सुहृत्सु तत्स्नेहसितः शिशूनां
कलाक्षराणामनुरक्तचित्तः ॥११॥
पुत्रान्स्मरंस्ता दुहितॄर्हृदय्या
भ्रातॄन् स्वसॄर्वा पितरौ च दीनौ ।
गृहान् मनोज्ञोरुपरिच्छदांश्च
वृत्तीश्च कुल्याः पशुभृत्यवर्गान् ॥१२॥
त्यजेत कोशस्कृदिवेहमानः
कर्माणि लोभादवितृप्तकामः ।
औपस्थ्यजैह्वं बहुमन्यमानः
कथं विरज्येत दुरन्तमोहः ॥१३॥

kathaṁ priyāyā anukampitāyāḥ
saṅgaṁ rahasyaṁ rucirāṁś ca mantrān
suhṛtsu tat-sneha-sitaḥ śiśūnāṁ
kalākṣarāṇām anurakta-cittaḥ

putrān smaraṁs tā duhitṝr hṛdayyā
bhrātṝn svasṝr vā pitarau ca dīnau
gṛhān manojñoru-paricchadāṁś ca
vṛttīś ca kulyāḥ paśu-bhṛtya-vargān

tyajeta kośas-kṛd ivehamānaḥ
karmāṇi lobhād avitṛpta-kāmaḥ
aupasthya-jaihvaṁ bahu-manyamānaḥ
kathaṁ virajyeta duranta-mohaḥ

katham—how; *priyāyāḥ*—of the dearmost wife; *anukampitāyāḥ*—always affectionate and compassionate; *saṅgam*—the association; *rahasyam*—solitary; *rucirān*—very pleasing and acceptable; *ca*—and; *mantrān*—instructions; *suhṛtsu*—to the wife and children; *tat-sneha-sitaḥ*—being bound by their affection; *śiśūnām*—to the small children; *kala-akṣarāṇām*—speaking in broken language; *anurakta-cittaḥ*—a person whose mind is attracted; *putrān*—the sons; *smaran*—thinking of; *tāḥ*—them; *duhitṝḥ*—the daughters (married and staying at the homes of their husbands); *hṛdayyāḥ*—always situated in the core of the heart; *bhrātṝn*—the brothers; *svasṝḥ vā*—or the sisters; *pitarau*—father and mother; *ca*—and; *dīnau*—who in old age are mostly invalids; *gṛhān*—household affairs; *manojña*—very attractive; *uru*—much; *paricchadān*—furniture; *ca*—and; *vṛttīḥ*—big sources of income (industry, business); *ca*—and; *kulyāḥ*—connected with the family; *paśu*—of animals (cows, elephants and other household animals); *bhṛtya*—servants and maidservants; *vargān*—groups; *tyajeta*—can give up; *kośaḥ-kṛt*—the silkworm; *iva*—like; *īhamānaḥ*—performing; *karmāṇi*—different activities; *lobhāt*—because of insatiable desires; *avitṛpta-kāmaḥ*—whose increasing desires are not satisfied; *aupasthya*—pleasure from the genitals; *jaihvam*—and the tongue; *bahu-manyamānaḥ*—considering as very important; *katham*—how; *virajyeta*—is able to give up; *duranta-mohaḥ*—being in great illusion.

TRANSLATION

How can a person who is most affectionate to his family, the core of his heart being always filled with their pictures, give up their association? Specifically, a wife is always very kind and sympathetic and always pleases her husband in a solitary place. Who could give up the association of such a dear and affectionate wife? Small children talk in broken language, very pleasing to hear, and their affectionate father always thinks of their sweet words. How could he give up their association? One's elderly parents and one's sons and daughters are also very dear. A daughter is especially dear to her father, and while living at her husband's house she is always in his mind. Who could give up that association? Aside from this, in household affairs there are many decorated items of household furniture, and there are also animals and servants. Who could give up such comforts? The attached householder is like a silkworm, which weaves a cocoon in which it becomes imprisoned, unable to get out. Simply for the satisfaction of two important senses—the genitals and the tongue—one is bound by material conditions. How can one escape?

PURPORT

In household affairs the first attraction is the beautiful and pleasing wife, who increases household attraction more and more. One enjoys his wife with two prominent sense organs, namely the tongue and the genitals. The wife speaks very sweetly. This is certainly an attraction. Then she prepares very palatable foods to satisfy the tongue, and when the tongue is satisfied one gains strength in the other sense organs, especially the genitals. Thus the wife gives pleasure in sexual intercourse. Household life means sex life (*yan maithunādi-gṛhamedhi-sukhaṁ hi tuccham*). This is encouraged by the tongue. Then there are children. A baby gives pleasure by speaking sweet words in broken language, and when the sons and daughters are grown up one becomes involved in their education and marriage. Then there are one's own father and mother to be taken care of, and one also becomes concerned with the social atmosphere and with pleasing his brothers and sisters. A man becomes increasingly entangled in household affairs, so much so that leaving them becomes almost impossible. Thus the household becomes *gṛham andha-kūpam*, a dark well into which the man has fallen. For such a man to get out is extremely difficult unless he is helped by a strong person, the spiritual master, who helps the fallen person with the strong rope of spiritual instructions. A fallen person should take advantage of this rope, and then the spiritual master, or the Supreme Personality of Godhead, Kṛṣṇa, will take him out of the dark well.

TEXT 14

कुटुम्बपोषाय वियन् निजायु-
न बुध्यतेऽर्थं विहतं प्रमत्तः ।
सर्वत्र तापत्रयदुःखितात्मा
निर्विद्यते न स्वकुटुम्बरामः ॥१४॥

kuṭumba-poṣāya viyan nijāyur
na budhyate 'rthaṁ vihataṁ pramattaḥ
sarvatra tāpa-traya-duḥkhitātmā
nirvidyate na sva-kuṭumba-rāmaḥ

kuṭumba—of family members; *poṣāya*—for the maintenance; *viyat*—declining; *nija-āyuḥ*—his lifetime; *na*—not; *budhyate*—understands; *artham*—the interest or purpose of life; *vihatam*—spoiled; *pramattaḥ*—being mad in material conditions; *sarvatra*—everywhere; *tāpa-traya*—by the threefold miserable conditions (*adhyātmika, adhidaivika* and *adhibautika*); *duḥkhita*—being distressed; *ātmā*—himself; *nirvidyate*—becomes remorseful; *na*—not; *sva-kuṭumba-rāmaḥ*—enjoying simply by maintaining the members of the family.

TRANSLATION

One who is too attached cannot understand that he is wasting his valuable life for the maintenance of his family. He also fails to understand that the purpose of human life, a life suitable for realization of the Absolute Truth, is being imperceptibly spoiled. However, he is very cleverly attentive to seeing that not a single

farthing is lost by mismanagement. Thus although an attached person in material existence always suffers from threefold miseries, he does not develop a distaste for the way of material existence.

PURPORT

A foolish man does not understand the values of human life, nor does he understand how he is wasting his valuable life simply for the maintenance of his family members. He is expert in calculating the loss of pounds, shillings and pence, but he is so foolish that he does not know how much money he is losing, even according to material considerations. Cāṇakya Paṇḍita gives the example that a moment of life cannot be purchased in exchange for millions of dollars. A foolish person, however, wastes such a valuable life without knowing how much he is losing, even according to monetary calculations. Although a materialistic person is expert in calculating costs and doing business, he does not realize that he is misusing his costly life for want of knowledge. Even though such a materialistic person is always suffering threefold miseries, he is not intelligent enough to cease his materialistic way of life.

TEXT 15

वित्तेषु नित्याभिनिविष्टचेता
विद्वांश्च दोषं परवित्तहर्तुः ।
प्रेत्येह वाथाप्यजितेन्द्रियस्त-
दशान्तकामो हरते कुटुम्बी ॥१५॥

vitteṣu nityābhiniviṣṭa-cetā
vidvāṁś ca doṣaṁ para-vitta-hartuḥ
pretyeha vāthāpy ajitendriyas tad
aśānta-kāmo harate kuṭumbī

vitteṣu—in material wealth; *nitya-abhiniviṣṭa-cetāḥ*—whose mind is always absorbed; *vidvān*—having learned; *ca*—also; *doṣam*—the fault; *para-vitta-hartuḥ*—of one who steals the money of others by cheating or by transactions on the black market; *pretya*—after dying; *iha*—in this material world; *vā*—or; *athāpi*—still; *ajita-indriyaḥ*—because of being unable to control the senses; *tat*—that; *aśānta-kāmaḥ*—whose desires are unsatiated; *harate*—steals; *kuṭumbī*—too fond of his family.

TRANSLATION

If a person too attached to the duties of family maintenance is unable to control his senses, the core of his heart is immersed in how to accumulate money. Although he knows that one who takes the wealth of others will be punished by the law of the government, and by the laws of Yamarāja after death, he continues cheating others to acquire money.

PURPORT

Especially in these days, people do not believe in a next life or in the court of Yamarāja and the various punishments of the sinful. But at least one should know that one who cheats others to acquire money will be punished by the laws of the government. Nonetheless, people do not care about the laws of this life or those governing the next. Despite whatever knowledge one has, one cannot stop his sinful activities if he is unable to control his senses.

TEXT 16

विद्वानपीत्थं दनुजाः कुटुम्बं
पुष्णन्स्वलोकाय न कल्पते वै ।
यः स्वीयपारक्यविभिन्नभाव-
स्तमः प्रपद्येत यथा विमूढः ॥१६॥

vidvān apītthaṁ danujāḥ kuṭumbaṁ
puṣṇan sva-lokāya na kalpate vai
yaḥ svīya-pārakya-vibhinna-bhāvas
tamaḥ prapadyeta yathā vimūḍhaḥ

vidvān—knowing (the inconvenience of material existence, especially in household life); *api*—although; *ittham*—thus; *danu-jāḥ*—O sons of demons; *kuṭumbam*—the family members or extended family members (like one's community, society, nation or union of nations); *puṣṇan*—providing with all the necessities of life; *sva-lokāya*—in understanding himself; *na*—not; *kalpate*—capable; *vai*—indeed; *yaḥ*—he who; *svīya*—my own; *pārakya*—belonging to others; *vibhinna*—separate; *bhāvaḥ*—having a conception of life; *tamaḥ*—nothing but darkness; *prapadyeta*—enters; *yathā*—just as; *vimūḍhaḥ*—a person without education, or one who is like an animal.

TRANSLATION

O my friends, sons of demons! In this material world, even those who are apparently advanced in education have the propensity to consider, "This is mine, and that is for others." Thus they are always engaged in providing the necessities of life to their families in a limited conception of family life, just like uneducated cats and dogs. They are unable to take to spiritual knowledge; instead, they are bewildered and overcome by ignorance.

PURPORT

In human society there are attempts to educate the human being, but for animal society there is no such system, nor are animals able to be educated. Therefore animals and unintelligent men are called *vimūḍha*, or ignorant, bewildered, whereas an educated person is called *vidvān*. The real *vidvān* is one who tries to understand his own position within this material world. For example, when Sanātana Gosvāmī submitted to the lotus feet of Śrī Caitanya Mahāprabhu, his first question was *'ke āmi'*, *'kene āmāya jāre tāpa-traya'*. In other words, he wanted to know his constitutional position and why he was suffering from the threefold miseries of material existence. This is the process of education. If one does not ask, "Who am I? What is the goal of my life?" but instead follows the same animal propensities as cats and dogs, what is the use of his education? As discussed in the previous verse, a living being is entrapped by his fruitive activities, exactly like a silkworm trapped in its own cocoon. Foolish persons are generally encaged by their fruitive actions (*karma*) because of a strong desire to enjoy this material world. Such attracted persons become involved in society, community and nation and waste their time, not having profited from having obtained human forms. Especially in this age, Kali-yuga, great leaders, politicians, philosophers and scientists are all engaged in foolish activities, thinking, "This is mine, and this is yours." The scientists invent nuclear weapons and collaborate with the big leaders to protect the interests of their own nation or society. In this verse, however, it is clearly stated that despite their so-called advanced knowledge, they actually have the same mentality as cats and dogs. As cats, dogs and other animals, not knowing their true interest in life, become increasingly involved in ignorance, the so-called educated person who does not know his own self-interest or the true goal of life becomes increasingly involved in materialism. Therefore Prahlāda Mahārāja advises everyone to follow the principles of *varṇāśrama-dharma.* Specifically, at a certain point one must give up family life and take to the renounced order of life to cultivate spiritual knowledge and thus become liberated. This is further discussed in the following verses.

TEXTS 17–18

यतो न कश्चित् क्व च कुत्रचिद् वा
दीनः स्वमात्मानमलं समर्थः ।
विमोचितुं कामदृशां विहार-
क्रीडामृगो यन्निगडो विसर्गः ॥१७॥
ततो विदूरात् परिहृत्य दैत्या
दैत्येषु सङ्गं विषयात्मकेषु ।
उपेत नारायणमादिदेवं
स मुक्तसङ्गैरिषितोऽपवर्गः ॥१८॥

yato na kaścit kva ca kutracid vā
dīnaḥ svam ātmānam alaṁ samarthaḥ
vimocituṁ kāma-dṛśāṁ vihāra-
krīḍā-mṛgo yan-nigaḍo visargaḥ

tato vidūrāt parihṛtya daityā
daityeṣu saṅgaṁ viṣayātmakeṣu
upeta nārāyaṇam ādi-devaṁ
sa mukta-saṅgair iṣito 'pavargaḥ

yataḥ—because; *na*—never; *kaścit*—anyone; *kva*—in any place; *ca*—also; *kutracit*—at any time; *vā*—or; *dīnaḥ*—having a poor fund of knowledge; *svam*—own; *ātmānam*—self; *alam*—exceedingly; *samarthaḥ*—able; *vimocitum*—to liberate; *kāma-dṛśām*—of lusty women; *vihāra*—in the sexual enjoyment; *krīḍā-mṛgaḥ*—a playboy; *yat*—in whom; *nigaḍaḥ*—which is the shackle of material bondage; *visargaḥ*—the expansions of family relationships; *tataḥ*—in such circumstances; *vidūrāt*—from far away; *parihṛtya*—giving up; *daityāḥ*—O my friends, sons of the demons; *daityeṣu*—among the demons; *saṅgam*—association; *viṣaya-ātma-keṣu*—who are too addicted to sense enjoyment; *upeta*—one should approach; *nārāyaṇam*—Lord Nārāyaṇa, the Supreme Personality of Godhead; *ādi-devam*—the origin of all the demigods; *saḥ*—He; *mukta-saṅgaiḥ*—by the association of liberated persons; *iṣitaḥ*—desired; *apavargaḥ*—the path of liberation.

TRANSLATION

My dear friends, O sons of the demons, it is certain that no one bereft of knowledge of the Supreme Personality of Godhead has been able to liberate himself from material bondage at any time or in any country. Rather, those bereft of knowledge of the Lord are bound by the material laws. They are factually addicted to sense gratification, and their target is woman. Indeed, they are actually playthings in the hands of attractive women. Victimized by such a conception of life, they become surrounded by children, grandchildren and great-grandchildren, and thus they are shackled to material bondage. Those who are very much addicted to this conception of life are called demons. Therefore, although you are sons of demons, keep aloof from such persons and take shelter of the Supreme Personality of Godhead, Nārāyaṇa, the origin of all the demigods, because the ultimate goal for the devotees of Nārāyaṇa is liberation from the bondage of material existence.

PURPORT

Prahlāda Mahārāja has maintained the philosophical point of view that one should give up the dark well of family life and go to the forest to take shelter of the lotus feet of the Supreme Personality of Godhead (*hitvātma-pātaṁ gṛham andha-kūpaṁ vanaṁ gato yad dharim āśrayeta*). In this verse also, he stresses the same point. In the history of human society, no one, at any time or any place, has been liberated because of too much affection and attachment for his family. Even in those who are apparently very educated, the same family attachment is there. They cannot give up the association of their families, even in old age or invalidity, for they are attached to sense enjoyment. As we have several times discussed, *yan maithunādi-gṛhamedhi-sukhaṁ hi tuccham:* so-called householders are simply attracted by sexual enjoyment. Thus they keep themselves shackled in family life, and furthermore they want their children to be shackled in the same way. Playing the parts of playboys in the hands of women, they glide down to the darkest regions of material existence. *Adānta-gobhir viśatāṁ tamisraṁ punaḥ punaś carvita-carvaṇānām.* Because they are unable to control their senses, they continue a life of chewing the chewed and therefore descend to the darkest material regions. One should give up the association of such demons and adhere to the association of devotees. Thus one will be able to be liberated from material bondage.

TEXT 19

न ह्यच्युतं प्रीणयतो बह्वायासोऽसुरात्मजाः ।
आत्मत्वात् सर्वभूतानां सिद्धत्वादिह सर्वतः ॥१९॥

na hy acyutaṁ prīṇayato
bahv-āyāso 'surātmajāḥ
ātmatvāt sarva-bhūtānāṁ
siddhatvād iha sarvataḥ

na—not; *hi*—indeed; *acyutam*—the infallible Supreme Personality of Godhead; *prīṇayataḥ*—satisfying; *bahu*—much; *āyāsaḥ*—endeavor; *asura-ātma-jāḥ*—O sons of demons; *ātmatvāt*—because of being intimately related as the Supersoul; *sarva-bhūtānām*—of all living entities; *siddhatvāt*—because of being established; *iha*—in this world; *sarvataḥ*—in all directions, in all times and from all angles of vision.

TRANSLATION

My dear sons of demons, the Supreme Personality of Godhead, Nārāyaṇa, is the original Supersoul, the father of all living entities.

Consequently there are no impediments to pleasing Him or worshiping Him under any conditions, whether one be a child or an old man. The relationship between the living entities and the Supreme Personality of Godhead is always a fact, and therefore there is no difficulty in pleasing the Lord.

PURPORT

One may ask, "One is certainly very attached to family life, but if one gives up family life to be attached to the service of the Lord, one must undergo the same endeavor and trouble. Therefore, what is the benefit of taking the trouble to engage in the service of the Lord?" This is not a valid objection. The Lord asserts in *Bhagavad-gītā* (14.4):

sarva-yoniṣu kaunteya
mūrtayaḥ sambhavanti yāḥ
tāsāṁ brahma mahad yonir
ahaṁ bīja-pradaḥ pitā

"It should be understood that all species of life, O son of Kuntī, are made possible by birth in this material nature, and that I am the seed-giving father." The Supreme Lord, Nārāyaṇa, is the seed-giving father of all living entities because the living entities are parts and parcels of the Supreme Lord (*mamaivāṁśo . . . jīva-bhūtaḥ*). As there is no difficulty in establishing the intimate relationship between a father and son, there is no difficulty in reestablishing the natural, intimate relationship between Nārāyaṇa and the living entities. *Svalpam apy asya dharmasya trāyate mahato bhayāt:* if one performs even very slight devotional service, Nārāyaṇa is always ready to save one from the greatest danger. The definite example is Ajāmila. Ajāmila separated himself from the Supreme Personality of Godhead by performing many sinful activities and was condemned by Yamarāja to be very severely punished, but because at the time of death he chanted the name of Nārāyaṇa, although he was calling not for the Supreme Lord Nārāyaṇa but for his son named Nārāyaṇa, he was saved from the hands of Yamarāja. Therefore, pleasing Nārāyaṇa does not require as much endeavor as pleasing one's family, community and nation. We have seen important political leaders killed for a slight discrepancy in their behavior. Therefore pleasing one's society, family, community and nation is extremely difficult. Pleasing Nārāyaṇa, however, is not at all difficult; it is very easy.

One's duty is to revive one's relationship with Nārāyaṇa. A slight endeavor in this direction will make the attempt successful, whereas one will never be successful in pleasing his so-called family, society and nation, even if one endeavors to sacrifice his life. The simple endeavor involved in the devotional service of *śravaṇaṁ kīrtanaṁ viṣṇoḥ*, hearing and chanting the holy name of the Lord, can make one successful in pleasing the Supreme Personality of Godhead. Śrī Caitanya Mahāprabhu has therefore bestowed His blessings by saying, *paraṁ vijayate śrī-kṛṣṇa-saṅkīrtanam:* "All glories to Śrī Kṛṣṇa *saṅkīrtana!*" If one wants to derive the actual benefit from this human form, he must take to the chanting of the holy name of the Lord.

TEXTS 20–23

परावरेषु भूतेषु ब्रह्मान्तस्थावरादिषु ।
भौतिकेषु विकारेषु भूतेष्वथ महत्सु च ॥२०॥

गुणेषु गुणसाम्ये च गुणव्यतिकरे तथा ।
एक एव परो ह्यात्मा भगवानीश्वरोऽव्ययः ॥२१॥

प्रत्यगात्मस्वरूपेण दृश्यरूपेण च स्वयम् ।
व्याप्यव्यापकनिर्देश्यो ह्यनिर्देश्योऽविकल्पितः ॥२२॥

केवलानुभवानन्दस्वरूपः परमेश्वरः ।
माययान्तर्हितैश्वर्य ईयते गुणसर्गया ॥२३॥

parāvareṣu bhūteṣu
brahmānta-sthāvarādiṣu
bhautikeṣu vikāreṣu
bhūteṣv atha mahatsu ca

guṇeṣu guṇa-sāmye ca
guṇa-vyatikare tathā

eka eva paro hy ātmā
bhagavān īśvaro 'vyayaḥ

pratyag-ātma-svarūpeṇa
dṛśya-rūpeṇa ca svayam
vyāpya-vyāpaka-nirdeśyo
hy anirdeśyo 'vikalpitaḥ

kevalānubhavānanda-
svarūpaḥ parameśvaraḥ
māyayāntarhitaiśvarya
īyate guṇa-sargayā

para-avareṣu—in exalted or hellish conditions of life; *bhūteṣu*—in the living beings; *brahma-anta*—ending with Lord Brahmā; *sthāvara-ādiṣu*—beginning with the nonmoving forms of life, the trees and plants; *bhautikeṣu*—of the material elements; *vikāreṣu*—in the transformations; *bhūteṣu*—in the five gross elements of material nature; *atha*—moreover; *mahatsu*—in the *mahat-tattva*, the total material energy; *ca*—also; *guṇeṣu*—in the modes of material nature; *guṇa-sāmye*—in an equilibrium of material qualities; *ca*—and; *guṇa-vyatikare*—in the uneven manifestation of the modes of material nature; *tathā*—as well; *ekaḥ*—one; *eva*—only; *paraḥ*—transcendental; *hi*—indeed; *ātmā*—the original source; *bhagavān*—the Supreme Personality of Godhead; *īśvaraḥ*—the controller; *avyayaḥ*—without deteriorating; *pratyak*—inner; *ātma-svarūpeṇa*—by His original constitutional position as the Supersoul; *dṛśya-rūpeṇa*—by His visible forms; *ca*—also; *svayam*—personally; *vyāpya*—pervaded; *vyāpaka*—all-pervading; *nirdeśyaḥ*—to be described; *hi*—certainly; *anirdeśyaḥ*—not to be described (because of fine, subtle existence); *avikalpitaḥ*—without differentiation; *kevala*—only; *anubhava-ānanda-svarūpaḥ*—whose form is blissful and full of knowledge; *parama-īśvaraḥ*—the Supreme Personality of Godhead, the supreme ruler; *māyayā*—by *māyā*, the illusory energy; *antarhita*—covered; *aiśvaryaḥ*—whose unlimited opulence; *īyate*—is mistaken as; *guṇa-sargayā*—the interaction of the material modes of nature.

TRANSLATION

The Supreme Personality of Godhead, the supreme controller, who is infallible and indefatigable, is present in different forms of life, from the inert living beings [sthāvara], such as the plants, to Brahmā, the foremost created living being. He is also present in the varieties of material creations and in the material elements, the total material energy and the modes of material nature [sattva-guṇa, rajo-guṇa and tamo-guṇa], as well as the unmanifested material nature and the false ego. Although He is one, He is present everywhere, and He is also the transcendental Supersoul, the cause of all causes, who is present as the observer in the cores of the hearts of all living entities. He is indicated as that which is pervaded and as the all-pervading Supersoul, but actually He cannot be indicated. He is changeless and undivided. He is simply perceived as the supreme sac-cid-ānanda [eternity, knowledge and bliss]. Being covered by the curtain of the external energy, to the atheist He appears nonexistent.

PURPORT

Not only is the Supreme Personality of Godhead present as the Supersoul of all living entities; at the same time, He pervades everything in the entire creation. He exists in all circumstances and at all times. He exists in the heart of Lord Brahmā and also in the cores of the hearts of the hogs, dogs, trees, plants and so on. He is present everywhere. He is present not only in the heart of the living entity, but also in material things, even in the atoms, protons and electrons being explored by material scientists.

The Lord is present in three features—as Brahman, Paramātmā and Bhagavān. Because He is present everywhere, He is described as *sarvaṁ khalv idaṁ brahma.* Viṣṇu exists beyond Brahman. *Bhagavad-gītā* confirms that Kṛṣṇa, by His Brahman feature, is all-pervading (*mayā tatam idaṁ sarvam*), but Brahman depends upon Kṛṣṇa (*brahmaṇo hi pratiṣṭhāham*). Without Kṛṣṇa, there could be no existence of Brahman or Paramātmā. Therefore, Bhagavān, the Supreme Personality of Godhead, is the ultimate realization of the Absolute Truth. Although He is present as the Paramātmā in the core of everyone's heart, He is nonetheless one, either as an individual or as the all-pervading Brahman.

The supreme cause is Kṛṣṇa, and devotees who have surrendered to the Supreme Personality of Godhead can realize Him and His presence within the universe and within the atom (*aṇḍāntara-stha-paramāṇu-cayāntara-stham*). This realization is possible only for devotees who have fully surrendered unto the lotus feet of the Lord; for others it is not possible. This is confirmed by the Lord Himself in *Bhagavad-gītā* (7.14):

daivī hy eṣā guṇamayī
mama māyā duratyayā
mām eva ye prapadyante
māyām etāṁ taranti te

The process of surrender in a devotional attitude is accepted by a fortunate living being. After wandering through many varieties of life on many planetary systems, when one comes to the real understanding of the Absolute Truth by the grace of a devotee, one surrenders to the Supreme Personality of Godhead, as confirmed in *Bhagavad-gītā* (*bahūnāṁ janmanām ante jñānavān māṁ prapadyate*).

Prahlāda Mahārāja's class friends, who were born of Daitya families, thought that realizing the Absolute was extremely difficult. Indeed, we have experience that many, many people say this very thing. Actually, however, this is not so. The Absolute, the Supreme Personality of Godhead, is most intimately related to all living entities. Therefore if one understands the Vaiṣṇava philosophy, which explains how He is present everywhere and how He acts everywhere, to worship the Supreme Lord or to realize Him is not at all difficult. Realization of the Lord, however, is possible only in the association of devotees. Therefore Śrī Caitanya Mahāprabhu, in His teachings to Rūpa Gosvāmī said (Cc. *Madhya* 19.151):

brahmāṇḍa bhramite kona bhāgyavān jīva
guru-kṛṣṇa-prasāde pāya bhakti-latā-bīja

The living entity in the material condition wanders through many varieties of life and many varieties of circumstances, but if he comes in contact with a pure devotee and is intelligent enough to take instructions from the pure devotee regarding the process of devotional service, he can understand the Supreme Personality of Godhead, the origin of Brahman and Paramātmā, without difficulty. In this regard, Śrīla Madhvācārya says:

antaryāmī pratyag-ātmā
vyāptaḥ kālo hariḥ smṛtaḥ
prakṛtyā tamasāvṛtatvāt
harer aiśvaryaṁ na jñāyate

The Lord is present as *antaryāmī* in everyone's heart and is visible in the individual soul covered by a body. Indeed, He is everywhere at every time and every condition, but because He is covered by the curtain of material energy, to an ordinary person there appears to be no God.

TEXT 24

तस्मात् सर्वेषु भूतेषु दयां कुरुत सौहृदम् ।
भावमासुरमुन्मुच्य यया तुष्यत्यधोक्षजः ॥२४॥

tasmāt sarveṣu bhūteṣu
dayāṁ kuruta sauhṛdam
bhāvam āsuram unmucya
yayā tuṣyaty adhokṣajaḥ

tasmāt—therefore; *sarveṣu*—to all; *bhūteṣu*—living entities; *dayām*—mercy; *kuruta*—show; *sauhṛdam*—friendliness; *bhāvam*—the attitude; *āsuram*—of the demons (who separate friends and enemies); *unmucya*—giving up; *yayā*—by which; *tuṣyati*—is satisfied; *adhokṣajaḥ*—the Supreme Lord, who is beyond the perception of the senses.

TRANSLATION

Therefore, my dear young friends born of demons, please act in such a way that the Supreme Lord, who is beyond the conception of material knowledge, will be satisfied. Give up your demoniac

nature and act without enmity or duality. Show mercy to all living entities by enlightening them in devotional service, thus becoming their well-wishers.

PURPORT

The Lord says in *Bhagavad-gītā* (18.55), *bhaktyā mām abhijānāti yāvān yaś cāsmi tattvataḥ:* "One can understand the Supreme Personality as He is only by devotional service." Prahlāda Mahārāja ultimately instructed his class friends, the sons of the demons, to accept the process of devotional service by preaching the science of Kṛṣṇa consciousness to everyone. Preaching is the best service to the Lord. The Lord will immediately be extremely satisfied with one who engages in this service of preaching Kṛṣṇa consciousness. This is confirmed by the Lord Himself in *Bhagavad-gītā* (18.69). *Na ca tasmān manuṣyeṣu kaścin me priya-kṛttamaḥ:* "There is no servant in this world more dear to Me than he, nor will there ever be one more dear." If one sincerely tries his best to spread Kṛṣṇa consciousness by preaching the glories of the Lord and His supremacy, even if he is imperfectly educated, he becomes the dearmost servant of the Supreme Personality of Godhead. This is *bhakti.* As one performs this service for humanity, without discrimination between friends and enemies, the Lord becomes satisfied, and the mission of one's life is fulfilled. Śrī Caitanya Mahāprabhu therefore advised everyone to become a *guru*-devotee and preach Kṛṣṇa consciousness (*yāre dekha, tāre kaha 'kṛṣṇa'-upadeśa*). That is the easiest way to realize the Supreme Personality of Godhead. By such preaching, the preacher becomes satisfied, and those to whom he preaches are also satisfied. This is the process of bringing peace and tranquility to the entire world.

bhoktāraṁ yajña-tapasāṁ
sarva-loka-maheśvaram
suhṛdaṁ sarva-bhūtānāṁ
jñātvā māṁ śāntim ṛcchati

One is expected to understand these three formulas of knowledge concerning the Supreme Lord—that He is the supreme enjoyer, that He is the proprietor of everything, and that He is the best well-wisher and friend of everyone. A preacher should personally understand these truths and preach them to everyone. Then there will be peace and tranquility all over the world.

The word *sauhṛdam* ("friendliness") is very significant in this verse. People are generally ignorant of Kṛṣṇa consciousness, and therefore to become their best well-wisher one should teach them about Kṛṣṇa consciousness without discrimination. Since the Supreme Lord, Viṣṇu, is situated in the core of everyone's heart, every body is a temple of Viṣṇu. One should not misuse this understanding as an excuse for such words as *daridra-nārāyaṇa.* If Nārāyaṇa lives in the house of a *daridra,* a poor man, this does not mean that Nārāyaṇa becomes poor. He lives everywhere—in the houses of the poor and those of the rich—but in all circumstances He remains Nārāyaṇa; to think that He becomes either poor or rich is a material calculation. He is always *ṣaḍ-aiśvarya-pūrṇa,* full in six opulences, in all circumstances.

TEXT 25

तुष्टे च तत्र किमलभ्यमनन्त आद्ये
किं तैर्गुणव्यतिकरादिह ये स्वसिद्धाः ।
धर्मादयः किमगुणेन च काङ्क्षितेन
सारंजुषां चरणयोरुपगायतां नः ॥२५॥

tuṣṭe ca tatra kim alabhyam ananta ādye
kiṁ tair guṇa-vyatikarād iha ye sva-siddhāḥ
dharmādayaḥ kim aguṇena ca kāṅkṣitena
sāraṁ juṣāṁ caraṇayor upagāyatāṁ naḥ

tuṣṭe—when satisfied; *ca*—also; *tatra*—that; *kim*—what; *alabhyam*—unobtainable; *anante*—the Supreme Personality of Godhead; *ādye*—the original source of everything, the cause of all causes; *kim*—what need; *taiḥ*—with them; *guṇa-vyatikarāt*—due to the actions of the modes of material nature; *iha*—in this world; *ye*—which; *sva-siddhāḥ*—automatically achieved; *dharma-ādayaḥ*—the three principles of material advancement, namely religion, economic development and sense gratification; *kim*—what need; *aguṇena*—with liberation into the Supreme; *ca*—and; *kāṅkṣitena*—desired; *sāram*—essence; *juṣām*—

relishing; *caraṇayoḥ*—of the two lotus feet of the Lord; *upagāyatām*—who glorify the qualities of the Lord; *naḥ*—of us.

TRANSLATION

Nothing is unobtainable for devotees who have satisfied the Supreme Personality of Godhead, who is the cause of all causes, the original source of everything. The Lord is the reservoir of unlimited spiritual qualities. For devotees, therefore, who are transcendental to the modes of material nature, what is the use of following the principles of religion, economic development, sense gratification and liberation, which are all automatically obtainable under the influence of the modes of nature? We devotees always glorify the lotus feet of the Lord, and therefore we need not ask for anything in terms of dharma, kāma, artha and mokṣa.

PURPORT

In an advanced civilization, people are eager to be religious, to be economically well situated, to satisfy their senses to the fullest extent, and at last to attain liberation. However, these are not to be magnified as desirable. Indeed, for a devotee these are all very easily available. Bilvamaṅgala Ṭhākura said, *muktiḥ svayaṁ mukulitāñjali sevate 'smān dharmārtha-kāma-gatayaḥ samaya-pratīkṣāḥ.* Liberation always stands at the door of a devotee, ready to carry out his orders. Material advancement in religion, economic development, sense gratification and liberation simply wait to serve a devotee at the first opportunity. A devotee is already in a transcendental position; he does not need further qualifications to be liberated. As confirmed in *Bhagavad-gītā* (14.26), *sa guṇān samatītyaitān brahma-bhūyāya kalpate:* a devotee is transcendental to the actions and reactions of the three modes of material nature because he is situated on the Brahman platform.

Prahlāda Mahārāja said, *aguṇena ca kāṅkṣitena:* if one is engaged in the transcendental loving service of the lotus feet of the Lord, he does not need anything in terms of *dharma, artha, kāma* or *mokṣa.* In *Śrīmad-Bhāgavatam,* therefore, in the beginning of the transcendental literature, it is said, *dharmaḥ projjhita-kaitavo 'tra. Dharma, artha, kāma* and *mokṣa* are *kaitava*—false and unnecessary. *Nirmatsarāṇām,* persons who are completely transcendental to the material activities of separateness, who make no distinction between "mine" and "yours," but who simply engage in the devotional service of the Lord, are actually fit to accept *bhāgavata-dharma* (*dharmān bhagavatān iha*). Because they are *nirmatsara,* not jealous of anyone, they want to make others devotees, even their enemies. In this regard, Śrīla Madhvācārya remarks, *kāṅkṣate mokṣa-gam api sukhaṁ nākāṅkṣato yathā.* Devotees are not desirous of any material happiness, including the happiness derived from liberation. This is called *anyābhilāṣitā-śūnyaṁ jñāna-karmādy-anāvṛtam. Karmīs* desire material happiness, and *jñānīs* desire liberation, but a devotee does not desire anything; he is simply satisfied by rendering transcendental loving service at the lotus feet of the Lord and glorifying Him everywhere by preaching, which is his life and soul.

TEXT 26

धर्मार्थकाम इति योऽभिहितस्त्रिवर्ग
ईक्षा त्रयी नयदमौ विविधा च वार्ता ।
मन्ये तदेतदखिलं निगमस्य सत्यं
स्वात्मार्पणं स्वसुहृदः परमस्य पुंसः ॥२६॥

dharmārtha-kāma iti yo 'bhihitas tri-varga
īkṣā trayī naya-damau vividhā ca vārtā
manye tad etad akhilaṁ nigamasya satyaṁ
svātmārpaṇaṁ sva-suhṛdaḥ paramasya puṁsaḥ

dharma—religion; *artha*—economic development; *kāmaḥ*—regulated sense gratification; *iti*—thus; *yaḥ*—which; *abhihitaḥ*—prescribed; *tri-vargaḥ*—the group of three; *īkṣā*—self-realization; *trayī*—the Vedic ritualistic ceremonies; *naya*—logic; *damau*—and the science of law and order; *vividhā*—varieties of; *ca*—also; *vārtā*—occupational duties, or one's livelihood; *manye*—I consider; *tat*—them; *etat*—these; *akhilam*—all; *nigamasya*—of the *Vedas; satyam*—truth; *sva-ātma-arpaṇam*—the full surrendering of one's self; *sva-suhṛdaḥ*—unto the supreme friend; *paramasya*—the ultimate; *puṁsaḥ*—personality.

TRANSLATION

Religion, economic development and sense gratification—these are described in the Vedas as tri-varga, or three ways to salvation. Within these three categories are education and self-realization; ritualistic ceremonies performed according to Vedic injunction; logic; the science of law and order; and the various means of earning one's livelihood. These are the external subject matters of study in the Vedas, and therefore I consider them material. However, I consider surrender to the lotus feet of Lord Viṣṇu to be transcendental.

PURPORT

These instructions of Prahlāda Mahārāja stress the transcendental position of devotional service. As confirmed in *Bhagavad-gītā* (14.26):

māṁ ca yo 'vyabhicāreṇa
bhakti-yogena sevate
sa guṇān samatītyaitān
brahma-bhūyāya kalpate

"One who engages in full devotional service, who does not fall down in any circumstance, at once transcends the modes of material nature and thus comes to the level of Brahman." One who fully engages in the devotional service of the Lord is immediately raised to the transcendental position, which is the *brahma-bhūta* stage. Any education or activity not on the *brahma-bhūta* platform, the platform of self-realization, is considered to be material, and Prahlāda Mahārāja says that anything material cannot be the Absolute Truth, for the Absolute Truth is on the spiritual platform. This is also confirmed by Lord Kṛṣṇa in *Bhagavad-gītā* (2.45), where He says, *traiguṇya-viṣayā vedā nistraiguṇyo bhavārjuna:* "The *Vedas* mainly deal with the subject of the three modes of material nature. Rise above these modes, O Arjuna. Be transcendental to all of them." To act on the material platform, even if one's activities are sanctioned by the *Vedas*, is not the ultimate goal of life. The ultimate goal of life is to stay on the spiritual platform, fully surrendered to the *parama-puruṣa*, the supreme person. This is the object of the human mission. In summary, the Vedic ritualistic ceremonies and injunctions are not to be discounted; they are means of being promoted to the spiritual platform. But if one does not come to the spiritual platform, the Vedic ceremonies are simply a waste of time. This is confirmed in *Śrīmad-Bhāgavatam* (1.2.8):

dharmaḥ svanuṣṭhitaḥ puṁsāṁ
viṣvaksena-kathāsu yaḥ
notpādayed yadi ratiṁ
śrama eva hi kevalam

"Duties [*dharma*] executed by men, regardless of occupation, are only so much useless labor if they do not provoke attraction for the message of the Supreme Lord." If one very strictly performs the various duties of religion but does not ultimately come to the platform of surrendering to the Supreme Lord, his methods of attaining salvation or elevation are simply a waste of time and energy.

TEXT 27

ज्ञानं तदेतदमलं दुरवापमाह
नारायणो नरसखः किल नारदाय ।
एकान्तिनां भगवतस्तदकिञ्चनानां
पादारविन्दरजसाप्लुतदेहिनां स्यात् ॥२७॥

jñānaṁ tad etad amalaṁ duravāpam āha
nārāyaṇo nara-sakhaḥ kila nāradāya
ekāntināṁ bhagavatas tad akiñcanānāṁ
pādāravinda-rajasāpluta-dehināṁ syāt

jñānam—knowledge; *tat*—that; *etat*—this; *amalam*—without material contamination; *duravāpam*—very difficult to understand (without the mercy of a devotee); *āha*—explained; *nārāyaṇaḥ*—Lord Nārāyaṇa, the Supreme Personality of Godhead; *nara-sakhaḥ*—the friend of all living entities (especially human beings); *kila*—certainly; *nāradāya*—unto the great sage Nārada; *ekāntinām*—of those who have surrendered exclusively to the Supreme Personality of Godhead; *bhagavataḥ*—of the Supreme Personality of Godhead; *tat*—that (knowledge);

akiñcanānām—who do not claim any material possessions; *pāda-aravinda*—of the lotus feet of the Lord; *rajasā*—by the dust; *āpluta*—bathed; *dehinām*—whose bodies; *syāt*—is possible.

TRANSLATION

Nārāyaṇa, the Supreme Personality of Godhead, the well-wisher and friend of all living entities, formerly explained this transcendental knowledge to the great saint Nārada. Such knowledge is extremely difficult to understand without the mercy of a saintly person like Nārada, but everyone who has taken shelter of Nārada's disciplic succession can understand this confidential knowledge.

PURPORT

It is stated here that this confidential knowledge is extremely difficult to understand, yet it is very easy to understand if one takes shelter of a pure devotee. This confidential knowledge is also mentioned at the end of *Bhagavad-gītā*, where the Lord says, *sarva-dharmān parityajya mām ekaṁ śaraṇaṁ vraja:* "Abandon all varieties of religion and just surrender unto Me." This knowledge is an extremely confidential secret, but it can be understood if one approaches the Supreme Personality of Godhead through the bona fide agent, the spiritual master in the disciplic succession from Nārada. Prahlāda Mahārāja wanted to impress upon the sons of the demons that although such knowledge can be understood only by a saintly person like Nārada, they should not be disappointed, for if one takes shelter of Nārada instead of material teachers, this knowledge is possible to understand. Understanding does not depend upon high parentage. The living entity is certainly pure on the spiritual platform, and therefore anyone who attains the spiritual platform by the grace of the spiritual master can also understand this confidential knowledge.

TEXT 28

श्रुतमेतन्मया पूर्वं ज्ञानं विज्ञानसंयुतम् ।
धर्मं भागवतं शुद्धं नारदाद् देवदर्शनात् ॥२८॥

śrutam etan mayā pūrvaṁ
jñānaṁ vijñāna-saṁyutam

dharmaṁ bhāgavataṁ śuddhaṁ
nāradād deva-darśanāt

śrutam—heard; *etat*—this; *mayā*—by me; *pūrvam*—formerly; *jñānam*—confidential knowledge; *vijñāna-saṁyutam*—combined with its practical application; *dharmam*—transcendental religion; *bhāgavatam*—in relationship with the Supreme Personality of Godhead; *śuddham*—having nothing to do with material activities; *nāradāt*—from the great saint Nārada; *deva*—the Supreme Lord; *darśanāt*—who always sees.

TRANSLATION

Prahlāda Mahārāja continued: I received this knowledge from the great saint Nārada Muni, who is always engaged in devotional service. This knowledge, which is called bhāgavata-dharma, is fully scientific. It is based on logic and philosophy and is free from all material contamination.

TEXTS 29–30

श्रीदैत्यपुत्रा ऊचुः
प्रह्राद त्वं वयं चापि नर्तेऽन्यं विद्महे गुरुम् ।
एताभ्यां गुरुपुत्राभ्यां बालानामपि हीश्वरौ ॥२९॥

बालस्यान्तःपुरस्थस्य महत्सङ्गो दुरन्वयः ।
छिन्धि नः संशयं सौम्य स्याच्चेद्विस्रम्भकारणम् ॥३०॥

śrī-daitya-putrā ūcuḥ
prahrāda tvaṁ vayaṁ cāpi
narte 'nyaṁ vidmahe gurum
etābhyāṁ guru-putrābhyāṁ
bālānām api hīśvarau

bālasyāntaḥpura-sthasya
mahat-saṅgo duranvayaḥ
chindhi naḥ saṁśayaṁ saumya
syāc ced visrambha-kāraṇam

śrī-daitya-putrāḥ ūcuḥ—the sons of the demons said; *prahrāda*—O dear friend Prahlāda; *tvam*—you; *vayam*—we; *ca*—and; *api*—also; *na*—not; *ṛte*—except; *anyam*—any other; *vidmahe*—know; *gurum*—spiritual master; *etābhyām*—these two; *guru-putrābhyām*—the sons of Śukrācārya; *bālānām*—of little children; *api*—although; *hi*—indeed; *īśvarau*—the two controllers; *bālasya*—of a child; *antaḥpura-sthasya*—remaining inside the house or palace; *mahat-saṅgaḥ*—the association of a great person like Nārada; *duranvayaḥ*—very difficult; *chindhi*—please dispel; *naḥ*—our; *saṁśayam*—doubt; *saumya*—O gentle one; *syāt*—there may be; *cet*—if; *visrambha-kāraṇam*—cause of faith (in your words).

TRANSLATION

The sons of the demons replied: Dear Prahlāda, neither you nor we know any teacher or spiritual master other than Ṣaṇḍa and Amarka, the sons of Śukrācārya. After all, we are children and they our controllers. For you especially, who always remain within the palace, it is very difficult to associate with a great personality. Dear friend, most gentle one, would you kindly explain how it was possible for you to hear Nārada? Kindly dispel our doubts in this regard.

Thus end the Bhaktivedanta purports of the Seventh Canto, Sixth Chapter, of the Śrīmad-Bhāgavatam, *entitled, "Prahlāda Instructs His Demoniac Schoolmates."*

CHAPTER SEVEN

What Prahlāda Learned in the Womb

In this chapter, to dissipate the doubts of his class friends, the sons of the demons, Prahlāda Mahārāja states how, within the womb of his mother, he had heard from the mouth of Nārada Muni, who had instructed him in *bhāgavata-dharma.*

When Hiraṇyakaśipu left his kingdom and went to the mountain known as Mandarācala to execute severe austerities, all the demons scattered. Hiraṇyakaśipu's wife, Kayādhu, was pregnant at that time, and the demigods, mistakenly thinking that she carried another demon in her womb, arrested her. Their plan was that as soon as the child took birth they would kill him. While they were taking Kayādhu to the heavenly planets, they met Nārada Muni, who stopped them from taking her away and took her to his *āśrama* until Hiraṇyakaśipu's return. In Nārada Muni's *āśrama,* Kayādhu prayed for the protection of the baby in her womb, and Nārada Muni reassured her and gave her instructions on spiritual knowledge. Taking advantage of those instructions, Prahlāda Mahārāja, although a small baby within the womb, listened very carefully. The spirit soul is always apart from the material body. There is no change in the spiritual form of the living entity. Any person above the bodily conception of life is pure and can receive transcendental knowledge. This transcendental knowledge is devotional service, and Prahlāda Mahārāja, while living in the womb of his mother, received instructions in devotional service from Nārada Muni. Any person engaged in the service of the Lord through the instructions of a bona fide spiritual master is immediately liberated, and being free from the clutches of *māyā,* he is relieved of all ignorance and material desires. The duty of everyone is to take shelter of the Supreme Lord and thus become free from all material desires. Regardless of the material condition in which one is situated, one can achieve this perfection. Devotional service is not dependent on the material activities of austerity, penance, mystic *yoga* or piety. Even without such assets, one can achieve devotional service through the mercy of a pure devotee.

TEXT 1

श्रीनारद उवाच

एवं दैत्यसुतैः पृष्टो महाभागवतोऽसुरः ।
उवाच तान्स्मयमानः स्मरन् मदनुभाषितम् ॥ १ ॥

śrī-nārada uvāca
evaṁ daitya-sutaiḥ pṛṣṭo
mahā-bhāgavato 'suraḥ
uvāca tān smayamānaḥ
smaran mad-anubhāṣitam

śrī-nāradaḥ uvāca—the great saint Nārada Muni said; *evam*—thus; *daitya-sutaiḥ*—by the sons of the demons; *pṛṣṭaḥ*—being questioned; *mahā-bhāgavataḥ*—the exalted devotee of the Lord; *asuraḥ*—born in a family of demons; *uvāca*—spoke; *tān*—unto them (the sons of the demons); *smayamānaḥ*—smiling; *smaran*—remembering; *mat-anubhāṣitam*—what was spoken by me.

TRANSLATION

Nārada Muni said: Although Prahlāda Mahārāja was born in a family of asuras, he was the greatest of all devotees. Having thus been questioned by his class friends, the sons of the asuras, he remembered the words spoken to him by me and replied to his friends as follows.

PURPORT

When he was in the womb of his mother, Prahlāda Mahārāja listened to the words of Nārada Muni. One cannot imagine how the baby in embryo could hear Nārada, but this is spiritual life; progress in spiritual life cannot be obstructed by any material condition. This is called *ahaituky apratihatā.* Reception of spiritual knowledge is never checked by any material condition. Thus Prahlāda Mahārāja, from his very childhood, spoke spiritual knowledge to his class friends, and certainly it was effective, although all of them were children.

TEXT 2

श्रीप्रह्राद उवाच

पितरि प्रस्थितेऽस्माकं तपसे मन्दराचलम् ।
युद्धोद्यमं परं चक्रुर्विबुधा दानवान्प्रति ॥ २ ॥

śrī-prahrāda uvāca
pitari prasthite 'smākaṁ
tapase mandarācalam
yuddhodyamaṁ paraṁ cakrur
vibudhā dānavān prati

śrī-prahrādaḥ uvāca—Prahlāda Mahārāja said; *pitari*—when the demon father, Hiraṇyakaśipu; *prasthite*—left for; *asmākam*—our; *tapase*—to execute austerities; *mandara-acalam*—the hill known as Mandarācala; *yuddha-udyamam*—exertion of warfare; *param*—very great; *cakruḥ*—executed; *vibudhāḥ*—the demigods, headed by King Indra; *dānavān*—the demons; *prati*—toward.

TRANSLATION

Prahlāda Mahārāja said: When our father, Hiraṇyakaśipu, went to Mandarācala Mountain to execute severe austerities, in his absence the demigods, headed by King Indra, made a severe attempt to subdue all the demons in warfare.

TEXT 3

पिपीलिकैरहिरिव दिष्टया लोकोपतापनः ।
पापेन पापोऽभक्षीति वदन्तो वासवादयः ॥ ३ ॥

pipīlikair ahir iva
diṣṭyā lokopatāpanaḥ
pāpena pāpo 'bhakṣīti
vadanto vāsavādayaḥ

pipīlikaiḥ—by small ants; *ahiḥ*—a serpent; *iva*—like; *diṣṭyā*—thank heaven; *loka-upatāpanaḥ*—always oppressing everyone; *pāpena*—by his own sinful activities; *pāpaḥ*—the sinful Hiraṇyakaśipu; *abhakṣi*—has now been eaten; *iti*—thus; *vadantaḥ*—saying; *vāsava-ādayaḥ*—the demigods, headed by King Indra.

TRANSLATION

"Alas, as a serpent is eaten by small ants, so the troublesome Hiraṇyakaśipu, who always inflicted miseries upon all types of people, has now been defeated by the reactions of his own sinful activities." Saying this, the demigods, headed by King Indra, arranged to fight the demons.

TEXTS 4–5

तेषामतिबलोद्योगं निशम्यासुरयूथपाः ।
वध्यमानाः सुरैर्भीता दुद्रुवुः सर्वतोदिशम् ॥ ४ ॥
कलत्रपुत्रवित्ताप्तान्गृहान्पशुपरिच्छदान् ।
नावेक्ष्यमाणास्त्वरिताः सर्वे प्राणपरीप्सवः ॥ ५ ॥

teṣām atibalodyogaṁ
niśamyāsura-yūthapāḥ
vadhyamānāḥ surair bhītā
dudruvuḥ sarvato diśam

kalatra-putra-vittāptān
gṛhān paśu-paricchadān
nāvekṣyamāṇās tvaritāḥ
sarve prāṇa-parīpsavaḥ

teṣām—of the demigods, headed by King Indra; *atibala-udyogam*—the great exertion and strength; *niśamya*—hearing of; *asura-yūthapāḥ*—the great leaders of the demons; *vadhyamānāḥ*—being killed one after another; *suraiḥ*—by the demigods; *bhītāḥ*—afraid; *dudruvuḥ*—ran away; *sarvataḥ*—in all; *diśam*—directions; *kalatra*—wives; *putra-vitta*—children and wealth; *āptān*—relatives; *gṛhān*—homes; *paśu-paricchadān*—animals and paraphernalia of household life; *na*—not; *avekṣyamāṇāḥ*—seeing to; *tvaritāḥ*—very hasty; *sarve*—all of them; *prāṇa-parīpsavaḥ*—very much desiring to live.

TRANSLATION

When the great leaders of the demons, who were being killed one after another, saw the unprecedented exertion of the demigods in fighting, they began to flee, scattering themselves in all directions. Simply to protect their lives, they hastily fled from their homes, wives, children, animals and household paraphernalia. Paying no heed to all these, the demons simply fled.

TEXT 6

व्यलुम्पन् राजशिबिरममरा जयकाङ्क्षिणः ।
इन्द्रस्तु राजमहिषीं मातरं मम चाग्रहीत् ॥ ६ ॥

vyalumpan rāja-śibiram
amarā jaya-kāṅkṣiṇaḥ
indras tu rāja-mahiṣīṁ
mātaraṁ mama cāgrahīt

vyalumpan—plundered; *rāja-śibiram*—the palace of my father, Hiraṇyakaśipu; *amarāḥ*—the demigods; *jaya-kāṅkṣiṇaḥ*—eager to be victorious; *indraḥ*—the head of the demigods, King Indra; *tu*—but; *rāja-mahiṣīm*—the Queen; *mātaram*—mother; *mama*—my; *ca*—also; *agrahīt*—captured.

TRANSLATION

The victorious demigods plundered the palace of Hiraṇyakaśipu, the King of the demons, and destroyed everything within it. Then Indra, King of heaven, arrested my mother, the Queen.

TEXT 7

नीयमानां भयोद्विग्नां रुदतीं कुररीमिव ।
यदृच्छयागतस्तत्र देवर्षिर्ददृशे पथि ॥ ७ ॥

nīyamānāṁ bhayodvignāṁ
rudatīṁ kurarīm iva
yadṛcchayāgatas tatra
devarṣir dadṛśe pathi

nīyamānām—being taken away; *bhaya-udvignām*—disturbed and full of fear; *rudatīm*—crying; *kurarīm iva*—like a *kurarī* (osprey); *yadṛcchayā*—by chance; *āgataḥ*—arrived; *tatra*—on the spot; *deva-ṛṣiḥ*—the great saint Nārada; *dadṛśe*—he saw; *pathi*—on the road.

TRANSLATION

As she was being led away, crying in fear like a kurarī captured by a vulture, the great sage Nārada, who at that time had no engagement, appeared on the scene and saw her in that condition.

TEXT 8

प्राह नैनां सुरपते नेतुमर्हस्यनागसम् ।
मुञ्च मुञ्च महाभाग सतीं परपरिग्रहम् ॥ ८ ॥

prāha naināṁ sura-pate
netum arhasy anāgasam
muñca muñca mahā-bhāga
satīṁ para-parigraham

prāha—he said; *na*—not; *enām*—this; *sura-pate*—O King of the demigods; *netum*—to drag away; *arhasi*—you deserve; *anāgasam*—not at all sinful; *muñca muñca*—release, release; *mahā-bhāga*—O greatly fortunate one; *satīm*—chaste; *para-parigraham*—the wife of another person.

TRANSLATION

Nārada Muni said: O Indra, King of the demigods, this woman is certainly sinless. You should not drag her off in this merciless way. O greatly fortunate one, this chaste woman is the wife of another. You must immediately release her.

TEXT 9

श्रीइन्द्र उवाच

आस्तेऽस्या जठरे वीर्यमविषह्यं सुरद्विषः ।
आस्यतां यावत्प्रसवं मोक्ष्येऽर्थपदवीं गतः ॥ ९ ॥

śrī-indra uvāca
āste 'syā jaṭhare vīryam
aviṣahyaṁ sura-dviṣaḥ
āsyatāṁ yāvat prasavaṁ
mokṣye 'rtha-padavīṁ gataḥ

śrī-indraḥ uvāca—King Indra said; *āste*—there is; *asyāḥ*—of her; *jaṭhare*—within the abdomen; *vīryam*—the seed; *aviṣahyam*—intolerable; *sura-dviṣaḥ*—of the enemy of the demigods; *āsyatām*—let her remain (in our prison); *yāvat*—until; *prasavam*—the delivery of the child; *mokṣye*—I shall release; *artha-padavīm*—the path of my object; *gataḥ*—obtained.

TRANSLATION

King Indra said: In the womb of this woman, the wife of the demon Hiraṇyakaśipu, is the seed of that great demon. Therefore, let her remain in our custody until her child is delivered, and then we shall release her.

PURPORT

Indra, the King of heaven, decided to arrest Prahlāda Mahārāja's mother because he thought that another demon, another Hiraṇyakaśipu, was within her womb. The best course, he thought, was to kill the child when the child was born, and then the woman could be released.

TEXT 10

श्रीनारद उवाच
अयं निष्किल्बिषः साक्षान्महाभागवतो महान् ।
त्वया न प्राप्स्यते संस्थामनन्तानुचरो बली ॥१०॥

śrī-nārada uvāca
ayaṁ niṣkilbiṣaḥ sākṣān
mahā-bhāgavato mahān
tvayā na prāpsyate saṁsthām
anantānucaro balī

śrī-nāradaḥ uvāca—the great saint Nārada Muni said; *ayam*—this (child within the womb); *niṣkilbiṣaḥ*—completely sinless; *sākṣāt*—directly; *mahā-bhāgavataḥ*—a saintly devotee; *mahān*—very great; *tvayā*—by you; *na*—not; *prāpsyate*—will obtain; *saṁsthām*—his death; *ananta*—of the Supreme Personality of Godhead; *anucaraḥ*—a servant; *balī*—extremely powerful.

TRANSLATION

Nārada Muni replied: The child within this woman's womb is faultless and sinless. Indeed, he is a great devotee, a powerful servant of the Supreme Personality of Godhead. Therefore you will not be able to kill him.

PURPORT

There have been many instances in which demons or nondevotees have attempted to kill a devotee, but they have never been able to destroy a great devotee of the Supreme Personality of Godhead. The Lord promises in *Bhagavad-gītā* (9.31), *kaunteya pratijānīhi na me bhaktaḥ praṇaśyati.* This is a declaration by the Supreme Personality of Godhead that His devotee cannot be killed by demons. Prahlāda Mahārāja is the vivid example of the truth of this promise. Nārada Muni told the King of heaven, "It would be impossible for you to kill the child, even though you are demigods, and certainly it would be impossible for others."

TEXT 11

इत्युक्तस्तां विहायेन्द्रो देवर्षेर्मानयन्वचः ।
अनन्तप्रियभक्त्यैनां परिक्रम्य दिवं ययौ ॥११॥

ity uktas tāṁ vihāyendro
devarṣer mānayan vacaḥ
ananta-priya-bhaktyaināṁ
parikramya divaṁ yayau

iti—thus; *uktaḥ*—addressed; *tām*—her; *vihāya*—releasing; *indraḥ*—the King of heaven; *deva-ṛṣeḥ*—of the saint Nārada Muni; *mānayan*—honoring; *vacaḥ*—the words; *ananta-priya*—for one who is very dear to the Supreme Personality of Godhead; *bhaktyā*—by devotion; *enām*—this (woman); *parikramya*—circumambulating; *divam*—to the heavenly planets; *yayau*—returned.

TRANSLATION

When the great saint Nārada Muni had thus spoken, King Indra, being respectful to Nārada's words, immediately released my mother. Because of my being a devotee of the Lord, all the demigods circumambulated her. Then they returned to their celestial kingdom.

PURPORT

Although King Indra and the other demigods are exalted personalities, they were so obedient to Nārada Muni that King Indra immediately accepted Nārada Muni's words concerning Prahlāda Mahārāja. This is called understanding by the *paramparā* system. Indra and the demigods did not know that a great devotee was in the womb of Kayādhu, the wife of Hiraṇyakaśipu, but they accepted the authoritative statements of Nārada Muni and immediately offered their respects to the devotee by circumambulating the woman in whose womb he was living. To understand God and the devotee by the *paramparā* system is the process of knowledge. There is no need to speculate about God and His devotee. One should accept the statements of a bona fide devotee and thus try to understand.

TEXT 12

ततो मे मातरमृषिः समानीय निजाश्रमे ।
आश्वास्येहोष्यतां वत्से यावत् ते भर्तुरागमः ॥१२॥

tato me mātaram ṛṣiḥ
samānīya nijāśrame
āśvāsyehoṣyatāṁ vatse
yāvat te bhartur āgamaḥ

tataḥ—thereafter; *me*—my; *mātaram*—mother; *ṛṣiḥ*—the great saint Nārada Ṛṣi; *samānīya*—bringing; *nija-āśrame*—to his own *āśrama;* *āśvāsya*—giving her assurance; *iha*—here; *uṣyatām*—stay; *vatse*—my dear child; *yāvat*—until; *te*—your; *bhartuḥ*—of the husband; *āgamaḥ*—the coming.

TRANSLATION

Prahlāda Mahārāja continued: The great saint Nārada Muni brought my mother to his āśrama and assured her of all protection, saying, "My dear child, please remain at my āśrama until the arrival of your husband."

TEXT 13

तथेत्यवात्सीद् देवर्षेरन्तिके साकुतोभया ।
यावद् दैत्यपतिर्घोरात् तपसो न न्यवर्तत ॥१३॥

tathety avātsīd devarṣer
antike sākuto-bhayā
yāvad daitya-patir ghorāt
tapaso na nyavartata

tathā—so be it; *iti*—thus; *avātsīt*—lived; *deva-ṛṣeḥ*—Devarṣi Nārada; *antike*—near; *sā*—she (my mother); *akuto-bhayā*—without fear from any direction; *yāvat*—as long as; *daitya-patiḥ*—my father, Hiraṇyakaśipu, the lord of the demons; *ghorāt*—from very severe; *tapasaḥ*—austerities; *na*—not; *nyavartata*—ceased.

TRANSLATION

After accepting the instructions of Devarṣi Nārada, my mother stayed in his care, without fear from any direction, as long as my father, the King of the Daityas, had not become free from his severe austerities.

TEXT 14

ऋषिं पर्यचरत् तत्र भक्त्या परमया सती ।
अन्तर्वत्नी स्वगर्भस्य क्षेमायेच्छाप्रसूतये ॥१४॥

ṛṣiṁ paryacarat tatra
bhaktyā paramayā satī
antarvatnī sva-garbhasya
kṣemāyecchā-prasūtaye

ṛṣim—unto Nārada Muni; *paryacarat*—rendered service; *tatra*—there (in the *āśrama* of Nārada Muni); *bhaktyā*—with devotion and faith; *paramayā*—great; *satī*—the faithful woman; *antarvatnī*—pregnant; *sva-garbhasya*—of her embryo; *kṣemāya*—for the welfare; *icchā*—according to desire; *prasūtaye*—for deliverance of the child.

TRANSLATION

My mother, being pregnant, desired the safety of her embryo and desired to give birth after her husband's arrival. Thus she stayed at Nārada Muni's āśrama, where she rendered service unto Nārada Muni with great devotion.

PURPORT

It is stated in *Śrīmad-Bhāgavatam* (9.19.17)

mātrā svasrā duhitrā vā
nāviviktāsano bhavet
balavān indriya-grāmo
vidvāṁsam api karṣati

One should not remain in a secluded place with a woman, even one's mother, sister, or daughter. Nonetheless, although one is strictly prohibited from staying with a woman in a secluded place, Nārada Muni gave shelter to Prahlāda Mahārāja's young mother, who rendered service to him with great devotion and faith. Does this mean that Nārada Muni transgressed the Vedic injunctions? Certainly he did not. Such injunctions are intended for mundane creatures, but Nārada Muni is transcendental to mundane categories. Nārada Muni is a great saint and is transcendentally situated. Therefore, although he was a young man, he could give shelter to a young woman and accept her service. Haridāsa Ṭhākura also spoke with a young woman, a prostitute, in the dead of night, but the woman could not deviate his mind. Instead, she became a Vaiṣṇavī, a pure devotee, by the benediction of Haridāsa Ṭhākura. Ordinary persons, however, should not imitate such highly elevated devotees. Ordinary persons must strictly observe the rules and regulations by staying aloof from the association of women. No one should imitate Nārada Muni or Haridāsa Ṭhākura. It is said, *vaiṣṇavera kriyā-mudrā vijñe nā bujhaya.* Even if a man is very advanced in learning, he cannot understand the behavior of a Vaiṣṇava. Anyone can take shelter of a pure Vaiṣṇava, without fear. Therefore in the previous verse it has been distinctly said, *devarṣer antike sākuto-bhayā:* Kayādhu, the mother of Prahlāda Mahārāja, stayed under the protection of Nārada Muni without fear from any direction. Similarly, Nārada Muni, in his transcendental position, stayed with the young woman without fear of deviation. Nārada Muni, Haridāsa Ṭhākura and similar *ācāryas* especially empowered to broadcast the glories of the Lord cannot be brought down to the material platform. Therefore one is strictly forbidden to think that the *ācārya* is an ordinary human being (*guruṣu nara-matiḥ*).

TEXT 15

ऋषिः कारुणिकस्तस्याः प्रादादुभयमीश्वरः ।
धर्मस्य तत्त्वं ज्ञानं च मामप्युद्दिश्य निर्मलम् ॥१५॥

ṛṣiḥ kāruṇikas tasyāḥ
prādād ubhayam īśvaraḥ

dharmasya tattvaṁ jñānaṁ ca
mām apy uddiśya nirmalam

ṛṣiḥ—the great sage Nārada Muni; *kāruṇikaḥ*—naturally very affectionate or merciful to the fallen souls; *tasyāḥ*—to her; *prādāt*—gave instructions; *ubhayam*—both; *īśvaraḥ*—a powerful controller who can do whatever he likes (Nārada Muni); *dharmasya*—of religion; *tattvam*—the truth; *jñānam*—knowledge; *ca*—and; *mām*—me; *api*—especially; *uddiśya*—indicating; *nirmalam*—without material contamination.

TRANSLATION

Nārada Muni delivered his instructions both to me, who was within the womb, and to my mother, who was engaged in rendering him service. Because he is naturally extremely kind to the fallen souls, being in a transcendental position, he gave instructions on religion and transcendental knowledge. These instructions were free from all material contamination.

PURPORT

Here it is said, *dharmasya tattvaṁ jñānaṁ ca . . . nirmalam.* The word *nirmalam* refers to spotless *dharma,* spotless religion—or, in other words, *bhāgavata-dharma.* Ordinary ritualistic activities constitute contaminated religion, by which one benefits by developing material wealth and prosperity, but uncontaminated, pure religion consists of understanding one's relationship with God and acting accordingly, thus fulfilling the highest mission of life and returning home, back to Godhead. Prahlāda Mahārāja advised that one elevate oneself to the standard of *bhāgavata-dharma* from the very beginning of life (*kaumāra ācaret prājño dharmān bhāgavatān iha*). The Lord Himself also speaks of pure, uncontaminated religion when He says, *sarva-darmān parityajya mām ekaṁ śaraṇaṁ vraja:* "Abandon all varieties of religion and just surrender unto Me." (Bg. 18.66) One must understand one's relationship with God and then act accordingly. This is *bhāgavata-dharma. Bhāgavata-dharma* means *bhakti-yoga.*

vāsudeve bhagavati
bhakti-yogaḥ prayojitaḥ
janayaty āśu vairāgyaṁ
jñānaṁ ca yad ahaitukam

"By rendering devotional service unto the Personality of Godhead, Śrī Kṛṣṇa, one immediately acquires causeless knowledge and detachment from the world." (*Bhāg.* 1.2.7) To be situated on the platform of pure religion, one should perform *bhakti-yoga* in relationship with Kṛṣṇa, Vāsudeva.

TEXT 16

तत्तु कालस्य दीर्घत्वात् स्त्रीत्वान्मातुस्तिरोदधे ।
ऋषिणानुगृहीतं मां नाधुनाप्यजहात् स्मृतिः ॥१६॥

tat tu kālasya dīrghatvāt
strītvān mātus tirodadhe
ṛṣiṇānugṛhītaṁ māṁ
nādhunāpy ajahāt smṛtiḥ

tat—that (instruction on religion and knowledge); *tu*—indeed; *kālasya*—of time; *dīrghatvāt*—because of the longness; *strītvāt*—because of being a woman; *mātuḥ*—of my mother; *tirodadhe*—disappeared; *ṛṣiṇā*—by the sage; *anugṛhītam*—being blessed; *mām*—me; *na*—not; *adhunā*—today; *api*—even; *ajahāt*—left; *smṛtiḥ*—the memory (of Nārada Muni's instructions).

TRANSLATION

Because of the long duration of time that has passed and because of her being a woman and therefore less intelligent, my mother has forgotten all those instructions; but the great sage Nārada blessed me, and therefore I could not forget them.

PURPORT

In *Bhagavad-gītā* (9.32) the Lord says:

mām hi pārtha vyapāśritya
ye 'pi syuḥ pāpa-yonayaḥ
striyo vaiśyās tathā śūdrās
te 'pi yānti parām gatim

"O son of Pṛthā, those who take shelter in Me—though they be lowborn, women, *vaiśyas* [merchants] or *śūdras* [workers]—can approach the supreme destination." The word *pāpa-yoni* refers to those who are less than *śūdras*, but even though a woman may not be *pāpa-yoni*, because of being less intelligent she sometimes forgets devotional instructions. For those who are strong enough, however, there is no question of forgetting. Women are generally attached to material enjoyment, and because of this tendency they sometimes forget devotional instructions. But if even a woman practices devotional service strictly, according to the rules and regulations, the statement by the Lord Himself that she can return to Godhead (*te 'pi yānti parām gatim*) is not at all astonishing. One must take shelter of the Lord and rigidly follow the rules and regulations. Then, regardless of what one is, one will return home, back to Godhead. Prahlāda Mahārāja's mother was more concerned with protecting the child in the womb and was very anxious to see her husband return. Therefore she could not consider very seriously the sublime instructions of Nārada Muni.

TEXT 17

भवतामपि भूयान्मे यदि श्रद्दधते वचः ।
वैशारदी धीः श्रद्धातः स्त्रीबालानां च मे यथा ॥१७॥

bhavatām api bhūyān me
yadi śraddadhate vacaḥ
vaiśāradī dhīḥ śraddhātaḥ
strī-bālānām ca me yathā

bhavatām—of yourselves; *api*—also; *bhūyāt*—it may be; *me*—of me; *yadi*—if; *śraddadhate*—you believe in; *vacaḥ*—the words; *vaiśāradī*—of the most expert, or in relation with the Supreme Lord;

dhīḥ—intelligence; *śraddhātaḥ*—because of firm faith; *strī*—of women; *bālānām*—of small boys; *ca*—also; *me*—of me; *yathā*—just as.

TRANSLATION

Prahlāda Mahārāja continued: My dear friends, if you can place your faith in my words, simply by that faith you can also understand transcendental knowledge, just like me, although you are small children. Similarly, a woman can also understand transcendental knowledge and know what is spirit and what is matter.

PURPORT

These words of Prahlāda Mahārāja are very important in regard to knowledge descending by the disciplic succession. Even when Prahlāda Mahārāja was a baby within the womb of his mother, he became fully convinced of the existence of the supreme power because of hearing the powerful instructions of Nārada and understood how to attain perfection in life by *bhakti-yoga.* These are the most important understandings in spiritual knowledge.

yasya deve parā bhaktir
yathā deve tathā gurau
tasyaite kathitā hy arthāḥ
prakāśante mahātmanaḥ

"Unto those great souls who have implicit faith in both the Lord and the spiritual master, all the imports of Vedic knowledge are automatically revealed." (*Śvetāśvatara Upaniṣad* 6.23)

ataḥ śrī-kṛṣṇa-nāmādi
na bhaved grāhyam indriyaiḥ
sevonmukhe hi jihvādau
svayam eva sphuraty adaḥ

"No one can understand Kṛṣṇa as He is by the blunt material senses. But He reveals Himself to the devotees, being pleased with them for their transcendental loving service unto Him." (*Bhakti-rasāmṛta-sindhu* 1.2.234)

bhaktyā mām abhijānāti
yāvān yaś cāsmi tattvataḥ
tato māṁ tattvato jñātvā
viśate tad-anantaram

"One can understand the Supreme Personality as He is only by devotional service. And when one is in full consciousness of the Supreme Lord by such devotion, he can enter into the kingdom of God." (Bg. 18.55)

These are Vedic instructions. One must have full faith in the words of the spiritual master and similar faith in the Supreme Personality of Godhead. Then the real knowledge of *ātmā* and Paramātmā and the distinction between matter and spirit will be automatically revealed. This *ātma-tattva*, or spiritual knowledge, will be revealed within the core of a devotee's heart because of his having taken shelter of the lotus feet of a *mahājana* such as Prahlāda Mahārāja.

In this verse the word *bhūyāt* may be understood to mean "let there be." Prahlāda Mahārāja offers his blessings to his class friends, saying, "Also become faithful like me. Become bona fide Vaiṣṇavas." A devotee of the Lord desires for everyone to take to Kṛṣṇa consciousness. Unfortunately, however, people sometimes do not have staunch faith in the words of the spiritual master who comes by the disciplic succession, and therefore they are unable to understand transcendental knowledge. The spiritual master must be in the line of authorized disciplic succession, like Prahlāda Mahārāja, who received the knowledge from Nārada. If the class friends of Prahlāda Mahārāja, the sons of demons, were to accept the truth through Prahlāda, they would certainly also become fully aware of transcendental knowledge.

The words *vaiśāradī dhīḥ* refer to intelligence concerning the Supreme Personality of Godhead, who is extremely expert. The Lord has created wonderful universes by His expert knowledge. Unless one is extremely expert, he cannot understand the expert management of the supreme expert. One can understand, however, if one is fortunate enough to meet a bona fide spiritual master coming in the disciplic succession from Lord Brahmā, Lord Śiva, Mother Lakṣmī or the Kumāras. These four *sampradāyas*, or disciplic successions of knowledge and transcendence, are called the Brahma-sampradāya, Rudra-sampradāya,

Śrī-sampradāya, and Kumāra-sampradāya. *Sampradāya-vihīnā ye mantrās te niṣphalā matāḥ.* The knowledge of the Supreme received from such a *sampradāya,* or disciplic succession, can give one enlightenment. If one does not take to the path of disciplic succession, it is not possible for one to understand the Supreme Personality of Godhead. If one understands the Supreme Lord through devotional service with faith in the disciplic succession and then advances further, he awakens his natural love for God, and then his success in life is assured.

TEXT 18

जन्माद्याः षडिमे भावा दृष्टा देहस्य नात्मनः ।
फलानामिव वृक्षस्य कालेनेश्वरमूर्तिना ॥१८॥

janmādyāḥ ṣaḍ ime bhāvā
dṛṣṭā dehasya nātmanaḥ
phalānām iva vṛkṣasya
kāleneśvara-mūrtinā

janma-ādyāḥ—beginning with birth; *ṣaṭ*—the six (birth, existence, growth, transformation, dwindling and at last death); *ime*—all these; *bhāvāḥ*—different conditions of the body; *dṛṣṭāḥ*—seen; *dehasya*—of the body; *na*—not; *ātmanaḥ*—of the soul; *phalānām*—of the fruits; *iva*—like; *vṛkṣasya*—of a tree; *kālena*—in due course of time; *īśvara-mūrtinā*—whose form is the ability to transform or control the bodily activities.

TRANSLATION

Just as the fruits and flowers of a tree in due course of time undergo six changes—birth, existence, growth, transformation, dwindling and then death—the material body, which is obtained by the spirit soul under different circumstances, undergoes similar changes. However, there are no such changes for the spirit soul.

PURPORT

This is a very important verse in understanding the difference between the spiritual soul and the material body. The soul is eternal, as stated in *Bhagavad-gītā* (2.20):

na jāyate mriyate vā kadācin
nāyaṁ bhūtvā bhavitā vā na bhūyaḥ
ajo nityaḥ śāśvato 'yaṁ purāṇo
na hanyate hanyamāne śarīre

"For the soul there is never birth nor death. Nor, having once been, does he ever cease to be. He is unborn, eternal, ever-existing, undying and primeval. He is not slain when the body is slain." The spirit soul is eternal, being freed from waste and change, which take place because of the material body. The example of a tree and its fruits and flowers is very simple and clear. A tree stands for many, many years, but with the seasonal changes its fruits and flowers undergo six transformations. The foolish theory of modern chemists that life can be produced by chemical interactions cannot be accepted as truth. The birth of a human being's material body takes place due to a mixture of the ovum and semen, but the history of birth is that although the ovum and semen mix together after sex, there is not always pregnancy. Unless the soul enters the mixture, there is no possibility of pregnancy, but when the soul takes shelter of the mixture the body takes birth, exists, grows, transforms and dwindles, and ultimately it is vanquished. The fruits and flowers of a tree seasonally come and go, but the tree continues to stand. Similarly, the transmigrating soul accepts various bodies, which undergo six transformations, but the soul remains permanently the same (*ajo nityaḥ śāśvato 'yaṁ purāṇo na hanyate hanyamāne śarīre*). The soul is eternal and ever existing, but the bodies accepted by the soul are changing.

There are two kinds of soul—the Supreme Soul (the Personality of Godhead) and the individual soul (the living entity). As various bodily changes take place in the individual soul, different millenniums of creation take place in the Supreme Soul. In this regard, Madhvācārya says:

ṣaḍ vikārāḥ śarīrasya
na viṣṇos tad-gatasya ca
tad-adhīnaṁ śarīraṁ ca
jñātvā tan mamatāṁ tyajet

Since the body is the external feature of the soul, the soul is not dependent on the body; rather, the body is dependent on the soul. One who understands this truth should not be very much anxious about the maintenance of his body. There is no possibility of maintaining the body permanently or eternally. *Antavanta ime dehā nityasyoktāḥ śarīriṇaḥ.* This is the statement of *Bhagavad-gītā* (2.18). The material body is *antavat* (perishable), but the soul within the body is eternal (*nityasyoktāḥ śarīriṇaḥ*). Lord Viṣṇu and the individual souls, who are part and parcel of Him, are both eternal. *Nityo nityānāṁ cetanaś cetanānām.* Lord Viṣṇu is the chief living being, whereas the individual living entities are parts of Lord Viṣṇu. All the various grades of bodies—from the gigantic universal body to the small body of an ant—are perishable, but the Supersoul and the soul, being equal in quality, both exist eternally. This is further explained in the next verses.

TEXTS 19–20

आत्मा नित्योऽव्ययः शुद्ध एकः क्षेत्रज्ञ आश्रयः ।
अविक्रियः स्वदृग् हेतुर्व्यापकोऽसङ्ग्यनावृतः ॥१९॥
एतैर्द्वादशभिर्विद्वानात्मनो लक्षणैः परैः ।
अहं ममेत्यसद्भावं देहादौ मोहजं त्यजेत् ॥२०॥

ātmā nityo 'vyayaḥ śuddha
ekaḥ kṣetra-jña āśrayaḥ
avikriyaḥ sva-dṛg hetur
vyāpako 'saṅgy anāvṛtaḥ

etair dvādaśabhir vidvān
ātmano lakṣaṇaiḥ paraiḥ
ahaṁ mamety asad-bhāvaṁ
dehādau mohajaṁ tyajet

ātmā—the spirit soul, the part of the Supreme Personality of Godhead; *nityaḥ*—without birth or death; *avyayaḥ*—with no possibility of dwindling; *śuddhaḥ*—without the material contamination of attachment and detachment; *ekaḥ*—individual; *kṣetra-jñaḥ*—who knows and is therefore different from the material body; *āśrayaḥ*—the original foundation;[1] *avikriyaḥ*—not undergoing changes like the body;[2] *sva-dṛk*—self-illuminated;[3] *hetuḥ*—the cause of all causes; *vyāpakaḥ*—spreading throughout the body in the form of consciousness; *asaṅgī*—not depending on the body (free to transmigrate from one body to another); *anāvṛtaḥ*—not covered by material contamination; *etaiḥ*—by all these; *dvādaśabhiḥ*—twelve; *vidvān*—a person who is not foolish but fully aware of things as they are; *ātmanaḥ*—of the spirit soul; *lakṣaṇaiḥ*—symptoms; *paraiḥ*—transcendental; *aham*—I ("I am this body"); *mama*—mine ("everything in relationship with this body is mine"); *iti*—thus; *asat-bhāvam*—a false conception of life; *deha-ādau*—identifying oneself with the material body and then with one's wife, children, family, community, nation and so on; *moha-jam*—produced from illusory knowledge; *tyajet*—must give up.

TRANSLATION

"Ātmā" refers to the Supreme Lord or the living entities. Both of them are spiritual, free from birth and death, free from deterioration and free from material contamination. They are individual, they are the knowers of the external body, and they are the foundation or shelter of everything. They are free from material change, they are self-illuminated, they are the cause of all causes, and they are all-pervading. They have nothing to do with the material body, and therefore they are always uncovered. With these transcendental qualities, one who is actually learned must give up the illusory conception of life, in which one thinks, "I am this material body, and everything in relationship with this body is mine."

---

[1] Without the shelter of the spirit soul, the material body cannot exist.

[2] As already explained, the fruits and flowers of a tree take birth, exist, grow, transform, dwindle and die according to seasonal changes, but the tree, through all these changes, remains the same. Similarly, the *ātmā* is free from all changes.

[3] One does not need to make the soul prominent; it is automatically prominent. One can very easily understand that in the living body there is a spiritual soul.

PURPORT

In *Bhagavad-gītā* (15.7) Lord Kṛṣṇa clearly says, *mamaivāṁśo jīva-loke jīva-bhūtaḥ:* "All the living entities are part of Me." Therefore the living entities are qualitatively the same as the Supreme Personality of Godhead, who is the leader, the Supreme among all the living entities. In the *Vedas* it is said, *nityo nityānāṁ cetanaś cetanānām:* the Lord is the chief individual living entity, the leader of the subordinate living entities. Because the living entities are parts or samples of God, their qualities are not different from those of the Supreme Lord. The living entities have the same qualities as the Lord, just as a drop of sea water is composed of the same chemicals as the great sea itself. Thus there is oneness in quality but a difference in quantity. One can understand the Supreme Personality of Godhead by understanding the sample, the living entity, because all the qualities of God exist in a minute quantity in the living entities. There is oneness, but God is great whereas the living entities are extremely small. *Aṇor aṇīyān mahato mahīyān* (*Kaṭha Upaniṣad* 1.2.20). The living entities are smaller than the atom, but God is greater than the greatest. Our conception of greatness may be represented by the sky because we think of the sky as being unlimitedly big, but God is bigger than the sky. Similarly, we have knowledge that the living entities are smaller than atoms, being one ten-thousandth the size of the tip of a hair, yet the quality of being the supreme cause of all causes exists in the living entity as well as in the Supreme Personality of Godhead. Indeed, it is due to the presence of the living entity that the body exists and bodily changes take place. Similarly, it is because the Supreme Lord is within this universe that the changes dictated by the material laws occur.

The word *ekaḥ,* meaning "individual," is significant. As explained in *Bhagavad-gītā* (9.4), *mat-sthāni sarva-bhūtāni na cāhaṁ teṣv avasthitaḥ.* Everything, material and spiritual, including earth, water, air, fire, sky and the living entities, exists on the platform of spirit soul. Although everything is an emanation from the Supreme Personality of Godhead, one should not think that the Supreme Lord is dependent upon anything else.

Both God and the living entity are fully conscious. As living entities, we are conscious of our bodily existence. Similarly, the Lord is conscious of the gigantic cosmic manifestation. This is confirmed in the *Vedas. Yasmin dyauḥ pṛthivī cāntarīkṣam. Vijñātāram adhikena vijānīyāt. Ekam evādvitīyam. Ātma-jyotiḥ samrāḍ ihovāca. Sa imān lokān asṛjata. Satyaṁ jñānam anantam. Asaṅgo hy ayaṁ puruṣaḥ. Pūrṇasya pūrṇam ādāya pūrṇam evāvaśiṣyate.* All these Vedic injunctions prove that both the Supreme Personality of Godhead and the minute soul are individual. One is great, and the other is small, but both of them are the cause of all causes—the corporally limited and the universally unlimited.

We should always remember that although we are equal to the Supreme Personality of Godhead in quality, we are never equal to Him in quantity. Persons with a small fund of intelligence, finding themselves equal in quality with God, foolishly think that they are equal in quantity also. Their intelligence is called *aviśuddha-buddhayaḥ*—unpolished or contaminated intelligence. When such persons, after endeavoring hard for many, many lives to understand the supreme cause, are finally in actual knowledge of Kṛṣṇa, Vāsudeva, they surrender unto Him (*vāsudevaḥ sarvam iti sa mahātmā sudurlabhaḥ*). Thus they become great *mahātmās*, perfect souls. If one is fortunate enough to understand his relationship with God, knowing that God is great (*vibhu*) whereas the living entity is small (*aṇu*), he is perfect in knowledge. The individual exists in darkness when he thinks that he is the material body and that everything in relationship with the material body belongs to him. This is called *ahaṁ mama* (*janasya moho 'yam ahaṁ mameti*). This is illusion. One must give up his illusory conception and thus become fully aware of everything.

TEXT 21

स्वर्णं यथा ग्रावसु हेमकारः
क्षेत्रेषु योगैस्तदभिज्ञ आप्नुयात् ।
क्षेत्रेषु देहेषु तथात्मयोगै-
रध्यात्मविद् ब्रह्मगतिं लभेत ॥२१॥

svarṇaṁ yathā grāvasu hema-kāraḥ
kṣetreṣu yogais tad-abhijña āpnuyāt
kṣetreṣu deheṣu tathātma-yogair
adhyātma-vid brahma-gatiṁ labheta

svarṇam—gold; *yathā*—just as; *grāvasu*—in the stones of gold ore; *hema-kāraḥ*—the expert who knows about gold; *kṣetreṣu*—in the gold mines; *yogaiḥ*—by various processes; *tat-abhijñaḥ*—an expert who can understand where gold is; *āpnuyāt*—very easily obtains; *kṣetreṣu*—within the material fields; *deheṣu*—the human bodies and all the rest of the 8,400,000 different bodily forms; *tathā*—similarly; *ātma-yogaiḥ*—by spiritual processes; *adhyātma-vit*—one who is expert in understanding the distinction between spirit and matter; *brahma-gatim*—perfection in spiritual life; *labheta*—may obtain.

TRANSLATION

An expert geologist can understand where there is gold and by various processes can extract it from the gold ore. Similarly, a spiritually advanced person can understand how the spiritual particle exists within the body, and thus by cultivating spiritual knowledge he can attain perfection in spiritual life. However, as one who is not expert cannot understand where there is gold, a foolish person who has not cultivated spiritual knowledge cannot understand how the spirit exists within the body.

PURPORT

Here is a very good example concerning spiritual understanding. Foolish rascals, including so-called *jñānīs*, philosophers and scientists, cannot understand the existence of the soul within the body because they are lacking in spiritual knowledge. The *Vedas* enjoin, *tad-vijñānārthaṁ sa gurum evābhigacchet:* to understand spiritual knowledge, one must approach a bona fide spiritual master. Unless one has been trained in geology, one cannot detect gold in stone. Similarly, unless one has been trained by a spiritual master, he cannot understand what is spirit and what is matter. Here it is said, *yogais tad-abhijñaḥ.* This indicates that one who has connected himself with spiritual knowledge can understand that there is a spiritual soul within the body. However, one who is in an animalistic conception of life and has no spiritual culture cannot understand. As an expert minerologist or geologist can understand where there is gold and can then invest his money to dig there and chemically separate the gold from the ore, an expert spiritualist can understand where the soul is within matter. One who has not been trained cannot distinguish between gold and stone. Similarly, fools and rascals who have not learned from an expert spiritual master what is soul and what is matter cannot understand the existence of the soul within the body. To understand such knowledge, one must be trained in the mystic *yoga* system, or, finally, in the *bhakti-yoga* system. As stated in *Bhagavad-gītā* (18.55), *bhaktyā mām abhijānāti.* Unless one takes shelter of the *bhakti-yoga* process, one cannot understand the existence of the soul within the body. Therefore *Bhagavad-gītā* begins by teaching:

dehino 'smin yathā dehe
kaumāraṁ yauvanaṁ jarā
tathā dehāntara-prāptir
dhīras tatra na muhyati

"As the embodied soul continually passes, in this body, from boyhood to youth to old age, the soul similarly passes into another body at death. The self-realized soul is not bewildered by such a change." (Bg. 2.13) Thus the first instruction is that one should understand that the soul is within the body and is transmigrating from one body to another. This is the beginning of spiritual knowledge. Any person who is not expert in understanding this science or is unwilling to understand it remains in the bodily conception of life, or the animalistic conception of life, as confirmed in *Śrīmad-Bhāgavatam* (*yasyātma-buddhiḥ kuṇape tri-dhātuke . . . sa eva go-kharaḥ*). Every member of human society should clearly understand the instructions of *Bhagavad-gītā*, for only in this way can one be spiritually elevated and automatically give up the false, illusory knowledge by which one thinks, "I am this body, and everything belonging to this body is mine [*ahaṁ mameti*]." This doggish conception should be rejected immediately. One should be prepared to understand the spirit soul and the supreme spirit, God, who are eternally related. Thus one may return home, back to Godhead, having solved all the problems of life.

TEXT 22

अष्टौ प्रकृतयः प्रोक्तास्त्रय एव हि तद्गुणाः ।
विकाराः षोडशाचार्यैः पुमानेकः समन्वयात् ॥२२॥

aṣṭau prakṛtayaḥ proktās
traya eva hi tad-guṇāḥ
vikārāḥ ṣoḍaśācāryaiḥ
pumān ekaḥ samanvayāt

aṣṭau—eight; *prakṛtayaḥ*—material energies; *proktāḥ*—it is said; *trayaḥ*—three; *eva*—certainly; *hi*—indeed; *tat-guṇāḥ*—the modes of material energy; *vikārāḥ*—transformations; *ṣoḍaśa*—sixteen; *ācāryaiḥ*—by the authorities; *pumān*—the living entity; *ekaḥ*—one; *samanvayāt*—from conjunction.

TRANSLATION

The Lord's eight separated material energies, the three modes of material nature and the sixteen transformations [the eleven senses and the five gross material elements like earth and water]—within all these, the one spiritual soul exists as the observer. Therefore all the great ācāryas have concluded that the individual soul is conditioned by these material elements.

PURPORT

As explained in the previous verse, *kṣetreṣu deheṣu tathātma-yogair adhyātma-vid brahma-gatiṁ labheta:* "A spiritually advanced person can understand how the spiritual particle exists within the body, and thus by cultivating spiritual knowledge he can attain perfection in spiritual life." The intelligent person who is expert in finding the self within the body must understand the eight external energies, which are listed in *Bhagavad-gītā* (7.4):

bhūmir āpo 'nalo vāyuḥ
khaṁ mano buddhir eva ca
ahaṅkāra itīyaṁ me
bhinnā prakṛtir aṣṭadhā

"Earth, water, fire, air, ether, mind, intelligence and false ego—all together these eight comprise My separated material energies." *Bhūmi*, earth, includes all the objects of sense perception—*rūpa* (form), *rasa* (taste), *gandha* (smell), *śabda* (sound) and *sparśa* (touch). Within the earth are the fragrance of roses, the taste of sweet fruit, and whatever else we want. As stated in *Śrīmad-Bhāgavatam* (1.10.4), *sarva-kāma-dughā mahī:* the earth (*mahī*) contains all our requirements. Thus the objects of sense perception are all present in *bhūmi*, or the earth. The gross material elements and subtle material elements (mind, intelligence and *ahaṅkāra*, false ego) constitute the total material energy.

Within the total material energy are the three material modes or qualities. These qualities—*sattva-guṇa*, *rajo-guṇa* and *tamo-guṇa*—belong not to the soul but to the material energy. It is because of the interaction of these three material modes of nature that the five knowledge-gathering senses, the five working senses and their controller, the mind, are manifested. Then, according to these modes, the living entity gets the opportunity to perform different types of *karma* with different types of knowledge, thinking, feeling and willing. Thus the bodily machine begins to work.

This has all been properly analyzed in *sāṅkhya-yoga* by the great *ācāryas*, especially by the Supreme Personality of Godhead, Kṛṣṇa, in His incarnation as Devahūti-putra Kapila. This is indicated here by the word *ācāryaiḥ*. We need not follow anyone who is not an authorized *ācārya*. *Ācāryavān puruṣo veda:* one can understand the truth fully when he has taken shelter of an expert *ācārya*.

The living entity is individual, but the body is a composition of many material elements. This is proved by the fact that as soon as the living entity quits this combination of material elements, it becomes a mere conglomeration of matter. The matter is qualitatively one, and the spiritual soul is qualitatively one with the Supreme. The Supreme is one, and the individual soul is one, but the individual soul is understood to be the master of the individual combination of material energy, whereas the Supreme Lord is the controller of the total material energy. The living entity is the master of his particular body, and according to his activities he is subjected to different types of pains and pleasures. However, although the Supreme Person, the Paramātmā, is also one, He is present as an individual in all the different bodies.

The material energy is in fact divided into twenty-four elements. The individual soul, the owner of the individual body, is a twenty-fifth subject, and above everything is Lord Viṣṇu as Paramātmā, the supreme controller, who is the twenty-sixth subject. When one understands all of these twenty-six subjects, he becomes *adhyātma-vit,* an expert in understanding the distinction between matter and spirit. As stated in *Bhagavad-gītā* (13.3), *kṣetra-kṣetrajñayor jñānam:* understanding of the *kṣetra* (the constitution of the body) and of the individual soul and the Supersoul constitutes real *jñāna,* or knowledge. Unless one ultimately understands that the Supreme Lord is eternally related with the individual soul, one's knowledge is imperfect. This is confirmed in *Bhagavad-gītā* (7.19):

bahūnāṁ janmanām ante
jñānavān māṁ prapadyate
vāsudevaḥ sarvam iti
sa mahātmā sudurlabhaḥ

"After many births and deaths, he who is actually in knowledge surrenders unto Me, knowing Me to be the cause of all causes and all that is. Such a great soul is very rare." Everything, material and spiritual, consists of various energies of Vāsudeva, to whom the individual soul, the spiritual part of the Supreme Lord, is subordinate. Upon understanding this perfect knowledge, one surrenders to the Supreme Personality of Godhead (*vāsudevaḥ sarvam iti sa mahātmā sudurlabhaḥ*).

TEXT 23

देहस्तु सर्वसंघातो जगत् तस्थुरिति द्विधा ।
अत्रैव मृग्यः पुरुषो नेति नेतीत्यतत् त्यजन् ॥२३॥

dehas tu sarva-saṅghāto
jagat tasthur iti dvidhā
atraiva mṛgyaḥ puruṣo
neti netīty atat tyajan

dehaḥ—the body; *tu*—but; *sarva-saṅghātaḥ*—the combination of all the twenty-four elements; *jagat*—seen to be moving; *tasthuḥ*—and standing in one place; *iti*—thus; *dvidhā*—two kinds; *atra eva*—in this matter; *mṛgyaḥ*—to be searched for; *puruṣaḥ*—the living entity, the soul; *na*—not; *iti*—thus; *na*—not; *iti*—thus; *iti*—in this way; *atat*—what is not spirit; *tyajan*—giving up.

TRANSLATION

There are two kinds of bodies for every individual soul—a gross body made of five gross elements and a subtle body made of three subtle elements. Within these bodies, however, is the spirit soul. One must find the soul by analysis, saying, "This is not it. This is not it." Thus one must separate spirit from matter.

PURPORT

As previously stated, *svarṇaṁ yathā grāvasu hema-kāraḥ kṣetreṣu yogais tad-abhijña āpnuyāt.* An expert in the study of soil can find out where gold is and then dig there. He can then analyze the stone and test the gold with nitric acid. Similarly, one must analyze the whole body to find within the body the spirit soul. In studying one's own body, one must ask himself whether his head is his soul, his fingers are his soul, his hand is his soul, and so on. In this way, one must gradually reject all the material elements and the combinations of material elements in the body. Then, if one is expert and follows the *ācārya*, he can understand that he is the spiritual soul living within the body. The greatest *ācārya*, Kṛṣṇa, begins His teachings in *Bhagavad-gītā* by saying:

dehino 'smin yathā dehe
kaumāraṁ yauvanaṁ jarā
tathā dehāntara-prāptir
dhīras tatra na muhyati

"As the embodied soul continually passes, in this body, from boyhood to youth to old age, the soul similarly passes into another body at death. The self-realized soul is not bewildered by such a change." (Bg. 2.13) The spirit soul possesses the body and is within the body. This is the real analysis. The soul never mixes with the bodily elements. Although the soul is within the body, it is separate and always pure. One must analyze and understand his self. This is self-realization. *Neti neti* is the analytical process of rejecting matter. By expertly conducting such an analysis, one can understand where the soul is. One who is not expert, however, cannot distinguish gold from earth, nor the soul from the body.

TEXT 24

अन्वयव्यतिरेकेण विवेकेनोशतात्मना ।
स्वर्गस्थानसमाम्नायैर्विमृशद्भिरसत्वरैः ॥२४॥

anvaya-vyatirekeṇa
vivekenośatātmanā
svarga-sthāna-samāmnāyair
vimṛśadbhir asatvaraiḥ

anvaya—directly; *vyatirekeṇa*—and indirectly; *vivekena*—by mature discrimination; *uśatā*—purified; *ātmanā*—with the mind; *svarga*—creation; *sthāna*—maintenance; *samāmnāyaiḥ*—and with destruction; *vimṛśadbhiḥ*—by those making a serious analysis; *asatvaraiḥ*—very sober.

TRANSLATION

Sober and expert persons should search for the spirit soul with minds purified through analytical study in terms of the soul's connection with and distinction from all things that undergo creation, maintenance and destruction.

PURPORT

A sober person can study himself and distinguish the soul from the body by analytical study. For example, when one considers his body—his head, his hands and so on—one can certainly understand the difference between the spirit soul and the body. No one says, "I head." Everyone says, "My head." Thus there are two entities—the head and "I." They are not identical, although they appear to be one conglomeration.

One may argue, "When we analyze the body we find a head, hands, legs, a belly, blood, bones, urine, stool and so on, but after everything is considered, where is the existence of the soul?" A sober man, however, avails himself of this Vedic instruction:

yato vā imāni bhūtāni jāyante. yena jātāni jīvanti. yat prayanty abhisaṁviśanti. tad vijijñāsasva. tad brahmeti. (*Taittirīya Upaniṣad* 3.1.1)

Thus he can understand that the head, hands, legs and indeed the entire body have grown on the basis of the soul. If the soul is within, the body, head, hands and legs grow, but otherwise they do not. A dead child does not grow up, for the soul is not present. If by a careful analysis of the body one still cannot find the existence of the soul, this is due to his ignorance. How can a gross man fully engaged in materialistic activities understand the soul, which is a small particle of spirit one ten-thousandth the size of the tip of a hair? Such a person foolishly thinks that the material body has grown from a combination of chemicals, although he cannot find them. The *Vedas* inform us, however, that chemical combinations do not constitute the living force; the living force is the *ātmā* and Paramātmā, and the body grows on the basis of that living force. The fruit of a tree grows and undergoes six kinds of change because of the presence of the tree. If there were no tree, there could be no question of the growth and maturity of fruit. Therefore, beyond the existence of the body are the Paramātmā and *ātmā* within the body. This is the first understanding of spiritual knowledge explained in *Bhagavad-gītā. Dehino 'smin yathā dehe.* The body exists because of the presence of the Supreme Lord and the *jīva,* which is part of the Lord. This is further explained by the Lord Himself in *Bhagavad-gītā* (9.4):

mayā tatam idaṁ sarvaṁ
jagad avyakta-mūrtinā
mat-sthāni sarva-bhūtāni
na cāhaṁ teṣv avasthitaḥ

"By Me, in My unmanifested form, this entire universe is pervaded. All beings are in Me, but I am not in them." The Supreme Soul exists everywhere. The *Vedas* enjoin, *sarvaṁ khalv idaṁ brahma:* everything is Brahman or an expansion of Brahman's energies. *Sūtre maṇi-gaṇā iva:* everything rests on the Lord, just like pearls strung together on a thread. The thread is the principal Brahman. He is the supreme cause, the

Supreme Lord upon whom everything rests (*mattaḥ parataraṁ nānyat*). Thus we must study the *ātmā* and Paramātmā—the individual soul and the Supersoul—upon whom the entire material cosmic manifestation rests. This is explained by the Vedic statement *yato vā imāni bhūtāni jāyante. yena jātāni jīvanti.*

TEXT 25

बुद्धेर्जागरणं स्वप्नः सुषुप्तिरिति वृत्तयः ।
ता येनैवानुभूयन्ते सोऽध्यक्षः पुरुषः परः ॥२५॥

buddher jāgaraṇaṁ svapnaḥ
suṣuptir iti vṛttayaḥ
tā yenaivānubhūyante
so 'dhyakṣaḥ puruṣaḥ paraḥ

buddheḥ—of the intelligence; *jāgaraṇam*—the waking or active state of the gross senses; *svapnaḥ*—dreaming (the activity of the senses without the gross body); *suṣuptiḥ*—deep sleep or cessation of all activities (although the living entity is the seer); *iti*—thus; *vṛttayaḥ*—the various transactions; *tāḥ*—they; *yena*—by whom; *eva*—indeed; *anubhūyante*—are perceived; *saḥ*—that; *adhyakṣaḥ*—overseer (who is different from the activities); *puruṣaḥ*—the enjoyer; *paraḥ*—transcendental.

TRANSLATION

Intelligence can be perceived in three states of activity—wakefulness, dreaming and deep sleep. The person who perceives these three is to be considered the original master, the ruler, the Supreme Personality of Godhead.

PURPORT

Without intelligence one cannot understand the direct activities of the senses, nor can he understand dreaming or the cessation of all gross and subtle activities. The seer and controller is the Supreme Personality of Godhead, the Supreme Soul, by whose direction the individual soul can understand when he is awake, when he is sleeping, and when he is completely in trance. In *Bhagavad-gītā* (15.15) the Lord says, *sarvasya cāhaṁ hṛdi sanniviṣṭo mattaḥ smṛtir jñānam apohanaṁ ca:* "I am seated in everyone's heart, and from Me come remembrance, knowledge and forgetfulness." The living entities are completely absorbed in the three states of wakefulness, dreaming and deep sleep through their intelligence. This intelligence is supplied by the Supreme Personality of Godhead, who accompanies the individual soul as a friend. Śrīla Madhvācārya says that the living entity is sometimes described as *sattva-buddhi* when his intelligence acts directly to perceive pains and pleasures above activities. There is a dreaming state in which understanding comes from the Supreme Personality of Godhead (*mattaḥ smṛtir jñānam apohanaṁ ca*). The Supreme Personality of Godhead, the Supersoul, is the supreme controller, and under His direction the living entities are subcontrollers. One must understand the Supreme Personality of Godhead with one's intelligence.

TEXT 26

एभिस्त्रिवर्णैः पर्यस्तैर्बुद्धिभेदैः क्रियोद्भवैः ।
स्वरूपमात्मनो बुध्येद् गन्धैर्वायुमिवान्वयात् ॥२६॥

ebhis tri-varṇaiḥ paryastair
buddhi-bhedaiḥ kriyodbhavaiḥ
svarūpam ātmano budhyed
gandhair vāyum ivānvayāt

ebhiḥ—by these; *tri-varṇaiḥ*—composed of the three modes of nature; *paryastaiḥ*—completely rejected (due to not touching the living force); *buddhi*—of intelligence; *bhedaiḥ*—the differentiations; *kriyā-udbhavaiḥ*—produced from different activities; *svarūpam*—the constitutional position; *ātmanaḥ*—of the self; *budhyet*—one should understand; *gandhaiḥ*—by the aromas; *vāyum*—the air; *iva*—exactly like; *anvayāt*—from close connection.

TRANSLATION

As one can understand the presence of the air by the aromas it carries, so, under the guidance of the Supreme Personality of

Godhead, one can understand the living soul by these three divisions of intelligence. These three divisions, however, are not the soul; they are constituted of the three modes and are born of activities.

PURPORT

As already explained, there are three states to our existence, namely wakefulness, dreaming and deep sleep. In all three states, we have different experiences. Thus the soul is the observer of these three states. Actually, the activities of the body are not the activities of the soul. The soul is different from the body. Just as aromas are distinct from the material vehicle in which they are carried, the soul is unattached to material activities. This analysis can be considered by a person who is fully under the shelter of the lotus feet of the Supreme Lord. This is confirmed by the Vedic injunction *yasmin vijñāte sarvam evaṁ vijñātaṁ bhavati.* If one can understand the Supreme Personality of Godhead, one can automatically understand everything else. Because of not taking shelter of the Lord's lotus feet, even great scholars, scientists, philosophers and religionists are always bewildered. This is confirmed in *Śrīmad-Bhāgavatam* (10.2.32):

ye 'nye 'ravindākṣa vimukta-māninas
tvayy asta-bhāvād aviśuddha-buddhayaḥ

Even though one may artificially think himself liberated from material contamination, if he has not taken shelter of the Lord's lotus feet his intelligence is polluted. As stated in *Bhagavad-gītā* (3.42):

indriyāṇi parāṇy āhur
indriyebhyaḥ paraṁ manaḥ
manasas tu parā buddhir
yo buddheḥ paratas tu saḥ

Above the senses is the mind, above the mind is the intelligence, and above the intelligence is the soul. Ultimately, when one's intelligence becomes clear through devotional service, one is situated in *buddhi-yoga.* This also is explained in *Bhagavad-gītā* (*dadāmi buddhi-yogaṁ taṁ yena māṁ upayānti te*). When devotional service develops and one's intelligence becomes clear, one can use his intelligence to return home, back to Godhead.

TEXT 27

एतद्द्वारो हि संसारो गुणकर्मनिबन्धनः ।
अज्ञानमूलोऽपार्थोऽपि पुंसः स्वप्न इवार्प्यते ॥२७॥

etad dvāro hi saṁsāro
guṇa-karma-nibandhanaḥ
ajñāna-mūlo 'pārtho 'pi
puṁsaḥ svapna ivārpyate

etat—this; *dvāraḥ*—whose door; *hi*—indeed; *saṁsāraḥ*—material existence, in which one suffers threefold miseries; *guṇa-karma-nibandhanaḥ*—captivation by the three modes of material nature; *ajñāna-mūlaḥ*—whose root is ignorance; *apārthaḥ*—without factual meaning; *api*—even; *puṁsaḥ*—of the living entity; *svapnaḥ*—a dream; *iva*—like; *arpyate*—is placed.

TRANSLATION

Through polluted intelligence one is subjected to the modes of nature, and thus one is conditioned by material existence. Like a dreaming state in which one falsely suffers, material existence, which is due to ignorance, must be considered unwanted and temporary.

PURPORT

The unwanted condition of temporary life is called ignorance. One can very easily understand that the material body is temporary, for it is generated at a certain date and ends at a certain date, after undergoing the six kinds of change, namely birth, death, growth, maintenance, transformation and dwindling. This condition of the eternal soul is due to his ignorance, and although it is temporary, it is unwanted. Because of ignorance one is put into temporary bodies one after another. The spirit soul, however, does not need to enter such temporary bodies. He does so only due to his ignorance or his forgetfulness of Kṛṣṇa. Therefore in the human form of life, when one's intelligence is developed, one should change his consciousness by trying to understand Kṛṣṇa. Then one can be liberated. This is confirmed in *Bhagavad-gītā* (4.9), where the Lord says:

janma karma ca me divyam
evaṁ yo vetti tattvataḥ
tyaktvā dehaṁ punar janma
naiti mām eti so 'rjuna

"One who knows the transcendental nature of My appearance and activities does not, upon leaving the body, take his birth again in this material world, but attains My eternal abode, O Arjuna." Unless one understands Kṛṣṇa and comes to Kṛṣṇa consciousness, one must continue in material bondage. To end this conditional life, one must surrender to the Supreme Personality of Godhead. Indeed, that is demanded by the Supreme Lord. *Sarva-dharmān parityajya mām ekaṁ śaraṇaṁ vraja.*

As advised by Mahārāja Ṛṣabhadeva, *na sādhu manye yata ātmano 'yam asann api kleśada āsa dehaḥ.* One must be intelligent enough to understand that although one's body is temporary and will not endure for long, as long as one has a body he must undergo the pangs of material existence. Therefore, if by good association, by the instructions of a bona fide spiritual master, one takes to Kṛṣṇa consciousness, his conditional life of material existence is vanquished, and his original consciousness, known as Kṛṣṇa consciousness, is revived. When one is Kṛṣṇa conscious, he can realize that material existence, whether one is awake or dreaming, is nothing but a dream and has no factual value. This realization is possible by the grace of the Supreme Lord. This grace is also present in the form of the instructions of *Bhagavad-gītā.* Therefore Śrī Caitanya Mahāprabhu's mission is for everyone to engage in welfare activities to awaken the foolish living entity, especially in human society, so that he may come to the platform of Kṛṣṇa consciousness and benefit by liberation from conditional life.

In this connection, Śrīla Madhvācārya cites the following verses:

duḥkha-rūpo 'pi saṁsāro
buddhi-pūrvam avāpyate

yathā svapne śiraś chedaṁ
svayaṁ kṛtvātmano vaśaḥ

tato duḥkham avāpyeta
tathā jāgarito 'pi tu
jānann apy ātmano duḥkham
avaśas tu pravartate

One must realize that the material condition of life is full of distresses. One can realize this with purified intelligence. When one's intelligence is purified, he can understand that unwanted, temporary, material life is just like a dream. Just as one suffers pain when his head is cut off in a dream, in ignorance one suffers not only while dreaming but also while awake. Without the mercy of the Supreme Personality of Godhead, one continues in ignorance and is thus subjected to material distresses in various ways.

TEXT 28

तस्माद्भवद्भिः कर्तव्यं कर्मणां त्रिगुणात्मनाम् ।
बीजनिर्हरणं योगः प्रवाहोपरमो धियः ॥२८॥

tasmād bhavadbhiḥ kartavyaṁ
karmaṇāṁ tri-guṇātmanām
bīja-nirharaṇaṁ yogaḥ
pravāhoparamo dhiyaḥ

tasmāt—therefore; *bhavadbhiḥ*—by your good selves; *kartavyam*—to be done; *karmaṇām*—of all material activities; *tri-guṇa-ātmanām*—conditioned by the three modes of material nature; *bīja-nirharaṇam*—burning of the seed; *yogaḥ*—the process by which one can be linked with the Supreme; *pravāha*—of the continuous current in the form of wakefulness, dreaming and deep sleep; *uparamaḥ*—the cessation; *dhiyaḥ*—of the intelligence.

TRANSLATION

Therefore, my dear friends, O sons of the demons, your duty is to take to Kṛṣṇa consciousness, which can burn the seed of fruitive

activities artificially created by the modes of material nature and stop the flow of the intelligence in wakefulness, dreaming and deep sleep. In other words, when one takes to Kṛṣṇa consciousness, his ignorance is immediately dissipated.

PURPORT

This is confirmed in *Bhagavad-gītā* (14.26):

māṁ ca yo 'vyabhicāreṇa
bhakti-yogena sevate
sa guṇān samatītyaitān
brahma-bhūyāya kalpate

"One who engages in full devotional service, who does not fall down in any circumstance, at once transcends the modes of material nature and thus comes to the level of Brahman." By the practice of *bhakti-yoga,* one immediately comes to the spiritual platform, transcendental to the actions and reactions of the three modes of material nature. The root of ignorance is material consciousness, which must be killed by spiritual consciousness, or Kṛṣṇa consciousness. The word *bīja-nirharaṇam* refers to burning the root cause of material life to ashes. In the Medinī dictionary, *yoga* is explained by its result: *yoge 'pūrvārtha-samprāptau saṅgati-dhyāna-yuktiṣu.* When one is put into an awkward position because of ignorance, the process by which one can be freed from this entanglement is called *yoga.* This is also called liberation. *Muktir hitvānyathā-rūpaṁ svarūpeṇa vyavasthitiḥ. Mukti* means giving up one's position in ignorance or illusion, by which one thinks in a way contrary to his constitutional position. Returning to one's constitutional position is called *mukti,* and the process by which one does this is called *yoga.* Thus *yoga* is above *karma, jñāna* and *sāṅkhya.* Indeed, *yoga* is the ultimate goal of life. Kṛṣṇa therefore advised Arjuna to become a *yogī* (*tasmād yogī bhavārjuna*). Lord Kṛṣṇa further advised in *Bhagavad-gītā* that the first-class *yogī* is he who has come to the platform of devotional service.

yoginām api sarveṣāṁ
mad-gatenāntarātmanā

śraddhāvān bhajate yo māṁ
sa me yuktatamo mataḥ

"Of all *yogīs*, he who always abides in Me with great faith, worshiping Me in transcendental loving service, is most intimately united with Me in *yoga* and is the highest of all." (Bg. 6.47) Thus one who always thinks of Kṛṣṇa within the core of his heart is the best *yogī*. By practicing this best of all *yoga* systems, one is liberated from the material condition.

TEXT 29

तत्रोपायसहस्राणामयं भगवतोदितः ।
यदीश्वरे भगवति यथा यैरञ्जसा रतिः ॥२९॥

tatropāya-sahasrāṇām
ayaṁ bhagavatoditaḥ
yad īśvare bhagavati
yathā yair añjasā ratiḥ

tatra—in that connection (getting out of the entanglement of material conditioning); *upāya*—of processes; *sahasrāṇām*—of many thousands; *ayam*—this; *bhagavatā uditaḥ*—given by the Supreme Personality of Godhead; *yat*—which; *īśvare*—to the Lord; *bhagavati*—the Supreme Personality of Godhead; *yathā*—as much as; *yaiḥ*—by which; *añjasā*—quickly; *ratiḥ*—attachment with love and affection.

TRANSLATION

Of the different processes recommended for disentanglement from material life, the one personally explained and accepted by the Supreme Personality of Godhead should be considered all-perfect. That process is the performance of duties by which love for the Supreme Lord develops.

PURPORT

Among the linking processes that elevate one from bondage to material contamination, the one recommended by the Supreme Personality of Godhead should be accepted as the best. That process is clearly explained in *Bhagavad-gītā,* where the Lord says, *sarva-dharmān parityajya mām ekaṁ śaraṇaṁ vraja:* "Abandon all varieties of religion and just surrender unto Me." This process is the best because the Lord assures, *ahaṁ tvāṁ sarva-pāpebhyo mokṣayiṣyāmi mā śucaḥ:* "I shall deliver you from all sinful reaction. Do not fear." There is no need to be worried, for the Lord Himself assures that He will care for His devotee and save him from the reactions of sinful activities. Material bondage is a result of sinful activity. Therefore, since the Lord assures that He will dissipate the results of fruitive material activities, there is no need to be worried. This process of understanding one's position as a spirit soul and then engaging oneself in devotional service is therefore the best. The entire Vedic program is based on this principle, and one can understand it as recommended in the *Vedas:*

yasya deve parā bhaktir
yathā deve tathā gurau
tasyaite kathitā hy arthāḥ
prakāśante mahātmanaḥ

"Unto those great souls who have implicit faith in both the Lord and the spiritual master, all the imports of Vedic knowledge are automatically revealed." (*Śvetāśvatara Upaniṣad* 6.23) One must accept the pure devotee, the representative of God, as one's *guru* and then offer him all the respects one would offer the Supreme Personality of Godhead. This is the secret of success. For one who adopts this method, the perfect process is revealed. In this verse, the words *yair añjasā ratiḥ* indicate that by offering service and surrendering to the spiritual master, one is elevated to devotional service, and by performing devotional service one gradually becomes attached to the Supreme Personality of Godhead. Because of this attachment to the Lord, one can understand the Lord. In other words, one can understand what the Lord's position is, what our position is and what our relationship is. All this can be understood very easily by the simple method of *bhakti-yoga.* As soon as one is situated on the platform of *bhakti-yoga,* the root cause of one's suffering and material bondage is destroyed. This is clearly explained in the next verse, which gives the secret of success.

TEXTS 30–31

गुरुशुश्रूषया भक्त्या सर्वलब्धार्पणेन च ।
सङ्गेन साधुभक्तानामीश्वराराधनेन च ॥३०॥
श्रद्धया तत्कथायां च कीर्तनैर्गुणकर्मणाम् ।
तत्पादाम्बुरुहध्यानात् तल्लिङ्गेक्षार्हणादिभिः ॥३१॥

guru-śuśrūṣayā bhaktyā
sarva-labdhārpaṇena ca
saṅgena sādhu-bhaktānām
īśvarārādhanena ca

śraddhayā tat-kathāyāṁ ca
kīrtanair guṇa-karmaṇām
tat-pādāmburuha-dhyānāt
tal-liṅgekṣārhaṇādibhiḥ

guru-śuśrūṣayā—by rendering service to the bona fide spiritual master; *bhaktyā*—with faith and devotion; *sarva*—all; *labdha*—of material gains; *arpaṇena*—by offering (to the *guru*, or to Kṛṣṇa through the spiritual master); *ca*—and; *saṅgena*—by the association; *sādhu-bhaktānām*—of devotees and saintly persons; *īśvara*—of the Supreme Personality of Godhead; *ārādhanena*—by the worship; *ca*—and; *śraddhayā*—with great faith; *tat-kathāyām*—in discourses about the Lord; *ca*—and; *kīrtanaiḥ*—by glorifications; *guṇa-karmaṇām*—of the transcendental qualities and activities of the Lord; *tat*—His; *pāda-amburuha*—on the lotus feet; *dhyānāt*—by meditation; *tat*—His; *liṅga*—forms (Deities); *īkṣa*—observing; *arhaṇa-ādibhiḥ*—and by worshiping.

TRANSLATION

One must accept the bona fide spiritual master and render service unto him with great devotion and faith. Whatever one has in one's possession should be offered to the spiritual master, and in the association of saintly persons and devotees one should worship the Lord, hear the glories of the Lord with faith, glorify the

transcendental qualities and activities of the Lord, always meditate on the Lord's lotus feet, and worship the Deity of the Lord strictly according to the injunctions of the śāstra and guru.

PURPORT

In the previous verse it has been said that the process which immediately increases one's love and affection for the Supreme Personality of Godhead is the best of the many thousands of ways to become free from the entanglement of material existence. It is also said, *dharmasya tattvaṁ nihitaṁ guhāyām:* actually the truth of religious principles is extremely confidential. Nonetheless, it can be understood very easily if one actually adopts the principles of religion. As it is said, *dharmaṁ tu sākṣād bhagavat-praṇītam:* the process of religion is enunciated by the Supreme Lord because He is the supreme authority. This is also indicated in the previous verse by the word *bhagavatoditaḥ.* The injunctions or directions of the Lord are infallible, and their benefits are fully assured. According to His directions, which are explained in this verse, the perfect form of religion is *bhakti-yoga.*

To practice *bhakti-yoga,* one must first accept a bona fide spiritual master. Śrīla Rūpa Gosvāmī, in his *Bhakti-rasāmṛta-sindhu* (1.2.74–75), advises:

guru-pādāśrayas tasmāt
kṛṣṇa-dīkṣādi-śikṣaṇam
viśrambheṇa guroḥ sevā
sādhu-vartmānuvartanam

sad-dharma-pṛcchā bhogādi-
tyāgaḥ kṛṣṇasya hetave

One's first duty is to accept a bona fide spiritual master. The student or disciple should be very inquisitive; he should be eager to know the complete truth about eternal religion (*sanātana-dharma*). The words *guru-śuśrūṣayā* mean that one should personally serve the spiritual master by giving him bodily comforts, helping him in bathing, dressing, sleeping, eating and so on. This is called *guru-śuśrūṣaṇam.* A disciple should serve the spiritual master as a menial servant, and whatever he has in his possession should be dedicated to the spiritual master. *Prāṇair arthair dhiyā vācā.* Everyone has his life, his wealth, his intelligence and his words, and all of them should be offered to the Supreme Personality of Godhead through the via medium of the spiritual master. Everything should be offered to the spiritual master as a matter of duty, but the offering should be made to the spiritual master with heart and soul, not artificially to gain material prestige. This offering is called *arpaṇa.* Moreover, one should live among devotees, saintly persons, to learn the etiquette and proper behavior of devotional service. Śrīla Viśvanātha Cakravartī Ṭhākura remarks in this connection that whatever is offered to the spiritual master should be offered with love and affection, not for material adoration. Similarly, it is recommended that one associate with devotees, but there must be some discrimination. Actually, a *sādhu,* a saintly person, must be saintly in his behavior (*sādhavaḥ sad-ācārāḥ*). Unless one adheres to the standard behavior, one's position as a *sādhu,* a saintly person, is not complete. Therefore a Vaiṣṇava, a *sādhu,* must completely adhere to the standard of behavior. Śrīla Viśvanātha Cakravartī Ṭhākura says that a Vaiṣṇava, a person initiated into the Vaiṣṇava cult, should be offered the respect befitting a Vaiṣṇava, which means that he should be offered service and prayers. However, one should not associate with him if he is not a fit person with whom to associate.

TEXT 32

हरिः सर्वेषु भूतेषु भगवानास्त ईश्वरः ।
इति भूतानि मनसा कामैस्तैः साधु मानयेत् ॥३२॥

hariḥ sarveṣu bhūteṣu
bhagavān āsta īśvaraḥ
iti bhūtāni manasā
kāmais taiḥ sādhu mānayet

hariḥ—the Supreme Personality of Godhead; *sarveṣu*—in all; *bhūteṣu*—living entities; *bhagavān*—the supreme personality; *āste*—is situated; *īśvaraḥ*—the supreme controller; *iti*—thus; *bhūtāni*—all living entities; *manasā*—by such understanding; *kāmaiḥ*—by desires; *taiḥ*—those; *sādhu mānayet*—one should highly esteem.

TRANSLATION

One should always remember the Supreme Personality of Godhead in His localized representation as the Paramātmā, who is situated in the core of every living entity's heart. Thus one should offer respect to every living entity according to that living entity's position or manifestation.

PURPORT

Hariḥ sarveṣu bhūteṣu. This statement is sometimes misunderstood by unscrupulous persons who wrongly conclude that because Hari, the Supreme Personality of Godhead, is situated in every living entity, every living entity is therefore Hari. Such foolish persons do not distinguish between the *ātmā* and the Paramātmā, who are situated in every body. The *ātmā* is the living entity, and the Paramātmā is the Supreme Personality of Godhead. The individual living entity, however, is different from the Paramātmā, the Supreme Lord. Therefore *hariḥ sarveṣu bhūteṣu* means that Hari is situated as Paramātmā, not as *ātmā*, although *ātmā* is a part of Paramātmā. Offering respect to every living entity means offering respect to the Paramātmā situated in every living entity. One should not misunderstand every living entity to be the Paramātmā. Sometimes unscrupulous persons designate a living entity as *daridra-nārāyaṇa*, *svāmī-nārāyaṇa*, this Nārāyaṇa or that Nārāyaṇa. One should clearly understand that although Nārāyaṇa is situated in the core of the heart of every living entity, the living entity never becomes Nārāyaṇa.

TEXT 33

एवं निर्जितषड्वर्गैः क्रियते भक्तिरीश्वरे ।
वासुदेवे भगवति यया संलभ्यते रतिः ॥३३॥

evaṁ nirjita-ṣaḍ-vargaiḥ
kriyate bhaktir īśvare
vāsudeve bhagavati
yayā saṁlabhyate ratiḥ

evam—thus; *nirjita*—subdued; *ṣaṭ-vargaiḥ*—by the six symptoms of the senses (lusty desires, anger, greed, illusion, madness and jealousy);

kriyate—is rendered; *bhaktiḥ*—devotional service; *īśvare*—unto the supreme controller; *vāsudeve*—to Lord Vāsudeva; *bhagavati*—the Supreme Personality of Godhead; *yayā*—by which; *saṁlabhyate*—is obtained; *ratiḥ*—attachment.

TRANSLATION

By these activities [as mentioned above] one is able to cut down the influence of the enemies, namely lust, anger, greed, illusion, madness and jealousy, and when thus situated, one can render service to the Lord. In this way one surely attains the platform of loving service to the Supreme Personality of Godhead.

PURPORT

As mentioned in verses thirty and thirty-one, one's first duty is to approach the spiritual master, the representative of the Supreme Personality of Godhead, to begin rendering service to him. Prahlāda Mahārāja proposed that from the very beginning of life (*kaumāra ācaret prājñaḥ*) a small child should be trained to serve the spiritual master while living at the *guru-kula*. *Brahmacārī guru-kule vasan dānto guror hitam* (*Bhāg.* 7.12.1). This is the beginning of spiritual life. *Guru-pādāśrayaḥ, sādhu-vartmānuvartanam, sad-dharma-pṛcchā.* By following the instructions of the *guru* and the *śāstras,* the disciple attains the stage of devotional service and becomes unattached to possessions. Whatever he possesses he offers to the spiritual master, the *guru,* who engages him in *śravaṇaṁ kīrtanaṁ viṣṇoḥ.* The disciple follows strictly and in this way learns how to control his senses. Then, by using his pure intelligence, he gradually becomes a lover of the Supreme Personality of Godhead, as confirmed by Śrīla Rūpa Gosvāmī (*ādau śraddhā tataḥ sādhu-saṅgaḥ*). In this way one's life becomes perfect, and his attachment for Kṛṣṇa becomes positively manifested. In that stage, he is situated in ecstasy, experiencing *bhāva* and *anubhāva,* as explained in the following verse.

TEXT 34

निशम्य कर्माणि गुणानतुल्यान्
वीर्याणि लीलातनुभिः कृतानि ।

यदातिहर्षोत्पुलकाश्रुगद्गदं
प्रोत्कण्ठ उद्गायति रौति नृत्यति ॥३४॥

niśamya karmāṇi guṇān atulyān
vīryāṇi līlā-tanubhiḥ kṛtāni
yadātiharṣotpulakāśru-gadgadaṁ
protkaṇṭha udgāyati rauti nṛtyati

niśamya—hearing; *karmāṇi*—transcendental activities; *guṇān*—spiritual qualities; *atulyān*—uncommon (not generally visible in an ordinary person); *vīryāṇi*—very powerful; *līlā-tanubhiḥ*—by different pastime forms; *kṛtāni*—performed; *yadā*—when; *atiharṣa*—because of great jubilation; *utpulaka*—horripilation; *aśru*—tears in the eyes; *gadgadam*—faltering voice; *protkaṇṭhaḥ*—with an open voice; *udgāyati*—chants very loudly; *rauti*—cries; *nṛtyati*—dances.

TRANSLATION

One who is situated in devotional service is certainly the controller of his senses, and thus he is a liberated person. When such a liberated person, the pure devotee, hears of the transcendental qualities and activities of the Lord's incarnations for the performance of various pastimes, his hair stands on end on his body, tears fall from his eyes, and in his spiritual realization his voice falters. Sometimes he very openly dances, sometimes he sings loudly, and sometimes he cries. Thus he expresses his transcendental jubilation.

PURPORT

The Lord's activities are uncommon. For example, when He appeared as Lord Rāmacandra, He performed uncommon activities like bridging the ocean. Similarly, when Lord Kṛṣṇa appeared He raised the Govardhana Hill when He was only seven years of age. These are uncommon activities. Fools and rascals, who are not in the transcendental position, consider these uncommon activities of the Lord to be mythological, but when the pure devotee, the liberated person, hears about these uncommon activities of the Lord, he immediately becomes ecstatic and exhibits the symptoms of chanting, dancing, and crying very loudly and jubilantly. This is the difference between a devotee and a nondevotee.

TEXT 35

यदा ग्रहग्रस्त इव क्वचिद्धस-
त्याक्रन्दते ध्यायति वन्दते जनम् ।
मुहुः श्वसन्वक्ति हरे जगत्पते
नारायणेत्यात्ममतिर्गतत्रपः ॥३५॥

yadā graha-grasta iva kvacid dhasaty
ākrandate dhyāyati vandate janam
muhuḥ śvasan vakti hare jagat-pate
nārāyaṇety ātma-matir gata-trapaḥ

yadā—when; *graha-grastaḥ*—haunted by a ghost; *iva*—like; *kvacit*—sometimes; *hasati*—laughs; *ākrandate*—cries loudly (remembering the transcendental qualities of the Lord); *dhyāyati*—meditates; *vandate*—offers respects; *janam*—to all living entities (thinking all of them to be engaged in the service of the Lord); *muhuḥ*—constantly; *śvasan*—breathing heavily; *vakti*—he speaks; *hare*—O my Lord; *jagat-pate*—O master of the whole world; *nārāyaṇa*—O Lord Nārāyaṇa; *iti*—thus; *ātma-matiḥ*—fully absorbed in thoughts of the Supreme Lord; *gata-trapaḥ*—without shame.

TRANSLATION

When a devotee becomes like a person haunted by a ghost, he laughs and very loudly chants about the qualities of the Lord. Sometimes he sits to perform meditation, and he offers respects to every living entity, considering him a devotee of the Lord. Constantly breathing very heavily, he becomes careless of social etiquette and loudly chants like a madman, "Hare Kṛṣṇa, Hare Kṛṣṇa! O my Lord, O master of the universe!"

PURPORT

When one chants the holy name of the Lord in ecstasy, not caring for outward social conventions, it is to be understood that he is *ātma-mati.* In other words, his consciousness is turned toward the Supreme Personality of Godhead.

TEXT 36

तदा पुमान्मुक्तसमस्तबन्धन-
स्तद्भावभावानुकृताशयाकृतिः ।
निर्दग्धबीजानुशयो महीयसा
भक्तिप्रयोगेण समेत्यधोक्षजम् ॥३६॥

tadā pumān mukta-samasta-bandhanas
tad-bhāva-bhāvānukṛtāśayākṛtiḥ
nirdagdha-bījānuśayo mahīyasā
bhakti-prayogeṇa samety adhokṣajam

tadā—at that time; *pumān*—the living entity; *mukta*—liberated; *samasta-bandhanaḥ*—from all material obstacles on the path of devotional service; *tat-bhāva*—of the situation of the Supreme Lord's activities; *bhāva*—by thinking; *anukṛta*—made similar; *āśaya-ākṛtiḥ*—whose mind and body; *nirdagdha*—completely burned up; *bīja*—the seed or original cause of material existence; *anuśayaḥ*—desire; *mahīyasā*—very powerful; *bhakti*—of devotional service; *prayogeṇa*—by the application; *sameti*—achieves; *adhokṣajam*—the Supreme Personality of Godhead, who is beyond the reach of the material mind and knowledge.

TRANSLATION

The devotee is then freed from all material contamination because he constantly thinks of the Lord's pastimes and because his mind and body have been converted to spiritual qualities. Because of his intense devotional service, his ignorance, material consciousness and all kinds of material desires are completely burnt to ashes. This is the stage at which one can achieve the shelter of the Lord's lotus feet.

PURPORT

When a devotee is completely purified, he becomes *anyābhilāṣitā-śūnya.* In other words, all of his material desires become zero, being burnt to ashes, and he exists either as the Lord's servant, friend, father, mother or conjugal lover. Because one thinks constantly in this way, one's present material body and mind are fully spiritualized, and the needs of one's material body completely vanish from one's existence. An iron rod put into a fire becomes warmer and warmer, and when it is red hot it is no longer an iron rod but fire. Similarly, when a devotee constantly engages in devotional service and thinks of the Lord in his original Kṛṣṇa consciousness, he no longer has any material activities, for his body is spiritualized. Advancement in Kṛṣṇa consciousness is very powerful, and therefore even during this life such a devotee has achieved the shelter of the lotus feet of the Lord. This transcendental ecstatic existence of a devotee was completely exhibited by Śrī Caitanya Mahāprabhu. In this regard, Śrīla Madhvācārya writes as follows:

tad-bhāva-bhāvaḥ tad yathā svarūpaṁ bhaktiḥ
kecid bhaktā vinṛtyanti gāyanti ca yathepsitam
kecit tuṣṇīṁ japanty eva kecit śobhaya-kāriṇaḥ

The ecstatic condition of devotional service was completely exhibited by Śrī Caitanya Mahāprabhu, who sometimes danced, sometimes cried, sometimes sang, sometimes remained silent, and sometimes chanted the holy name of the Lord. That is perfect spiritual existence.

TEXT 37

अधोक्षजालम्भमिहाशुभात्मनः
शरीरिणः संसृतिचक्रशातनम् ।
तद् ब्रह्मनिर्वाणसुखं विदुर्बुधा-
स्ततो भजध्वं हृदये हृदीश्वरम् ॥३७॥

adhokṣajālambham ihāśubhātmanaḥ
śarīriṇaḥ saṁsṛti-cakra-śātanam
tad brahma-nirvāṇa-sukhaṁ vidur budhās
tato bhajadhvaṁ hṛdaye hṛd-īśvaram

adhokṣaja—with the Supreme Personality of Godhead, who is beyond the reach of the materialistic mind or experimental knowledge;

ālambham—being constantly in contact; *iha*—in this material world; *aśubha-ātmanaḥ*—whose mind is materially contaminated; *śarīriṇaḥ*—of a living entity who has accepted a material body; *saṁsṛti*—of material existence; *cakra*—the cycle; *śātanam*—completely stopping; *tat*—that; *brahma-nirvāṇa*—connected with the Supreme Brahman, the Absolute Truth; *sukham*—transcendental happiness; *viduḥ*—understand; *budhāḥ*—those who are spiritually advanced; *tataḥ*—therefore; *bhajadhvam*—engage in devotional service; *hṛdaye*—within the core of the heart; *hṛt-īśvaram*—to the Supreme Personality of Godhead, the Supersoul within the heart.

TRANSLATION

The real problem of life is the repetition of birth and death, which is like a wheel rolling repeatedly up and down. This wheel, however, completely stops when one is in touch with the Supreme Personality of Godhead. In other words, by the transcendental bliss realized from constant engagement in devotional service, one is completely liberated from material existence. All learned men know this. Therefore, my dear friends, O sons of the asuras, immediately begin meditating upon and worshiping the Supersoul within everyone's heart.

PURPORT

Generally it is understood that by merging into the existence of Brahman, the impersonal feature of the Absolute Truth, one becomes completely happy. The words *brahma-nirvāṇa* refer to connecting with the Absolute Truth, who is realized in three features: *brahmeti paramātmeti bhagavān iti śabdyate.* One feels *brahma-sukha,* spiritual happiness, by merging into the impersonal Brahman because the *brahmajyoti* is the effulgence of the Supreme Personality of Godhead. *Yasya prabhā prabhavato jagad-aṇḍa-koṭi. Yasya prabhā,* the impersonal Brahman, consists of the rays of Kṛṣṇa's transcendental body. Therefore whatever transcendental bliss one feels from merging in Brahman is due to contact with Kṛṣṇa. Contact with Kṛṣṇa is perfect *brahma-sukha.* When the mind is in touch with the impersonal Brahman one becomes satisfied, but one must advance further to render service to the Supreme Personality of Godhead, for one's remaining merged in the Brahman effulgence is not always assured. As it is said, *āruhya kṛcchreṇa paraṁ padaṁ tataḥ patanty adho 'nādṛta-yuṣmad-aṅghrayaḥ:* one may merge in the Brahman feature of the Absolute Truth, but there is a chance that one may fall because of not being acquainted with Adhokṣaja, or Vāsudeva. Of course, such *brahma-sukha* undoubtedly eliminates material happiness, but when one advances through impersonal Brahman and localized Paramātmā to approach the Supreme Personality of Godhead in relationship with Him as a servant, friend, parent or conjugal lover, one's happiness becomes all-pervading. Then one automatically feels transcendental bliss, just as one becomes happy seeing the shining of the moon. One acquires natural happiness upon seeing the moon, but when one can see the Supreme Personality of Godhead, one's transcendental happiness increases hundreds and thousands of times. As soon as one is very intimately connected with the Supreme Personality of Godhead, one surely becomes free from all material contamination. *Yā nirvṛtis tanu-bhṛtām.* This cessation of all material happiness is called *nirvṛti* or *nirvāṇa.* Śrīla Rūpa Gosvāmī says in *Bhakti-rasāmṛta-sindhu* (1.1.38):

brahmānando bhaved eṣa
cet parārdha-guṇīkṛtaḥ
naiti bhakti-sukhāmbhodheḥ
paramāṇu-tulām api

"If *brahmānanda,* the bliss of merging in the Brahman effulgence, were multiplied one hundred trillion times, it would still not equal even an atomic fragment of the ocean of transcendental bliss felt in devotional service."

brahma-bhūtaḥ prasannātmā
na śocati na kāṅkṣati
samaḥ sarveṣu bhūteṣu
mad-bhaktiṁ labhate parām

"One who is transcendentally situated at once realizes the Supreme Brahman and becomes fully joyful. He never laments nor desires to have anything; he is equally disposed toward all living entities. In that state he attains pure devotional service unto the Lord." (Bg. 18.54) If one advances further from the *brahma-nirvāṇa* platform, one enters the stage of devotional service (*mad-bhaktiṁ labhate parām*). The word *adhokṣajālambham* refers to keeping the mind always engaged in the Absolute Truth, who is beyond the mind and material speculation. *Sa vai manaḥ kṛṣṇa-padāravindayoḥ.* This is the result of Deity worship. By constantly engaging in the service of the Lord and thinking of His lotus feet, one is automatically freed from all material contamination. Thus the word *brahma-nirvāṇa-sukham* indicates that when one is in touch with the Absolute Truth, material sense gratification is completely nullified.

TEXT 38

कोऽतिप्रयासोऽसुरबालका हरे-
रुपासने स्वे हृदि छिद्रवत् सतः ।
स्वस्यात्मनः सख्युरशेषदेहिनां
सामान्यतः किं विषयोपपादनैः ॥३८॥

ko 'ti-prayāso 'sura-bālakā harer
upāsane sve hṛdi chidravat sataḥ
svasyātmanaḥ sakhyur aśeṣa-dehināṁ
sāmānyataḥ kiṁ viṣayopapādanaiḥ

kaḥ—what; *ati-prayāsaḥ*—difficult endeavor; *asura-bālakāḥ*—O sons of demons; *hareḥ*—of the Supreme Personality of Godhead; *upāsane*—in discharging the devotional service; *sve*—in one's own; *hṛdi*—core of the heart; *chidra-vat*—just like the space; *sataḥ*—who always exists; *svasya*—of one's self or of the living entity; *ātmanaḥ*—of the Supersoul; *sakhyuḥ*—of the well-wishing friend; *aśeṣa*—unlimited; *dehinām*—of the embodied souls; *sāmānyataḥ*—generally; *kim*—what is the need; *viṣaya-upapādanaiḥ*—with activities delivering the objects of the senses for sense enjoyment.

TRANSLATION

O my friends, sons of the asuras, the Supreme Personality of Godhead in His Supersoul feature always exists within the cores of

the hearts of all living entities. Indeed, He is the well-wisher and friend of all living entities, and there is no difficulty in worshiping the Lord. Why, then, should people not engage in His devotional service? Why are they so addicted to unnecessarily producing artificial paraphernalia for sense gratification?

PURPORT

Because the Personality of Godhead is supreme, no one is equal to Him, and no one is greater than Him. Nonetheless, if one is a devotee of the Supreme Personality of Godhead, the Lord is easily obtainable. The Lord is compared to the sky because the sky is vast yet within the reach of all, not only of human beings but even of the animals. The Supreme Lord, in His Paramātmā feature, exists as the best well-wisher and friend. As confirmed in the *Vedas, sayujau sakhāyau.* The Lord, in His Supersoul feature, always stays in the heart along with the living entity. The Lord is so friendly to the living entity that He remains within the heart so that one can always contact Him without difficulty. One can do this simply by devotional service (*śravaṇaṁ kīrtanaṁ viṣṇoḥ smaranaṁ pāda-sevanam*). As soon as one hears of the Supreme Personality of Godhead (*kṛṣṇa-kīrtana*), one immediately comes in touch with the Lord. A devotee immediately comes in touch with the Lord by any or all of the items of devotional service:

śravaṇaṁ kīrtanaṁ viṣṇoḥ
smaraṇaṁ pāda-sevanam
arcanaṁ vandanaṁ dāsyaṁ
sakhyam ātma-nivedanam

Therefore there is no difficulty in coming in contact with the Supreme Lord (*ko 'ti-prayāsaḥ*). On the other hand, going to hell requires great endeavor. If one wants to go to hell by illicit sex, meat-eating, gambling and intoxication, he must acquire so many things. For illicit sex he must arrange for money for brothels, for meat-eating he must arrange for many slaughterhouses, for gambling he must arrange for casinos and hotels, and for intoxication he must open many breweries. Clearly, therefore, if one wants to go to hell he must endeavor very much, but if he wants to return home, back to Godhead, there is no difficult endeavor.

To go back to Godhead, one may live alone anywhere, in any condition, and simply sit down, meditate upon the Supersoul and chant and hear about the Lord. Thus there is no difficulty in approaching the Lord. *Adānta-gobhir viśatāṁ tamisram.* Because of inability to control the senses, one must go through great endeavor to go to hell, but if one is sensible he can very easily obtain the favor of the Supreme Personality of Godhead because the Lord is always with him. By the simple method of *śravaṇaṁ kīrtanaṁ viṣṇoḥ*, the Lord is satisfied. Indeed, the Lord says:

patraṁ puṣpaṁ phalaṁ toyaṁ
yo me bhaktyā prayacchati
tad ahaṁ bhakty-upahṛtam
aśnāmi prayatātmanaḥ

"If one offers Me with love and devotion a leaf, a flower, fruit or water, I will accept it." (Bg. 9.26) One can meditate upon the Lord anywhere and everywhere. Thus Prahlāda Mahārāja advised his friends, the sons of the demons, to take this path back home, back to Godhead, without difficulty.

TEXT 39

रायः कलत्रं पशवः सुतादयो
गृहा मही कुञ्जरकोशभूतयः ।
सर्वेऽर्थकामाः क्षणभङ्गुरायुषः
कुर्वन्ति मर्त्यस्य कियत् प्रियं चलाः ॥३९॥

rāyaḥ kalatraṁ paśavaḥ sutādayo
gṛhā mahī kuñjara-kośa-bhūtayaḥ
sarve 'rtha-kāmāḥ kṣaṇa-bhaṅgurāyuṣaḥ
kurvanti martyasya kiyat priyaṁ calāḥ

rāyaḥ—wealth; *kalatram*—one's wife and feminine friends; *paśavaḥ*—domestic animals like cows, horses, asses, cats and dogs; *suta-ādayaḥ*—children and so on; *gṛhāḥ*—big buildings and residences; *mahī*—land; *kuñjara*—elephants; *kośa*—treasury house; *bhūtayaḥ*—and other luxuries for sense gratification and material enjoyment;

sarve—all; *artha*—economic development; *kāmāḥ*—and sense gratification; *kṣaṇa-bhaṅgura*—perishable in a moment; *āyuṣaḥ*—of one whose duration of life; *kurvanti*—effect or bring; *martyasya*—of one who is destined to die; *kiyat*—how much; *priyam*—pleasure; *calāḥ*—flickering and temporary.

TRANSLATION

One's riches, beautiful wife and female friends, one's sons and daughters, one's residence, one's domestic animals like cows, elephants and horses, one's treasury, economic development and sense gratification—indeed, even the lifetime in which one can enjoy all these material opulences—are certainly temporary and flickering. Since the opportunity of human life is temporary, what benefit can these material opulences give to a sensible man who has understood himself to be eternal?

PURPORT

This verse describes how the advocates of economic development are frustrated by the laws of nature. As the previous verse asks, *kiṁ viṣayopapādanaiḥ:* what is the actual benefit of so-called economic development? The history of the world has factually proved that attempts to increase economic development for bodily comfort through the advancement of material civilization have done nothing to remedy the inevitability of birth, death, old age and disease. Everyone has knowledge of huge empires throughout the history of the world—the Roman Empire, the Moghul Empire, the British Empire and so on—but all the societies engaged in such economic development (*sarve 'rtha-kāmāḥ*) have been frustrated by the laws of nature through periodic wars, pestilence, famine and so on. Thus all their attempts have been flickering and temporary. In this verse, therefore, it is said, *kurvanti martyasya kiyat priyaṁ calāḥ:* one may be very proud of possessing a vast empire, but such empires are impermanent; after one hundred or two hundred years, everything is finished. All such positions of economic development, although created with great endeavor and hardship, are vanquished very soon. Therefore they have been described as *calāḥ*. An intelligent man should conclude that material economic development is not at all pleasing. The entire world is described in *Bhagavad-gītā* as *duḥkhālayam aśāśvatam*—miserable and temporary. Economic development may be pleasing for some time, but it cannot endure. Thus many big businessmen are now very morose because they are being harassed by various plundering governments. In conclusion, why should one waste his time for so-called economic development, which is neither permanent nor pleasing to the soul?

On the other hand, our relationship with Kṛṣṇa, the Supreme Personality of Godhead, is eternal. *Nitya-siddha kṛṣṇa-prema.* The pure souls are eternally in love with Kṛṣṇa, and this permanent love, either as a servant, a friend, a parent or a conjugal lover, is not at all difficult to revive. Especially in this age, the concession is that simply by chanting the Hare Kṛṣṇa *mantra* (*harer nāma harer nāma harer nāmaiva kevalam*) one revives his original relationship with God and thus becomes so happy that he does not want anything material. As enunciated by Śrī Caitanya Mahāprabhu, *na dhanaṁ na janaṁ na sundarīṁ kavitāṁ vā jagad-īśa kāmaye.* A very advanced devotee in Kṛṣṇa consciousness does not want riches, followers or possessions. *Rāyaḥ kalatraṁ paśavaḥ sutādayo gṛhā mahī kuñjara-kośa-bhūtayaḥ.* The satisfaction of possessing material opulences, although perhaps of a different standard, is available even in the lives of dogs and hogs, who cannot revive their eternal relationship with Kṛṣṇa. In human life, however, our eternal, dormant relationship with Kṛṣṇa is possible to revive. Therefore Prahlāda Mahārāja has described this life as *arthadam.* Consequently, instead of wasting our time for economic development, which cannot give us any happiness, if we simply try to revive our eternal relationship with Kṛṣṇa, we will properly utilize our lives.

TEXT 40

एवं हि लोकाः क्रतुभिः कृता अमी
क्षयिष्णवः सातिशया न निर्मलाः ।
तस्माददृष्टश्रुतदूषणं परं
भक्त्योक्तयेशं भजतात्मलब्धये ॥४०॥

evaṁ hi lokāḥ kratubhiḥ kṛtā amī
kṣayiṣṇavaḥ sātiśayā na nirmalāḥ

tasmād adṛṣṭa-śruta-dūṣaṇaṁ paraṁ
bhaktyoktayeśaṁ bhajatātma-labdhaye

evam—similarly (as earthly wealth and possessions are impermanent); *hi*—indeed; *lokāḥ*—higher planetary systems like heaven, the moon, the sun and Brahmaloka; *kratubhiḥ*—by performing great sacrifices; *kṛtāḥ*—achieved; *amī*—all those; *kṣayiṣṇavaḥ*—perishable, impermanent; *sātiśayāḥ*—although more comfortable and pleasing; *na*—not; *nirmalāḥ*—pure (free from disturbances); *tasmāt*—therefore; *adṛṣṭa-śruta*—never seen or heard; *dūṣaṇam*—whose fault; *param*—the Supreme; *bhaktyā*—with great devotional love; *uktayā*—as described in the Vedic literature (not mixed with *jñāna* or *karma*); *īśam*—the Supreme Lord; *bhajata*—worship; *ātma-labdhaye*—for self-realization.

TRANSLATION

It is learned from Vedic literature that by performing great sacrifices one may elevate himself to the heavenly planets. However, although life on the heavenly planets is hundreds and thousands of times more comfortable than life on earth, the heavenly planets are not pure [nirmalam], or free from the taint of material existence. The heavenly planets are also temporary, and therefore they are not the goal of life. The Supreme Personality of Godhead, however, has never been seen or heard to possess inebriety. Consequently, for your own benefit and self-realization, you must worship the Lord with great devotion, as described in the revealed scriptures.

PURPORT

As stated in *Bhagavad-gītā, kṣīṇe puṇye martya-lokaṁ viśanti.* Even if one is promoted to the higher planetary systems by performing great sacrifices, which are accompanied by the sinful act of sacrificing animals, the standard of happiness in Svargaloka is also not free of disturbances. There is a similar struggle for existence even for the King of heaven, Indra. Thus there is no practical benefit in promoting oneself to the heavenly planets. Indeed, from the heavenly planets one must return to this earth after one has exhausted the results of his pious activities. In the *Vedas* it is said, *tad yatheha karma-jito lokaḥ kṣīyate evam evāmutra puṇya-jito lokaḥ kṣīyata.* As the material positions we acquire here by hard work are vanquished in due course of time, one's residence in the heavenly planets is also eventually vanquished. According to one's activities of piety in different degrees, one obtains different standards of life, but none of them are permanent, and therefore they are all impure. Consequently, one should not endeavor to be promoted to the higher planetary systems, only to return to this earth or descend still lower to the hellish planets. To stop this cycle of going up and coming down, one must take to Kṛṣṇa consciousness. Śrī Caitanya Mahāprabhu therefore said:

brahmāṇḍa bhramite kona bhāgyavān jīva
guru-kṛṣṇa-prasāde pāya bhakti-latā-bīja
(Cc. *Madhya* 19.151)

The living entity is rotating in the cycle of birth and death, going sometimes to the higher planets and sometimes to the lower planets, but that is not the solution to the problems of life. But if by the grace of Kṛṣṇa one is fortunate enough to meet a *guru,* a representative of Kṛṣṇa, one gets the clue to returning home, back to Godhead, having achieved self-realization. This is what is actually desirable. *Bhajatātma-labdhaye:* one must take to Kṛṣṇa consciousness for self-realization.

TEXT 41

यदर्थ इह कर्माणि विद्वन्मान्यसकृन्नरः ।
करोत्यतो विपर्यासममोघं विन्दते फलम् ॥४१॥

yad-artha iha karmāṇi
vidvan-māny asakṛn naraḥ
karoty ato viparyāsam
amoghaṁ vindate phalam

yat—of which; *arthe*—for the purpose; *iha*—in this material world; *karmāṇi*—many activities (in factories, industries, speculation and so on); *vidvat*—advanced in knowledge; *mānī*—thinking himself to be; *asakṛt*—again and again; *naraḥ*—a person; *karoti*—performs; *ataḥ*—

from this; *viparyāsam*—the opposite; *amogham*—unfailingly; *vindate*—achieves; *phalam*—result.

TRANSLATION

A materialistic person, thinking himself very advanced in intelligence, continually acts for economic development. But again and again, as enunciated in the Vedas, he is frustrated by material activities, either in this life or in the next. Indeed, the results one obtains are inevitably the opposite of those one desires.

PURPORT

No one has ever achieved the results he desired from material activities. On the contrary, everyone has been frustrated again and again. Therefore one must not waste his time in such material activities for sensual pleasure, either in this life or in the next. So many nationalists, economists and other ambitious persons have tried for happiness, individually or collectively, but history proves that they have all been frustrated. In recent history we have seen many political leaders work hard for individual and collective economic development, but they have all failed. This is the law of nature, as clearly explained in the next verse.

TEXT 42

सुखाय दुःखमोक्षाय सङ्कल्प इह कर्मिणः ।
सदाप्नोतीहया दुःखमनीहायाः सुखावृतः ॥४२॥

sukhāya duḥkha-mokṣāya
saṅkalpa iha karmiṇaḥ
sadāpnotīhayā duḥkham
anīhāyāḥ sukhāvṛtaḥ

sukhāya—for achieving happiness by a so-called higher standard of life; *duḥkha-mokṣāya*—for becoming free from misery; *saṅkalpaḥ*—the determination; *iha*—in this world; *karmiṇaḥ*—of the living entity trying for economic development; *sadā*—always; *āpnoti*—achieves; *īhayā*—by activity or ambition; *duḥkham*—only unhappiness;

anīhāyāḥ—and from not desiring economic development; *sukha*—by happiness; *āvṛtaḥ*—covered.

TRANSLATION

In this material world, every materialist desires to achieve happiness and diminish his distress, and therefore he acts accordingly. Actually, however, one is happy as long as one does not endeavor for happiness; as soon as one begins his activities for happiness, his conditions of distress begin.

PURPORT

Every conditioned soul is bound by the laws of material nature, as described in *Bhagavad-gītā* (*prakṛteḥ kriyamāṇāni guṇaiḥ karmāṇi sarvaśaḥ*). Everyone has achieved a certain type of body given by material nature according to the instructions of the Supreme Personality of Godhead.

īśvaraḥ sarva-bhūtānāṁ
hṛd-deśe 'rjuna tiṣṭhati
bhrāmayan sarva-bhūtāni
yantrārūḍhāni māyayā

"The Supreme Lord is situated in everyone's heart, O Arjuna, and is directing the wanderings of all living entities, who are seated as on a machine, made of the material energy." (Bg. 18.61) The Supreme Personality of Godhead, the Supersoul, is present in everyone's heart, and as the living entity desires, the Lord gives him facilities with which to work according to his ambitions in different grades of bodies. The body is just like an instrument by which the living entity moves according to false desires for happiness and thus suffers the pangs of birth, death, old age and disease in different standards of life. Everyone begins his activities with some plan and ambition, but actually, from the beginning of one's plan to the end, one does not derive any happiness. On the contrary, as soon as one begins acting according to his plan, his life of distress immediately begins. Therefore, one should not be ambitious to dissipate the unhappy conditions of life, for one cannot do anything about them. *Ahaṅkāra-vimūḍhātmā kartāham iti manyate.* Although one is acting according to false ambitions, he thinks he can improve his material conditions by his activities. The *Vedas* enjoin that one should not try to increase happiness or decrease distress, for this is futile. *Tasyaiva hetoḥ prayateta kovidaḥ.* One should work for self-realization, not for economic development, which is impossible to improve. Without endeavor, one can get the amount of happiness and distress for which he is destined, and one cannot change this. Therefore, it is better to use one's time for advancement in the spiritual life of Kṛṣṇa consciousness. One should not waste his valuable life as a human being. It is better to utilize this life for developing Kṛṣṇa consciousness, without ambitions for so-called happiness.

TEXT 43

कामान्कामयते काम्यैर्यदर्थमिह पूरुषः ।
स वै देहस्तु पारक्यो भङ्गुरो यात्युपैति च ॥४३॥

kāmān kāmayate kāmyair
yad-artham iha pūruṣaḥ
sa vai dehas tu pārakyo
bhaṅguro yāty upaiti ca

kāmān—things for sense gratification; *kāmayate*—one desires; *kāmyaiḥ*—by different desirable actions; *yat*—of which; *artham*—for the purpose; *iha*—in this material world; *pūruṣaḥ*—the living entity; *saḥ*—that; *vai*—indeed; *dehaḥ*—body; *tu*—but; *pārakyaḥ*—belongs to others (the dogs, vultures, etc.); *bhaṅguraḥ*—perishable; *yāti*—goes away; *upaiti*—embraces the spirit soul; *ca*—and.

TRANSLATION

A living entity desires comfort for his body and makes many plans for this purpose, but actually the body is the property of others. Indeed, the perishable body embraces the living entity and then leaves him aside.

PURPORT

Everyone desires comfort for his body and tries to make a suitable situation for this purpose, forgetting that the body is meant to be eaten by dogs, jackals or moths and thus turned into useless stool, ashes or earth. The living entity wastes his time in a futile attempt to gain material possessions for the comfort of one body after another.

TEXT 44

किमु व्यवहितापत्यदारागारधनादयः ।
राज्यकोशगजामात्यभृत्याप्ता ममतास्पदाः ॥४४॥

kim u vyavahitāpatya-
dārāgāra-dhanādayaḥ
rājya-kośa-gajāmātya-
bhṛtyāptā mamatāspadāḥ

kim u—what to speak of; *vyavahita*—separated; *apatya*—children; *dāra*—wives; *agāra*—residences; *dhana*—wealth; *ādayaḥ*—and so on; *rājya*—kingdoms; *kośa*—treasuries; *gaja*—big elephants and horses; *amātya*—ministers; *bhṛtya*—servants; *āptāḥ*—relatives; *mamatā-āspadāḥ*—false seats or abodes of intimate relationship ("mineness").

TRANSLATION

Since the body itself is ultimately meant to become stool or earth, what is the meaning of the paraphernalia related to the body, such as wives, residences, wealth, children, relatives, servants, friends, kingdoms, treasuries, animals and ministers? They are also temporary. What more can be said about this?

TEXT 45

किमेतैरात्मनस्तुच्छैः सह देहेन नश्वरैः ।
अनर्थैरर्थसंकाशैर्नित्यानन्दरसोदधेः ॥४५॥

kim etair ātmanas tucchaiḥ
saha dehena naśvaraiḥ
anarthair artha-saṅkāśair
nityānanda-rasodadheḥ

kim—what is the use; *etaiḥ*—with all these; *ātmanaḥ*—for the real self; *tucchaiḥ*—which are most insignificant; *saha*—with; *dehena*—the body; *naśvaraiḥ*—perishable; *anarthaiḥ*—unwanted; *artha-saṅkāśaiḥ*—appearing as if needed; *nitya-ānanda*—of eternal happiness; *rasa*—of the nectar; *udadheḥ*—for the ocean.

TRANSLATION

All this paraphernalia is very near and dear as long as the body exists, but as soon as the body is destroyed, all things related to the body are also finished. Therefore, actually one has nothing to do with them, but because of ignorance one accepts them as valuable. Compared to the ocean of eternal happiness, they are most insignificant. What is the use of such insignificant relationships for the eternal living being?

PURPORT

Kṛṣṇa consciousness, devotional service to Kṛṣṇa, is the ocean of eternal bliss. In comparison to this eternal bliss, the so-called happiness of society, friendship and love is simply useless and insignificant. One should therefore not be attached to temporary things. One should take to Kṛṣṇa consciousness and become eternally happy.

TEXT 46

निरूप्यतामिह स्वार्थः कियान्देहभृतोऽसुराः ।
निषेकादिष्ववस्थासु क्लिश्यमानस्य कर्मभिः ॥४६॥

nirūpyatām iha svārthaḥ
kiyān deha-bhṛto 'surāḥ
niṣekādiṣv avasthāsu
kliśyamānasya karmabhiḥ

nirūpyatām—let it be ascertained; *iha*—in this world; *sva-arthaḥ*—personal benefit; *kiyān*—how much; *deha-bhṛtaḥ*—of a living entity who has a material body; *asurāḥ*—O sons of demons; *niṣeka-ādiṣu*—beginning from the happiness derived from sex life; *avasthāsu*—in temporary conditions; *kliśyamānasya*—of one who is suffering in severe hardships; *karmabhiḥ*—by his previous material activities.

TRANSLATION

My dear friends, O sons of the asuras, the living entity receives different types of bodies according to his previous fruitive activities. Thus he is seen to suffer with reference to his particular body in all conditions of life, beginning with his infusion into the womb. Please tell me, therefore, after full consideration, what is the living entity's actual interest in fruitive activities, which result in hardship and misery?

PURPORT

Karmaṇā daiva-netreṇa jantur dehopapattaye. The living entity receives a particular type of body according to his *karma*, or fruitive activities. The material pleasure derived in the material world from one's particular body is based on sexual pleasure: *yan maithunādi-gṛhamedhi-sukhaṁ hi tuccham.* The entire world is working so hard only for sexual pleasure. To enjoy sexual pleasure and maintain the status quo of material life, one must work very hard, and because of such activities, one prepares himself another material body. Prahlāda Mahārāja places this matter to his friends, the *asuras*, for their consideration. *Asuras* generally cannot understand that the objects of sexual pleasure, the so-called pleasure of materialistic life, depend on extremely hard labor.

TEXT 47

कर्माण्यारभते देही देहेनात्मानुवर्तिना ।
कर्मभिस्तनुते देहमुभयं त्वविवेकतः ॥४७॥

karmāṇy ārabhate dehī
dehenātmānuvartinā
karmabhis tanute deham
ubhayaṁ tv avivekataḥ

karmāṇi—material fruitive activities; *ārabhate*—begins; *dehī*—a living entity who has accepted a particular type of body; *dehena*—with that body; *ātma-anuvartinā*—which is received according to his desire and past activities; *karmabhiḥ*—by such material activities; *tanute*—he expands; *deham*—another body; *ubhayam*—both of them; *tu*—indeed; *avivekataḥ*—due to ignorance.

TRANSLATION

The living entity, who has received his present body because of his past fruitive activity, may end the results of his actions in this life, but this does not mean that he is liberated from bondage to material bodies. The living entity receives one type of body, and by performing actions with that body he creates another. Thus he transmigrates from one body to another, through repeated birth and death, because of his gross ignorance.

PURPORT

The living entity's evolution through different types of bodies is conducted automatically by the laws of nature in bodies other than those of human beings. In other words, by the laws of nature (*prakṛteḥ kriyamāṇāni*) the living entity evolves from lower grades of life to the human form. Because of his developed consciousness, however, the human being must understand the constitutional position of the living entity and understand why he must accept a material body. This chance is given to him by nature, but if he nonetheless acts like an animal, what is the benefit of his human life? In this life one must select the goal of life and act accordingly. Having received instructions from the spiritual master and the *śāstra*, one must be sufficiently intelligent. In the human form of life, one should not remain foolish and ignorant, but must inquire about his constitutional position. This is called *athāto brahma-jijñāsā.* The human psychology gives rise to many questions, which various philosophers have considered and answered with various types of philosophy based upon mental concoction. This is not the way of liberation. The Vedic instructions say, *tad-vijñānārthaṁ sa gurum evābhigacchet:* to solve the problems of life, one must accept a spiritual master. *Tasmād guruṁ prapadyeta jijñāsuḥ śreya uttamam:* if one is actually serious in inquiring about the solution to material existence, one must approach a bona fide *guru.*

tad viddhi praṇipātena
paripraśnena sevayā
upadekṣyanti te jñānaṁ
jñāninas tattva-darśinaḥ

"Just try to learn the truth by approaching a spiritual master. Inquire from him submissively and render service unto him. The self-realized soul can impart knowledge unto you because he has seen the truth." (Bg. 4.34) One must approach a bona fide spiritual master by surrendering himself (*praṇipātena*) and rendering service. An intelligent person must inquire from the spiritual master about the goal of life. A bona fide spiritual master can answer all such questions because he has seen the real truth. Even in ordinary activities, we first consider gain and loss, and then we act. Similarly, an intelligent person must consider the entire process of material existence and then act intelligently, following the directions of the bona fide spiritual master.

TEXT 48

तस्मादर्थाश्च कामाश्च धर्माश्च यदपाश्रयाः ।
भजतानीहयात्मानमनीहं हरिमीश्वरम् ॥४८॥

tasmād arthāś ca kāmāś ca
dharmāś ca yad-apāśrayāḥ
bhajatānīhayātmānam
anīhaṁ harim īśvaram

tasmāt—therefore; *arthāḥ*—ambitions for economic development; *ca*—and; *kāmāḥ*—ambitions for satisfaction of the senses; *ca*—also; *dharmāḥ*—duties of religion; *ca*—and; *yat*—upon whom; *apāśrayāḥ*—dependent; *bhajata*—worship; *anīhayā*—without desire for them; *ātmānam*—the Supersoul; *anīham*—indifferent; *harim*—the Supreme Personality of Godhead; *īśvaram*—the Lord.

TRANSLATION

The four principles of advancement in spiritual life—dharma, artha, kāma and mokṣa—all depend on the disposition of the

Supreme Personality of Godhead. Therefore, my dear friends, follow in the footsteps of devotees. Without desire, fully depend upon the disposition of the Supreme Lord, worship Him, the Supersoul, in devotional service.

PURPORT

These are words of intelligence. Everyone should know that in every stage of life we are dependent upon the Supreme Personality of Godhead. Therefore the *dharma*, religion, which we accept should be that which is recommended by Prahlāda Mahārāja—*bhāgavata-dharma.* This is the instruction of Kṛṣṇa: *sarva-dharmān parityajya mām ekaṁ śaraṇaṁ vraja.* To take shelter of the lotus feet of Kṛṣṇa means to act according to the rules and regulations of *bhāgavata-dharma,* devotional service. As far as economic development is concerned, we should discharge our occupational duties but fully depend on the lotus feet of the Lord for the results. *Karmaṇy evādhikāras te mā phaleṣu kadācana:* "You have a right to perform your prescribed duty, but you are not entitled to the fruits of action." According to one's position, one should perform his duties, but for the results one should fully depend upon Kṛṣṇa. Narottama dāsa Ṭhākura sings that our only desire should be to perform the duties of Kṛṣṇa consciousness. We should not be misled by the *karma-mīmāṁsā* philosophy, which concludes that if we work seriously the results will come automatically. This is not a fact. The ultimate result depends upon the will of the Supreme Personality of Godhead. In devotional service, therefore, the devotee completely depends upon the Lord and honestly performs his occupational duties. Therefore Prahlāda Mahārāja advised his friends to depend completely on Kṛṣṇa and worship Him in devotional service.

TEXT 49

सर्वेषामपि भूतानां हरिरात्मेश्वरः प्रियः ।
भूतैर्महद्भिः स्वकृतैः कृतानां जीवसंज्ञितः ॥४९॥

sarveṣām api bhūtānāṁ
harir ātmeśvaraḥ priyaḥ
bhūtair mahadbhiḥ sva-kṛtaiḥ
kṛtānāṁ jīva-saṁjñitaḥ

sarveṣām—of all; *api*—certainly; *bhūtānām*—living entities; *hariḥ*—the Lord, who mitigates all the miseries of the living entity; *ātmā*—the original source of life; *īśvaraḥ*—the complete controller; *priyaḥ*—the dear; *bhūtaiḥ*—by the separated energies, the five material elements; *mahadbhiḥ*—emanating from the total material energy, the *mahat-tattva*; *sva-kṛtaiḥ*—which are manifested by Himself; *kṛtānām*—created; *jīva-saṁjñitaḥ*—who is also known as the living entity, since the living entities are expansions of His marginal energy.

TRANSLATION

The Supreme Personality of Godhead, Hari, is the soul and the Supersoul of all living entities. Every living entity is a manifestation of His energy in terms of the living soul and the material body. Therefore the Lord is the most dear, and He is the supreme controller.

PURPORT

The Supreme Personality of Godhead is manifested by His different energies—the material energy, the spiritual energy and the marginal energy. He is the original source of all living entities in the material world, and He is situated in everyone's heart as the Supersoul. Although the living entity is the cause of his various types of bodies, the body is given by material nature according to the order of the Lord.

īśvaraḥ sarva-bhūtānāṁ
hṛd-deśe 'rjuna tiṣṭhati
bhrāmayan sarva-bhūtāni
yantrārūḍhāni māyayā

"The Supreme Lord is situated in everyone's heart, O Arjuna, and is directing the wanderings of all living entities, who are seated as on a machine, made of the material energy." (Bg. 18.61) The body is just like a machine, a car, in which the living entity is given a chance to sit and move according to his desire. The Lord is the original cause of the material body and the soul, which is expanded by His marginal energy. The Supreme Lord is the dearmost object of all living entities. Prahlāda Mahārāja therefore advised his class friends, the sons of the demons, to take shelter of the Supreme Personality of Godhead again.

TEXT 50

देवोऽसुरो मनुष्यो वा यक्षो गन्धर्व एव वा ।
भजन् मुकुन्दचरणं स्वस्तिमान् स्याद् यथा वयम् ॥५०॥

devo 'suro manuṣyo vā
yakṣo gandharva eva vā
bhajan mukunda-caraṇaṁ
svastimān syād yathā vayam

devaḥ—a demigod; *asuraḥ*—a demon; *manuṣyaḥ*—a human being; *vā*—or; *yakṣaḥ*—a Yakṣa (a member of a demoniac species); *gandharvaḥ*—a Gandharva; *eva*—indeed; *vā*—or; *bhajan*—rendering service; *mukunda-caraṇam*—to the lotus feet of Mukunda, Lord Kṛṣṇa, who can give liberation; *svasti-mān*—full of all auspiciousness; *syāt*—becomes; *yathā*—just as; *vayam*—we (Prahlāda Mahārāja).

TRANSLATION

If a demigod, demon, human being, Yakṣa, Gandharva or anyone within this universe renders service to the lotus feet of Mukunda, who can deliver liberation, he is actually situated in the most auspicious condition of life, exactly like us [the mahājanas, headed by Prahlāda Mahārāja].

PURPORT

Prahlāda Mahārāja, by his living example, requested his friends to engage in devotional service. Whether in demigod society, *asura* society, human society or Gandharva society, every living entity should take shelter of the lotus feet of Mukunda and thus become perfect in good fortune.

TEXTS 51–52

नालं द्विजत्वं देवत्वमृषित्वं वासुरात्मजाः ।
प्रीणनाय मुकुन्दस्य न वृत्तं न बहुज्ञता ॥५१॥
न दानं न तपो नेज्या न शौचं न व्रतानि च ।
प्रीयतेऽमलया भक्त्या हरिरन्यद् विडम्बनम् ॥५२॥

nālaṁ dvijatvaṁ devatvam
ṛṣitvaṁ vāsurātmajāḥ
prīṇanāya mukundasya
na vṛttaṁ na bahu-jñatā

na dānaṁ na tapo nejyā
na śaucaṁ na vratāni ca
prīyate 'malayā bhaktyā
harir anyad viḍambanam

na—not; *alam*—sufficient; *dvijatvam*—being a perfect, highly qualified *brāhmaṇa*; *devatvam*—being a demigod; *ṛṣitvam*—being a saintly person; *vā*—or; *asura-ātma-jāḥ*—O descendants of *asuras*; *prīṇanāya*—for pleasing; *mukundasya*—of Mukunda, the Supreme Personality of Godhead; *na vṛttam*—not good conduct; *na*—not; *bahu-jñatā*—vast learning; *na*—neither; *dānam*—charity; *na tapaḥ*—no austerity; *na*—nor; *ijyā*—worship; *na*—nor; *śaucam*—cleanliness; *na vratāni*—nor execution of great vows; *ca*—also; *prīyate*—is satisfied; *amalayā*—by spotless; *bhaktyā*—devotional service; *hariḥ*—the Supreme Lord; *anyat*—other things; *viḍambanam*—only show.

TRANSLATION

My dear friends, O sons of the demons, you cannot please the Supreme Personality of Godhead by becoming perfect brāhmaṇas, demigods or great saints or by becoming perfectly good in etiquette or vast learning. None of these qualifications can awaken the pleasure of the Lord. Nor by charity, austerity, sacrifice, cleanliness or vows can one satisfy the Lord. The Lord is pleased only if one has unflinching, unalloyed devotion to Him. Without sincere devotional service, everything is simply a show.

PURPORT

Prahlāda Mahārāja concludes that one can become perfect by serving the Supreme Lord sincerely by all means. Material elevation to life as a *brāhmaṇa*, demigod, *ṛṣi* and so on are not causes for developing love of Godhead, but if one sincerely engages in the service of the Lord, his

Kṛṣṇa consciousness is complete. This is confirmed in *Bhagavad-gītā* (9.30):

api cet sudurācāro
bhajate mām ananya-bhāk
sādhur eva sa mantavyaḥ
samyag vyavasito hi saḥ

"Even if one commits the most abominable actions, if he is engaged in devotional service he is to be considered saintly because he is properly situated." To develop unalloyed love for Kṛṣṇa is the perfection of life. Other processes may be helpful, but if one does not develop his love for Kṛṣṇa, these other processes are simply a waste of time.

dharmaḥ svanuṣṭhitaḥ puṁsāṁ
viṣvaksena-kathāsu yaḥ
notpādayed yadi ratiṁ
śrama eva hi kevalam

"Duties [*dharma*] executed by men, regardless of occupation, are only so much useless labor if they do not provoke attraction for the message of the Supreme Lord." (*Bhāg.* 1.2.8) The test of perfection is one's unalloyed devotion to the Lord.

TEXT 53

ततो हरौ भगवति भक्तिं कुरुत दानवाः ।
आत्मौपम्येन सर्वत्र सर्वभूतात्मनीश्वरे ॥५३॥

tato harau bhagavati
bhaktiṁ kuruta dānavāḥ
ātmaupamyena sarvatra
sarva-bhūtātmanīśvare

tataḥ—therefore; *harau*—unto Lord Hari; *bhagavati*—the Supreme Personality of Godhead; *bhaktim*—devotional service; *kuruta*—execute; *dānavāḥ*—O my dear friends, O sons of demons; *ātma-aupamyena*—just as one's own self; *sarvatra*—everywhere; *sarva-bhūta-ātmani*—who is situated as the soul and Supersoul of all living entities; *īśvare*—unto the Supreme Lord, the controller.

TRANSLATION

My dear friends, O sons of the demons, in the same favorable way that one sees himself and takes care of himself, take to devotional service to satisfy the Supreme Personality of Godhead, who is present everywhere as the Supersoul of all living entities.

PURPORT

The word *ātmaupamyena* refers to thinking others to be like oneself. One can very intelligently conclude that without devotional service, without becoming Kṛṣṇa conscious, one cannot be happy. Therefore the duty of all devotees is to preach Kṛṣṇa consciousness everywhere all over the world, because all living entities without Kṛṣṇa consciousness are suffering the pangs of material existence. To preach Kṛṣṇa consciousness is the best welfare activity. Indeed, it is described by Śrī Caitanya Mahāprabhu as *para-upakāra,* work for the true benefit of others. The activities of *para-upakāra* have been especially entrusted to those who have taken birth in India as human beings.

bhārata-bhūmite haila manuṣya-janma yāra
janma sārthaka kari' kara para-upakāra
(Cc. *Ādi* 9.41)

The entire world is suffering for want of Kṛṣṇa consciousness. Therefore Śrī Caitanya Mahāprabhu advised all human beings born in India to make their lives perfect by Kṛṣṇa consciousness and then preach the gospel of Kṛṣṇa consciousness all over the world so that others may become happy by executing the principles of Kṛṣṇa consciousness.

TEXT 54

दैतेया यक्षरक्षांसि स्त्रियः शूद्रा व्रजौकसः ।
खगा मृगाः पापजीवाः सन्ति ह्यच्युततां गताः ॥५४॥

daiteyā yakṣa-rakṣāṁsi
striyaḥ śūdrā vrajaukasaḥ
khagā mṛgāḥ pāpa-jīvāḥ
santi hy acyutatāṁ gatāḥ

daiteyāḥ—O demons; *yakṣa-rakṣāṁsi*—the living entities known as the Yakṣas and Rākṣasas; *striyaḥ*—women; *śūdrāḥ*—the laborer class; *vraja-okasaḥ*—village cowherd men; *khagāḥ*—birds; *mṛgāḥ*—animals; *pāpa-jīvāḥ*—sinful living entities; *santi*—can become; *hi*—certainly; *acyutatām*—the qualities of Acyuta, the Supreme Lord; *gatāḥ*—obtained.

TRANSLATION

O my friends, O sons of demons, everyone, including you (the Yakṣas and Rākṣasas), the unintelligent women, śūdras and cowherd men, the birds, the lower animals and the sinful living entities, can revive his original, eternal spiritual life and exist forever simply by accepting the principles of bhakti-yoga.

PURPORT

The devotees are referred to as *acyuta-gotra*, or the dynasty of the Supreme Personality of Godhead. The Lord is called Acyuta, as indicated in *Bhagavad-gītā* (*senayor ubhayor madhye rathaṁ sthāpaya me 'cyuta*). The Lord is infallible in the material world because He is the supreme spiritual person. Similarly, the *jīvas*, who are part and parcel of the Lord, can also become infallible. Although Prahlāda's mother was in the conditional state and was the wife of a demon, even Yakṣas, Rākṣasas, women, *śūdras* and even birds and other lower living entities can be elevated to the *acyuta-gotra*, the family of the Supreme Personality of Godhead. That is the highest perfection. As Kṛṣṇa never falls, when we revive our spiritual consciousness, Kṛṣṇa consciousness, we never fall again to material existence. One should understand the position of the supreme Acyuta, Kṛṣṇa, who says in *Bhagavad-gītā* (4.9):

janma karma ca me divyam
evaṁ yo vetti tattvataḥ
tyaktvā dehaṁ punar janma
naiti mām eti so 'rjuna

"One who knows the transcendental nature of My appearance and activities does not, upon leaving the body, take his birth again in this material world, but attains My eternal abode, O Arjuna." One should understand Acyuta, the supreme infallible, and how we are related with Him, and one should take to the service of the Lord. This is the perfection of life. Śrīla Madhvācārya says, *acyutatāṁ cyuti-varjanam.* The word *acyutatām* refers to one who never falls to this material world but always remains in the Vaikuṇṭha world, fully engaged in the service of the Lord.

TEXT 55

एतावानेव लोकेऽस्मिन्पुंसः स्वार्थः परः स्मृतः ।
एकान्तभक्तिर्गोविन्दे यत् सर्वत्र तदीक्षणम् ॥५५॥

etāvān eva loke 'smin
puṁsaḥ svārthaḥ paraḥ smṛtaḥ
ekānta-bhaktir govinde
yat sarvatra tad-īkṣaṇam

etāvān—this much; *eva*—certainly; *loke asmin*—in this material world; *puṁsaḥ*—of the living entity; *sva-arthaḥ*—the real self-interest; *paraḥ*—transcendental; *smṛtaḥ*—regarded; *ekānta-bhaktiḥ*—unalloyed devotional service; *govinde*—to Govinda; *yat*—which; *sarvatra*—everywhere; *tat-īkṣaṇam*—seeing the relationship with Govinda, Kṛṣṇa.

TRANSLATION

In this material world, to render service to the lotus feet of Govinda, the cause of all causes, and to see Him everywhere, is the only goal of life. This much alone is the ultimate goal of human life, as explained by all the revealed scriptures.

PURPORT

In this verse the words *sarvatra tad-īkṣaṇam* describe the highest perfection of devotional service, in which one sees everything with reference to Govinda's activities. The highly elevated devotee never sees anything unrelated to Govinda.

sthāvara-jaṅgama dekhe, nā dekhe tāra mūrti
sarvatra haya nija iṣṭa-deva-sphūrti

"The *mahā-bhāgavata*, the advanced devotee, certainly sees everything mobile and immobile, but he does not exactly see their forms. Rather, everywhere he immediately sees manifest the form of the Supreme Lord." (Cc. *Madhya* 8.274) Even in this material world, a devotee does not see materially manifested things; instead he sees Govinda in everything. When he sees a tree or a human being, a devotee sees them in relation to Govinda. *Govindam ādi-puruṣam:* Govinda is the original source of everything.

īśvaraḥ paramaḥ kṛṣṇaḥ
sac-cid-ānanda-vigrahaḥ
anādir ādir govindaḥ
sarva-kāraṇa-kāraṇam

"Kṛṣṇa, who is known as Govinda, is the supreme controller. He has an eternal, blissful, spiritual body. He is the origin of all. He has no other origin, for He is the prime cause of all causes." (*Brahma-saṁhitā* 5.1) The test of a perfect devotee is that he sees Govinda everywhere in this universe, even in every atomic particle (*aṇḍāntara-stha-paramāṇu-cayāntara-stham*). This is the perfect vision of a devotee. It is therefore said:

nārāyaṇam ayaṁ dhīrāḥ
paśyanti paramārthinaḥ
jagad dhanamayaṁ lubdhāḥ
kāmukāḥ kāminīmayam

A devotee sees everyone and everything in relationship with Nārāyaṇa (*nārāyaṇam ayam*). Everything is an expansion of Nārāyaṇa's energy. Just as those who are greedy see everything as a source of money-making and those who are lusty see everything as being conducive to sex, the most perfect devotee, Prahlāda Mahārāja, saw Nārāyaṇa even within a stone column. This does not mean, however, that we must accept the words *daridra-nārāyaṇa*, which have been manufactured by some unscrupulous person. One who actually envisions Nārāyaṇa everywhere makes no distinction between the poor and the rich. To single out the *daridra-nārāyaṇas*, or poor Nārāyaṇa, and reject the *dhani-nārāyaṇa*, or rich Nārāyaṇa, is not the vision of a devotee. Rather, that is the imperfect vision of materialistic persons.

Thus end the Bhaktivedanta purports of the Seventh Canto, Seventh Chapter, of the Śrīmad-Bhāgavatam, *entitled "What Prahlāda Learned in the Womb."*

CHAPTER EIGHT

Lord Nṛsiṁhadeva Slays the King of the Demons

As described in this chapter, Hiraṇyakaśipu was ready to kill his own son Prahlāda Mahārāja, but the Supreme Personality of Godhead appeared in front of the demon as Śrī Nṛkeśarī, half lion and half man, and killed him.

Following the instructions of Prahlāda Mahārāja, all the sons of the demons became attached to Lord Viṣṇu, the Supreme Personality of Godhead. When this attachment became pronounced, their teachers, Ṣaṇḍa and Amarka, were very much afraid that the boys would become more and more devoted to the Lord. In a helpless condition, they approached Hiraṇyakaśipu and described in detail the effect of Prahlāda's preaching. After hearing of this, Hiraṇyakaśipu decided to kill his son Prahlāda. Hiraṇyakaśipu was so angry that Prahlāda Mahārāja fell down at his feet and said many things just to pacify him, but he was unsuccessful in satisfying his demoniac father. Hiraṇyakaśipu, as a typical demon, began to advertise himself as being greater than the Supreme Personality of Godhead, but Prahlāda Mahārāja challenged him, saying that Hiraṇyakaśipu was not God, and began to glorify the Supreme Personality of Godhead, declaring that the Lord is all-pervading, that everything is under Him, and that no one is equal to or greater than Him. Thus he requested his father to be submissive to the omnipotent Supreme Lord.

The more Prahlāda Mahārāja glorified the Supreme Personality of Godhead, the more angry and agitated the demon became. Hiraṇyakaśipu asked his Vaiṣṇava son whether his God existed within the columns of the palace, and Prahlāda Mahārāja immediately accepted that since the Lord is present everywhere, He was also present within the columns. When Hiraṇyakaśipu heard this philosophy from his young son, he derided the boy's statement as just the talk of a child and forcefully struck the pillar with his fist.

As soon as Hiraṇyakaśipu struck the column, there issued forth a tumultuous sound. At first Hiraṇyakaśipu, the King of the demons, could not see anything but the pillar, but to substantiate Prahlāda's statements, the Lord came out of the pillar in His wonderful incarnation as Narasiṁha, half lion and half man. Hiraṇyakaśipu could immediately understand that the extraordinarily wonderful form of the Lord was surely meant for his death, and thus he prepared to fight with the form of half lion and half man. The Lord performed His pastimes by fighting with the demon for some time, and in the evening, on the border between day and night, the Lord captured the demon, threw him on His lap, and killed him by piercing his abdomen with His nails. The Lord not only killed Hiraṇyakaśipu, the King of the demons, but also killed many of his followers. When there was no one else to fight, the Lord, roaring with anger, sat down on Hiraṇyakaśipu's throne.

The entire universe was thus relieved of the rule of Hiraṇyakaśipu, and everyone was jubilant in transcendental bliss. Then all the demigods, headed by Lord Brahmā, approached the Lord. These included the great saintly persons, the Pitās, the Siddhas, the Vidyādharas, the Nāgas, the Manus, the *prajāpatis*, the Gandharvas, the Cāraṇas, the Yakṣas, the Kimpuruṣas, the Vaitālikas, the Kinnaras and also many other varieties of beings in human form. All of them stood not far from the Supreme Personality of Godhead and began offering their prayers unto the Lord, whose spiritual effulgence was brilliant as He sat on the throne.

TEXT 1

श्रीनारद उवाच
अथ दैत्यसुताः सर्वे श्रुत्वा तदनुवर्णितम् ।
जगृहुर्निरवद्यत्वान्नैव गुर्वनुशिक्षितम् ॥ १ ॥

śrī-nārada uvāca
atha daitya-sutāḥ sarve
śrutvā tad-anuvarṇitam
jagṛhur niravadyatvān
naiva gurv-anuśikṣitam

śrī-nāradaḥ uvāca—Śrī Nārada Muni said; *atha*—thereupon; *daitya-sutāḥ*—the sons of the demons (the class friends of Prahlāda Mahārāja);

sarve—all; *śrutvā*—hearing; *tat*—by him (Prahlāda); *anuvarṇitam*—the statements about devotional life; *jagṛhuḥ*—accepted; *niravadyatvāt*—due to the supreme utility of that instruction; *na*—not; *eva*—indeed; *guru-anuśikṣitam*—that which was taught by their teachers.

TRANSLATION

Nārada Muni continued: All the sons of the demons appreciated the transcendental instructions of Prahlāda Mahārāja and took them very seriously. They rejected the materialistic instructions given by their teachers, Ṣaṇḍa and Amarka.

PURPORT

This is the effect of the preaching of a pure devotee like Prahlāda Mahārāja. If a devotee is qualified, sincere and serious about Kṛṣṇa consciousness and if he follows the instructions of a bona fide spiritual master, as Prahlāda Mahārāja did when preaching the instructions he had received from Nārada Muni, his preaching is effective. As it is said in the *Śrīmad-Bhāgavatam* (3.25.25):

satāṁ prasaṅgān mama vīrya-saṁvido
bhavanti hṛt-karṇa-rasāyanāḥ kathāḥ

If one tries to understand the discourses given by the *sat*, or pure devotees, those instructions will be very pleasing to the ear and appealing to the heart. Thus if one is inspired to take to Kṛṣṇa consciousness and if one practices the process in his life, he is surely successful in returning home, back to Godhead. By the grace of Prahlāda Mahārāja, all his class friends, the sons of the demons, became Vaiṣṇavas. They did not like hearing from their so-called teachers Ṣaṇḍa and Amarka, who were interested only in teaching them about diplomacy, politics, economic development and similar topics meant exclusively for sense gratification.

TEXT 2

अथाचार्यसुतस्तेषां बुद्धिमेकान्तसंस्थिताम् ।
आलक्ष्य भीतस्त्वरितो राज्ञ आवेदयद् यथा ॥ २ ॥

athācārya-sutas teṣāṁ
buddhim ekānta-saṁsthitām
ālakṣya bhītas tvarito
rājña āvedayad yathā

atha—thereupon; *ācārya-sutaḥ*—the son of Śukrācārya; *teṣām*—of them (the sons of the demons); *buddhim*—the intelligence; *ekānta-saṁsthitām*—fixed in one subject matter, devotional service; *ālakṣya*—realizing or seeing practically; *bhītaḥ*—being afraid; *tvaritaḥ*—as soon as possible; *rājñe*—unto the King (Hiraṇyakaśipu); *āvedayat*—submitted; *yathā*—fittingly.

TRANSLATION

When Ṣaṇḍa and Amarka, the sons of Śukrācārya, observed that all the students, the sons of the demons, were becoming advanced in Kṛṣṇa consciousness because of the association of Prahlāda Mahārāja, they were afraid. They approached the King of the demons and described the situation as it was.

PURPORT

The words *buddhim ekānta-saṁsthitām* indicate that as an effect of Prahlāda Mahārāja's preaching, the students who listened to him became fixed in the conclusion that Kṛṣṇa consciousness is the only object of human life. The fact is that anyone who associates with a pure devotee and follows his instructions becomes fixed in Kṛṣṇa consciousness and is not disturbed by materialistic consciousness. The teachers particularly observed this in their students, and therefore they were afraid because the whole community of students was gradually becoming Kṛṣṇa conscious.

TEXTS 3–4

कोपावेशचलद्गात्रः पुत्रं हन्तुं मनो दधे ।
क्षिप्त्वा परुषया वाचा प्रह्लादमतदर्हणम् ॥ ३ ॥
आहेक्षमाणः पापेन तिरश्चीनेन चक्षुषा ।
प्रश्रयावनतं दान्तं बद्धाञ्जलिमवस्थितम् ।
सर्पः पदाहत इव श्वसन्प्रकृतिदारुणः ॥ ४ ॥

kopāveśa-calad-gātraḥ
putraṁ hantuṁ mano dadhe
kṣiptvā paruṣayā vācā
prahrādam atad-arhaṇam

āhekṣamāṇaḥ pāpena
tiraścīnena cakṣuṣā
praśrayāvanataṁ dāntaṁ
baddhāñjalim avasthitam
sarpaḥ padāhata iva
śvasan prakṛti-dāruṇaḥ

kopa-āveśa—by a very angry mood; *calat*—trembling; *gātraḥ*—the whole body; *putram*—his son; *hantum*—to kill; *manaḥ*—mind; *dadhe*—fixed; *kṣiptvā*—rebuking; *paruṣayā*—with very harsh; *vācā*—words; *prahrādam*—Prahlāda Mahārāja; *a-tat-arhaṇam*—not fit to be chastised (due to his noble character and tender age); *āha*—said; *īkṣamāṇaḥ*—looking at him in anger; *pāpena*—because of his sinful activities; *tiraścīnena*—crooked; *cakṣuṣā*—with eyes; *praśraya-avanatam*—very gentle and mild; *dāntam*—very restrained; *baddha-añjalim*—having folded hands; *avasthitam*—situated; *sarpaḥ*—a snake; *pada-āhataḥ*—being trampled by the foot; *iva*—like; *śvasan*—hissing; *prakṛti*—by nature; *dāruṇaḥ*—very evil.

TRANSLATION

When Hiraṇyakaśipu understood the entire situation, he was extremely angry, so much so that his body trembled. Thus he finally decided to kill his son Prahlāda. Hiraṇyakaśipu was by nature very cruel, and feeling insulted, he began hissing like a snake trampled upon by someone's foot. His son Prahlāda was peaceful, mild and gentle, his senses were under control, and he stood before Hiraṇyakaśipu with folded hands. According to Prahlāda's age and behavior, he was not to be chastised. Yet with staring, crooked eyes, Hiraṇyakaśipu rebuked him with the following harsh words.

PURPORT

When one is impudent toward a highly authorized devotee, one is punished by the laws of nature. The duration of his life is diminished, and he loses the blessings of superior persons and the results of pious activities. Hiraṇyakaśipu, for example, had achieved such great power in the material world that he could subdue practically all the planetary systems in the universe, including the heavenly planets (Svargaloka). Yet now, because of his mistreatment of such a Vaiṣṇava as Prahlāda Mahārāja, all the results of his *tapasya* diminished. As stated in *Śrīmad-Bhāgavatam* (10.4.46):

āyuḥ śriyaṁ yaśo dharmaṁ
lokān āśiṣa eva ca
hanti śreyāṁsi sarvāṇi
puṁso mahad-atikramaḥ

"When one mistreats great souls, his life span, opulence, reputation, religion, possessions and good fortune are all destroyed."

TEXT 5

श्रीहिरण्यकशिपुरुवाच
हे दुर्विनीत मन्दात्मन्कुलभेदकराधम ।
स्तब्धं मच्छासनोद्वृत्तं नेष्ये त्वाद्य यमक्षयम् ॥ ५ ॥

śrī-hiraṇyakaśipur uvāca
he durvinīta mandātman
kula-bheda-karādhama
stabdhaṁ mac-chāsanodvṛttaṁ
neṣye tvādya yama-kṣayam

śrī-hiraṇyakaśipuḥ uvāca—the blessed Hiraṇyakaśipu said; *he*—O; *durvinīta*—most impudent; *manda-ātman*—O stupid fool; *kula-bheda-kara*—who are bringing about a disruption in the family; *adhama*—O lowest of mankind; *stabdham*—most obstinate; *mat-śāsana*—from my ruling; *udvṛttam*—going astray; *neṣye*—I shall bring; *tvā*—you; *adya*—today; *yama-kṣayam*—to the place of Yamarāja, the superintendent of death.

TRANSLATION

Hiraṇyakaśipu said: O most impudent, most unintelligent disruptor of the family, O lowest of mankind, you have violated my

power to rule you, and therefore you are an obstinate fool. Today I shall send you to the place of Yamarāja.

PURPORT

Hiraṇyakaśipu condemned his Vaiṣṇava son Prahlāda for being *durvinīta*—ungentle, uncivilized, or impudent. Śrīla Viśvanātha Cakravartī Ṭhākura, however, has derived a meaning from this word *durvinīta* by the mercy of the goddess of learning, Sarasvatī. He says that *duḥ* refers to this material world. This is confirmed by Lord Kṛṣṇa in His instruction in *Bhagavad-gītā* that this material world is *duḥkhālayam*, full of material conditions. *Vi* means *viśeṣa*, "specifically," and *nīta* means "brought in." By the mercy of the Supreme Lord, Prahlāda Mahārāja was especially brought to this material world to teach people how to get out of the material condition. Lord Kṛṣṇa says, *yadā yadā hi dharmasya glānir bhavati bhārata.* When the entire population, or part of it, becomes forgetful of its own duty, Kṛṣṇa comes. When Kṛṣṇa is not present the devotee is present, but the mission is the same: to free the poor conditioned souls from the clutches of the *māyā* that chastises them.

Śrīla Viśvanātha Cakravartī Ṭhākura further explains that the word *mandātman* means *manda*—very bad or very slow in spiritual realization. As stated in *Śrīmad-Bhāgavatam* (1.1.10), *mandāḥ sumanda-matayo manda-bhāgyā.* Prahlāda Mahārāja is the guide of all the *mandas*, or bad living entities who are under the influence of *māyā.* He is the benefactor even of the slow and bad living entities in this material world. *Kula-bheda-karādhama:* by his actions, Prahlāda Mahārāja made great personalities who established big, big families seem insignificant. Everyone is interested in his own family and in making his dynasty famous, but Prahlāda Mahārāja was so liberal that he made no distinction between one living entity and another. Therefore he was greater than the great *prajāpatis* who established their dynasties. The word *stabdham* means obstinate. A devotee does not care for the instructions of the *asuras.* When they give instructions, he remains silent. A devotee cares about the instructions of Kṛṣṇa, not those of demons or nondevotees. He does not give any respect to a demon, even though the demon be his father. *Mac-chāsanodvṛttam:* Prahlāda Mahārāja was disobedient to the orders of his demoniac father. *Yama-kṣayam:* every conditioned soul is under the control of Yamarāja, but Hiraṇyakaśipu said that he considered

Prahlāda Mahārāja his deliverer, for Prahlāda would stop Hiraṇyakaśipu's repetition of birth and death. Because Prahlāda Mahārāja, being a great devotee, was better than any *yogī*, Hiraṇyakaśipu was to be brought among the society of *bhakti-yogīs*. Thus Śrīla Viśvanātha Cakravartī Ṭhākura has explained these words in a very interesting way as they can be interpreted from the side of Sarasvatī, the mother of learning.

TEXT 6

क्रुद्धस्य यस्य कम्पन्ते त्रयो लोकाः सहेश्वराः ।
तस्य मेऽभीतवन्मूढ शासनं किं बलोऽत्यगाः ॥ ६ ॥

kruddhasya yasya kampante
trayo lokāḥ saheśvarāḥ
tasya me 'bhītavan mūḍha
śāsanaṁ kiṁ balo 'tyagāḥ

kruddhasya—when angered; *yasya*—he who; *kampante*—tremble; *trayaḥ lokāḥ*—the three worlds; *saha-īśvarāḥ*—with their leaders; *tasya*—of that; *me*—of me (Hiraṇyakaśipu); *abhīta-vat*—without fear; *mūḍha*—rascal; *śāsanam*—ruling order; *kim*—what; *balaḥ*—strength; *atyagāḥ*—have overstepped.

TRANSLATION

My son Prahlāda, you rascal, you know that when I am angry all the planets of the three worlds tremble, along with their chief rulers. By whose power has a rascal like you become so impudent that you appear fearless and overstep my power to rule you?

PURPORT

The relationship between a pure devotee and the Supreme Personality of Godhead is extremely relishable. A devotee never claims to be very powerful himself; instead, he fully surrenders to the lotus feet of Kṛṣṇa, being confident that in all dangerous conditions Kṛṣṇa will protect His devotee. Kṛṣṇa Himself says in *Bhagavad-gītā* (9.31), *kaunteya pratijānīhi na me bhaktaḥ praṇaśyati:* "O son of Kuntī, declare boldly that

My devotee never perishes." The Lord requested Arjuna to declare this instead of declaring it Himself because sometimes Kṛṣṇa changes His view and therefore people might not believe Him. Thus Kṛṣṇa asked Arjuna to declare that a devotee of the Lord is never vanquished.

Hiraṇyakaśipu was perplexed about how his five-year-old boy could be so fearless that he did not care for the order of his very great and powerful father. A devotee cannot execute the order of anyone except the Supreme Personality of Godhead. This is the position of a devotee. Hiraṇyakaśipu could understand that this boy must have been very powerful, since the boy did not heed his orders. Hiraṇyakaśipu asked his son, *kiṁ balaḥ:* "How have you overcome my order? By whose strength have you done this?"

TEXT 7

श्रीप्रह्राद उवाच
न केवलं मे भवतश्च राजन्
स वै बलं बलिनां चापरेषाम् ।
परेऽवरेऽमी स्थिरजङ्गमा ये
ब्रह्मादयो येन वशं प्रणीताः ॥ ७ ॥

śrī-prahrāda uvāca
na kevalaṁ me bhavataś ca rājan
sa vai balaṁ balināṁ cāpareṣām
pare 'vare 'mī sthira-jaṅgamā ye
brahmādayo yena vaśaṁ praṇītāḥ

śrī-prahrādaḥ uvāca—Prahlāda Mahārāja replied; *na*—not; *kevalam*—only; *me*—of me; *bhavataḥ*—of yourself; *ca*—and; *rājan*—O great King; *saḥ*—he; *vai*—indeed; *balam*—strength; *balinām*—of the strong; *ca*—and; *apareṣām*—of others; *pare*—exalted; *avare*—subordinate; *amī*—those; *sthira-jaṅgamāḥ*—moving or nonmoving living entities; *ye*—who; *brahma-ādayaḥ*—beginning from Lord Brahmā; *yena*—by whom; *vaśam*—under control; *praṇītāḥ*—brought.

TRANSLATION

Prahlāda Mahārāja said: My dear King, the source of my strength, of which you are asking, is also the source of yours.

Indeed, the original source of all kinds of strength is one. He is not only your strength or mine, but the only strength for everyone. Without Him, no one can get any strength. Whether moving or not moving, superior or inferior, everyone, including Lord Brahmā, is controlled by the strength of the Supreme Personality of Godhead.

PURPORT

Lord Kṛṣṇa says in *Bhagavad-gītā* (10.41):

yad yad vibhūtimat sattvaṁ
śrīmad ūrjitam eva vā
tat tad evāvagaccha tvaṁ
mama tejo-'ṁśa-sambhavam

"Know that all beautiful, glorious and mighty creations spring from but a spark of My splendor." This is confirmed by Prahlāda Mahārāja. If one sees extraordinary strength or power anywhere, it is derived from the Supreme Personality of Godhead. To give an example, there are different grades of fire, but all of them derive heat and light from the sun. Similarly, all living entities, big or small, are dependent on the mercy of the Supreme Personality of Godhead. One's only duty is to surrender, for one is a servant and cannot independently attain the position of master. One can attain the position of master only by the mercy of the master, not independently. Unless one understands this philosophy, he is still a *mūḍha;* in other words, he is not very intelligent. The *mūḍhas*, the asses who do not have this intelligence, cannot surrender unto the Supreme Personality of Godhead.

Understanding the subordinate position of the living entity takes millions of births, but when one is actually wise he surrenders unto the Supreme Personality of Godhead. The Lord says in *Bhagavad-gītā* (7.19):

bahūnāṁ janmanām ante
jñānavān māṁ prapadyate
vāsudevaḥ sarvam iti
sa mahātmā sudurlabhaḥ

"After many births and deaths, he who is actually in knowledge surrenders unto Me, knowing Me to be the cause of all causes and all that is. Such a great soul is very rare." Prahlāda Mahārāja was a great soul, a *mahātmā*, and therefore he completely surrendered unto the lotus feet of the Lord. He was confident that Kṛṣṇa would give him protection under all circumstances.

TEXT 8

स ईश्वरः काल उरुक्रमोऽसा-
वोजःसहःसत्त्वबलेन्द्रियात्मा ।
स एव विश्वं परमः स्वशक्तिभिः
सृजत्यवत्यत्ति गुणत्रयेशः ॥ ८ ॥

sa īśvaraḥ kāla urukramo 'sāv
ojaḥ sahaḥ sattva-balendriyātmā
sa eva viśvaṁ paramaḥ sva-śaktibhiḥ
sṛjaty avaty atti guṇa-trayeśaḥ

saḥ—He (the Supreme Personality of Godhead); *īśvaraḥ*—the supreme controller; *kālaḥ*—the time factor; *urukramaḥ*—the Lord, whose every action is uncommon; *asau*—that one; *ojaḥ*—the strength of the senses; *sahaḥ*—the strength of the mind; *sattva*—steadiness; *bala*—bodily strength; *indriya*—and of the senses themselves; *ātmā*—the very self; *saḥ*—He; *eva*—indeed; *viśvam*—the whole universe; *paramaḥ*—the supreme; *sva-śaktibhiḥ*—by His multifarious transcendental potencies; *sṛjati*—creates; *avati*—maintains; *atti*—winds up; *guṇa-traya-īśaḥ*—the master of the material modes.

TRANSLATION

The Supreme Personality of Godhead, who is the supreme controller and time factor, is the power of the senses, the power of the mind, the power of the body, and the vital force of the senses. His influence is unlimited. He is the best of all living entities, the controller of the three modes of material nature. By His own power, He creates this cosmic manifestation, maintains it and annihilates it also.

PURPORT

Since the material world is being moved by the three material modes and since the Lord is their master, the Lord can create, maintain and destroy the material world.

TEXT 9

जह्यासुरं भावमिमं त्वमात्मनः
समं मनो धत्स्व न सन्ति विद्विषः ।
ऋतेऽजितादात्मन उत्पथे स्थितात्
तद्धि ह्यनन्तस्य महत् समर्हणम् ॥ ९ ॥

jahy āsuraṁ bhāvam imaṁ tvam ātmanaḥ
samaṁ mano dhatsva na santi vidviṣaḥ
ṛte 'jitād ātmana utpathe sthitāt
tad dhi hy anantasya mahat samarhaṇam

jahi—just give up; *āsuram*—demoniac; *bhāvam*—tendency; *imam*—this; *tvam*—you (my dear father); *ātmanaḥ*—of yourself; *samam*—equal; *manaḥ*—the mind; *dhatsva*—make; *na*—not; *santi*—are; *vidviṣaḥ*—enemies; *ṛte*—except; *ajitāt*—uncontrolled; *ātmanaḥ*—the mind; *utpathe*—on the mistaken path of undesirable tendencies; *sthitāt*—being situated; *tat hi*—that (mentality); *hi*—indeed; *anantasya*—of the unlimited Lord; *mahat*—the best; *samarhaṇam*—method of worship.

TRANSLATION

Prahlāda Mahārāja continued: My dear father, please give up your demoniac mentality. Do not discriminate in your heart between enemies and friends; make your mind equipoised toward everyone. Except for the uncontrolled and misguided mind, there is no enemy within this world. When one sees everyone on the platform of equality, one then comes to the position of worshiping the Lord perfectly.

PURPORT

Unless one is able to fix the mind at the lotus feet of the Lord, the mind is impossible to control. As Arjuna says in *Bhagavad-gītā* (6.34):

cañcalaṁ hi manaḥ kṛṣṇa
pramāthi balavad dṛḍham
tasyāhaṁ nigrahaṁ manye
vāyor iva suduṣkaram

"For the mind is restless, turbulent, obstinate and very strong, O Kṛṣṇa, and to subdue it, it seems to me, is more difficult than controlling the wind." The only bona fide process for controlling the mind is to fix the mind by service to the Lord. We create enemies and friends according to the dictation of the mind, but actually there are no enemies and friends. *Paṇḍitāḥ sama-darśinaḥ. Samaḥ sarveṣu bhūteṣu mad-bhaktiṁ labhate parām.* To understand this is the preliminary condition for entering into the kingdom of devotional service.

TEXT 10

दस्यून्पुरा षण् न विजित्य लुम्पतो
मन्यन्त एके स्वजिता दिशो दश ।
जितात्मनो ज्ञस्य समस्य देहिनां
साधोः स्वमोहप्रभवाः कुतः परे ॥१०॥

dasyūn purā ṣaṇ na vijitya lumpato
manyanta eke sva-jitā diśo daśa
jitātmano jñasya samasya dehināṁ
sādhoḥ sva-moha-prabhavāḥ kutaḥ pare

dasyūn—plunderers; *purā*—in the beginning; *ṣaṭ*—six; *na*—not; *vijitya*—conquering; *lumpataḥ*—stealing all one's possessions; *manyante*—consider; *eke*—some; *sva-jitāḥ*—conquered; *diśaḥ daśa*—the ten directions; *jita-ātmanaḥ*—one who has conquered the senses; *jñasya*—learned; *samasya*—equipoised; *dehinām*—to all living entities; *sādhoḥ*—of such a saintly person; *sva-moha-prabhavāḥ*—created by one's own illusion; *kutaḥ*—where; *pare*—enemies or opposing elements.

TRANSLATION

In former times there were many fools like you who did not conquer the six enemies that steal away the wealth of the body.

These fools were very proud, thinking, "I have conquered all enemies in all the ten directions." But if a person is victorious over the six enemies and is equipoised toward all living entities, for him there are no enemies. Enemies are merely imagined by one in ignorance.

PURPORT

In this material world, everyone thinks that he has conquered his enemies, not understanding that his enemies are his uncontrolled mind and five senses (*manaḥ ṣaṣṭhānīndriyāṇi prakṛti-sthāni karṣati*). In this material world, everyone has become a servant of the senses. Originally everyone is a servant of Kṛṣṇa, but in ignorance one forgets this, and thus one is engaged in the service of *māyā* through lusty desires, anger, greed, illusion, madness and jealousy. Everyone is actually dependent on the reactions of material laws, but still one thinks himself independent and thinks that he has conquered all directions. In conclusion, one who thinks that he has many enemies is an ignorant man, whereas one who is in Kṛṣṇa consciousness knows that there are no enemies but those within oneself—the uncontrolled mind and senses.

TEXT 11

श्रीहिरण्यकशिपुरुवाच

व्यक्तं त्वं मर्तुकामोऽसि योऽतिमात्रं विकत्थसे ।
मुमूर्षूणां हि मन्दात्मन् ननु स्युर्विक्लवा गिरः ॥११॥

śrī-hiraṇyakaśipur uvāca
vyaktaṁ tvaṁ martu-kāmo 'si
yo 'timātraṁ vikatthase
mumūrṣūṇāṁ hi mandātman
nanu syur viklavā giraḥ

śrī-hiraṇyakaśipuḥ uvāca—the blessed Hiraṇyakaśipu said; *vyaktam*—evidently; *tvam*—you; *martu-kāmaḥ*—desirous of death; *asi*—are; *yaḥ*—one who; *atimātram*—without limit; *vikatthase*—are boasting (as if you had conquered your senses whereas your father could not do so); *mumūrṣūṇām*—of persons who are about to meet immediate death; *hi*—indeed; *manda-ātman*—O unintelligent rascal; *nanu*—certainly; *syuḥ*—become; *viklavāḥ*—confused; *giraḥ*—the words.

TRANSLATION

Hiraṇyakaśipu replied: You rascal, you are trying to minimize my value, as if you were better than me at controlling the senses. This is over-intelligent. I can therefore understand that you desire to die at my hands, for this kind of nonsensical talk is indulged in by those about to die.

PURPORT

It is said in *Hitopadeśa, upadeśo hi mūrkhāṇāṁ prokopāya na śāntaye.* If good instructions are given to a foolish person, he does not take advantage of them, but becomes more and more angry. Prahlāda Mahārāja's authorized instructions to his father were not accepted by Hiraṇyakaśipu as truth; instead Hiraṇyakaśipu became increasingly angry at his great son, who was a pure devotee. This kind of difficulty always exists when a devotee preaches Kṛṣṇa consciousness to persons like Hiraṇyakaśipu, who are interested in money and women. (The word *hiraṇya* means "gold," and *kaśipu* refers to cushions or good bedding.) Moreover, a father does not like to be instructed by his son, especially if the father is a demon. Prahlāda Mahārāja's Vaiṣṇava preaching to his demoniac father was indirectly effective, for because of Hiraṇyakaśipu's excessive jealousy of Kṛṣṇa and His devotee, he was inviting Nṛsiṁhadeva to kill him very quickly. Thus he was expediting his being killed by the Lord Himself. Although Hiraṇyakaśipu was a demon, he is described here by the added word *śrī.* Why? The answer is that fortunately he had such a great devotee son as Prahlāda Mahārāja. Thus although he was a demon, he would attain salvation and return home, back to Godhead.

TEXT 12

यस्त्वया मन्दभाग्योक्तो मदन्यो जगदीश्वरः ।
क्वासौ यदि स सर्वत्र कस्मात् स्तम्भे न दृश्यते ॥१२॥

yas tvayā manda-bhāgyokto
mad-anyo jagad-īśvaraḥ

kvāsau yadi sa sarvatra
kasmāt stambhe na dṛśyate

yaḥ—the one who; *tvayā*—by you; *manda-bhāgya*—O unfortunate one; *uktaḥ*—described; *mat-anyaḥ*—besides me; *jagat-īśvaraḥ*—the supreme controller of the universe; *kva*—where; *asau*—that one; *yadi*—if; *saḥ*—He; *sarvatra*—everywhere (all-pervading); *kasmāt*—why; *stambhe*—in the pillar before me; *na dṛśyate*—not seen.

TRANSLATION

O most unfortunate Prahlāda, you have always described a supreme being other than me, a supreme being who is above everything, who is the controller of everyone, and who is all-pervading. But where is He? If He is everywhere, then why is He not present before me in this pillar?

PURPORT

Demons sometimes declare to a devotee that they cannot accept the existence of God because they cannot see Him. But what the demon does not know is stated by the Lord Himself in *Bhagavad-gītā* (7.25): *nāhaṁ prakāśaḥ sarvasya yogamāyā-samāvṛtaḥ.* "I am never manifest to the foolish and unintelligent. For them I am covered by *yogamāyā.*" The Lord is open to being seen by devotees, but nondevotees cannot see Him. The qualification for seeing God is stated in *Brahma-saṁhitā* (5.38): *premāñjana-cchurita-bhakti-vilocanena santaḥ sadaiva hṛdayeṣu vilokayanti.* A devotee who has developed a genuine love for Kṛṣṇa can always see Him everywhere, whereas a demon, not having a clear understanding of the Supreme Lord, cannot see Him. When Hiraṇyakaśipu was threatening to kill Prahlāda Mahārāja, Prahlāda certainly saw the column standing before him and his father, and he saw that the Lord was present in the pillar to encourage him not to fear his demoniac father's words. The Lord was present to protect him. Hiraṇyakaśipu marked Prahlāda's observation and asked him, "Where is your God?" Prahlāda Mahārāja replied, "He is everywhere." Then Hiraṇyakaśipu asked, "Why is He not in this pillar before me?" Thus in all circumstances the devotee can always see the Supreme Lord, whereas the nondevotee cannot.

Prahlāda Mahārāja has here been addressed by his father as "the most unfortunate." Hiraṇyakaśipu thought himself extremely fortunate because he possessed the property of the universe. Prahlāda Mahārāja, his legitimate son, was to have inherited this vast property, but because of his impudence, he was going to die at his father's hands. Therefore the demoniac father considered Prahlāda the most unfortunate because Prahlāda would not be able to inherit his property. Hiraṇyakaśipu did not know that Prahlāda Mahārāja was the most fortunate person within the three worlds because Prahlāda was protected by the Supreme Personality of Godhead. Such are the misunderstandings of demons. They do not know that a devotee is protected by the Lord in all circumstances (*kaunteya pratijānīhi na me bhaktaḥ praṇaśyati*).

TEXT 13

सोऽहं विकत्थमानस्य शिरः कायाद्धरामि ते ।
गोपायेत हरिस्त्वाद्य यस्ते शरणमीप्सितम् ॥१३॥

so 'haṁ vikatthamānasya
śiraḥ kāyād dharāmi te
gopāyeta haris tvādya
yas te śaraṇam īpsitam

saḥ—he; *aham*—I; *vikatthamānasya*—who are speaking such nonsense; *śiraḥ*—the head; *kāyāt*—from the body; *harāmi*—I shall take away; *te*—of you; *gopāyeta*—let Him protect; *hariḥ*—the Supreme Personality of Godhead; *tvā*—you; *adya*—now; *yaḥ*—He who; *te*—your; *śaraṇam*—protector; *īpsitam*—desired.

TRANSLATION

Because you are speaking so much nonsense, I shall now sever your head from your body. Now let me see your most worshipable God come to protect you. I want to see it.

PURPORT

Demons always think that the God of the devotees is fictitious. They think that there is no God and that the so-called religious feeling of devotion to God is but an opiate, a kind of illusion, like the illusions derived from LSD and opium. Hiraṇyakaśipu did not believe Prahlāda Mahārāja when Prahlāda asserted that his Lord is present everywhere. Because Hiraṇyakaśipu, as a typical demon, was convinced that there is no God and that no one could protect Prahlāda, he felt encouraged to kill his son. He challenged the idea that the devotee is always protected by the Supreme Lord.

TEXT 14

एवं दुरुक्तैर्मुहुरर्दयन्रुषा
सुतं महाभागवतं महासुरः ।
खड्गं प्रगृह्योत्पतितो वरासनात्
स्तम्भं तताडातिबलः स्वमुष्टिना ॥१४॥

evaṁ duruktair muhur ardayan ruṣā
sutaṁ mahā-bhāgavataṁ mahāsuraḥ
khaḍgaṁ pragṛhyotpatito varāsanāt
stambhaṁ tatāḍātibalaḥ sva-muṣṭinā

evam—thus; *duruktaiḥ*—by harsh words; *muhuḥ*—constantly; *ardayan*—chastising; *ruṣā*—with unnecessary anger; *sutam*—his son; *mahā-bhāgavatam*—who was a most exalted devotee; *mahā-asuraḥ*—Hiraṇyakaśipu, the great demon; *khaḍgam*—sword; *pragṛhya*—taking up; *utpatitaḥ*—having gotten up; *vara-āsanāt*—from his exalted throne; *stambham*—the column; *tatāḍa*—struck; *ati-balaḥ*—very strong; *sva-muṣṭinā*—by his fist.

TRANSLATION

Being obsessed with anger, Hiraṇyakaśipu, who was very great in bodily strength, thus chastised his exalted devotee-son Prahlāda with harsh words. Cursing him again and again, Hiraṇyakaśipu took up his sword, got up from his royal throne, and with great anger struck his fist against the column.

TEXT 15

तदैव तस्मिन् निनदोऽतिभीषणो
बभूव येनाण्डकटाहमस्फुटत् ।

यं वै स्वधिष्ण्योपगतं त्वजादयः
श्रुत्वा स्वधामात्ययमङ्ग मेनिरे ॥१५॥

tadaiva tasmin ninado 'tibhīṣaṇo
babhūva yenāṇḍa-kaṭāham asphuṭat
yaṁ vai sva-dhiṣṇyopagataṁ tv ajādayaḥ
śrutvā sva-dhāmātyayam aṅga menire

tadā—at that time; *eva*—just; *tasmin*—within (the pillar); *ninadaḥ*—a sound; *ati-bhīṣaṇaḥ*—very fearful; *babhūva*—there was; *yena*—by which; *aṇḍa-kaṭāham*—the covering of the universe; *asphuṭat*—appeared to crack; *yam*—which; *vai*—indeed; *sva-dhiṣṇya-upagatam*—reaching their respective abodes; *tu*—but; *aja-ādayaḥ*—the demigods, headed by Lord Brahmā; *śrutvā*—hearing; *sva-dhāma-atyayam*—the destruction of their abodes; *aṅga*—my dear Yudhiṣṭhira; *menire*—thought.

TRANSLATION

Then from within the pillar came a fearful sound, which appeared to crack the covering of the universe. O my dear Yudhiṣṭhira, this sound reached even the abodes of the demigods like Lord Brahmā, and when the demigods heard it, they thought, "Oh, now our planets are being destroyed!"

PURPORT

As we sometimes become very much afraid at the sound of a thunderbolt, perhaps thinking that our houses will be destroyed, the great demigods like Lord Brahmā feared the thundering sound that came from the pillar in front of Hiraṇyakaśipu.

TEXT 16

स विक्रमन् पुत्रवधेप्सुरोजसा
निशम्य निर्ह्रादमपूर्वमद्भुतम् ।
अन्तःसभायां न ददर्श तत्पदं
वितत्रसुर्येन सुरारियूथपाः ॥१६॥

sa vikraman putra-vadhepsur ojasā
niśamya nirhrādam apūrvam adbhutam
antaḥ-sabhāyāṁ na dadarśa tat-padaṁ
vitatrasur yena surāri-yūtha-pāḥ

saḥ—he (Hiraṇyakaśipu); *vikraman*—exhibiting his prowess; *putra-vadha-īpsuḥ*—desirous of killing his own son; *ojasā*—with great strength; *niśamya*—hearing; *nirhrādam*—the fierce sound; *apūrvam*—never heard before; *adbhutam*—very wonderful; *antaḥ-sabhāyām*—within the jurisdiction of the great assembly; *na*—not; *dadarśa*—saw; *tat-padam*—the source of that tumultuous sound; *vitatrasuḥ*—became afraid; *yena*—by which sound; *sura-ari-yūtha-pāḥ*—the other leaders of the demons (not only Hiraṇyakaśipu).

TRANSLATION

While showing his extraordinary prowess, Hiraṇyakaśipu, who desired to kill his own son, heard that wonderful, tumultuous sound, which had never before been heard. Upon hearing the sound, the other leaders of the demons were afraid. None of them could find the origin of that sound in the assembly.

PURPORT

In *Bhagavad-gītā* (7.8), Kṛṣṇa explains Himself by saying:

raso 'ham apsu kaunteya
prabhāsmi śaśi sūryayoḥ
praṇavaḥ sarva-vedeṣu
śabdaḥ khe pauruṣaṁ nṛṣu

"O son of Kuntī [Arjuna], I am the taste of water, the light of the sun and the moon, the syllable *om* in the Vedic *mantras;* I am the sound in ether and ability in man." Here the Lord exhibited His presence everywhere by the tumultuous sound in the sky (*śabdaḥ khe*). The tumultuous thundering sound was proof of the Lord's presence. The demons like Hiraṇyakaśipu could now realize the supreme ruling power of the Lord, and thus Hiraṇyakaśipu became afraid. However powerful a man may be, he always fears the sound of a thunderbolt. Similarly, Hiraṇyakaśipu and all the demons who were his associates were extremely afraid because of the presence of the Supreme Lord in the form of sound, although they could not trace out the source of the sound.

TEXT 17

सत्यं विधातुं निजभृत्यभाषितं
व्याप्तिं च भूतेष्वखिलेषु चात्मनः ।
अदृश्यतात्यद्भुतरूपमुद्वहन्
स्तम्भे सभायां न मृगं न मानुषम् ॥१७॥

satyaṁ vidhātuṁ nija-bhṛtya-bhāṣitaṁ
vyāptiṁ ca bhūteṣv akhileṣu cātmanaḥ
adṛśyatātyadbhuta-rūpam udvahan
stambhe sabhāyāṁ na mṛgaṁ na mānuṣam

satyam—true; *vidhātum*—to prove; *nija-bhṛtya-bhāṣitam*—the words of His own servant (Prahlāda Mahārāja, who had said that his Lord is present everywhere); *vyāptim*—the pervasion; *ca*—and; *bhūteṣu*—among the living entities and elements; *akhileṣu*—all; *ca*—also; *ātmanaḥ*—of Himself; *adṛśyata*—was seen; *ati*—very; *adbhuta*—wonderful; *rūpam*—form; *udvahan*—taking; *stambhe*—in the pillar; *sabhāyām*—within the assembly; *na*—not; *mṛgam*—an animal; *na*—nor; *mānuṣam*—a human being.

TRANSLATION

To prove that the statement of His servant Prahlāda Mahārāja was substantial—in other words, to prove that the Supreme Lord is present everywhere, even within the pillar of an assembly hall—the Supreme Personality of Godhead, Hari, exhibited a wonderful form never before seen. The form was neither that of a man nor that of a lion. Thus the Lord appeared in His wonderful form in the assembly hall.

PURPORT

When Hiraṇyakaśipu asked Prahlāda Mahārāja, "Where is your Lord? Is He present in this pillar?" Prahlāda Mahārāja fearlessly replied, "Yes, my Lord is present everywhere." Therefore, to convince Hiraṇyakaśipu that the statement of Prahlāda Mahārāja was unmistakably true, the Lord appeared from the pillar. The Lord appeared as half lion and half man so that Hiraṇyakaśipu could not understand whether the great giant was a lion or a human being. To substantiate Prahlāda's statement, the Lord proved that His devotee, as declared in *Bhagavad-gītā*, is never vanquished (*kaunteya pratijānīhi na me bhaktaḥ praṇaśyati*). Prahlāda Mahārāja's demoniac father had repeatedly threatened to kill Prahlāda, but Prahlāda was confident that he could not be killed, since he was protected by the Supreme Lord. By appearing from the pillar, the Lord encouraged His devotee, saying in effect, "Don't worry. I am present here." By manifesting His form as Nṛsiṁhadeva, the Lord also preserved the truth of Lord Brahmā's promise that Hiraṇyakaśipu was not to be killed by any animal or any man. The Lord appeared in a form that could not be said to be fully a man or a lion.

TEXT 18

स सत्त्वमेनं परितो विपश्यन्
स्तम्भस्य मध्यादनुनिर्जिहानम् ।
नायं मृगो नापि नरो विचित्र-
महो किमेतन्नृमृगेन्द्ररूपम् ॥१८॥

sa sattvam enaṁ parito vipaśyan
stambhasya madhyād anunirjihānam
nāyaṁ mṛgo nāpi naro vicitram
aho kim etan nṛ-mṛgendra-rūpam

saḥ—he (Hiraṇyakaśipu, the King of the Daityas); *sattvam*—living being; *enam*—that; *paritaḥ*—all around; *vipaśyan*—looking; *stambhasya*—of the pillar; *madhyāt*—from the midst; *anunirjihānam*—having come out; *na*—not; *ayam*—this; *mṛgaḥ*—animal; *na*—not; *api*—indeed; *naraḥ*—human being; *vicitram*—very wonderful; *aho*—alas; *kim*—what; *etat*—this; *nṛ-mṛga-indra-rūpam*—the form of both a man and the king of the beasts, the lion.

TRANSLATION

While Hiraṇyakaśipu looked all around to find the source of the sound, that wonderful form of the Lord, which could not be ascertained to be either a man or a lion, emerged from the pillar. In amazement, Hiraṇyakaśipu wondered, "What is this creature that is half man and half lion?"

PURPORT

A demon cannot calculate the unlimited potency of the Supreme Lord. As stated in the *Vedas, parāsya śaktir vividhaiva śrūyate svābhāvikī jñāna-bala-kriyā ca:* the different potencies of the Lord are always working as an automatic exhibition of His knowledge. For a demon it is certainly wonderful that the form of a lion and the form of a man can be united, since a demon has no experience of the inconceivable power for which the Supreme Lord is called "all-powerful." Demons cannot understand the omnipotence of the Lord. They simply compare the Lord to one of them (*avajānanti māṁ mūḍhā mānuṣīṁ tanum āśritam*). *Mūḍhas,* rascals, think that Kṛṣṇa is an ordinary human being who appears for the benefit of other human beings. *Paraṁ bhāvam ajānantaḥ:* fools, rascals and demons cannot realize the supreme potency of the Lord, but He can do anything and everything; indeed, He can do whatever He likes. When Hiraṇyakaśipu received benedictions from Lord Brahmā, he thought that he was safe, since he received the benediction that he would not be killed either by an animal or by a human being. He never thought that an animal and human being would be combined so that demons like him would be puzzled by such a form. This is the meaning of the Supreme Personality of Godhead's omnipotence.

TEXTS 19–22

मीमांसमानस्य समुत्थितोऽग्रतो ।
नृसिंहरूपस्तदलं भयानकम् ॥१९॥
प्रतप्तचामीकरचण्डलोचनं
स्फुरत्सटाकेशरजृम्भिताननम् ।

करालदंष्ट्रं करवालचञ्चल-
क्षुरान्तजिह्वं भ्रुकुटीमुखोल्बणम् ॥२०॥
स्तब्धोर्ध्वकर्णं गिरिकन्दराद्भुत-
व्यात्तास्यनासं हनुभेदभीषणम् ।
दिविस्पृशत्कायमदीर्घपीवर-
ग्रीवोरुवक्षःस्थलमल्पमध्यमम् ॥२१॥
चन्द्रांशुगौरैश्छुरितं तनूरुहै-
र्विष्वग्भुजानीकशतं नखायुधम् ।
दुरासदं सर्वनिजेतरायुध-
प्रवेकविद्रावितदैत्यदानवम् ॥२२॥

mīmāṁsamānasya samutthito 'grato
nṛsiṁha-rūpas tad alaṁ bhayānakam

pratapta-cāmīkara-caṇḍa-locanaṁ
sphurat saṭā-keśara-jṛmbhitānanam
karāla-daṁṣṭraṁ karavāla-cañcala-
kṣurānta-jihvaṁ bhrukuṭī-mukholbaṇam

stabdhordhva-karṇaṁ giri-kandarādbhuta-
vyāttāsya-nāsaṁ hanu-bheda-bhīṣaṇam
divi-spṛśat kāyam adīrgha-pīvara-
grīvoru-vakṣaḥ-sthalam alpa-madhyamam

candrāṁśu-gauraiś churitaṁ tanūruhair
viṣvag bhujānīka-śataṁ nakhāyudham
durāsadaṁ sarva-nijetarāyudha-
praveka-vidrāvita-daitya-dānavam

mīmāṁsamānasya—of Hiraṇyakaśipu, who was contemplating the wonderful form of the Lord; *samutthitaḥ*—appeared; *agrataḥ*—in front; *nṛsiṁha-rūpaḥ*—the form of Nṛsiṁhadeva (half lion and half man); *tat*—that; *alam*—extraordinarily; *bhayānakam*—very fearful;

pratapta—like molten; *cāmīkara*—gold; *caṇḍa-locanam*—having fierce eyes; *sphurat*—flashing; *saṭā-keśara*—by His mane; *jṛmbhita-ānanam*—whose face was expanded; *karāla*—deadly; *daṁṣṭram*—with a set of teeth; *karavāla-cañcala*—waving like a sharp sword; *kṣura-anta*—and as sharp as a razor; *jihvam*—whose tongue; *bhrukuṭī-mukha*—due to His frowning face; *ulbaṇam*—dreadful; *stabdha*—motionless; *ūrdhva*—extending upward; *karṇam*—whose ears; *giri-kandara*—like the caves of a mountain; *adbhuta*—very wonderful; *vyāttāsya*—with a widely opened mouth; *nāsam*—and nostrils; *hanu-bheda-bhīṣaṇam*—causing fear due to the separation of the jaws; *divi-spṛśat*—touching the sky; *kāyam*—whose body; *adīrgha*—short; *pīvara*—fat; *grīva*—neck; *uru*—broad; *vakṣaḥ-sthalam*—chest; *alpa*—small; *madhyamam*—middle portion of the body; *candra-aṁśu*—like the rays of the moon; *gauraiḥ*—whitish; *churitam*—covered; *tanūruhaiḥ*—with hairs; *viṣvak*—in all directions; *bhuja*—of arms; *anīka-śatam*—with a hundred rows; *nakha*—having nails; *āyudham*—as fatal weapons; *durāsadam*—very difficult to conquer; *sarva*—all; *nija*—personal; *itara*—and other; *āyudha*—of weapons; *praveka*—by use of the best; *vidrāvita*—caused to run; *daitya*—by whom the demons; *dānavam*—and the rogues (atheists).

TRANSLATION

Hiraṇyakaśipu studied the form of the Lord, trying to decide who the form of Nṛsiṁhadeva standing before him was. The Lord's form was extremely fearsome because of His angry eyes, which resembled molten gold; His shining mane, which expanded the dimensions of His fearful face; His deadly teeth; and His razor-sharp tongue, which moved about like a dueling sword. His ears were erect and motionless, and His nostrils and gaping mouth appeared like caves of a mountain. His jaws parted fearfully, and His entire body touched the sky. His neck was very short and thick, His chest broad, His waist thin, and the hairs on His body as white as the rays of the moon. His arms, which resembled flanks of soldiers, spread in all directions as He killed the demons, rogues and atheists with His conchshell, disc, club, lotus and other natural weapons.

TEXT 23

प्रायेण मेऽयं हरिणोरुमायिना
वधः स्मृतोऽनेन समुद्यतेन किम् ।
एवं ब्रुवंस्त्वभ्यपतद् गदायुधो
नदन् नृसिंहं प्रति दैत्यकुञ्जरः ॥२३॥

prāyeṇa me 'yaṁ hariṇorumāyinā
vadhaḥ smṛto 'nena samudyatena kim
evaṁ bruvaṁs tv abhyapatad gadāyudho
nadan nṛsiṁhaṁ prati daitya-kuñjaraḥ

prāyeṇa—probably; *me*—of me; *ayam*—this; *hariṇā*—by the Supreme Lord; *uru-māyinā*—who possesses the great mystic power; *vadhaḥ*—the death; *smṛtaḥ*—planned; *anena*—with this; *samudyatena*—endeavor; *kim*—what use; *evam*—in this way; *bruvan*—murmuring; *tu*—indeed; *abhyapatat*—attacked; *gadā-āyudhaḥ*—armed with his weapon, the club; *nadan*—loudly roaring; *nṛ-siṁham*—the Lord, appearing in the form of half lion and half man; *prati*—toward; *daitya-kuñjaraḥ*—Hiraṇyakaśipu, who was like an elephant.

TRANSLATION

Hiraṇyakaśipu murmured to himself, "Lord Viṣṇu, who possesses great mystic power, has made this plan to kill me, but what is the use of such an attempt? Who can fight with me?" Thinking like this and taking up his club, Hiraṇyakaśipu attacked the Lord like an elephant.

PURPORT

In the jungle there are sometimes fights between lions and elephants. Here the Lord appeared like a lion, and Hiraṇyakaśipu, unafraid of the Lord, attacked Him like an elephant. Generally the elephant is defeated by the lion, and therefore the comparison in this verse is appropriate.

TEXT 24

अलक्षितोऽग्नौ पतितः पतङ्गमो
यथा नृसिंहौजसि सोऽसुरस्तदा ।

न तद् विचित्रं खलु सत्त्वधामनि
स्वतेजसा यो नु पुरापिबत् तमः ॥२४॥

alakṣito 'gnau patitaḥ pataṅgamo
yathā nṛsiṁhaujasi so 'suras tadā
na tad vicitraṁ khalu sattva-dhāmani
sva-tejasā yo nu purāpibat tamaḥ

alakṣitaḥ—invisible; *agnau*—in the fire; *patitaḥ*—fallen; *pataṅgamaḥ*—an insect; *yathā*—just as; *nṛsiṁha*—of Lord Nṛsiṁhadeva; *ojasi*—in the effulgence; *saḥ*—he; *asuraḥ*—Hiraṇyakaśipu; *tadā*—at that time; *na*—not; *tat*—that; *vicitram*—wonderful; *khalu*—indeed; *sattva-dhāmani*—in the Supreme Personality of Godhead, who is situated in pure goodness; *sva-tejasā*—by His own effulgence; *yaḥ*—He who (the Lord); *nu*—indeed; *purā*—formerly; *apibat*—swallowed up; *tamaḥ*—the darkness within the material creation.

TRANSLATION

Just as a small insect falls forcefully into a fire and the insignificant creature becomes invisible, when Hiraṇyakaśipu attacked the Lord, who was full of effulgence, Hiraṇyakaśipu became invisible. This is not at all astonishing, for the Lord is always situated in pure goodness. Formerly, during creation, He entered the dark universe and illuminated it by His spiritual effulgence.

PURPORT

The Lord is situated transcendentally, in pure goodness. The material world is generally controlled by *tamo-guṇa*, the quality of ignorance, but the spiritual world, because of the presence of the Lord and His effulgence, is free from all contamination by darkness, passion or contaminated goodness. Although there is a tinge of goodness in this material world in terms of the brahminical qualifications, such qualifications sometimes become invisible because of the strong prevalence of the modes of passion and ignorance. But because the Lord is always transcendentally situated, the material modes of passion and ignorance cannot touch Him. Whenever the Lord is present, there cannot be any darkness from the mode of ignorance. It is stated in *Caitanya-caritāmṛta* (*Madhya* 22.31):

kṛṣṇa——sūrya-sama, māyā haya andhakāra
yāhāṅ kṛṣṇa, tāhāṅ nāhi māyāra adhikāra

"Godhead is light. Nescience is darkness. Where there is Godhead there is no nescience." This material world is full of darkness and ignorance of spiritual life, but by *bhakti-yoga* this ignorance is dissipated. The Lord appeared because of the *bhakti-yoga* exhibited by Prahlāda Mahārāja, and as soon as the Lord appeared, the influence of Hiraṇyakaśipu's passion and ignorance was vanquished as the Lord's quality of pure goodness, or the Brahman effulgence, became prominent. In that prominent effulgence, Hiraṇyakaśipu became invisible, or his influence became insignificant. An example illustrating how the darkness of the material world is vanquished is given in the *śāstra.* When Brahmā was created from the lotus stem growing from the abdomen of Garbhodakaśāyī Viṣṇu, Lord Brahmā saw everything to be dark, but when he received knowledge from the Supreme Personality of Godhead, everything became clear, as everything becomes clear when one comes from night to sunshine. The important point is that as long as we are in the material modes of nature, we are always in darkness. This darkness cannot be dissipated without the presence of the Supreme Personality of Godhead, which is invoked by the practice of *bhakti-yoga. Bhakti-yoga* creates a transcendental situation with no tinges of material contamination.

TEXT 25

ततोऽभिपद्याभ्यहनन्महासुरो
रुषा नृसिंहं गदयोरुवेगया ।
तं विक्रमन्तं सगदं गदाधरो
महोरगं तार्क्ष्यसुतो यथाग्रहीत् ॥२५॥

tato 'bhipadyābhyahanan mahāsuro
ruṣā nṛsiṁhaṁ gadayoruvegayā

taṁ vikramantaṁ sagadaṁ gadādharo
mahoragaṁ tārkṣya-suto yathāgrahīt

tataḥ—thereafter; *abhipadya*—attacking; *abhyahanat*—struck; *mahā-asuraḥ*—the great demon (Hiraṇyakaśipu); *ruṣā*—with anger; *nṛsiṁham*—Lord Nṛsiṁhadeva; *gadayā*—by his club; *uru-vegayā*—moving with great force; *tam*—him (Hiraṇyakaśipu); *vikramantam*—showing his prowess; *sa-gadam*—with his club; *gadā-dharaḥ*—Lord Nṛsiṁhadeva, who also holds a club in His hand; *mahā-uragam*—a great snake; *tārkṣya-sutaḥ*—Garuḍa, the son of Tārkṣya; *yathā*—just as; *agrahīt*—captured.

TRANSLATION

Thereafter, the great demon Hiraṇyakaśipu, who was extremely angry, swiftly attacked Nṛsiṁhadeva with his club and began to beat Him. Lord Nṛsiṁhadeva, however, captured the great demon, along with his club, just as Garuḍa might capture a great snake.

TEXT 26

स तस्य हस्तोत्कलितस्तदासुरो
विक्रीडतो यद्वदहिर्गरुत्मतः ।
असाध्वमन्यन्त हृतौकसोऽमरा
घनच्छदा भारत सर्वधिष्ण्यपाः ॥२६॥

sa tasya hastotkalitas tadāsuro
vikrīḍato yadvad ahir garutmataḥ
asādhv amanyanta hṛtaukaso 'marā
ghana-cchadā bhārata sarva-dhiṣṇya-pāḥ

saḥ—he (Hiraṇyakaśipu); *tasya*—of Him (Lord Nṛsiṁhadeva); *hasta*—from the hands; *utkalitaḥ*—slipped; *tadā*—at that time; *asuraḥ*—the King of the demons, Hiraṇyakaśipu; *vikrīḍataḥ*—playing; *yadvat*—exactly like; *ahiḥ*—a snake; *garutmataḥ*—of Garuḍa; *asādhu*—not very good; *amanyanta*—considered; *hṛta-okasaḥ*—whose abodes were taken by Hiraṇyakaśipu; *amarāḥ*—the demigods;

ghana-cchadāḥ—situated behind a cover of clouds; *bhārata*—O great son of Bharata; *sarva-dhiṣṇya-pāḥ*—the rulers of the heavenly planets.

TRANSLATION

O Yudhiṣṭhira, O great son of Bharata, when Lord Nṛsiṁhadeva gave Hiraṇyakaśipu a chance to slip from His hand, just as Garuḍa sometimes plays with a snake and lets it slip from his mouth, the demigods, who had lost their abodes and who were hiding behind the clouds for fear of the demon, did not consider that incident very good. Indeed, they were perturbed.

PURPORT

When Hiraṇyakaśipu was in the process of being killed by Lord Nṛsiṁhadeva, the Lord gave the demon a chance to slip from His clutches. This incident was not very much appreciated by the demigods, for they were greatly afraid of Hiraṇyakaśipu. They knew that if somehow or other Hiraṇyakaśipu escaped from Nṛsiṁhadeva's hands and saw that the demigods were looking forward to his death with great pleasure, he would take great revenge upon them. Therefore they were very much afraid.

TEXT 27

तं मन्यमानो निजवीर्यशङ्कितं
यद्धस्तमुक्तो नृहरिं महासुरः ।
पुनस्तमासज्जत खड्गचर्मणी
प्रगृह्य वेगेन गतश्रमो मृधे ॥२७॥

taṁ manyamāno nija-vīrya-śaṅkitaṁ
yad dhasta-mukto nṛhariṁ mahāsuraḥ
punas tam āsajjata khaḍga-carmaṇī
pragṛhya vegena gata-śramo mṛdhe

tam—Him (Lord Nṛsiṁhadeva); *manyamānaḥ*—thinking; *nija-vīrya-śaṅkitam*—afraid of his prowess; *yat*—because; *hasta-muktaḥ*—freed from the clutches of the Lord; *nṛ-harim*—Lord Nṛsiṁhadeva;

mahā-asuraḥ—the great demon; *punaḥ*—again; *tam*—Him; *āsajjata*—attacked; *khaḍga-carmaṇī*—his sword and shield; *pragṛhya*—taking up; *vegena*—with great force; *gata-śramaḥ*—his fatigue having gone; *mṛdhe*—in the battle.

TRANSLATION

When Hiraṇyakaśipu was freed from the hands of Nṛsiṁhadeva, he falsely thought that the Lord was afraid of his prowess. Therefore, after taking a little rest from the fight, he took up his sword and shield and again attacked the Lord with great force.

PURPORT

When a sinful man enjoys material facilities, foolish people sometimes think, "How is it that this sinful man is enjoying whereas a pious man is suffering?" By the will of the Supreme, a sinful man is sometimes given the chance to enjoy the material world as if he were not under the clutches of material nature, just so that he may be fooled. A sinful man who acts against the laws of nature must be punished, but sometimes he is given a chance to play, exactly like Hiraṇyakaśipu when he was released from the hands of Nṛsiṁhadeva. Hiraṇyakaśipu was destined to be ultimately killed by Nṛsiṁhadeva, but just to see the fun, the Lord gave him a chance to slip from His hands.

TEXT 28

तं श्येनवेगं शतचन्द्रवर्त्मभि-
श्चरन्तमच्छिद्रमुपर्यधो हरिः ।
कृत्वाट्टहासं खरमुत्स्वनोल्बणं
निमीलिताक्षं जगृहे महाजवः ॥२८॥

taṁ śyena-vegaṁ śata-candra-vartmabhiś
carantam acchidram upary-adho hariḥ
kṛtvāṭṭa-hāsaṁ kharam utsvanolbaṇaṁ
nimīlitākṣaṁ jagṛhe mahā-javaḥ

tam—him (Hiraṇyakaśipu); *śyena-vegam*—possessing the speed of a hawk; *śata-candra-vartmabhiḥ*—by the maneuvers of his sword and his shield, which was marked with a hundred moonlike spots; *carantam*—moving; *acchidram*—without any weak spot; *upari-adhaḥ*—up and down; *hariḥ*—the Supreme Personality of Godhead; *kṛtvā*—making; *aṭṭa-hāsam*—loud laughter; *kharam*—extremely shrill; *utsvana-ulbaṇam*—very fearful due to its great sound; *nimīlita*—closed; *akṣam*—eyes; *jagṛhe*—captured; *mahā-javaḥ*—the greatly powerful Lord.

TRANSLATION

Making a loud, shrill sound of laughter, the Supreme Personality of Godhead, Nārāyaṇa, who is extremely strong and powerful, captured Hiraṇyakaśipu, who was protecting himself with his sword and shield, leaving no gaps open. With the speed of a hawk, Hiraṇyakaśipu moved sometimes in the sky and sometimes on the earth, his eyes closed because of fear of Nṛsiṁhadeva's laughter.

TEXT 29

विष्वक् स्फुरन्तं ग्रहणातुरं हरि-
र्व्यालो यथाखुं कुलिशाक्षतत्वचम् ।
द्वार्यूरुमापत्य ददार लीलया
नखैर्यथाहिं गरुडो महाविषम् ॥२९॥

viṣvak sphurantaṁ grahaṇāturaṁ harir
vyālo yathākhuṁ kuliśākṣata-tvacam
dvāry ūrum āpatya dadāra līlayā
nakhair yathāhiṁ garuḍo mahā-viṣam

viṣvak—all around; *sphurantam*—moving his limbs; *grahaṇa-āturam*—afflicted because of being captured; *hariḥ*—the Supreme Personality of Godhead, Nṛsiṁhadeva; *vyālaḥ*—a snake; *yathā*—just as; *ākhum*—a mouse; *kuliśa-akṣata*—not cut even by the thunderbolt thrown by Indra; *tvacam*—whose skin; *dvāri*—on the threshold of the door; *ūrum*—on His thigh; *āpatya*—placing; *dadāra*—pierced; *līlayā*—very easily; *nakhaiḥ*—with the nails; *yathā*—just as; *ahim*—a snake; *garuḍaḥ*—Garuḍa, the carrier of Lord Viṣṇu; *mahā-viṣam*—very venomous.

TRANSLATION

As a snake captures a mouse or Garuḍa captures a very venomous snake, Lord Nṛsiṁhadeva captured Hiraṇyakaśipu, who could not be pierced even by the thunderbolt of King Indra. As Hiraṇyakaśipu moved his limbs here, there and all around, very much afflicted at being captured, Lord Nṛsiṁhadeva placed the demon on His lap, supporting him with His thighs, and in the doorway of the assembly hall the Lord very easily tore the demon to pieces with the nails of His hand.

PURPORT

Hiraṇyakaśipu had received from Lord Brahmā the benediction that he would not die on the land or in the sky. Therefore, to keep the promise of Lord Brahmā intact, Nṛsiṁhadeva placed Hiraṇyakaśipu's body on His lap, which was neither land nor sky. Hiraṇyakaśipu had received the benediction that he would not die either during the day or at night. Therefore, to keep this promise of Brahmā, the Lord killed Hiraṇyakaśipu in the evening, which is the end of day and the beginning of night but is neither day nor night. Hiraṇyakaśipu had taken a benediction from Lord Brahmā that he would not die from any weapon or be killed by any person, dead or alive. Therefore, just to keep the word of Lord Brahmā, Lord Nṛsiṁhadeva pierced Hiraṇyakaśipu's body with His nails, which were not weapons and were neither living nor dead. Indeed, the nails can be called dead, but at the same time they can be said to be alive. To keep intact all of Lord Brahmā's benedictions, Lord Nṛsiṁhadeva paradoxically but very easily killed the great demon Hiraṇyakaśipu.

TEXT 30

संरम्भदुष्प्रेक्ष्यकराललोचनो
व्यात्ताननान्तं विलिहन्स्वजिह्वया ।
असृग्लवाक्तारुणकेशराननो
यथान्त्रमाली द्विपहत्यया हरिः ॥३०॥

saṁrambha-duṣprekṣya-karāla-locano
vyāttānanāntaṁ vilihan sva-jihvayā

asṛg-lavāktāruṇa-keśarānano
yathāntra-mālī dvipa-hatyayā hariḥ

saṁrambha—because of great anger; *duṣprekṣya*—very difficult to look at; *karāla*—very fearful; *locanaḥ*—eyes; *vyātta*—expanded; *ānana-antam*—the edge of the mouth; *vilihan*—licking; *sva-jihvayā*—with His tongue; *asṛk-lava*—with spots of blood; *ākta*—smeared; *aruṇa*—reddish; *keśara*—mane; *ānanaḥ*—and face; *yathā*—just as; *antra-mālī*—decorated with a garland of intestines; *dvipa-hatyayā*—by the killing of an elephant; *hariḥ*—the lion.

TRANSLATION

Lord Nṛsiṁhadeva's mouth and mane were sprinkled with drops of blood, and His fierce eyes, full of anger, were impossible to look at. Licking the edge of His mouth with His tongue, the Supreme Personality of Godhead, Nṛsiṁhadeva, decorated with a garland of intestines taken from Hiraṇyakaśipu's abdomen, resembled a lion that has just killed an elephant.

PURPORT

The hair on Lord Nṛsiṁhadeva's face, being sprinkled with drops of blood, was reddish and looked very beautiful. Lord Nṛsiṁhadeva pierced Hiraṇyakaśipu's abdomen with His nails, pulled out the demon's intestines and wore them as a garland, which enhanced His beauty. Thus the Lord became very fearsome, like a lion engaged in fighting an elephant.

TEXT 31

नखाङ्कुरोत्पाटितहृत्सरोरुहं
विसृज्य तस्यानुचरानुदायुधान् ।
अहन् समस्तान्नखशस्त्रपाणिभि-
र्दोर्दण्डयूथोऽनुपथान् सहस्रशः ॥३१॥

nakhāṅkurotpāṭita-hṛt-saroruhaṁ
visṛjya tasyānucarān udāyudhān
ahan samastān nakha-śastra-pāṇibhir
dordaṇḍa-yūtho 'nupathān sahasraśaḥ

nakha-aṅkura—by the pointed nails; *utpāṭita*—torn out; *hṛt-saroruham*—whose heart, which was like a lotus flower; *visṛjya*—leaving aside; *tasya*—of him; *anucarān*—the followers (soldiers and bodyguards); *udāyudhān*—having raised weapons; *ahan*—He killed; *samastān*—all; *nakha-śastra-pāṇibhiḥ*—with His nails and other weapons in His hands; *dordaṇḍa-yūthaḥ*—having unlimited arms; *anupathān*—the attendants of Hiraṇyakaśipu; *sahasraśaḥ*—by thousands.

TRANSLATION

The Supreme Personality of Godhead, who had many, many arms, first uprooted Hiraṇyakaśipu's heart and then threw him aside and turned toward the demon's soldiers. These soldiers had come in thousands to fight with Him with raised weapons and were very faithful followers of Hiraṇyakaśipu, but Lord Nṛsiṁhadeva killed all of them merely with the ends of His nails.

PURPORT

Since the creation of the material world, there have been two kinds of men—the *devas* and the *asuras*. The *devas* are always faithful to the Supreme Personality of Godhead, whereas the *asuras* are always atheists who defy the supremacy of the Lord. At the present moment, throughout the entire world, the atheists are extremely numerous. They are trying to prove that there is no God and that everything takes place due to combinations and permutations of material elements. Thus the material world is becoming more and more godless, and consequently everything is in a disturbed condition. If this continues, the Supreme Personality of Godhead will certainly take action, as He did in the case of Hiraṇyakaśipu. Within a second, Hiraṇyakaśipu and his followers were destroyed, and similarly if this godless civilization continues, it will be destroyed in a second, simply by the movement of one finger of the Supreme Personality of Godhead. The demons should therefore be careful and curtail their godless civilization. They should take advantage of the Kṛṣṇa consciousness movement and become faithful to the Supreme Personality of Godhead; otherwise they are doomed. As Hiraṇyakaśipu was killed in a second, the godless civilization can be destroyed at any moment.

TEXT 32

सटावधूता जलदाः परापतन्
ग्रहाश्च तद्दृष्टिविमुष्टरोचिषः ।
अम्भोधयः श्वासहता विचुक्षुभु-
र्निर्ह्रादभीता दिगिभा विचुक्रुशुः ॥३२॥

saṭāvadhūtā jaladāḥ parāpatan
grahāś ca tad-dṛṣṭi-vimuṣṭa-rociṣaḥ
ambhodhayaḥ śvāsa-hatā vicukṣubhur
nirhrāda-bhītā digibhā vicukruśuḥ

saṭā—by the hair on Lord Nṛsiṁhadeva's head; *avadhūtāḥ*—shaken; *jaladāḥ*—the clouds; *parāpatan*—scattered; *grahāḥ*—the luminous planets; *ca*—and; *tat-dṛṣṭi*—by His glaring glance; *vimuṣṭa*—taken away; *rociṣaḥ*—whose effulgence; *ambhodhayaḥ*—the water of the oceans and seas; *śvāsa-hatāḥ*—being struck by Lord Nṛsiṁhadeva's breathing; *vicukṣubhuḥ*—became turbulent; *nirhrāda-bhītāḥ*—frightened by Nṛsiṁhadeva's roaring; *digibhāḥ*—all the elephants guarding the quarters; *vicukruśuḥ*—cried out.

TRANSLATION

The hair on Nṛsiṁhadeva's head shook the clouds and scattered them here and there, His glaring eyes stole the effulgence of the luminaries in the sky, and His breathing agitated the seas and oceans. Because of His roaring, all the elephants in the world began to cry in fear.

PURPORT

As the Lord says in *Bhagavad-gītā* (10.41):

yad yad vibhūtimat sattvaṁ
śrīmad ūrjitam eva vā
tat tad evāvagaccha tvaṁ
mama tejo-'ṁśa-sambhavam

"Know that all beautiful, glorious and mighty creations spring from but a spark of My splendor." The illumination of the planets and stars in the sky is but a partial manifestation of the Lord's effulgence. There are many wonderful qualities of different living entities, but whatever extraordinary things exist are but part of the Lord's *tejas*, His illumination or brilliance. The deep waves of the seas and oceans and the many other wonders within the creation of the Supreme Personality of Godhead all become insignificant when the Lord, in His special feature, incarnates within this material world. Everything is insignificant in comparison to His personal, all-defeating transcendental qualities.

TEXT 33

द्यौस्तत्सटोत्क्षिप्तविमानसङ्कुला
प्रोत्सर्पत क्ष्मा च पदाभिपीडिता ।
शैलाः समुत्पेतुरमुष्य रंहसा
तत्तेजसा खं ककुभो न रेजिरे ॥३३॥

dyaus tat-saṭotkṣipta-vimāna-saṅkulā
protsarpata kṣmā ca padābhipīḍitā
śailāḥ samutpetur amuṣya raṁhasā
tat-tejasā khaṁ kakubho na rejire

dyauḥ—outer space; *tat-saṭā*—by His hair; *utkṣipta*—thrown up; *vimāna-saṅkulā*—filled with airplanes; *protsarpata*—slipped out of place; *kṣmā*—the planet earth; *ca*—also; *pada-abhipīḍitā*—distressed due to the heavy weight of the lotus feet of the Lord; *śailāḥ*—the hills and mountains; *samutpetuḥ*—sprang up; *amuṣya*—of that one (the Lord); *raṁhasā*—due to the intolerable force; *tat-tejasā*—by His effulgence; *kham*—the sky; *kakubhaḥ*—the ten directions; *na rejire*—did not shine.

TRANSLATION

Airplanes were thrown into outer space and the upper planetary system by the hair on Nṛsiṁhadeva's head. Because of the pressure of the Lord's lotus feet, the earth appeared to slip from its position, and all the hills and mountains sprang up due to His intolerable force. Because of the Lord's bodily effulgence, both the sky and all directions diminished in their natural illumination.

PURPORT

That there were airplanes flying in the sky long, long ago can be understood from this verse. *Śrīmad-Bhāgavatam* was spoken five thousand years ago, and the statements of this verse prove that the symptoms of a very advanced civilization then existed, even in the upper planetary systems, as well as in the lower planetary systems. Modern scientists and philosophers foolishly explain that there was no civilization prior to three thousand years ago, but the statement of this verse nullifies such whimsical judgments. The Vedic civilization existed millions and millions of years ago. It existed since the creation of this universe, and it included arrangements all over the universe with all the modern amenities and even more.

TEXT 34

ततः सभायामुपविष्टमुत्तमे
नृपासने संभृततेजसं विभुम् ।
अलक्षितद्वैरथमत्यमर्षणं
प्रचण्डवक्त्रं न बभाज कश्चन ॥३४॥

tataḥ sabhāyām upaviṣṭam uttame
nṛpāsane sambhṛta-tejasaṁ vibhum
alakṣita-dvairatham atyamarṣaṇaṁ
pracaṇḍa-vaktraṁ na babhāja kaścana

tataḥ—thereafter; *sabhāyām*—in the assembly house; *upaviṣṭam*—seated; *uttame*—on the best; *nṛpa-āsane*—throne (upon which King Hiraṇyakaśipu used to sit); *saṁbhṛta-tejasam*—in full effulgence; *vibhum*—the Supreme Lord; *alakṣita-dvairatham*—whose challenger or enemy was not seen; *ati*—very much; *amarṣaṇam*—fearsome (due to His anger); *pracaṇḍa*—terrible; *vaktram*—face; *na*—not; *babhāja*—worshiped; *kaścana*—anyone.

TRANSLATION

Manifesting a full effulgence and a fearsome countenance, Lord Nṛsiṁha, being very angry and finding no contestant to face His power and opulence, then sat down in the assembly hall on the ex-

cellent throne of the king. Because of fear and obedience, no one could come forward to serve the Lord directly.

PURPORT

When the Lord sat on the throne of Hiraṇyakaśipu, there was no one to protest; no enemy came forward on behalf of Hiraṇyakaśipu to fight with the Lord. This means that His supremacy was immediately accepted by the demons. Another point is that although Hiraṇyakaśipu treated the Lord as his bitterest enemy, he was the Lord's faithful servant in Vaikuṇṭha, and therefore the Lord had no hesitation in sitting on the throne that Hiraṇyakaśipu had so laboriously created. Śrīla Viśvanātha Cakravartī Ṭhākura remarks in this connection that sometimes, with great care and attention, great saintly persons and *ṛṣis* offer the Lord valuable seats dedicated with Vedic *mantras* and *tantras*, but still the Lord does not sit upon those thrones. Hiraṇyakaśipu, however, had formerly been Jaya, the doorkeeper at the Vaikuṇṭha gate, and although he had fallen because of the curse of the *brāhmaṇas* and had gotten the nature of a demon, and although he had never offered anything to the Lord as Hiraṇyakaśipu, the Lord is so affectionate to His devotee and servant that He nonetheless took pleasure in sitting on the throne that Hiraṇyakaśipu had created. In this regard it is to be understood that a devotee is fortunate in any condition of his life.

TEXT 35

निशाम्य लोकत्रयमस्तकज्वरं
तमादिदैत्यं हरिणा हतं मृधे ।
प्रहर्षवेगोत्कलितानना मुहुः
प्रसूनवर्षैर्ववृषुः सुरस्त्रियः ॥३५॥

niśāmya loka-traya-mastaka-jvaraṁ
tam ādi-daityaṁ hariṇā hataṁ mṛdhe
praharṣa-vegotkalitānanā muhuḥ
prasūna-varṣair vavṛṣuḥ sura-striyaḥ

niśāmya—hearing; *loka-traya*—of the three worlds; *mastaka-jvaram*—the headache; *tam*—him; *ādi*—the original; *daityam*—

demon; *hariṇā*—by the Supreme Personality of Godhead; *hatam*—killed; *mṛdhe*—in battle; *praharṣa-vega*—by an outburst of ecstasy; *utkalita-ānanāḥ*—whose faces blossomed; *muhuḥ*—again and again; *prasūna-varṣaiḥ*—with showers of flowers; *vavṛṣuḥ*—rained; *sura-striyaḥ*—the wives of the demigods.

TRANSLATION

Hiraṇyakaśipu had been exactly like a fever of meningitis in the head of the three worlds. Thus when the wives of the demigods in the heavenly planets saw that the great demon had been killed by the personal hands of the Supreme Personality of Godhead, their faces blossomed in great joy. The wives of the demigods again and again showered flowers from heaven upon Lord Nṛsiṁhadeva like rain.

TEXT 36

तदा विमानावलिभिर्नभस्तलं
दिदृक्षतां सङ्कुलमास नाकिनाम् ।
सुरानका दुन्दुभयोऽथ जघ्निरे
गन्धर्वमुख्या ननृतुर्जगुः स्त्रियः ॥३६॥

tadā vimānāvalibhir nabhastalaṁ
didṛkṣatāṁ saṅkulam āsa nākinām
surānakā dundubhayo 'tha jaghnire
gandharva-mukhyā nanṛtur jaguḥ striyaḥ

tadā—at that time; *vimāna-āvalibhiḥ*—with different types of airplanes; *nabhastalam*—the sky; *didṛkṣatām*—desirous of seeing; *saṅkulam*—crowded; *āsa*—became; *nākinām*—of the demigods; *sura-ānakāḥ*—the drums of the demigods; *dundubhayaḥ*—the kettledrums; *atha*—as well; *jaghnire*—were sounded; *gandharva-mukhyāḥ*—the chiefs of Gandharvaloka; *nanṛtuḥ*—began to dance; *jaguḥ*—sang; *striyaḥ*—heavenly society women.

TRANSLATION

At that time, the airplanes of the demigods, who desired to see the activities of the Supreme Lord, Nārāyaṇa, crowded the sky.

The demigods began beating drums and kettledrums, and upon hearing them the angelic women began to dance, while the chiefs of the Gandharvas sang sweetly.

TEXTS 37–39

तत्रोपव्रज्य विबुधा ब्रह्मेन्द्रगिरिशादयः ।
ऋषयः पितरः सिद्धा विद्याधरमहोरगाः ॥३७॥
मनवः प्रजानां पतयो गन्धर्वाप्सरचारणाः ।
यक्षाः किम्पुरुषास्तात वेतालाः सहकिन्नराः॥३८॥
ते विष्णुपार्षदाः सर्वे सुनन्दकुमुदादयः ।
मूर्ध्नि बद्धाञ्जलिपुटा आसीनं तीव्रतेजसम् ।
ईडिरे नरशार्दुलं नातिदूरचराः पृथक् ॥३९॥

tatropavrajya vibudhā
brahmendra-giriśādayaḥ
ṛṣayaḥ pitaraḥ siddhā
vidyādhara-mahoragāḥ

manavaḥ prajānāṁ patayo
gandharvāpsara-cāraṇāḥ
yakṣāḥ kimpuruṣās tāta
vetālāḥ saha-kinnarāḥ

te viṣṇu-pārṣadāḥ sarve
sunanda-kumudādayaḥ
mūrdhni baddhāñjali-puṭā
āsīnaṁ tīvra-tejasam
īḍire nara-śārdulaṁ
nātidūracarāḥ pṛthak

tatra—there (in the sky); *upavrajya*—coming (in their respective airplanes); *vibudhāḥ*—all the different demigods; *brahma-indra-giriśa-ādayaḥ*—headed by Lord Brahmā, King Indra and Lord Śiva; *ṛṣayaḥ*—the great saintly sages; *pitaraḥ*—the inhabitants of Pitṛloka; *siddhāḥ*—

the residents of Siddhaloka; *vidyādhara*—the residents of Vidyādhara-loka; *mahā-uragāḥ*—the residents of the planets where great serpents reside; *manavaḥ*—the Manus; *prajānām*—of the living entities (on different planets); *patayaḥ*—the chiefs; *gandharva*—the residents of Gandharvaloka; *apsara*—the residents of the angelic planet; *cāraṇāḥ*—the residents of Cāraṇaloka; *yakṣāḥ*—the Yakṣas; *kimpuruṣāḥ*—the Kimpuruṣas; *tāta*—O dear one; *vetālāḥ*—the Vetālas; *saha-kinnarāḥ*—along with the Kinnaras; *te*—they; *viṣṇu-pārṣadāḥ*—the personal associates of Lord Viṣṇu (in the Vaikuṇṭhalokas); *sarve*—all; *sunanda-kumuda-ādayaḥ*—headed by Sunanda and Kumuda; *mūrdhni*—on their heads; *baddha-añjali-puṭāḥ*—with folded hands; *āsīnam*—who was sitting on the throne; *tīvra-tejasam*—exposing His great spiritual effulgence; *īḍire*—offered respectful worship; *nara-śārdulam*—unto the Lord, who had appeared as half man and half lion; *na ati-dūracarāḥ*—coming near; *pṛthak*—individually.

TRANSLATION

My dear King Yudhiṣṭhira, the demigods then approached the Lord. They were headed by Lord Brahmā, King Indra and Lord Śiva and included great saintly persons and the residents of Pitṛloka, Siddhaloka, Vidyādhara-loka and the planet of the snakes. The Manus approached, and so did the chiefs of various other planets. The angelic dancers approached, as did the Gandharvas, the Cāraṇas, the Yakṣas, the inhabitants of Kinnaraloka, the Vetālas, the inhabitants of Kimpuruṣa-loka, and the personal servants of Viṣṇu like Sunanda and Kumuda. All of them came near the Lord, who glowed with intense light. They individually offered their obeisances and prayers, their hands folded at their heads.

TEXT 40

श्रीब्रह्मोवाच

नतोऽस्म्यनन्ताय दुरन्तशक्तये
विचित्रवीर्याय पवित्रकर्मणे ।
विश्वस्य सर्गस्थितिसंयमान् गुणैः
स्वलीलया सन्दधतेऽव्ययात्मने ॥४०॥

śrī-brahmovāca
nato 'smy anantāya duranta-śaktaye
vicitra-vīryāya pavitra-karmaṇe
viśvasya sarga-sthiti-saṁyamān guṇaiḥ
sva-līlayā sandadhate 'vyayātmane

śrī-brahmā uvāca—Lord Brahmā said; *nataḥ*—bowed down; *asmi*—I am; *anantāya*—unto the unlimited Lord; *duranta*—very difficult to find an end to; *śaktaye*—who possesses different potencies; *vicitra-vīryāya*—having varieties of prowess; *pavitra-karmaṇe*—whose actions have no reaction (even though doing contrary things, He remains without contamination by the material modes); *viśvasya*—of the universe; *sarga*—creation; *sthiti*—maintenance; *saṁyamān*—and annihilation; *guṇaiḥ*—by the material qualities; *sva-līlayā*—very easily; *sandadhate*—performs; *avyaya-ātmane*—whose personality never deteriorates.

TRANSLATION

Lord Brahmā prayed: My Lord, You are unlimited, and You possess unending potencies. No one can estimate or calculate Your prowess and wonderful influence, for Your actions are never polluted by the material energy. Through the material qualities, You very easily create the universe, maintain it and again annihilate it, yet You remain the same, without deterioration. I therefore offer my respectful obeisances unto You.

PURPORT

The activities of the Lord are always wonderful. His personal servants Jaya and Vijaya were confidential friends, yet they were cursed, and they accepted bodies of demons. Again, in the family of one such demon, Prahlāda Mahārāja was caused to take birth to exhibit the behavior of an exalted devotee, and then the Lord accepted the body of Nṛsiṁhadeva to kill that same demon, who by the Lord's own will had taken birth in a demoniac family. Therefore, who can understand the Lord's transcendental activities? Not to speak of understanding the transcendental activities of the Lord, no one can understand even the activities of His servants. In *Caitanya-caritāmṛta* (*Madhya* 23.39) it is said, *tāṅra vākya, kriyā, mudrā vijñeha nā bhujhaya:* no one can understand the activities of the Lord's servants. Therefore, what to speak of the activities of the Lord? Who can understand how Kṛṣṇa is benefiting the entire world? The Lord is addressed as *duranta-śakti* because no one can understand His potencies and how He acts.

TEXT 41

श्रीरुद्र उवाच
कोपकालो युगान्तस्ते हतोऽयमसुरोऽल्पकः ।
तत्सुतं पाह्युपसृतं भक्तं ते भक्तवत्सल ॥४१॥

śrī-rudra uvāca
kopa-kālo yugāntas te
hato 'yam asuro 'lpakaḥ
tat-sutaṁ pāhy upasṛtaṁ
bhaktaṁ te bhakta-vatsala

śrī-rudraḥ uvāca—Lord Śiva offered his prayer; *kopa-kālaḥ*—the right time for Your anger (for the purpose of annihilating the universe); *yuga-antaḥ*—the end of the millennium; *te*—by You; *hataḥ*—killed; *ayam*—this; *asuraḥ*—great demon; *alpakaḥ*—very insignificant; *tat-sutam*—his son (Prahlāda Mahārāja); *pāhi*—just protect; *upasṛtam*—who is surrendered and standing nearby; *bhaktam*—devotee; *te*—of Your Lordship; *bhakta-vatsala*—O my Lord, who are so affectionate to Your devotee.

TRANSLATION

Lord Śiva said: The end of the millennium is the time for Your anger. Now that this insignificant demon Hiraṇyakaśipu has been killed, O my Lord, who are naturally affectionate to Your devotee, kindly protect his son Prahlāda Mahārāja, who is standing nearby as Your fully surrendered devotee.

PURPORT

The Supreme Personality of Godhead is the creator of the material world. There are three processes in creation—namely creation, maintenance and finally annihilation. During the period of annihilation, at the end of each millennium, the Lord becomes angry, and the part of anger is played by Lord Śiva, who is therefore called Rudra. When the Lord appeared in great anger to kill Hiraṇyakaśipu, everyone was extremely afraid of the Lord's attitude, but Lord Śiva, knowing very well that the Lord's anger is also His *līlā*, was not afraid. Lord Śiva knew that he would have to play the part of anger for the Lord. *Kāla* means Lord Śiva (Bhairava), and *kopa* refers to the Lord's anger. These words, combined together as *kopa-kāla*, refer to the end of each millennium. Actually the Lord is always affectionate toward His devotees, even though He may appear very angry. Because He is *avyayātmā*—because He never falls down—even when angry the Lord is affectionate toward His devotees. Therefore Lord Śiva reminded the Lord to act like an affectionate father toward Prahlāda Mahārāja, who was standing by the Lord's side as an exalted, fully surrendered devotee.

TEXT 42

श्रीइन्द्र उवाच

प्रत्यानीताः परम भवता त्रायता नः स्वभागा
दैत्याक्रान्तं हृदयकमलं तद्गृहं प्रत्यबोधि ।
कालग्रस्तं कियदिदमहो नाथ शुश्रूषतां ते
मुक्तिस्तेषां न हि बहुमता नारसिंहापरैः किम् ॥४२॥

śrī-indra uvāca
pratyānītāḥ parama bhavatā trāyatā naḥ sva-bhāgā
daityākrāntaṁ hṛdaya-kamalaṁ tad-gṛhaṁ pratyabodhi
kāla-grastaṁ kiyad idam aho nātha śuśrūṣatāṁ te
muktis teṣāṁ na hi bahumatā nārasiṁhāparaiḥ kim

śrī-indraḥ uvāca—Indra, the King of heaven, said; *pratyānītāḥ*—recovered; *parama*—O Supreme; *bhavatā*—by Your Lordship; *trāyatā*—who are protecting; *naḥ*—us; *sva-bhāgāḥ*—shares in the sacrifices; *daitya-ākrāntam*—afflicted by the demon; *hṛdaya-kamalam*—the lotuslike cores of our hearts; *tat-gṛham*—which is actually Your residence; *pratyabodhi*—it has been illuminated; *kāla-*

grastam—devoured by time; *kiyat*—insignificant; *idam*—this (world); *aho*—alas; *nātha*—O Lord; *śuśrūṣatām*—for those who are always engaged in the service; *te*—of You; *muktiḥ*—liberation from material bondage; *teṣām*—of them (the pure devotees); *na*—not; *hi*—indeed; *bahumatā*—thought very important; *nāra-siṁha*—O Lord Nṛsiṁhadeva, half lion and half human being; *aparaiḥ kim*—then what is the use of other possessions.

TRANSLATION

King Indra said: O Supreme Lord, You are our deliverer and protector. Our shares of sacrifices, which are actually Yours, have been recovered from the demon by You. Because the demoniac king Hiraṇyakaśipu was most fearsome, our hearts, which are Your permanent abode, were all overtaken by him. Now, by Your presence, the gloom and darkness in our hearts have been dissipated. O Lord, for those who always engage in Your service, which is more exalted than liberation, all material opulence is insignificant. They do not even care for liberation, not to speak of the benefits of kāma, artha and dharma.

PURPORT

In this material world there are two kinds of people—the *devatās* (demigods) and the *asuras* (demons). Although the demigods are attached to material enjoyment, they are devotees of the Lord who act according to the rules and regulations of the Vedic injunctions. During the reign of Hiraṇyakaśipu, everyone was disturbed in the routine duties of Vedic civilization. When Hiraṇyakaśipu was killed, all the demigods, who had always been disturbed by Hiraṇyakaśipu, felt relief in their general way of life.

Because the government in Kali-yuga is full of demons, the living conditions of devotees are always disturbed. Devotees cannot perform *yajña*, and thus they cannot partake of the remnants of food offered in *yajña* for the worship of Lord Viṣṇu. The hearts of the demigods are always filled with fear of the demons, and therefore they cannot think of the Supreme Personality of Godhead. The engagement of the demigods is to think of the Lord always within the cores of their hearts. The Lord says in *Bhagavad-gītā* (6.47):

yoginām api sarveṣāṁ
mad gatenāntarātmanā
śraddhāvān bhajate yo māṁ
sa me yuktatamo mataḥ

"And of all *yogīs*, he who always abides in Me with great faith, worshiping Me in transcendental loving service, is most intimately united with Me in *yoga* and is the highest of all." The demigods fully absorb themselves in meditation upon the Supreme Personality of Godhead to become perfect *yogīs*, but because of the presence of demons, their hearts are filled with the activities of the demons. Thus their hearts, which are meant to be the abode of the Supreme Lord, are practically occupied by the demons. All the demigods felt relieved when Hiraṇyakaśipu was dead, for they could easily think of the Lord. They could then receive the results of sacrifices and become happy even though in the material world.

TEXT 43

श्रीऋषय ऊचुः
त्वं नस्तपः परममात्थ यदात्मतेजो
येनेदमादिपुरुषात्मगतं ससर्क्थ ।
तद् विप्रलुप्तममुनाद्य शरण्यपाल
रक्षागृहीतवपुषा पुनरन्वमंस्थाः ॥४३॥

śrī-ṛṣaya ūcuḥ
tvaṁ nas tapaḥ paramam āttha yad ātma-tejo
yenedam ādi-puruṣātma-gataṁ sasarktha
tad vipraluptam amunādya śaraṇya-pāla
rakṣā-gṛhīta-vapuṣā punar anvamaṁsthāḥ

śrī-ṛṣayaḥ ūcuḥ—the great sages said; *tvam*—You; *naḥ*—our; *tapaḥ*—austerity; *paramam*—topmost; *āttha*—instructed; *yat*—which; *ātma-tejaḥ*—Your spiritual power; *yena*—by which; *idam*—this (material world); *ādi-puruṣa*—O supreme original Personality of Godhead; *ātma-gatam*—merged within Yourself; *sasarktha*—(You) created; *tat*—that process of austerity and penance; *vipraluptam*—stolen; *amunā*—by that demon (Hiraṇyakaśipu); *adya*—now; *śaraṇya-pāla*—

O supreme maintainer of those who need to be sheltered; *rakṣā-gṛhīta-vapuṣā*—by Your body, which You accept to give protection; *punaḥ*—again; *anvamaṁsthāḥ*—You have approved.

TRANSLATION

All the saintly persons present offered their prayers in this way: O Lord, O supreme maintainer of those sheltered at Your lotus feet, O original Personality of Godhead, the process of austerity and penance, in which You instructed us before, is the spiritual power of Your very self. It is by austerity that You create the material world, which lies dormant within You. This austerity was almost stopped by the activities of this demon, but now, by Yourself appearing in the form of Nṛsiṁhadeva, which is meant just to give us protection, and by killing this demon, You have again approved the process of austerity.

PURPORT

The living entities wandering within the jurisdiction of the 8,400,000 species of life get the opportunity for self-realization in the human form and gradually in such other elevated forms as those of the demigods, Kinnaras and Cāraṇas, as will be described below. In the higher statuses of life, beginning from human life, the main duty is *tapasya,* or austerity. As Ṛṣabhadeva advised His sons, *tapo divyaṁ putrakā yena sattvaṁ śuddhyet.* To rectify our material existence, austerity (*tapasya*) is absolutely necessary. However, when people in general come under the control of a demon or a demoniac ruling power, they forget this process of *tapasya* and gradually also become demoniac. All the saintly persons, who were generally engaged in austerity, felt relieved when Hiraṇyakaśipu was killed by the Lord in the form of Nṛsiṁhadeva. They realized that the original instruction concerning human life—that it is meant for *tapasya* for self-realization—was reaffirmed by the Lord when He killed Hiraṇyakaśipu.

TEXT 44

श्रीपितर ऊचुः

श्राद्धानि नोऽधिबुभुजे प्रसभं तनूजै-
र्दत्तानि तीर्थसमयेऽप्यपिबत् तिलाम्बु ।

तस्योदरान्नखविदीर्णवपाद् य आर्च्छत्
तस्मै नमो नृहरयेऽखिलधर्मगोप्त्रे ॥४४॥

śrī-pitara ūcuḥ
śrāddhāni no 'dhibubhuje prasabhaṁ tanūjair
dattāni tīrtha-samaye 'py apibat tilāmbu
tasyodarān nakha-vidīrṇa-vapād ya ārcchat
tasmai namo nṛharaye 'khila-dharma-goptre

śrī-pitaraḥ ūcuḥ—the inhabitants of Pitṛloka said; *śrāddhāni*—the performances of the *śrāddha* ceremony (offering of food grains to dead forefathers by a particular process); *naḥ*—our; *adhibubhuje*—enjoyed; *prasabham*—by force; *tanūjaiḥ*—by our sons and grandsons; *dattāni*—offered; *tīrtha-samaye*—at the time of bathing in the holy places; *api*—even; *apibat*—drank; *tila-ambu*—offerings of water with sesame seeds; *tasya*—of the demon; *udarāt*—from the abdomen; *nakha-vidīrṇa*—pierced by the nails of the hand; *vapāt*—the skin of the intestines of which; *yaḥ*—He who (the Personality of Godhead); *ārcchat*—obtained; *tasmai*—unto Him (the Supreme Personality of Godhead); *namaḥ*—respectful obeisances; *nṛ-haraye*—who has appeared as half lion and half man (Nṛhari); *akhila*—universal; *dharma*—religious principles; *goptre*—who maintains.

TRANSLATION

The inhabitants of Pitṛloka prayed: Let us offer our respectful obeisances unto Lord Nṛsiṁhadeva, the maintainer of the religious principles of the universe. He has killed Hiraṇyakaśipu, the demon who by force enjoyed all the offerings of the śrāddha ceremonies performed by our sons and grandsons on the anniversaries of our death and who drank the water with sesame seeds offered in holy places of pilgrimage. By killing this demon, O Lord, You have taken back all this stolen property from his abdomen by piercing it with Your nails. We therefore wish to offer our respectful obeisances unto You.

PURPORT

It is the duty of all householders to offer food grains to all their departed forefathers, but during the time of Hiraṇyakaśipu this process was stopped; no one would offer *śrāddha* oblations of food grains to the forefathers with great respect. Thus when there is a demoniac rule, everything concerning the Vedic principles is turned upside down, all the religious ceremonies of *yajña* are stopped, the resources meant to be spent for *yajña* are taken away by the demoniac government, everything becomes chaotic, and consequently the entire world becomes hell itself. When the demons are killed by the presence of Nṛsiṁhadeva, everyone feels comfortable, irrespective of the planet upon which he lives.

TEXT 45

श्रीसिद्धा ऊचुः
यो नो गतिं योगसिद्धामसाधु-
रहार्षीद् योगतपोबलेन ।
नानादर्पं तं नखैर्विददार
तस्मै तुभ्यं प्रणताः स्मो नृसिंह ॥४५॥

śrī-siddhā ūcuḥ
yo no gatiṁ yoga-siddhām asādhur
ahārṣīd yoga-tapo-balena
nānā darpaṁ taṁ nakhair vidadāra
tasmai tubhyaṁ praṇatāḥ smo nṛsiṁha

śrī-siddhāḥ ūcuḥ—the inhabitants of Siddhaloka said; *yaḥ*—the person who; *naḥ*—our; *gatim*—perfection; *yoga-siddhām*—achieved by mystic *yoga; asādhuḥ*—most uncivilized and dishonest; *ahārṣīt*—stole away; *yoga*—of mysticism; *tapaḥ*—and austerities; *balena*—by the power; *nānā darpam*—proud due to wealth, opulence and strength; *tam*—him; *nakhaiḥ*—by the nails; *vidadāra*—pierced; *tasmai*—unto him; *tubhyam*—unto You; *praṇatāḥ*—bowed down; *smaḥ*—we are; *nṛsiṁha*—O Lord Nṛsiṁhadeva.

TRANSLATION

The inhabitants of Siddhaloka prayed: O Lord Nṛsiṁhadeva, because we belong to Siddhaloka, we automatically achieve perfection in all eight kinds of mystic power. Yet Hiraṇyakaśipu was so

dishonest that by the strength of his power and austerity, he took away our powers. Thus he became very proud of his mystic strength. Now, because this rogue has been killed by Your nails, we offer our respectful obeisances unto You.

PURPORT

On earth there are many *yogīs* who can exhibit some feeble mystic power by manufacturing pieces of gold like magic, but the inhabitants of the planet Siddhaloka are actually extremely powerful in mysticism. They can fly from one planet to another without airplanes. This is called *laghimā-siddhi.* They can actually become very light and fly in the sky. By a severe type of austerity, however, Hiraṇyakaśipu excelled all the inhabitants of Siddhaloka and created disturbances for them. The residents of Siddhaloka were also beaten by the powers of Hiraṇyakaśipu. Now that Hiraṇyakaśipu had been killed by the Lord, the inhabitants of Siddhaloka also felt relieved.

TEXT 46

श्रीविद्याधरा ऊचुः

विद्यां पृथग्धारणयानुराद्धां
न्यषेधदज्ञो बलवीर्यदृप्तः ।
स येन संख्ये पशुवद्धतस्तं
मायानृसिंहं प्रणताः स्म नित्यम् ॥४६॥

śrī-vidyādharā ūcuḥ
vidyāṁ pṛthag dhāraṇayānurāddhāṁ
nyaṣedhad ajño bala-vīrya-dṛptaḥ
sa yena saṅkhye paśuvad dhatas taṁ
māyā-nṛsiṁhaṁ praṇatāḥ sma nityam

śrī-vidyādharāḥ ūcuḥ—the inhabitants of Vidyādhara-loka prayed; *vidyām*—mystic formulas (by which one can appear and disappear); *pṛthak*—separately; *dhāraṇayā*—by various meditations within the mind; *anurāddhām*—attained; *nyaṣedhat*—stopped; *ajñaḥ*—this fool; *bala-vīrya-dṛptaḥ*—puffed up by bodily strength and his ability to conquer anyone; *saḥ*—he (Hiraṇyakaśipu); *yena*—by whom; *saṅkhye*—in battle; *paśu-vat*—exactly like an animal; *hataḥ*—killed; *tam*—unto Him; *māyā-nṛsiṁham*—appearing as Lord Nṛsiṁhadeva by the influence of His own energy; *praṇatāḥ*—fallen; *sma*—certainly; *nityam*—eternally.

TRANSLATION

The inhabitants of Vidyādhara-loka prayed: Our acquired power to appear and disappear in various ways according to varieties of meditation was banned by that foolish Hiraṇyakaśipu because of his pride in his superior bodily strength and his ability to conquer others. Now the Supreme Personality of Godhead has killed him just as if the demon were an animal. Unto that supreme pastime form of Lord Nṛsiṁhadeva, we eternally offer our respectful obeisances.

TEXT 47

श्रीनागा ऊचुः

येन पापेन रत्नानि स्त्रीरत्नानि हृतानि नः ।
तद्वक्षःपाटनेनासां दत्तानन्द नमोऽस्तु ते ॥४७॥

śrī-nāgā ūcuḥ
yena pāpena ratnāni
strī-ratnāni hṛtāni naḥ
tad-vakṣaḥ-pāṭanenāsāṁ
dattānanda namo 'stu te

śrī-nāgāḥ ūcuḥ—the inhabitants of Nāgaloka, who look like serpents, said; *yena*—by which person; *pāpena*—the most sinful (Hiraṇyakaśipu); *ratnāni*—the jewels on our heads; *strī-ratnāni*—beautiful wives; *hṛtāni*—taken away; *naḥ*—our; *tat*—his; *vakṣaḥ-pāṭanena*—by the piercing of the chest; *āsām*—of all the women (who were kidnapped); *datta-ānanda*—O Lord, You are the source of the pleasure; *namaḥ*—our respectful obeisances; *astu*—let there be; *te*—unto You.

TRANSLATION

The inhabitants of Nāgaloka said: The most sinful Hiraṇyakaśipu took away all the jewels on our hoods and all our beautiful wives. Now, since his chest has been pierced by Your nails, You are the source of all pleasure to our wives. Thus we together offer our respectful obeisances unto You.

PURPORT

No one is peaceful if his wealth and wife are forcibly taken away. All the inhabitants of Nāgaloka, which is situated below the earthly planetary system, were in great anxiety because their wealth had been stolen and their wives kidnapped by Hiraṇyakaśipu. Now, Hiraṇyakaśipu having been killed, their wealth and wives were returned, and their wives felt satisfied. The inhabitants of various *lokas*, or planets, offered their respectful obeisances unto the Lord because they were relieved by the death of Hiraṇyakaśipu. Disturbances similar to those created by Hiraṇyakaśipu are now taking place all over the world because of demoniac governments. As stated in the Twelfth Canto of *Śrīmad-Bhāgavatam*, the men of the governments of Kali-yuga will be no better than rogues and plunderers. Thus the populace will be harassed on one side by scarcity of food and on another by heavy taxation by the government. In other words, the people in most parts of the world in this age are harassed by the ruling principles of Hiraṇyakaśipu.

TEXT 48

श्रीमनव ऊचुः
मनवो वयं तव निदेशकारिणो
दितिजेन देव परिभूतसेतवः ।
भवता खलः स उपसंहृतः प्रभो
करवाम ते किमनुशाधि किङ्करान् ॥४८॥

śrī-manava ūcuḥ
manavo vayaṁ tava nideśa-kāriṇo
ditijena deva paribhūta-setavaḥ

bhavatā khalaḥ sa upasaṁhṛtaḥ prabho
karavāma te kim anuśādhi kiṅkarān

śrī-manavaḥ ūcuḥ—all the Manus offered their respectful obeisances by saying; *manavaḥ*—the leaders of the universal affairs (especially in connection with giving knowledge to humanity about how to live lawfully under the protection of the Supreme Personality of Godhead); *vayam*—we; *tava*—of Your Lordship; *nideśa-kāriṇaḥ*—the carriers of the orders; *diti-jena*—by Hiraṇyakaśipu, the son of Diti; *deva*—O Lord; *paribhūta*—disregarded; *setavaḥ*—whose laws of morality concerning the *varṇāśrama* system in human society; *bhavatā*—by Your Lordship; *khalaḥ*—the most envious rascal; *saḥ*—he; *upasaṁhṛtaḥ*—killed; *prabho*—O Lord; *karavāma*—shall we do; *te*—Your; *kim*—what; *anuśādhi*—please direct; *kiṅkarān*—Your eternal servants.

TRANSLATION

All the Manus offered their prayers as follows: As Your order carriers, O Lord, we, the Manus, are the law-givers for human society, but because of the temporary supremacy of this great demon, Hiraṇyakaśipu, our laws for maintaining varṇāśrama-dharma were destroyed. O Lord, now that You have killed this great demon, we are in our normal condition. Kindly order us, Your eternal servants, what to do now.

PURPORT

In many places in *Bhagavad-gītā*, the Supreme Lord, Kṛṣṇa, refers to the *varṇāśrama-dharma* of four *varṇas* and four *āśramas*. He teaches people about this *varṇāśrama-dharma* so that all of human society can live peacefully by observing the principles for the four social divisions and four spiritual divisions (*varṇa* and *āśrama*) and thus make advancement in spiritual knowledge. The Manus compiled the *Manu-saṁhitā*. The word *saṁhitā* means Vedic knowledge, and *manu* indicates that this knowledge is given by Manu. The Manus are sometimes incarnations of the Supreme Lord and sometimes empowered living entities. Formerly, many long years ago, Lord Kṛṣṇa instructed the sun-god. The Manus are generally sons of the sun-god. Therefore, while speaking to Arjuna about the importance of *Bhagavad-gītā*, Kṛṣṇa said, *imaṁ vivas-*

vate yogaṁ proktavān aham avyayam vivasvān manave prāha: "This instruction was given to Vivasvān, the sun-god, who in turn instructed his son Manu." Manu gave the law known as *Manu-saṁhitā,* which is full of directions based on *varṇa* and *āśrama* concerning how to live as a human being. These are very scientific ways of life, but under the rule of demons like Hiraṇyakaśipu, human society breaks all these systems of law and order and gradually becomes lower and lower. Thus there is no peace in the world. The conclusion is that if we want real peace and order in the human society, we must follow the principles laid down by the *Manu-saṁhitā* and confirmed by the Supreme Personality of Godhead, Kṛṣṇa.

TEXT 49

श्रीप्रजापतय ऊचुः
प्रजेशा वयं ते परेशाभिसृष्टा
न येन प्रजा वै सृजामो निषिद्धाः ।
स एष त्वया भिन्नवक्षा नु शेते
जगन्मङ्गलं सत्त्वमूर्तेऽवतारः ॥४९॥

śrī-prajāpataya ūcuḥ
prajeśā vayaṁ te pareśābhisṛṣṭā
na yena prajā vai sṛjāmo niṣiddhāḥ
sa eṣa tvayā bhinna-vakṣā nu śete
jagan-maṅgalaṁ sattva-mūrte 'vatāraḥ

śrī-prajāpatayaḥ ūcuḥ—the great personalities who created the various living beings offered their prayers by saying; *prajā-īśāḥ*—the *prajāpatis* created by Lord Brahmā, who have created generations of living entities; *vayam*—we; *te*—of You; *para-īśa*—O Supreme Lord; *abhisṛṣṭāḥ*—born; *na*—not; *yena*—by whom (Hiraṇyakaśipu); *prajāḥ*—living entities; *vai*—indeed; *sṛjāmaḥ*—we create; *niṣiddhāḥ*—being forbidden; *saḥ*—he (Hiraṇyakaśipu); *eṣaḥ*—this; *tvayā*—by You; *bhinna-vakṣāḥ*—whose chest has been split; *nu*—indeed; *śete*—lies down; *jagat-maṅgalam*—for the auspiciousness of the whole world; *sattva-mūrte*—in this transcendental form of pure goodness; *avatāraḥ*—this incarnation.

TRANSLATION

The prajāpatis offered their prayers as follows: O Supreme Lord, Lord of even Brahmā and Śiva, we, the prajāpatis, were created by You to execute Your orders, but we were forbidden by Hiraṇyakaśipu to create any more good progeny. Now the demon is lying dead before us, his chest pierced by You. Let us therefore offer our respectful obeisances unto You, whose incarnation in this form of pure goodness is meant for the welfare of the entire universe.

TEXT 50

श्रीगन्धर्वा ऊचुः

वयं विभो ते नटनाट्यगायका
येनात्मसाद् वीर्यबलौजसा कृताः ।
स एष नीतो भवता दशामिमां
किमुत्पथस्थः कुशलाय कल्पते ॥५०॥

śrī-gandharvā ūcuḥ
vayaṁ vibho te naṭa-nāṭya-gāyakā
yenātmasād vīrya-balaujasā kṛtāḥ
sa eṣa nīto bhavatā daśām imāṁ
kim utpathasthaḥ kuśalāya kalpate

śrī-gandharvāḥ ūcuḥ—the inhabitants of Gandharvaloka (who are usually engaged as musicians of the heavenly planets) said; *vayam*—we; *vibho*—O Lord; *te*—Your; *naṭa-nāṭya-gāyakāḥ*—dancers and singers in dramatic performances; *yena*—by whom; *ātmasāt*—under subjection; *vīrya*—of his valor; *bala*—and bodily strength; *ojasā*—by the influence; *kṛtāḥ*—made (brought); *saḥ*—he (Hiraṇyakaśipu); *eṣaḥ*—this; *nītaḥ*—brought; *bhavatā*—by Your Lordship; *daśām imām*—to this condition; *kim*—whether; *utpathasthaḥ*—anyone who is an upstart; *kuśalāya*—for auspiciousness; *kalpate*—is capable.

TRANSLATION

The inhabitants of Gandharvaloka prayed: Your Lordship, we ever engage in Your service by dancing and singing in dramatic

performances, but this Hiraṇyakaśipu, by the influence of his bodily strength and valor, brought us under his subjugation. Now he has been brought to this low condition by Your Lordship. What benefit can result from the activities of such an upstart as Hiraṇyakaśipu?

PURPORT

By being a very obedient servant of the Supreme Lord, one becomes extremely powerful in bodily strength, influence and effulgence, whereas the fate of demoniac upstarts is ultimately to fall down like Hiraṇyakaśipu. Hiraṇyakaśipu and persons like him may be very powerful for some time, but the obedient servants of the Supreme Personality of Godhead like the demigods remain powerful always. They are victorious over the influence of Hiraṇyakaśipu by the grace of the Supreme Lord.

TEXT 51

श्रीचारणा ऊचुः

हरे तवाङ्घ्रिपङ्कजं भवापवर्गमाश्रिताः ।
यदेष साधुहृच्छयस्त्वयासुरः समापितः ॥५१॥

śrī-cāraṇā ūcuḥ
hare tavāṅghri-paṅkajaṁ
bhavāpavargam āśritāḥ
yad eṣa sādhu-hṛc-chayas
tvayāsuraḥ samāpitaḥ

śrī-cāraṇāḥ ūcuḥ—the inhabitants of the Cāraṇa planet said; *hare*—O Lord; *tava*—Your; *aṅghri-paṅkajam*—lotus feet; *bhava-apavargam*—the only shelter for becoming free from the contamination of material existence; *āśritāḥ*—sheltered at; *yat*—because; *eṣaḥ*—this; *sādhu-hṛt-śayaḥ*—stake in the hearts of all honest persons; *tvayā*—by Your Lordship; *asuraḥ*—the demon (Hiraṇyakaśipu); *samāpitaḥ*—finished.

TRANSLATION

The inhabitants of the Cāraṇa planet said: O Lord, because You have destroyed the demon Hiraṇyakaśipu, who was always a stake

in the hearts of all honest men, we are now relieved, and we eternally take shelter of Your lotus feet, which award the conditioned soul liberation from materialistic contamination.

PURPORT

The Supreme Personality of Godhead in His transcendental form of Narahari, Nṛsiṁhadeva, is always ready to kill the demons, who always create disturbances in the minds of honest devotees. To spread the Kṛṣṇa consciousness movement, devotees have to face many dangers and impediments all over the world, but a faithful servant who preaches with great devotion to the Lord must know that Lord Nṛsiṁhadeva is always his protector.

TEXT 52

श्रीयक्षा ऊचुः

वयमनुचरमुख्याः कर्मभिस्ते मनोज्ञै-
स्त इह दितिसुतेन प्रापिता वाहकत्वम् ।
स तु जनपरितापं तत्कृतं जानता ते
नरहर उपनीतः पञ्चतां पञ्चविंश ॥५२॥

śrī-yakṣā ūcuḥ
vayam anucara-mukhyāḥ karmabhis te mano-jñais
ta iha diti-sutena prāpitā vāhakatvam
sa tu jana-paritāpaṁ tat-kṛtaṁ jānatā te
narahara upanītaḥ pañcatāṁ pañca-viṁśa

śrī-yakṣāḥ ūcuḥ—the inhabitants of the Yakṣa planet prayed; *vayam*—we; *anucara-mukhyāḥ*—the chief among Your many servants; *karmabhiḥ*—by services; *te*—unto You; *mano-jñaiḥ*—very pleasing; *te*—they; *iha*—at the present moment; *diti-sutena*—by Hiraṇyakaśipu, the son of Diti; *prāpitāḥ*—forced to engage as; *vāhakatvam*—the palanquin carriers; *saḥ*—he; *tu*—but; *jana-paritāpam*—the miserable condition of everyone; *tat-kṛtam*—caused by him; *jānatā*—knowing; *te*—by You; *nara-hara*—O Lord in the form of Nṛsiṁha; *upanītaḥ*—is put to;

pañcatām—death; *pañca-viṁśa*—O twenty-fifth principle (the controller of the other twenty-four elements).

TRANSLATION

The inhabitants of Yakṣaloka prayed: O controller of the twenty-four elements, we are considered the best servants of Your Lordship because of rendering services pleasing to You, yet we engaged as palanquin carriers by the order of Hiraṇyakaśipu, the son of Diti. O Lord in the form of Nṛsiṁhadeva, You know how this demon gave trouble to everyone, but now You have killed him, and his body is mixing with the five material elements.

PURPORT

The Supreme Lord is the controller of the ten senses, the five material elements, the five sense objects, the mind, the intelligence, the false ego and the soul. Therefore He is addressed as *pañca-viṁśa*, the twenty-fifth element. The inhabitants of the Yakṣa planet are supposed to be the best of all servants, but Hiraṇyakaśipu engaged them as palanquin carriers. The entire universe was in trouble because of Hiraṇyakaśipu, but now that Hiraṇyakaśipu's body was mixing with the five material elements—earth, water, fire, air and sky—everyone felt relief. Upon Hiraṇyakaśipu's death, the Yakṣas were reinstated in their original service to the Supreme Personality of Godhead. Thus they felt obliged to the Lord and offered their prayers.

TEXT 53

श्रीकिम्पुरुषा ऊचुः

वयं किम्पुरुषास्त्वं तु महापुरुष ईश्वरः ।
अयं कुपुरुषो नष्टो धिक्कृतः साधुभिर्यदा ॥५३॥

śrī-kimpuruṣā ūcuḥ
vayaṁ kimpuruṣās tvaṁ tu
mahā-puruṣa īśvaraḥ
ayaṁ kupuruṣo naṣṭo
dhik-kṛtaḥ sādhubhir yadā

śrī-kimpuruṣāḥ ūcuḥ—the inhabitants of Kimpuruṣa-loka said; *vayam*—we; *kimpuruṣāḥ*—the inhabitants of Kimpuruṣa-loka, or insignificant living entities; *tvam*—Your Lordship; *tu*—however; *mahā-puruṣaḥ*—the Supreme Personality of Godhead; *īśvaraḥ*—the supreme controller; *ayam*—this; *ku-puruṣaḥ*—most sinful person, Hiraṇyakaśipu; *naṣṭaḥ*—slain; *dhik-kṛtaḥ*—being condemned; *sādhubhiḥ*—by the saintly persons; *yadā*—when.

TRANSLATION

The inhabitants of Kimpuruṣa-loka said: We are insignificant living entities, and You are the Supreme Personality of Godhead, the supreme controller. Therefore how can we offer suitable prayers unto You? When this demon was condemned by devotees because they were disgusted with him, he was then killed by You.

PURPORT

The cause of the Supreme Lord's appearance upon this earth is stated in *Bhagavad-gītā* (4.7–8) by the Lord Himself:

yadā yadā hi dharmasya
glānir bhavati bhārata
abhyutthānam adharmasya
tadātmānaṁ sṛjāmy aham

paritrāṇāya sādhūnāṁ
vināśāya ca duṣkṛtām
dharma-saṁsthāpanārthāya
sambhavāmi yuge yuge

"Whenever and wherever there is a decrease in religious principles and a predominant rise in irreligion, at that time I descend Myself. To deliver the pious and annihilate the miscreants, as well as to reestablish the principles of religion, I advent Myself, millennium after millennium." The Lord appears in order to execute two kinds of activities—to kill the demons and to protect the devotees. When the devotees are too disturbed by the demons, the Lord certainly appears in different incarnations to give the devotees protection. The devotees following in the footsteps of

Prahlāda Mahārāja should not be disturbed by the demoniac activities of the nondevotees. Rather, they should stick to their principles as sincere servants of the Lord and rest assured that the demoniac activities directed against them will not be able to stop their devotional service.

TEXT 54

श्रीवैतालिका ऊचुः
सभासु सत्रेषु तवामलं यशो
गीत्वा सपर्यां महतीं लभामहे ।
यस्तामनैषीद्‌ वशमेष दुर्जनो
द्विष्ट्या हतस्ते भगवन्यथामयः ॥५४॥

śrī-vaitālikā ūcuḥ
sabhāsu satreṣu tavāmalaṁ yaśo
gītvā saparyāṁ mahatīṁ labhāmahe
yas tām anaiṣīd vaśam eṣa durjano
dviṣṭyā hatas te bhagavan yathāmayaḥ

śrī-vaitālikāḥ ūcuḥ—the inhabitants of Vaitālika-loka said; *sabhāsu*—in great assemblies; *satreṣu*—in the arenas of sacrifice; *tava*—Your; *amalam*—without any spot of material contamination; *yaśaḥ*—reputation; *gītvā*—singing; *saparyām*—respectful position; *mahatīm*—great; *labhāmahe*—we achieved; *yaḥ*—he who; *tām*—that (respectful position); *anaiṣīt*—brought under; *vaśam*—his control; *eṣaḥ*—this; *durjanaḥ*—crooked person; *dviṣṭyā*—by great fortune; *hataḥ*—killed; *te*—by You; *bhagavan*—O Lord; *yathā*—exactly like; *āmayaḥ*—a disease.

TRANSLATION

The inhabitants of Vaitālika-loka said: Dear Lord, because of chanting Your spotless glories in great assemblies and arenas of sacrifice, we were accustomed to great respect from everyone. This demon, however, usurped that position. Now, to our great fortune, You have killed this great demon, exactly as one cures a chronic disease.

TEXT 55

श्रीकिन्नरा ऊचुः
वयमीश किन्नरगणास्तवानुगा
दितिजेन विष्टिममुनानुकारिताः ।
भवता हरे स वृजिनोऽवसादितो
नरसिंह नाथ विभवाय नो भव ॥५५॥

śrī-kinnarā ūcuḥ
vayam īśa kinnara-gaṇās tavānugā
ditijena viṣṭim amunānukāritāḥ
bhavatā hare sa vṛjino 'vasādito
narasiṁha nātha vibhavāya no bhava

śrī-kinnarāḥ ūcuḥ—the inhabitants of the Kinnara planet said; *vayam*—we; *īśa*—O Lord; *kinnara-gaṇāḥ*—the inhabitants of the Kinnara planet; *tava*—Your; *anugāḥ*—faithful servants; *diti-jena*—by the son of Diti; *viṣṭim*—service without remuneration; *amunā*—by that; *anukāritāḥ*—caused to perform; *bhavatā*—by You; *hare*—O Lord; *saḥ*—he; *vṛjinaḥ*—most sinful; *avasāditaḥ*—destroyed; *narasiṁha*—O Lord Nṛsiṁhadeva; *nātha*—O master; *vibhavāya*—for the happiness and opulence; *naḥ*—of us; *bhava*—You please be.

TRANSLATION

The Kinnaras said: O supreme controller, we are ever-existing servants of Your Lordship, but instead of rendering service to You, we were engaged by this demon in his service, constantly and without remuneration. This sinful man has now been killed by You. Therefore, O Lord Nṛsiṁhadeva, our master, we offer our respectful obeisances unto You. Please continue to be our patron.

TEXT 56

श्रीविष्णुपार्षदा ऊचुः
अद्यैतद्धरिनररूपमद्भुतं ते
दृष्टं नः शरणद सर्वलोकशर्म ।

सोऽयं ते विधिकर ईश विप्रशप्त-
स्तस्येदं निधनमनुग्रहाय विद्मः ॥५६॥

śrī-viṣṇu-pārṣadā ūcuḥ
adyaitad dhari-nara-rūpam adbhutaṁ te
dṛṣṭaṁ naḥ śaraṇada sarva-loka-śarma
so 'yaṁ te vidhikara īśa vipra-śaptas
tasyedaṁ nidhanam anugrahāya vidmaḥ

śrī-viṣṇu-pārṣadāḥ ūcuḥ—the associates of Lord Viṣṇu in Vaikuṇṭhaloka said; *adya*—today; *etat*—this; *hari-nara*—of half lion and half human being; *rūpam*—form; *adbhutam*—very wonderful; *te*—Your; *dṛṣṭam*—seen; *naḥ*—of us; *śaraṇa-da*—the everlasting bestower of shelter; *sarva-loka-śarma*—which brings good fortune to all the various planets; *saḥ*—he; *ayam*—this; *te*—of Your Lordship; *vidhikaraḥ*—order carrier (servant); *īśa*—O Lord; *vipra-śaptaḥ*—being cursed by the *brāhmaṇas; tasya*—of him; *idam*—this; *nidhanam*—killing; *anugrahāya*—for the special favor; *vidmaḥ*—we understand.

TRANSLATION

The associates of Lord Viṣṇu in Vaikuṇṭha offered this prayer: O Lord, our supreme giver of shelter, today we have seen Your wonderful form as Lord Nṛsiṁhadeva, meant for the good fortune of all the world. O Lord, we can understand that Hiraṇyakaśipu was the same Jaya who engaged in Your service but was cursed by brāhmaṇas and who thus received the body of a demon. We understand that his having now been killed is Your special mercy upon him.

PURPORT

Hiraṇyakaśipu's coming to this earth and acting as the Lord's enemy was prearranged. Jaya and Vijaya were cursed by the *brāhmaṇas* Sanaka, Sanat-kumāra, Sanandana and Sanātana because Jaya and Vijaya checked these four Kumāras. The Lord accepted this cursing of His servants and agreed that they would have to go to the material world and would then return to Vaikuṇṭha after serving the term of the curse. Jaya and Vijaya were very much perturbed, but the Lord advised them to act as enemies, for then they would return after three births; otherwise, ordinarily, they would have to take seven births. With this authority, Jaya and Vijaya acted as the Lord's enemies, and now that these two were dead, all the Viṣṇudūtas understood that the Lord's killing of Hiraṇyakaśipu was special mercy bestowed upon them.

Thus end the Bhaktivedanta purports of the Seventh Canto, Eighth Chapter, of the Śrīmad-Bhāgavatam, *entitled "Lord Nṛsiṁhadeva Slays the King of the Demons."*

CHAPTER NINE

Prahlāda Pacifies Lord Nṛsiṁhadeva with Prayers

As related in this chapter, Prahlāda Mahārāja, following the order of Lord Brahmā, pacified the Lord when the Lord was extremely angry after having killed Hiraṇyakaśipu.

After Hiraṇyakaśipu was killed, the Lord continued to be very angry, and the demigods, headed by Lord Brahmā, could not pacify Him. Even mother Lakṣmī, the goddess of fortune, the constant companion of Nārāyaṇa, could not dare come before Lord Nṛsiṁhadeva. Then Lord Brahmā asked Prahlāda Mahārāja to go forward and pacify the Lord's anger. Prahlāda Mahārāja, being confident of the affection of his master, Lord Nṛsiṁhadeva, was not afraid at all. He very gravely appeared before the Lord's lotus feet and offered Him respectful obeisances. Lord Nṛsiṁhadeva, being very much affectionate toward Prahlāda Mahārāja, put His hand on Prahlāda's head, and because of being personally touched by the Lord, Prahlāda Mahārāja immediately achieved *brahma-jñāna,* spiritual knowledge. Thus he offered his prayers to the Lord in full spiritual knowledge and full devotional ecstasy. The instructions given by Prahlāda Mahārāja in the form of his prayers are as follows.

Prahlāda said, "I am not proud of being able to offer prayers to the Supreme Personality of Godhead. I simply take shelter of the mercy of the Lord, for without devotion one cannot appease Him. One cannot please the Supreme Personality of Godhead simply by dint of high parentage or great opulence, learning, austerity, penance or mystic power. Indeed, these are never pleasing to the Supreme Lord, for nothing can please Him but pure devotional service. Even if a nondevotee is a *brāhmaṇa* qualified with the twelve brahminical symptoms, he cannot be very dear to the Lord, whereas if a person born in a family of dog-eaters is a devotee, the Lord can accept his prayers. The Lord does not need anyone's prayers, but if a devotee offers his prayers to the Lord, the devotee benefits greatly. Ignorant persons born in low families, therefore, can sincerely offer heartfelt prayers to the Lord, and the Lord will accept them. As soon as one offers his prayers to the Lord, he is immediately situated on the Brahman platform.

Lord Nṛsiṁhadeva appeared for the benefit of all human society, not only for Prahlāda's personal benefit. The fierce form of Lord Nṛsiṁhadeva may appear most awful to a nondevotee, but to the devotee the Lord is always affectionate as He is in other forms. Conditioned life in the material world is actually extremely fearful; indeed, a devotee is not afraid of anything else. Fear of material existence is due to false ego. Therefore the ultimate goal of life for every living entity is to attain the position of being servant of the servant of the Lord. The miserable condition of the living entities in the material world can be remedied only by the mercy of the Lord. Although there are so-called material protectors like Lord Brahmā and the other demigods, or even one's own father, they are unable to do anything if one is neglected by the Supreme Personality of Godhead. However, one who has fully taken shelter of the Lord's lotus feet can be saved from the onslaught of material nature. Therefore every living entity should be unattracted by material so-called happiness and should take shelter of the Lord by all means. That is the mission of human life. To be attracted by sense gratification is simply foolish. Whether one is a devotee of the Lord or is a nondevotee does not depend upon one's birth in a high or low family. Even Lord Brahmā and the goddess of fortune cannot achieve the full favor of the Lord, whereas a devotee can very easily attain such devotional service. The Lord's mercy is bestowed equally upon everyone, regardless of whether one is high or low. Because Prahlāda Mahārāja was blessed by Nārada Muni, Prahlāda became a great devotee. The Lord always saves the devotee from impersonalists and voidists. The Lord is present in everyone's heart as the Supersoul to give the living being protection and all benefits. Thus the Lord acts sometimes as the killer and sometimes as the protector. One should not accuse the Lord for any discrepancies. It is His plan that we see varieties of life within this material world. All of them are ultimately His mercy.

Although the entire cosmic manifestation is nondifferent, the material world is nonetheless different from the spiritual world. Only by the mercy of the Supreme Lord can one understand how the wonderful material nature acts. For example, although Lord Brahmā appeared from the lotus seat that had grown from the abdomen of Garbhodakaśāyī Viṣṇu, he could not understand what to do after his appearance. He was attacked by two demons, Madhu and Kaiṭabha, who took away Vedic knowledge, but the Lord killed them and entrusted to Lord Brahmā the Vedic knowledge. Thus the Lord appears in every millennium in the societies of demigods, human beings, animals, saints and aquatics. All such incarnations are meant to protect the devotees and kill the demons, but this killing and protecting does not reflect any sense of partiality on the part of the Supreme Lord. The conditioned soul is always attracted by the external energy. Therefore he is subjected to lust and greed, and he suffers under the conditions of material nature. The Lord's causeless mercy toward His devotee is the only means by which to get out of material existence. Anyone engaged in glorifying the Lord's activities is always unafraid of this material world, whereas one who cannot glorify the Lord in that way is subjected to all lamentation.

Those interested in silently worshiping the Lord in solitary places may be eligible for liberation themselves, but a pure devotee is always aggrieved to see others suffering. Therefore, not caring for his own liberation, he always engages in preaching by glorifying the Lord. Prahlāda Mahārāja, therefore, had tried to deliver his class friends by preaching and had never remained silent. Although being silent, observing austerities and penances, learning the Vedic literature, undergoing ritualistic ceremonies, living in a solitary place and performing *japa* and transcendental meditation are approved means of liberation, they are meant for nondevotees or for cheaters who want to live at the expense of others. A pure devotee, however, being freed from all such deceptive activities, is able to see the Lord face to face.

The atomic theory of the composition of the cosmic manifestation is not factual. The Lord is the cause of everything, and therefore He is the cause of this creation. One should therefore always engage in devotional service by offering respectful obeisances to the Lord, offering prayers, working for the Lord, worshiping the Lord in the temple, always remembering the Lord and always hearing about His transcendental activities. Without these six kinds of activity, one cannot attain to devotional service.

Prahlāda Mahārāja thus offered his prayers to the Supreme Lord, begging His mercy at every step. Lord Nṛsiṁhadeva was pacified by

Prahlāda Mahārāja's prayers and wanted to give him benedictions by which Prahlāda could procure all kinds of material facilities. Prahlāda Mahārāja, however, was not misled by material facilities. Rather, he wanted to remain always a servant of the servant of the Lord.

TEXT 1

श्रीनारद उवाच

एवं सुरादयः सर्वे ब्रह्मरुद्रपुरःसराः ।
नोपैतुमशकन्मन्युसंरम्भं सुदुरासदम् ॥ १ ॥

śrī-nārada uvāca
evaṁ surādayaḥ sarve
brahma-rudra-puraḥ sarāḥ
nopaitum aśakan manyu-
saṁrambhaṁ sudurāsadam

śrī-nāradaḥ uvāca—the great saintly sage Nārada Muni said; *evam*—thus; *sura-ādayaḥ*—the groups of demigods; *sarve*—all; *brahma-rudra-puraḥ sarāḥ*—represented by Lord Brahmā and Lord Śiva; *na*—not; *upaitum*—to go before the Lord; *aśakan*—able; *manyu-saṁrambham*—in a completely angry mood; *su-durāsadam*—very difficult to approach (Lord Nṛsiṁhadeva).

TRANSLATION

The great saint Nārada Muni continued: The demigods, headed by Lord Brahmā, Lord Śiva and other great demigods, dared not come forward before the Lord, who at that time was extremely angry.

PURPORT

Śrīla Narottama dāsa Ṭhākura has sung in his *Prema-bhakti-candrikā*, *'krodha' bhakta-dveṣi-jane:* anger should be used to punish a demon who is envious of devotees. *Kāma, krodha, lobha, moha, mada* and *mātsarya*—lust, anger, greed, illusion, pride and envy—all have their proper use for the Supreme Personality of Godhead and His devotee. A devotee of the Lord cannot tolerate blasphemy of the Lord or His other devotees, and the Lord also cannot tolerate blasphemy of a devotee. Thus Lord Nṛsiṁhadeva was so very angry that the great demigods like Lord Brahmā and Lord Śiva and even the goddess of fortune, who is the Lord's constant companion, could not pacify Him, even after offering prayers of glorification and praise. No one was able to pacify the Lord in His anger, but because the Lord was willing to exhibit His affection for Prahlāda Mahārāja, all the demigods and the others present before the Lord pushed Prahlāda Mahārāja forward to pacify Him.

TEXT 2

साक्षात् श्रीः प्रेषिता देवैर्दृष्ट्वा तं महदद्भुतम् ।
अदृष्टाश्रुतपूर्वत्वात् सा नोपेयाय शङ्किता ॥ २ ॥

sākṣāt śrīḥ preṣitā devair
dṛṣṭvā taṁ mahad adbhutam
adṛṣṭāśruta-pūrvatvāt
sā nopeyāya śaṅkitā

sākṣāt—directly; *śrīḥ*—the goddess of fortune; *preṣitā*—being requested to go forward before the Lord; *devaiḥ*—by all the demigods (headed by Lord Brahmā and Lord Śiva); *dṛṣṭvā*—after seeing; *tam*—Him (Lord Nṛsiṁhadeva); *mahat*—very big; *adbhutam*—wonderful; *adṛṣṭa*—never seen; *aśruta*—never heard of; *pūrvatvāt*—due to being previously; *sā*—the goddess of fortune, Lakṣmī; *na*—not; *upeyāya*—went before the Lord; *śaṅkitā*—being very much afraid.

TRANSLATION

The goddess of fortune, Lakṣmījī, was requested to go before the Lord by all the demigods present, who because of fear could not do so. But even she had never seen such a wonderful and extraordinary form of the Lord, and thus she could not approach Him.

PURPORT

The Lord has unlimited forms and bodily features (*advaitam acyutam anādim ananta-rūpam*). These are all situated in Vaikuṇṭha, yet

Lakṣmīdevī, the goddess of fortune, being inspired by *līlā-śakti*, could not appreciate this unprecedented form of the Lord. In this regard, Śrīla Madhvācārya recites the following verses from the *Brahmāṇḍa Purāṇa:*

adṛṣṭāśruta-pūrvatvād
anyaiḥ sādhāraṇair janaiḥ
nṛsiṁhaṁ śaṅkiteva śrīr
loka-mohāyano yayau

prahrāde caiva vātsalya-
darśanāya harer api
jñātvā manas tathā brahmā
prahrādaṁ preṣayat tadā

ekatraikasya vātsalyaṁ
viśeṣād darśayed dhariḥ
avarasyāpi mohāya
krameṇaivāpi vatsalaḥ

In other words, for the common men the form of the Lord as Nṛsiṁhadeva is certainly unseen and wonderful, but for a devotee like Prahlāda Mahārāja such a fearsome form of the Lord is not at all extraordinary. By the grace of the Lord, a devotee can very easily understand how the Lord can appear in any form He likes. Therefore the devotee is never afraid of such a form. Because of special favor bestowed upon Prahlāda Mahārāja, he remained silent and unafraid, even though all the demigods, including even Lakṣmīdevī, were afraid of Lord Nṛsiṁhadeva. *Nārāyaṇa-parāḥ sarve na kutaścana bibhyati* (*Bhāg.* 6.17.28). Not only is a pure devotee of Nārāyaṇa like Prahlāda Mahārāja unafraid of any dangerous condition of material life, but also if the Lord appears to mitigate the fear of a devotee, the devotee maintains his status of fearlessness in all circumstances.

TEXT 3

प्रह्लादं प्रेषयामास ब्रह्मावस्थितमन्तिके ।
तात प्रशमयोपेहि स्वपित्रे कुपितं प्रभुम् ॥ ३ ॥

prahrādaṁ preṣayām āsa
brahmāvasthitam antike
tāta praśamayopehi
sva-pitre kupitaṁ prabhum

prahrādam—Prahlāda Mahārāja; *preṣayām āsa*—requested; *brahmā*—Lord Brahmā; *avasthitam*—being situated; *antike*—very near; *tāta*—my dear son; *praśamaya*—just try to appease; *upehi*—go near; *sva-pitre*—because of your father's demoniac activities; *kupitam*—greatly angered; *prabhum*—the Lord.

TRANSLATION

Thereafter Lord Brahmā requested Prahlāda Mahārāja, who was standing very near him: My dear son, Lord Nṛsiṁhadeva is extremely angry at your demoniac father. Please go forward and appease the Lord.

TEXT 4

तथेति शनकै राजन्महाभागवतोऽर्भकः ।
उपेत्य भुवि कायेन ननाम विधृताञ्जलिः ॥ ४ ॥

tatheti śanakai rājan
mahā-bhāgavato 'rbhakaḥ
upetya bhuvi kāyena
nanāma vidhṛtāñjaliḥ

tathā—so be it; *iti*—thus accepting the words of Lord Brahmā; *śanakaiḥ*—very slowly; *rājan*—O King (Yudhiṣṭhira); *mahā-bhāgavataḥ*—the great, exalted devotee (Prahlāda Mahārāja); *arbhakaḥ*—although only a small boy; *upetya*—gradually going near; *bhuvi*—on the ground; *kāyena*—by his body; *nanāma*—offered respectful obeisances; *vidhṛta-añjaliḥ*—folding his hands.

TRANSLATION

Nārada Muni continued: O King, although the exalted devotee Prahlāda Mahārāja was only a little boy, he accepted Lord Brahmā's

words. He gradually proceeded toward Lord Nṛsiṁhadeva and fell down to offer his respectful obeisances with folded hands.

TEXT 5

स्वपादमूले पतितं तमर्भकं
विलोक्य देवः कृपया परिप्लुतः ।
उत्थाप्य तच्छीर्ष्ण्यदधात् कराम्बुजं
कालाहिवित्रस्तधियां कृताभयम् ॥ ५ ॥

sva-pāda-mūle patitaṁ tam arbhakaṁ
vilokya devaḥ kṛpayā pariplutaḥ
utthāpya tac-chīrṣṇy adadhāt karāmbujaṁ
kālāhi-vitrasta-dhiyāṁ kṛtābhayam

sva-pāda-mūle—at His lotus feet; *patitam*—fallen; *tam*—him (Prahlāda Mahārāja); *arbhakam*—only a little boy; *vilokya*—seeing; *devaḥ*—Lord Nṛsiṁhadeva; *kṛpayā*—out of His causeless mercy; *pariplutaḥ*—very much afflicted (in ecstasy); *utthāpya*—raising; *tat-śīrṣṇi*—on his head; *adadhāt*—placed; *kara-ambujam*—His lotus hand; *kāla-ahi*—of the deadly snake of time, (which can cause immediate death); *vitrasta*—afraid; *dhiyām*—to all of those whose minds; *kṛta-abhayam*—which causes fearlessness.

TRANSLATION

When Lord Nṛsiṁhadeva saw the small boy Prahlāda Mahārāja prostrated at the soles of His lotus feet, He became most ecstatic in affection toward His devotee. Raising Prahlāda, the Lord placed His lotus hand upon the boy's head because His hand is always ready to create fearlessness in all of His devotees.

PURPORT

The necessities of the material world are four—*āhāra, nidrā, bhaya* and *maithuna* (eating, sleeping, defending and mating). In this material world, everyone is in fearful consciousness (*sadā samudvigna-dhiyām*), and the only means to make everyone fearless is Kṛṣṇa consciousness.

When Lord Nṛsiṁhadeva appeared, all the devotees became fearless. The devotee's hope of becoming fearless is to chant the holy name of Lord Nṛsiṁhadeva. *Yato yato yāmi tato nṛsiṁhaḥ:* wherever we go, we must always think of Lord Nṛsiṁhadeva. Thus there will be no fear for the devotee of the Lord.

TEXT 6

स तत्करस्पर्शधुताखिलाशुभः
सपद्यभिव्यक्तपरात्मदर्शनः ।
तत्पादपद्मं हृदि निर्वृतो दधौ
हृष्यत्तनुः क्लिन्नहृदश्रुलोचनः ॥ ६ ॥

sa tat-kara-sparśa-dhutākhilāśubhaḥ
sapady abhivyakta-parātma-darśanaḥ
tat-pāda-padmaṁ hṛdi nirvṛto dadhau
hṛṣyat-tanuḥ klinna-hṛd-aśru-locanaḥ

saḥ—he (Prahlāda Mahārāja); *tat-kara-sparśa*—because of being touched on the head by the lotus hand of Nṛsiṁhadeva; *dhuta*—being cleansed; *akhila*—all; *aśubhaḥ*—inauspiciousness or material desires; *sapadi*—immediately; *abhivyakta*—manifested; *para-ātma-darśanaḥ*—realization of the Supreme Soul (spiritual knowledge); *tat-pāda-padmam*—Lord Nṛsiṁhadeva's lotus feet; *hṛdi*—within the core of the heart; *nirvṛtaḥ*—full of transcendental bliss; *dadhau*—captured; *hṛṣyat-tanuḥ*—having transcendental ecstatic bliss manifested in the body; *klinna-hṛt*—whose heart was softened due to transcendental ecstasy; *aśru-locanaḥ*—with tears in his eyes.

TRANSLATION

By the touch of Lord Nṛsiṁhadeva's hand on Prahlāda Mahārāja's head, Prahlāda was completely freed of all material contaminations and desires, as if he had been thoroughly cleansed. Therefore he at once became transcendentally situated, and all the symptoms of ecstasy became manifest in his body. His heart filled with love, and his eyes with tears, and thus he was able to

completely capture the lotus feet of the Lord within the core of his heart.

PURPORT

As stated in *Bhagavad-gītā* (14.26):

māṁ ca yo 'vyabhicāreṇa
bhakti-yogena sevate
sa guṇān samatītyaitān
brahma-bhūyāya kalpate

"One who engages in full devotional service, who does not fall down in any circumstance, at once transcends the modes of material nature and thus comes to the level of Brahman." Elsewhere in *Bhagavad-gītā* (9.32) the Lord says:

māṁ hi pārtha vyapāśritya
ye 'pi syuḥ pāpa-yonayaḥ
striyo vaiśyās tathā śūdrās
te 'pi yānti parāṁ gatim

"O son of Pṛthā, those who take shelter in Me, though they be of lower birth—women, *vaiśyas* [merchants], as well as *śūdras* [workers]—can approach the supreme destination."

On the strength of these verses from *Bhagavad-gītā*, it is evident that although Prahlāda Mahārāja was born in a demoniac family and although virtually demoniac blood flowed within his body, he was cleansed of all material bodily contamination because of his exalted position as a devotee. In other words, such impediments on the spiritual path could not stop him from progressing, for he was directly in touch with the Supreme Personality of Godhead. Those who are physically and mentally contaminated by atheism cannot be situated on the transcendental platform, but as soon as one is freed from material contamination he is immediately fit to be situated in devotional service.

TEXT 7

अस्तौषीद्धरिमेकाग्रमनसा सुसमाहितः ।
प्रेमगद्गदया वाचा तन्न्यस्तहृदयेक्षणः ॥ ७ ॥

astauṣīd dharim ekāgra-
manasā susamāhitaḥ
prema-gadgadayā vācā
tan-nyasta-hṛdayekṣaṇaḥ

astauṣīt—he began to offer prayers; *harim*—unto the Supreme Personality of Godhead; *ekāgra-manasā*—the mind being completely fixed upon the lotus feet of the Lord; *su-samāhitaḥ*—very attentive (without diversion to any other subject); *prema-gadgadayā*—faltering because of feeling transcendental bliss; *vācā*—with a voice; *tat-nyasta*—being fully dedicated to Him (Lord Nṛsiṁhadeva); *hṛdaya-īkṣaṇaḥ*—with heart and sight.

TRANSLATION

Prahlāda Mahārāja fixed his mind and sight upon Lord Nṛsiṁhadeva with full attention in complete trance. With a fixed mind, he began to offer prayers in love with a faltering voice.

PURPORT

The word *susamāhitaḥ* means "very attentive" or "fully fixed." The ability to fix the mind in this way is a result of *yoga-siddhi,* mystic perfection. As it is stated in *Śrīmad-Bhāgavatam* (12.13.1), *dhyānāvasthita-tad-gatena manasā paśyanti yaṁ yoginaḥ.* One attains yogic perfection when he is freed from all material diversions and his mind is fixed upon the lotus feet of the Lord. This is called *samādhi* or trance. Prahlāda Mahārāja attained that stage beyond the senses. Because he was engaged in service, he felt transcendentally situated, and naturally his mind and attention became saturated in transcendence. In that condition, he began to offer his prayers as follows.

TEXT 8

श्रीप्रह्लाद उवाच
ब्रह्मादयः सुरगणा मुनयोऽथ सिद्धाः
सत्त्वैकतानगतयो वचसां प्रवाहैः ।
नाराधितुं पुरुगुणैरधुनापि पिप्रुः
किं तोष्टुमर्हति स मे हरिरुग्रजातेः ॥ ८ ॥

śrī-prahrāda uvāca
brahmādayaḥ sura-gaṇā munayo 'tha siddhāḥ
sattvaikatāna-gatayo vacasāṁ pravāhaiḥ
nārādhituṁ puru-guṇair adhunāpi pipruḥ
kiṁ toṣṭum arhati sa me harir ugra-jāteḥ

śrī-prahrādaḥ uvāca—Prahlāda Mahārāja prayed; *brahma-ādayaḥ*—headed by Lord Brahmā; *sura-gaṇāḥ*—the inhabitants of the upper planetary systems; *munayaḥ*—the great saintly persons; *atha*—as well (like the four Kumāras and others); *siddhāḥ*—who have attained perfection or full knowledge; *sattva*—to spiritual existence; *ekatāna-gatayaḥ*—who have taken without diversion to any material activities; *vacasām*—of descriptions or words; *pravāhaiḥ*—by streams; *na*—not; *ārādhitum*—to satisfy; *puru-guṇaiḥ*—although fully qualified; *adhunā*—until now; *api*—even; *pipruḥ*—were able; *kim*—whether; *toṣṭum*—to become pleased; *arhati*—is able; *saḥ*—He (the Lord); *me*—my; *hariḥ*—the Supreme Personality of Godhead; *ugra-jāteḥ*—who am born in an asuric family.

TRANSLATION

Prahlāda Mahārāja prayed: How is it possible for me, who have been born in a family of asuras, to offer suitable prayers to satisfy the Supreme Personality of Godhead? Even until now, all the demigods, headed by Lord Brahmā, and all the saintly persons, could not satisfy the Lord by streams of excellent words, although such persons are very qualified, being in the mode of goodness. Then what is to be said of me? I am not at all qualified.

PURPORT

A Vaiṣṇava who is fully qualified to serve the Lord still thinks himself extremely low while offering prayers to the Lord. For example, Kṛṣṇadāsa Kavirāja Gosvāmī, the author of *Caitanya-caritāmṛta*, says:

jagāi mādhāi haite muñi se pāpiṣṭha
purīṣera kīṭa haite muñi se laghiṣṭha
(Cc. *Ādi* 5.205)

Thus he considers himself unqualified, lower than the worms in stool, and more sinful than Jagāi and Mādhāi. A pure Vaiṣṇava actually thinks of himself in this way. Similarly, although Prahlāda Mahārāja was a pure, exalted Vaiṣṇava, he thought himself most unqualified to offer prayers to the Supreme Lord. *Mahājano yena gataḥ sa panthāḥ.* Every pure Vaiṣṇava should think like this. One should not be falsely proud of his Vaiṣṇava qualifications. Śrī Caitanya Mahāprabhu has therefore instructed us:

tṛṇād api sunīcena
taror iva sahiṣṇunā
amāninā mānadena
kīrtanīyaḥ sadā hariḥ

"One should chant the holy name of the Lord in a humble state of mind, thinking oneself lower than the straw in the street; one should be more tolerant than a tree, devoid of all sense of false prestige and should be ready to offer all respect to others. In such a state of mind one can chant the holy name of the Lord constantly." Unless one is meek and humble, to make progress in spiritual life is very difficult.

TEXT 9

मन्ये धनाभिजनरूपतपःश्रुतौज-
स्तेजःप्रभावबलपौरुषबुद्धियोगाः ।
नाराधनाय हि भवन्ति परस्य पुंसो
भक्त्या तुतोष भगवान्गजयूथपाय ॥ ९ ॥

manye dhanābhijana-rūpa-tapaḥ-śrutaujas-
tejaḥ-prabhāva-bala-pauruṣa-buddhi-yogāḥ
nārādhanāya hi bhavanti parasya puṁso
bhaktyā tutoṣa bhagavān gaja-yūtha-pāya

manye—I consider; *dhana*—riches; *abhijana*—aristocratic family; *rūpa*—personal beauty; *tapaḥ*—austerity; *śruta*—knowledge from studying the *Vedas; ojaḥ*—sensory prowess; *tejaḥ*—bodily effulgence;

prabhāva—influence; *bala*—bodily strength; *pauruṣa*—diligence; *buddhi*—intelligence; *yogāḥ*—mystic power; *na*—not; *ārādhanāya*—for satisfying; *hi*—indeed; *bhavanti*—are; *parasya*—of the transcendent; *puṁsaḥ*—Supreme Personality of Godhead; *bhaktyā*—simply by devotional service; *tutoṣa*—was satisfied; *bhagavān*—the Supreme Personality of Godhead; *gaja-yūtha-pāya*—unto the King of elephants (Gajendra).

TRANSLATION

Prahlāda Mahārāja continued: One may possess wealth, an aristocratic family, beauty, austerity, education, sensory expertise, luster, influence, physical strength, diligence, intelligence and mystic yogic power, but I think that even by all these qualifications one cannot satisfy the Supreme Personality of Godhead. However, one can satisfy the Lord simply by devotional service. Gajendra did this, and thus the Lord was satisfied with him.

PURPORT

No kind of material qualification is the means for satisfying the Supreme Personality of Godhead. As stated in *Bhagavad-gītā,* only by devotional service can the Lord be known (*bhaktyā mām abhijānāti*). Unless the Lord is pleased by the service of a devotee, the Lord does not reveal Himself (*nāhaṁ prakāśaḥ sarvasya yoga-māyā-samāvṛtaḥ*). This is the verdict of all *śāstras.* Neither by speculation nor by material qualifications can one understand or approach the Supreme Personality of Godhead.

TEXT 10

विप्राद् द्विषड्गुणयुतादरविन्दनाभ-
पादारविन्दविमुखात् श्वपचं वरिष्ठम् ।
मन्ये तदर्पितमनोवचनेहितार्थ-
प्राणं पुनाति स कुलं न तु भूरिमानः ॥१०॥

viprād dvi-ṣaḍ-guṇa-yutād aravinda-nābha-
pādāravinda-vimukhāt śvapacaṁ variṣṭham
manye tad-arpita-mano-vacanehitārtha-
prāṇaṁ punāti sa kulaṁ na tu bhūrimānaḥ

viprāt—than a *brāhmaṇa; dvi-ṣaṭ-guṇa-yutāt*—qualified with twelve brahminical qualities;* *aravinda-nābha*—Lord Viṣṇu, who has a lotus growing from His navel; *pāda-aravinda*—to the lotus feet of the Lord; *vimukhāt*—not interested in devotional service; *śva-pacam*—one born in a low family, or a dog-eater; *variṣṭham*—more glorious; *manye*—I consider; *tat-arpita*—surrendered unto the lotus feet of the Lord; *manaḥ*—his mind; *vacana*—words; *īhita*—every endeavor; *artha*—wealth; *prāṇam*—and life; *punāti*—purifies; *saḥ*—he (the devotee); *kulam*—his family; *na*—not; *tu*—but; *bhūrimānaḥ*—one who falsely thinks himself to be in a prestigious position.

TRANSLATION

If a brāhmaṇa has all twelve of the brahminical qualifications [as they are stated in the book called Sanat-sujāta] but is not a devotee and is averse to the lotus feet of the Lord, he is certainly lower than a devotee who is a dog-eater but who has dedicated everything—mind, words, activities, wealth and life—to the Supreme Lord. Such a devotee is better than such a brāhmaṇa because the devotee can purify his whole family, whereas the so-called brāhmaṇa in a position of false prestige cannot purify even himself.

PURPORT

Here is a statement by Prahlāda Mahārāja, one of the twelve authorities, regarding the distinction between a devotee and a *brāhmaṇa* expert in *karma-kāṇḍa*, or Vedic ritualistic ceremonies. There are four *varṇas* and four *āśramas*, which divide human society, but the central principle is to become a first-class pure devotee. It is said in the *Hari-bhakti-sudhodaya:*

bhagavad-bhakti-hīnasya
jātiḥ śāstraṁ japas tapaḥ

---

*These are the twelve qualities of a perfect *brāhmaṇa:* following religious principles, speaking truthfully, controlling the senses by undergoing austerities and penances, being free from jealousy, being intelligent, being tolerant, creating no enemies, performing *yajña*, giving charity, being steady, being well versed in Vedic study, and observing vows.

aprāṇasyaiva dehasya
maṇḍanaṁ loka-rañjanam

"If one is born in a high family like that of a *brāhmaṇa, kṣatriya* or *vaiśya* but is not a devotee of the Lord, all his good qualifications as a *brāhmaṇa, kṣatriya* or *vaiśya* are null and void. Indeed, they are considered decorations of a dead body."

In this verse Prahlāda Mahārāja speaks of the *vipras*, the learned *brāhmaṇas.* The learned *brāhmaṇa* is considered best among the divisions of *brāhmaṇa, kṣatriya, vaiśya* and *śūdra*, but a devotee born in a low *caṇḍāla* family is better than such *brāhmaṇas*, not to speak of the *kṣatriyas, vaiśyas* and others. A devotee is better than anyone, for he is in the transcendental position on the Brahman platform.

māṁ ca yo vyabhicāreṇa
bhakti-yogena sevate
sa guṇān samatītyaitān
brahma-bhūyāya kalpate

"One who engages in full devotional service, who does not fall down in any circumstance, at once transcends the modes of material nature and thus comes to the level of Brahman." (Bg. 14.26) The twelve qualities of a first-class *brāhmaṇa*, as stated in the book called *Sanat-sujāta*, are as follows:

jñānaṁ ca satyaṁ ca damaḥ śrutaṁ ca
hy amātsaryaṁ hrīs titikṣānasūyā
yajñaś ca dānaṁ ca dhṛtiḥ śamaś ca
mahā-vratā dvādaśa brāhmaṇasya

The European and American devotees in the Kṛṣṇa consciousness movement are sometimes accepted as *brāhmaṇas*, but the so-called caste *brāhmaṇas* are very much envious of them. In answer to such envy, Prahlāda Mahārāja says that one who has been born in a *brāhmaṇa* family but is falsely proud of his prestigious position cannot even purify himself, not to speak of his family, whereas if a *caṇḍāla*, a lowborn person, is a devotee and has fully surrendered unto the lotus feet of the Lord, he can purify his entire family. We have had actual experience of how Americans and Europeans, because of their full Kṛṣṇa consciousness, have purified their whole families, so much so that a mother of a devotee, at the time of her death, inquired about Kṛṣṇa with her last breath. Therefore it is theoretically true and has been practically proven that a devotee can give the best service to his family, his community, his society and his nation. The foolish accuse a devotee of following the principle of escapism, but actually the fact is that a devotee is the right person to elevate his family. A devotee engages everything in the service of the Lord, and therefore he is always exalted.

TEXT 11

नैवात्मनः प्रभुरयं निजलाभपूर्णो
मानं जनादविदुषः करुणो वृणीते ।
यद् यज्जनो भगवते विदधीत मानं
तच्चात्मने प्रतिमुखस्य यथा मुखश्रीः ॥११॥

naivātmanaḥ prabhur ayaṁ nija-lābha-pūrṇo
mānaṁ janād aviduṣaḥ karuṇo vṛṇīte
yad yaj jano bhagavate vidadhīta mānaṁ
tac cātmane prati-mukhasya yathā mukha-śrīḥ

na—nor; *eva*—certainly; *ātmanaḥ*—for His personal benefit; *prabhuḥ*—Lord; *ayam*—this; *nija-lābha-pūrṇaḥ*—is always satisfied in Himself (He does not need to be satisfied by the service of others); *mānam*—respect; *janāt*—from a person; *aviduṣaḥ*—who does not know that the aim of life is to please the Supreme Lord; *karuṇaḥ*—(the Supreme Personality of Godhead), who is so kind to this foolish, ignorant person; *vṛṇīte*—accepts; *yat yat*—whatever; *janaḥ*—a person; *bhagavate*—unto the Supreme Personality of Godhead; *vidadhīta*—may offer; *mānam*—worship; *tat*—that; *ca*—indeed; *ātmane*—for his own benefit; *prati-mukhasya*—of the reflection of the face in the mirror; *yathā*—just as; *mukha-śrīḥ*—the decoration of the face.

TRANSLATION

The Supreme Lord, the Supreme Personality of Godhead, is always fully satisfied in Himself. Therefore when something is

offered to Him, the offering, by the Lord's mercy, is for the benefit of the devotee, for the Lord does not need service from anyone. To give an example, if one's face is decorated, the reflection of one's face in a mirror is also seen to be decorated.

PURPORT

In *bhakti-yoga* it is recommended that a devotee follow nine principles: *śravaṇaṁ kīrtanaṁ viṣṇoḥ smaraṇaṁ pāda-sevanam/ arcanaṁ vandanaṁ dāsyaṁ sakhyam ātma-nivedanam.* This service of glorifying the Lord by hearing, chanting and so on is not, of course, meant for the benefit of the Lord; this devotional service is recommended for the benefit of the devotee. The Lord is always glorious, whether the devotee glorifies Him or not, but if the devotee engages in glorifying the Lord, the devotee himself automatically becomes glorious. *Ceto-darpaṇa-mārjanaṁ bhava-mahā-dāvāgni-nirvāpaṇam.* By glorifying the Lord constantly, the living entity becomes purified in the core of his heart, and thus he can understand that he does not belong to the material world but is a spirit soul whose actual activity is to advance in Kṛṣṇa consciousness so that he may become free from the material clutches. Thus the blazing fire of material existence is immediately extinguished (*bhava-mahā-dāvāgni-nirvāpaṇam*). A foolish person is amazed that Kṛṣṇa orders, *sarva-dharmān parityajya mām ekaṁ śaraṇaṁ vraja:* "Abandon all varieties of religious activities and just surrender unto Me." Some foolish scholars even say that this is too much to demand. But this demand is not for the benefit of the Supreme Personality of Godhead; rather, it is for the benefit of human society. If human beings individually and collectively surrender everything to the Supreme Personality of Godhead in full Kṛṣṇa consciousness, all of human society will benefit. One who does not dedicate everything to the Supreme Lord is described in this verse as *aviduṣa*, a rascal. In *Bhagavad-gītā* (7.15), the Lord Himself speaks in the same way:

na māṁ duṣkṛtino mūḍhāḥ
prapadyante narādhamāḥ
māyayāpahṛta-jñānā
āsuraṁ bhāvam āśritāḥ

"Those miscreants who are grossly foolish, lowest among mankind, whose knowledge is stolen by illusion, and who partake of the atheistic nature of demons, do not surrender unto Me." Because of ignorance and misfortune, the atheists and the *narādhamas,* the lowest of men, do not surrender unto the Supreme Personality of Godhead. Therefore although the Supreme Lord, Kṛṣṇa, is full in Himself, He appears in different *yugas* to demand the surrender of the conditioned souls so that they will benefit by becoming free from the material clutches. In conclusion, the more we engage in Kṛṣṇa consciousness and render service unto the Lord, the more we benefit. Kṛṣṇa does not need service from any of us.

TEXT 12

तस्मादहं विगतविक्लव ईश्वरस्य
सर्वात्मना महि गृणामि यथामनीषम् ।
नीचोऽजया गुणविसर्गमनुप्रविष्टः
पूयेत येन हि पुमाननुवर्णितेन ॥१२॥

tasmād ahaṁ vigata-viklava īśvarasya
sarvātmanā mahi gṛṇāmi yathā manīṣam
nīco 'jayā guṇa-visargam anupraviṣṭaḥ
pūyeta yena hi pumān anuvarṇitena

tasmāt—therefore; *aham*—I; *vigata-viklavaḥ*—having given up contemplation of being unfit; *īśvarasya*—of the Supreme Personality of Godhead; *sarva-ātmanā*—in full surrender; *mahi*—glory; *gṛṇāmi*—I shall chant or describe; *yathā manīṣam*—according to my intelligence; *nīcaḥ*—although lowborn (my father being a great demon, devoid of all good qualities); *ajayā*—because of ignorance; *guṇa-visargam*—the material world (wherein the living entity takes birth according to the contamination of the modes of nature); *anupraviṣṭaḥ*—entered into; *pūyeta*—may be purified; *yena*—by which (the glory of the Lord); *hi*—indeed; *pumān*—a person; *anuvarṇitena*—being chanted or recited.

TRANSLATION

Therefore, although I was born in a demoniac family, I may without a doubt offer prayers to the Lord with full endeavor, as far as my intelligence allows. Anyone who has been forced by

ignorance to enter the material world may be purified of material life if he offers prayers to the Lord and hears the Lord's glories.

PURPORT

It is clearly understood that a devotee does not need to be born in a very high family, to be rich, to be aristocratic or to be very beautiful. None of these qualifications will engage one in devotional service. With devotion one should feel, "God is great, and I am very small. Therefore my duty is to offer my prayers to the Lord." Only on this basis can one understand and render service to the Lord. As the Lord says in *Bhagavad-gītā* (18.55):

bhaktyā mām abhijānāti
yāvān yaś cāsmi tattvataḥ
tato māṁ tattvato jñātvā
viśate tad-anantaram

"One can understand the Supreme Personality as He is only by devotional service. And when one is in full consciousness of the Supreme Lord by such devotion, he can enter into the kingdom of God." Thus Prahlāda Mahārāja decided to offer his best prayers to the Lord, without consideration of his material position.

TEXT 13

सर्वे ह्यमी विधिकरास्तव सत्त्वधाम्नो
ब्रह्मादयो वयमिवेश न चोद्विजन्तः ।
क्षेमाय भूतय उतात्मसुखाय चास्य
विक्रीडितं भगवतो रुचिरावतारैः ॥१३॥

sarve hy amī vidhi-karās tava sattva-dhāmno
brahmādayo vayam iveśa na codvijantaḥ
kṣemāya bhūtaya utātma-sukhāya cāsya
vikrīḍitaṁ bhagavato rucirāvatāraiḥ

sarve—all; *hi*—certainly; *amī*—these; *vidhi-karāḥ*—executors of orders; *tava*—Your; *sattva-dhāmnaḥ*—being always situated in the transcendental world; *brahma-ādayaḥ*—the demigods, headed by Lord Brahmā; *vayam*—we; *iva*—like; *īśa*—O my Lord; *na*—not; *ca*—and; *udvijantaḥ*—who are afraid (of Your fearful appearance); *kṣemāya*—for the protection; *bhūtaye*—for the increase; *uta*—it is said; *ātma-sukhāya*—for personal satisfaction by such pastimes; *ca*—also; *asya*—of this (material world); *vikrīḍitam*—manifested; *bhagavataḥ*—of Your Lordship; *rucira*—very pleasing; *avatāraiḥ*—by Your incarnations.

TRANSLATION

O my Lord, all the demigods, headed by Lord Brahmā, are sincere servants of Your Lordship, who are situated in a transcendental position. Therefore they are not like us [Prahlāda and his father, the demon Hiraṇyakaśipu]. Your appearance in this fearsome form is Your pastime for Your own pleasure. Such an incarnation is always meant for the protection and improvement of the universe.

PURPORT

Prahlāda Mahārāja wanted to assert that his father and the other members of his family were all unfortunate because they were demoniac, whereas the devotees of the Lord are always fortunate because they are always ready to follow the orders of the Lord. When the Supreme Lord appears in this material world in His various incarnations, He performs two functions—saving the devotee and vanquishing the demon (*paritrāṇāya sādhūnāṁ vināśāya ca duṣkṛtām*). Lord Nṛsiṁhadeva, for example, appeared for the protection of His devotee. Such pastimes as those of Nṛsiṁhadeva are certainly not meant to create a fearful situation for the devotees, but nonetheless the devotees, being very simple and faithful, were afraid of the fierce incarnation of the Lord. Therefore Prahlāda Mahārāja, in the following prayer, requests the Lord to give up His anger.

TEXT 14

तद् यच्छ मन्युमसुरश्च हतस्त्वयाद्य
मोदेत साधुरपि वृश्चिकसर्पहत्या ।
लोकाश्च निर्वृतिमिताः प्रतियन्ति सर्वे
रूपं नृसिंह विभयाय जनाः स्मरन्ति ॥१४॥

tad yaccha manyum asuraś ca hatas tvayādya
modeta sādhur api vṛścika-sarpa-hatyā
lokāś ca nirvṛtim itāḥ pratiyanti sarve
rūpaṁ nṛsiṁha vibhayāya janāḥ smaranti

tat—therefore; *yaccha*—kindly give up; *manyum*—Your anger; *asuraḥ*—my father, Hiraṇyakaśipu, the great demon; *ca*—also; *hataḥ*—killed; *tvayā*—by You; *adya*—today; *modeta*—take pleasure; *sādhuḥ api*—even a saintly person; *vṛścika-sarpa-hatyā*—by killing a snake or a scorpion; *lokāḥ*—all the planets; *ca*—indeed; *nirvṛtim*—pleasure; *itāḥ*—have achieved; *pratiyanti*—are waiting (for pacification of Your anger); *sarve*—all of them; *rūpam*—this form; *nṛsiṁha*—O Lord Nṛsiṁhadeva; *vibhayāya*—for mitigating their fear; *janāḥ*—all the people of the universe; *smaranti*—will remember.

TRANSLATION

My Lord Nṛsiṁhadeva, please, therefore, cease Your anger now that my father, the great demon Hiraṇyakaśipu, has been killed. Since even saintly persons take pleasure in the killing of a scorpion or a snake, all the worlds have achieved great satisfaction because of the death of this demon. Now they are confident of their happiness, and they will always remember Your auspicious incarnation in order to be free from fear.

PURPORT

The most important point in this verse is that although saintly persons never desire the killing of any living entity, they take pleasure in the killing of envious living entities like snakes and scorpions. Hiraṇyakaśipu was killed because he was worse than a snake or a scorpion, and therefore everyone was happy. Now there was no need for the Lord to be angry. The devotees can always remember the form of Nṛsiṁhadeva when they are in danger, and therefore the appearance of Nṛsiṁhadeva was not at all inauspicious. The Lord's appearance is always worshipable and auspicious for all sane persons and devotees.

TEXT 15

नाहं बिभेम्यजित तेऽतिभयानकास्य-
जिह्वार्कनेत्रभ्रुकुटीरभसोग्रदंष्ट्रात् ।
आन्त्रस्रजः क्षतजकेशरशङ्कुकर्णा-
न्निर्ह्राद‌भीतदिगिभादरिभिन्नखाग्रात् ॥१५॥

nāhaṁ bibhemy ajita te 'tibhayānakāsya-
jihvārka-netra-bhrukuṭī-rabhasogra-daṁṣṭrāt
āntra-srajaḥ-kṣataja-keśara-śaṅku-karṇān
nirhrāda-bhīta-digibhād ari-bhin-nakhāgrāt

na—not; *aham*—I; *bibhemi*—am afraid; *ajita*—O supreme victorious person, who are never conquered by anyone; *te*—Your; *ati*—very much; *bhayānaka*—fearful; *āsya*—mouth; *jihvā*—tongue; *arka-netra*—eyes shining like the sun; *bhrukuṭī*—frowning brows; *rabhasa*—strong; *ugra-daṁṣṭrāt*—ferocious teeth; *āntra-srajaḥ*—garlanded by intestines; *kṣataja*—bloody; *keśara*—manes; *śaṅku-karṇāt*—wedgelike ears; *nirhrāda*—by a roaring sound (caused by You); *bhīta*—frightened; *digibhāt*—from which even the great elephants; *ari-bhit*—piercing the enemy; *nakha-agrāt*—the tips of whose nails.

TRANSLATION

My Lord, who are never conquered by anyone, I am certainly not afraid of Your ferocious mouth and tongue, Your eyes bright like the sun or Your frowning eyebrows. I do not fear Your sharp, pinching teeth, Your garland of intestines, Your mane soaked with blood, or Your high, wedgelike ears. Nor do I fear Your tumultuous roaring, which makes elephants flee to distant places, or Your nails, which are meant to kill Your enemies.

PURPORT

Lord Nṛsiṁhadeva's fierce appearance was certainly most dangerous for the nondevotees, but for Prahlāda Mahārāja such a fearful appearance was not at all disturbing. The lion is very fearsome for other animals, but its cubs are not at all afraid of the lion. The water of the sea is certainly dreadful for all living entities on the land, but within the sea even the small fish is unafraid. Why? Because the small fish has taken shelter of the big ocean. It is said that although great elephants are taken away by the flooding waters of the river, the small fish swim opposite the current. Therefore although the Lord sometimes assumes a fierce appearance to kill the *duṣkṛtīs*, the devotees worship Him. *Keśava dhṛta-nara-hari-rūpa jaya jagadīśa hare.* The devotee always takes pleasure in worshiping the Lord and glorifying the Lord in any form, either pleasing or fierce.

TEXT 16

त्रस्तोऽस्म्यहं कृपणवत्सल दुःसहोग्र-
संसारचक्रकदनाद् ग्रसतां प्रणीतः ।
बद्धः स्वकर्मभिरुशत्तम तेऽङ्घ्रिमूलं
प्रीतोऽपवर्गशरणं ह्वयसे कदा नु ॥१६॥

trasto 'smy ahaṁ kṛpaṇa-vatsala duḥsahogra-
saṁsāra-cakra-kadanād grasatāṁ praṇītaḥ
baddhaḥ sva-karmabhir uśattama te 'ṅghri-mūlaṁ
prīto 'pavarga-śaraṇaṁ hvayase kadā nu

trastaḥ—frightened; *asmi*—am; *aham*—I; *kṛpaṇa-vatsala*—O my Lord, who are so kind to the fallen souls (who have no spiritual knowledge); *duḥsaha*—intolerable; *ugra*—ferocious; *saṁsāra-cakra*—of the cycle of birth and death; *kadanāt*—from such a miserable condition; *grasatām*—among other conditioned souls, who devour one another; *praṇītaḥ*—being thrown; *baddhaḥ*—bound; *sva-karmabhiḥ*—the course by the reactions of my own activities; *uśattama*—O great insurmountable; *te*—Your; *aṅghri-mūlam*—to the soles of the lotus feet; *prītaḥ*—being pleased (with me); *apavarga-śaraṇam*—which are the shelter meant for liberation from this horrible condition of material existence; *hvayase*—You will call (me); *kadā*—when; *nu*—indeed.

TRANSLATION

O most powerful, insurmountable Lord, who are kind to the fallen souls, I have been put into the association of demons as a

result of my activities, and therefore I am very much afraid of my condition of life within this material world. When will that moment come when You will call me to the shelter of Your lotus feet, which are the ultimate goal for liberation from conditional life?

PURPORT

Being in the material world is certainly miserable, but certainly when one is put into the association of *asuras*, or atheistic men, it is intolerably so. One may ask why the living entity is put into the material world. Indeed, sometimes foolish people deride the Lord for having put them here. Actually, everyone is put into conditional life according to his *karma*. Therefore Prahlāda Mahārāja, representing all the other conditioned souls, admits that he was put into life among the *asuras* because of the results of his *karma*. The Lord is known as *kṛpaṇa-vatsala* because He is extremely kind to the conditioned souls. As stated in *Bhagavad-gītā*, therefore, the Lord appears whenever there are discrepancies in the execution of religious principles (*yadā yadā hi dharmasya glānir bhavati bhārata . . . tadātmānaṁ sṛjāmy aham*). The Lord is extremely anxious to deliver the conditioned souls, and therefore He instructs all of us to return home, back to Godhead (*sarva-dharmān parityajya māṁ ekaṁ śaraṇaṁ vraja*). Thus Prahlāda Mahārāja expected that the Lord, by His kindness, would call him again to the shelter of His lotus feet. In other words, everyone should be eager to return home, back to Godhead, taking shelter of the lotus feet of the Lord and thus being fully trained in Kṛṣṇa consciousness.

TEXT 17

यस्मात् प्रियाप्रियवियोगसंयोगजन्म-
शोकाग्निना सकलयोनिषु दह्यमानः ।
दुःखौषधं तदपि दुःखमतद्धियाहं
भूमन्भ्रमामि वद मे तव दास्ययोगम् ॥१७॥

yasmāt priyāpriya-viyoga-saṁyoga-janma-
śokāgninā sakala-yoniṣu dahyamānaḥ
duḥkhauṣadhaṁ tad api duḥkham atad-dhiyāhaṁ
bhūman bhramāmi vada me tava dāsya-yogam

yasmāt—because of which (because of existing in the material world); *priya*—pleasing; *apriya*—not pleasing; *viyoga*—by separation; *saṁyoga*—and combination; *janma*—whose birth; *śoka-agninā*—by the fire of lamentation; *sakala-yoniṣu*—in any type of body; *dahyamānaḥ*—being burned; *duḥkha-auṣadham*—remedial measures for miserable life; *tat*—that; *api*—also; *duḥkham*—suffering; *a-tat-dhiyā*—by accepting the body as the self; *aham*—I; *bhūman*—O great one; *bhramāmi*—am wandering (within the cycle of birth and death); *vada*—kindly instruct; *me*—unto me; *tava*—Your; *dāsya-yogam*—activities of service.

TRANSLATION

O great one, O Supreme Lord, because of combination with pleasing and displeasing circumstances and because of separation from them, one is placed in a most regrettable position, within heavenly or hellish planets, as if burning in a fire of lamentation. Although there are many remedies by which to get out of miserable life, any such remedies in the material world are more miserable than the miseries themselves. Therefore I think that the only remedy is to engage in Your service. Kindly instruct me in such service.

PURPORT

Prahlāda Mahārāja aspired to engage in the service of the lotus feet of the Lord. After the death of his father, who was materially very opulent, Prahlāda would have inherited his father's property, which extended throughout the world, but Prahlāda Mahārāja was not inclined to accept such material opulence, for whether one is in the heavenly or hellish planets or is a rich or a poor man's son, material conditions are everywhere. Therefore no condition of life is at all pleasing. If one wants the uncontaminated pleasure of blissful life, he must engage himself in the transcendental loving service of the Lord. Material opulence may be somewhat pleasing for the time being, but to come to that temporary pleasing condition one must work extremely hard. When a poor man is rich he may be better situated, but to come to that position he had to accept many miseries. The fact is that in material life, whether one is miserable or happy, both conditions are miserable. If one actually wants happy, blissful life, one must become Kṛṣṇa conscious and constantly engage in the transcendental loving service of the Lord. That is the real remedy. The entire world is under the illusion that people will be happy by advancing in materialistic measures to counteract the miseries of conditional life, but this attempt will never be successful. Humanity must be trained to engage in the transcendental loving service of the Lord. That is the purpose of the Kṛṣṇa consciousness movement. There can be no happiness in changing one's material conditions, for everywhere there is trouble and misery.

TEXT 18

सोऽहं प्रियस्य सुहृदः परदेवताया
लीलाकथास्तव नृसिंह विरिञ्चगीताः ।
अञ्जस्तितर्म्यनुगृणन्गुणविप्रमुक्तो
दुर्गाणि ते पदयुगालयहंससङ्गः ॥१८॥

so 'haṁ priyasya suhṛdaḥ paradevatāyā
līlā-kathās tava nṛsiṁha viriñca-gītāḥ
añjas titarmy anugṛṇan guṇa-vipramukto
durgāṇi te pada-yugālaya-haṁsa-saṅgaḥ

saḥ—that; *aham*—I (Prahlāda Mahārāja); *priyasya*—of the dearmost; *suhṛdaḥ*—well-wisher; *paradevatāyāḥ*—of the Supreme Personality of Godhead; *līlā-kathāḥ*—narrations of the pastimes; *tava*—Your; *nṛsiṁha*—O my Lord Nṛsiṁhadeva; *viriñca-gītāḥ*—given by Lord Brahmā by the disciplic succession; *añjaḥ*—easily; *titarmi*—I shall cross; *anugṛṇan*—constantly describing; *guṇa*—by the modes of material nature; *vipramuktaḥ*—specifically being uncontaminated; *durgāṇi*—all miserable conditions of life; *te*—of You; *pada-yuga-ālaya*—fully absorbed in meditation on the lotus feet; *haṁsa-saṅgaḥ*—having the association of the *haṁsas*, or liberated persons (who have no connection with material activities).

TRANSLATION

O my Lord Nṛsiṁhadeva, by engaging in Your transcendental loving service in the association of devotees who are liberated

souls [haṁsas], I shall become completely uncontaminated by the association of the three modes of material nature and be able to chant the glories of Your Lordship, who are so dear to me. I shall chant Your glories, following exactly in the footsteps of Lord Brahmā and his disciplic succession. In this way I shall undoubtedly be able to cross the ocean of nescience.

PURPORT

A devotee's life and duty are very well explained herein. As soon as a devotee can chant the holy name and glories of the Supreme Lord, he certainly comes to the liberated position. Attachment for glorifying the Lord by hearing and chanting the holy name and activities of the Lord (*śravaṇaṁ kīrtanaṁ viṣṇoḥ*) certainly brings one to the position where material contamination is absent. One should chant the bona fide songs received from the disciplic succession. In *Bhagavad-gītā* it is said that the chanting is powerful when one follows the disciplic succession (*evaṁ paramparā-prāptam imaṁ rājarṣayo viduḥ*). Manufacturing many ways of chanting will never be effective. However, chanting the song or the narration left by the previous *ācāryas* (*mahājano yena gataḥ sa panthāḥ*) is extremely effective, and this process is very easy. Therefore in this verse Prahlāda Mahārāja uses the word *añjaḥ* ("easily"). Accepting the thoughts of exalted authorities through disciplic succession is certainly much easier than the method of mental speculation, by which one tries to invent some means to understand the Absolute Truth. The best process is to accept the instructions of the previous *ācāryas* and follow them. Then God realization and self-realization become extremely easy. By following this easy method, one is liberated from the contamination of the material modes of nature, and thus one can certainly cross the ocean of nescience, in which there are many miserable conditions. By following in the footsteps of the great *ācāryas*, one associates with the *haṁsas* or *paramahaṁsas*, those who are completely freed from material contamination. Indeed, by following the instructions of the *ācāryas* one is always freed from all material contamination, and thus one's life becomes successful, for one reaches the goal of life. This material world is miserable, regardless of one's standard of life. Of this there is no doubt. Attempts to mitigate the miseries of material existence by material methods will never be successful. One must take to Kṛṣṇa consciousness to become really happy; otherwise happiness is impossible. One might say that becoming advanced in spiritual life also involves *tapasya,* voluntary acceptance of some inconvenience. However, such inconvenience is not as dangerous as material attempts to mitigate all miseries.

TEXT 19

बालस्य नेह शरणं पितरौ नृसिंह
नार्तस्य चागदमुदन्वति मज्जतो नौः ।
तप्तस्य तत्प्रतिविधिर्य इहाञ्जसेष्ट-
स्तावद् विभो तनुभृतां त्वदुपेक्षितानाम् ॥१९॥

bālasya neha śaraṇaṁ pitarau nṛsiṁha
nārtasya cāgadam udanvati majjato nauḥ
taptasya tat-pratividhir ya ihāñjaseṣṭas
tāvad vibho tanu-bhṛtāṁ tvad-upekṣitānām

bālasya—of a little child; *na*—not; *iha*—in this world; *śaraṇam*—shelter (protection); *pitarau*—the father and mother; *nṛsiṁha*—O my Lord Nṛsiṁhadeva; *na*—neither; *ārtasya*—of a person suffering from some disease; *ca*—also; *agadam*—medicine; *udanvati*—in the water of the ocean; *majjataḥ*—of a person who is drowning; *nauḥ*—the boat; *taptasya*—of a person suffering from a condition of material misery; *tat-pratividhiḥ*—the counteraction (invented for stopping the suffering of material existence); *yaḥ*—that which; *iha*—in this material world; *añjasā*—very easily; *iṣṭaḥ*—accepted (as a remedy); *tāvat*—similarly; *vibho*—O my Lord, O Supreme; *tanu-bhṛtām*—of the living entities who have accepted material bodies; *tvat-upekṣitānām*—who are neglected by You and not accepted by You.

TRANSLATION

My Lord Nṛsiṁhadeva, O Supreme, because of a bodily conception of life, embodied souls neglected and not cared for by You cannot do anything for their betterment. Whatever remedies they accept, although perhaps temporarily beneficial, are certainly impermanent. For example, a father and mother cannot protect their

child, a physician and medicine cannot relieve a suffering patient, and a boat on the ocean cannot protect a drowning man.

PURPORT

Through parental care, through remedies for different kinds of disease, and through means of protection on the water, in the air and on land, there is always an endeavor for relief from various kinds of suffering in the material world, but none of them are guaranteed measures for protection. They may be beneficial temporarily, but they afford no permanent benefit. Despite the presence of a father and mother, a child cannot be protected from accidental death, disease and various other miseries. No one can help, including the parents. Ultimately the shelter is the Lord, and one who takes shelter of the Lord is protected. This is guaranteed. As the Lord says in *Bhagavad-gītā* (9.31), *kaunteya pratijānīhi na me bhaktaḥ praṇaśyati:* "O son of Kuntī, declare it boldly that My devotee never perishes." Therefore, unless one is protected by the mercy of the Lord, no remedial measure can act effectively. One should consequently depend fully on the causeless mercy of the Lord. Although as a matter of routine duty one must of course accept other remedial measures, no one can protect one who is neglected by the Supreme Personality of Godhead. In this material world, everyone is trying to counteract the onslaught of material nature, but everyone is ultimately fully controlled by material nature. Therefore even though so-called philosophers and scientists try to surmount the onslaught of material nature, they have not been able to do so. Kṛṣṇa says in *Bhagavad-gītā* (13.9) that the real sufferings of the material world are four—*janma-mṛtyu-jarā-vyādhi* (birth, death, old age and disease). In the history of the world, no one has been successful in conquering these miseries imposed by material nature. *Prakṛteḥ kriyamāṇāni guṇaiḥ karmāṇi sarvaśaḥ.* Nature (*prakṛti*) is so strong that no one can overcome her stringent laws. So-called scientists, philosophers, religionists and politicians should therefore conclude that they cannot offer facilities to the people in general. They should make vigorous propaganda to awaken the populace and raise them to the platform of Kṛṣṇa consciousness. Our humble attempt to propagate the Kṛṣṇa consciousness movement all over the world is the only remedy that can bring about a peaceful and happy life. We can never be happy without the mercy of the Supreme Lord (*tvad-upekṣitānām*). If we keep displeasing our supreme father, we shall never be happy within this material world, in either the upper or lower planetary systems.

TEXT 20

यस्मिन्यतो यर्हि येन च यस्य यस्माद्
यस्मै यथा यदुत यस्त्वपरः परो वा ।
भावः करोति विकरोति पृथक्स्वभावः
सञ्चोदितस्तदखिलं भवतः स्वरूपम् ॥२०॥

yasmin yato yarhi yena ca yasya yasmād
yasmai yathā yad uta yas tv aparaḥ paro vā
bhāvaḥ karoti vikaroti pṛthak svabhāvaḥ
sañcoditas tad akhilaṁ bhavataḥ svarūpam

yasmin—in any condition of life; *yataḥ*—because of anything; *yarhi*—at any time (past, present or future); *yena*—by something; *ca*—also; *yasya*—in relationship with anyone; *yasmāt*—from any causal representative; *yasmai*—unto anyone (without discrimination in regard to place, person or time); *yathā*—in any manner; *yat*—whatever it may be; *uta*—certainly; *yaḥ*—anyone who; *tu*—but; *aparaḥ*—the other; *paraḥ*—the supreme; *vā*—or; *bhāvaḥ*—being; *karoti*—does; *vikaroti*—changes; *pṛthak*—separate; *svabhāvaḥ*—nature (under the influence of different modes of material nature); *sañcoditaḥ*—being influenced; *tat*—that; *akhilam*—all; *bhavataḥ*—of Your Lordship; *svarūpam*—emanated from Your different energies.

TRANSLATION

My dear Lord, everyone in this material world is under the modes of material nature, being influenced by goodness, passion and ignorance. Everyone—from the greatest personality, Lord Brahmā, down to the small ant—works under the influence of these modes. Therefore everyone in this material world is influenced by Your energy. The cause for which they work, the place where they work, the time when they work, the matter due to which they work, the goal of life they have considered final, and

the process for obtaining this goal—all are nothing but manifestations of Your energy. Indeed, since the energy and energetic are identical, all of them are but manifestations of You.

PURPORT

Whether one thinks himself protected by his parents, by the government, by some place or by some other cause, everything is due to the various potencies of the Supreme Personality of Godhead. Everything that is done, whether in the higher, middle or lower planetary systems, is due to the supervision or control of the Supreme Lord. It is therefore said, *karmaṇā daiva-netreṇa jantur dehopapattaye.* The Supreme Personality of Godhead, the Supersoul within the core of everyone's heart, gives inspirations for action according to one's mentality. All of these mentalities are merely facilities given by Kṛṣṇa to the person acting. *Bhagavad-gītā* therefore says, *mattaḥ smṛtir jñānam apohanaṁ ca:* everyone works according to the inspiration given by the Supersoul. Because everyone has a different goal of life, everyone acts differently, as guided by the Supreme Personality of Godhead.

The words *yasmin yato yarhi yena ca yasya yasmāt* indicate that all activities, whatever they may be, are but different features of the Supreme Personality of Godhead. All of them are created by the living entity and fulfilled by the mercy of the Lord. Although all such activities are nondifferent from the Lord, the Lord nonetheless directs, *sarva-dharmān parityajya mām ekaṁ śaraṇaṁ vraja:* "Give up all other duties and surrender unto Me." When we accept this direction from the Lord, we can actually become happy. As long as we work according to our material senses we are in material life, but as soon as we act according to the real, transcendental direction of the Lord, our position is spiritual. The activities of *bhakti,* devotional service, are directly under the control of the Supreme Personality of Godhead. The *Nārada-pañcarātra* states:

sarvopādhi-vinirmuktaṁ
tat-paratvena nirmalam
hṛṣīkeṇa hṛṣīkeśa-
sevanaṁ bhaktir ucyate

When one gives up materially designated positions and works directly under the Supreme Personality of Godhead, one's spiritual life is revived. This is described as *svarūpena avasthiti,* being situated in one's original constitutional position. This is the real description of *mukti,* or liberation from material bondage.

TEXT 21

माया मनः सृजति कर्ममयं बलीयः
कालेन चोदितगुणानुमतेन पुंसः ।
छन्दोमयं यदजयार्पितषोडशारं
संसारचक्रमज कोऽतितरेत् त्वदन्यः ॥२१॥

māyā manaḥ sṛjati karmamayaṁ balīyaḥ
kālena codita-guṇānumatena puṁsaḥ
chandomayaṁ yad ajayārpita-ṣoḍaśāraṁ
saṁsāra-cakram aja ko 'titaret tvad-anyaḥ

māyā—the external energy of the Supreme Personality of Godhead; *manaḥ*—the mind;* *sṛjati*—creates; *karma-mayam*—producing hundreds and thousands of desires and acting accordingly; *balīyaḥ*—extremely powerful, insurmountable; *kālena*—by time; *codita-guṇa*—whose three modes of material nature are agitated; *anumatena*—permitted by the mercy of the glance (time); *puṁsaḥ*—of the plenary portion, Lord Viṣṇu, the expansion of Lord Kṛṣṇa; *chandaḥ-mayam*—chiefly influenced by the directions in the *Vedas; yat*—which; *ajayā*—because of dark ignorance; *arpita*—offered; *ṣoḍaśa*—sixteen; *aram*—the spokes; *saṁsāra-cakram*—the wheel of repeated birth and death in different species of life; *aja*—O unborn Lord; *kaḥ*—who (is there); *atitaret*—able to get out; *tvat-anyaḥ*—without taking shelter at Your lotus feet.

---

*The mind is always planning how to remain in the material world and struggle for existence. It is the chief part of the subtle body, which consists of the mind, intelligence and false ego.

TRANSLATION

O Lord, O supreme eternal, by expanding Your plenary portion You have created the subtle bodies of the living entities through the agency of Your external energy, which is agitated by time. Thus the mind entraps the living entity in unlimited varieties of desires to be fulfilled by the Vedic directions of karma-kāṇḍa [fruitive activity] and the sixteen elements. Who can get free from this entanglement unless he takes shelter at Your lotus feet?

PURPORT

If the hand of the Supreme Personality of Godhead is present in everything, where is the question of being liberated from material encagement to spiritual, blissful life? Indeed, it is a fact that Kṛṣṇa is the source of everything, as we understand from Kṛṣṇa Himself in *Bhagavad-gītā* (*ahaṁ sarvasya prabhavaḥ*). All the activities in both the spiritual and material world are certainly conducted by the orders of the Supreme Personality of Godhead through the agency of either the material or spiritual nature. As further confirmed in *Bhagavad-gītā* (9.10), *mayādhyakṣeṇa prakṛtiḥ sūyate sacarācaram:* without the direction of the Supreme Lord, material nature cannot do anything; it cannot act independently. Therefore, in the beginning the living entity wanted to enjoy the material energy, and to give the living entity all facility, Kṛṣṇa, the Supreme Personality of Godhead, created this material world and gave the living entity the facility to concoct different ideas and plans through the mind. These facilities offered by the Lord to the living entity constitute the sixteen kinds of perverted support in terms of the knowledge-gathering senses, the working senses, the mind and the five material elements. The wheel of repeated birth and death is created by the Supreme Personality of Godhead, but to direct the bewildered living entity in progress toward liberation according to varied stages of advancement, different directions are given in the *Vedas* (*chandomayam*). If one wants to be elevated to the higher planetary systems, he may follow the Vedic directions. As the Lord states in *Bhagavad-gītā* (9.25):

yānti deva-vratā devān
pitṝn yānti pitṛ-vratāḥ

bhūtāni yānti bhūtejyā
yānti mad-yājino 'pi mām

"Those who worship the demigods will take birth among the demigods; those who worship ghosts and spirits will take birth among such beings; those who worship ancestors go to the ancestors; and those who worship Me will live with Me." The real purpose of the *Vedas* is to direct one back home, back to Godhead, but the living entity, not knowing the real goal of his life, wants to go sometimes here and sometimes there and do sometimes this and sometimes that. In this way he wanders throughout the entire universe, imprisoned in various species and thus engaging in various activities for which he must suffer the reactions. Śrī Caitanya Mahāprabhu therefore says:

brahmāṇḍa bhramite kona bhāgyavān jīva
guru-kṛṣṇa-prasāde pāya bhakti-latā-bīja
(Cc. *Madhya* 19.151)

The fallen, conditioned living entity, trapped by the external energy, loiters in the material world, but if by good fortune he meets a bona fide representative of the Lord who gives him the seed of devotional service, and if he takes advantage of such a *guru*, or representative of God, he receives the *bhakti-latā-bīja*, the seed of devotional service. If he properly cultivates Kṛṣṇa consciousness, he is then gradually elevated to the spiritual world. The ultimate conclusion is that one must surrender to the principles of *bhakti-yoga*, for then one will gradually attain liberation. No other method of liberation from the material struggle is at all possible.

TEXT 22

स त्वं हि नित्यविजितात्मगुणः स्वधाम्ना
कालो वशीकृतविसृज्यविसर्गशक्तिः ।
चक्रे विसृष्टमजयेश्वर षोडशारे
निष्पीड्यमानमुपकर्ष विभो प्रपन्नम् ॥२२॥

sa tvaṁ hi nitya-vijitātma-guṇaḥ sva-dhāmnā
kālo vaśī-kṛta-visṛjya-visarga-śaktiḥ

cakre visṛṣṭam ajayeśvara ṣoḍaśāre
niṣpīḍyamānam upakarṣa vibho prapannam

saḥ—that one (the supreme independent person who, through His external energy, has created the material mind, which is the cause of all suffering in this material world); *tvam*—You (are); *hi*—indeed; *nitya*—eternally; *vijita-ātma*—conquered; *guṇaḥ*—whose property of the intelligence; *sva-dhāmnā*—by Your personal spiritual energy; *kālaḥ*—the time element (which creates and annihilates); *vaśī-kṛta*—brought under Your control; *visṛjya*—by which all effects; *visarga*—and causes; *śaktiḥ*—the energy; *cakre*—in the wheel of time (the repetition of birth and death); *visṛṣṭam*—being thrown; *ajayā*—by Your external energy, the mode of ignorance; *īśvara*—O supreme controller; *ṣoḍaśa-are*—with sixteen spokes (the five material elements, the ten senses, and the leader of the senses, namely the mind); *niṣpīḍyamānam*—being crushed (under that wheel); *upakarṣa*—kindly take me (to the shelter of Your lotus feet); *vibho*—O supreme great; *prapannam*—who am fully surrendered unto You.

TRANSLATION

My dear Lord, O supreme great, You have created this material world of sixteen constituents, but You are transcendental to their material qualities. In other words, these material qualities are under Your full control, and You are never conquered by them. Therefore the time element is Your representation. My Lord, O Supreme, no one can conquer You. As for me, however, I am being crushed by the wheel of time, and therefore I surrender fully unto You. Now kindly take me under the protection of Your lotus feet.

PURPORT

The wheel of material miseries is also a creation of the Supreme Personality of Godhead, but He is not under the control of the material energy. Rather, He is the controller of the material energy, whereas we, the living entities, are under its control. When we give up our constitutional position (*jīvera 'svarūpa' haya—kṛṣṇera 'nitya-dāsa'*), the Supreme Personality of Godhead creates this material energy and her influence over the conditioned soul. Therefore He is the Supreme, and only He can deliver the conditioned soul from the onslaught of material nature (*mām eva ye prapadyante māyām etāṁ taranti te*). *Māyā*, the external energy, continuously imposes upon the conditioned souls the suffering of the threefold miseries of this material world. Therefore, in the previous verse, Prahlāda Mahārāja prayed to the Lord, "But for Your Lordship, no one can save me." Prahlāda Mahārāja has also explained that a child's protectors, his parents, cannot save the child from the onslaught of birth and death, nor can medicine and a physician save one from death, nor can a boat or similar means of protection save a person drowning in the water, for everything is controlled by the Supreme Personality of Godhead. Therefore suffering humanity must surrender to Kṛṣṇa, as Kṛṣṇa Himself demands in the last instruction of *Bhagavad-gītā* (18.66):

sarva-dharmān parityajya
mām ekaṁ śaraṇaṁ vraja
ahaṁ tvāṁ sarva-pāpebhyo
mokṣayiṣyāmi mā śucaḥ

"Abandon all varieties of religion and just surrender unto Me. I shall deliver you from all sinful reaction. Do not fear." All of human society must take advantage of this offer and thus be saved by Kṛṣṇa from the danger of being crushed by the wheel of time, the wheel of past, present and future.

The word *niṣpīḍyamānam* ("being crushed") is very significant. Every living entity in the material condition is actually being crushed again and again, and to be saved from this position one must take shelter of the Supreme Personality of Godhead. Then one will be happy. The word *prapannam* is also very significant, for unless one fully surrenders to the Supreme Lord one cannot be saved from being crushed. A criminal is put in prison and punished by the government, but the same government, if it likes, can release the criminal from imprisoned life. Similarly, we must know conclusively that our material condition of suffering has been allotted to us by the Supreme Personality of Godhead, and if we want to be saved from this suffering, we must appeal to the same controller. Thus one can be saved from this material condition.

TEXT 23

दृष्टा मया दिवि विभोऽखिलधिष्ण्यपाना-
मायुः श्रियो विभव इच्छति याञ्जनोऽयम् ।
येऽस्मत्पितुः कुपितहासविजृम्भितभ्रू-
विस्फूर्जितेन लुलिताः स तु ते निरस्तः ॥२३॥

dṛṣṭā mayā divi vibho 'khila-dhiṣṇya-pānām
āyuḥ śriyo vibhava icchati yāñ jano 'yam
ye 'smat pituḥ kupita-hāsa-vijṛmbhita-bhrū-
visphūrjitena lulitāḥ sa tu te nirastaḥ

dṛṣṭāḥ—have been seen practically; *mayā*—by me; *divi*—in the higher planetary systems; *vibho*—O my Lord; *akhila*—all; *dhiṣṇya-pānām*—of the chiefs of different states or planets; *āyuḥ*—the duration of life; *śriyaḥ*—the opulences; *vibhavaḥ*—glories, influence; *icchati*—desire; *yān*—all of which; *janaḥ ayam*—these people in general; *ye*—all of which (duration of life, opulence, etc.); *asmat pituḥ*—of our father, Hiraṇyakaśipu; *kupita-hāsa*—by his critical laughing when angry; *vijṛmbhita*—being expanded; *bhrū*—of the eyebrows; *visphūrjitena*—simply by the feature; *lulitāḥ*—pulled down or finished; *saḥ*—he (my father); *tu*—but; *te*—by You; *nirastaḥ*—completely vanquished.

TRANSLATION

My dear Lord, people in general want to be elevated to the higher planetary systems for a long duration of life, opulence and enjoyment, but I have seen all of these through the activities of my father. When my father was angry and he laughed sarcastically at the demigods, they were immediately vanquished simply by seeing the movements of his eyebrows. Yet my father, who was so powerful, has now been vanquished by You within a moment.

PURPORT

Within this material world, one should understand by practical experience the value of material opulence, longevity and influence. We have actual experience that even on this planet there have been many great politicians and military commanders like Napolean, Hitler, Shubhash Chandra Bose and Gandhi, but as soon as their lives were finished, their popularity, influence and everything else were finished also. Prahlāda Mahārāja formerly gathered the same experience by seeing the activities of Hiraṇyakaśipu, his great father. Therefore Prahlāda Mahārāja did not give any importance to anything in this material world. No one can maintain his body or material achievements forever. A Vaiṣṇava can understand that nothing within this material world, not even that which is powerful, opulent or influential, can endure. At any time such things may be vanquished. And who can vanquish them? The Supreme Personality of Godhead. Therefore one should conclusively understand that no one is greater than the Supreme Great. Since the Supreme Great demands, *sarva-dharmān parityajya mām ekaṁ śaraṇaṁ vraja*, every intelligent man must agree to this proposal. One must surrender unto the Lord to be saved from the wheel of repeated birth, death, old age and disease.

TEXT 24

तस्मादमूस्तनुभृतामहमाशिषोऽज्ञ
आयुः श्रियं विभवमैन्द्रियमाविरिञ्च्यात् ।
नेच्छामि ते विलुलितानुरुविक्रमेण
कालात्मनोपनय मां निजभृत्यपार्श्वम् ॥२४॥

tasmād amūs tanu-bhṛtām aham āśiṣo 'jña
āyuḥ śriyaṁ vibhavam aindriyam āviriñcyāt
necchāmi te vilulitān uruvikrameṇa
kālātmanopanaya māṁ nija-bhṛtya-pārśvam

tasmāt—therefore; *amūḥ*—all those (opulences); *tanu-bhṛtām*—with reference to living entities possessing material bodies; *aham*—I; *āśiṣaḥ ajñaḥ*—knowing well the results of such benedictions; *āyuḥ*—a long duration of life; *śriyam*—material opulences; *vibhavam*—influence and glories; *aindriyam*—all meant for sense gratification; *āviriñcyāt*—beginning from Lord Brahmā (down to the small ant); *na*—not;

icchāmi—I want; *te*—by You; *vilulitān*—subject to be finished; *uru-vikrameṇa*—who are extremely powerful; *kāla-ātmanā*—as the master of the time factor; *upanaya*—kindly take to; *mām*—me; *nija-bhṛtya-pārśvam*—the association of Your faithful servant, Your devotee.

TRANSLATION

My dear Lord, now I have complete experience concerning the worldly opulence, mystic power, longevity and other material pleasures enjoyed by all living entities, from Lord Brahmā down to the ant. As powerful time, You destroy them all. Therefore, because of my experience, I do not wish to possess them. My dear Lord, I request You to place me in touch with Your pure devotee and let me serve him as a sincere servant.

PURPORT

By studying *Śrīmad-Bhāgavatam*, every intelligent man can get experience like that of Prahlāda Mahārāja through the historical incidents mentioned in this great literature of spiritual knowledge. By following in the footsteps of Prahlāda Mahārāja, one should gain thorough experience that all material opulence is perishable at every moment. Even this body, for which we try to acquire so many sensual pleasures, may perish at any time. The soul, however, is eternal. *Na hanyate hanyamāne śarīre:* the soul is never vanquished, even when the body is destroyed. An intelligent man, therefore, should care for the happiness of the spirit soul, not of the body. Even if one receives a body with a long duration of life, like those of Lord Brahmā and the other great demigods, it will also be destroyed, and therefore an intelligent man should be concerned with the imperishable spirit soul.

To save oneself, one must take shelter of a pure devotee. Narottama dāsa Ṭhākura therefore says, *chāḍiyā vaiṣṇava-sevā nistāra pāyeche kebā.* If one wants to save himself from material nature's onslaughts, which arise because of the material body, one must become Kṛṣṇa conscious and try to fully understand Kṛṣṇa. As stated in *Bhagavad-gītā* (4.9), *janma karma ca me divyam evaṁ yo vetti tattvataḥ.* One should understand Kṛṣṇa in truth, and this one can do only by serving a pure devotee. Thus Prahlāda Mahārāja prays that Lord Nṛsiṁhadeva place him in touch with a pure devotee and servant instead of awarding him material opulence. Every intelligent man within this material world must follow Prahlāda Mahārāja. *Mahājano yena gataḥ sa panthāḥ.* Prahlāda Mahārāja did not want to enjoy the estate left by his father; rather, he wanted to become a servant of the servant of the Lord. The illusory human civilization that perpetually endeavors for happiness through material advancement is rejected by Prahlāda Mahārāja and those who strictly follow in his footsteps.

There are different types of material opulence, known technically as *bhukti, mukti* and *siddhi. Bhukti* refers to being situated in a very good position, like a position with the demigods in the higher planetary systems, where one can enjoy material sense gratification to the greatest extent. *Mukti* refers to being disgusted with material advancement and thus desiring to become one with the Supreme. *Siddhi* refers to executing a severe type of meditation, like that of the *yogīs*, to attain eight kinds of perfection (*aṇimā, laghimā, mahimā,* etc.). All who desire some material advancement through *bhukti, mukti* or *siddhi* are punishable in due course of time, and they return to material activities. Prahlāda Mahārāja rejected them all; he simply wanted to engage as an apprentice under the guidance of a pure devotee.

TEXT 25

कुत्राशिषः श्रुतिसुखा मृगतृष्णिरूपाः
क्वेदं कलेवरमशेषरुजां विरोहः ।
निर्विद्यते न तु जनो यदपीति विद्वान्
कामानलं मधुलवैः शमयन्दुरापैः ॥२५॥

kutrāśiṣaḥ śruti-sukhā mṛgatṛṣṇi-rūpāḥ
kvedaṁ kalevaram aśeṣa-rujāṁ virohaḥ
nirvidyate na tu jano yad apīti vidvān
kāmānalaṁ madhu-lavaiḥ śamayan durāpaiḥ

kutra—where; *āśiṣaḥ*—benedictions; *śruti-sukhāḥ*—simply pleasing to hear of; *mṛgatṛṣṇi-rūpāḥ*—exactly like a mirage in the desert; *kva*—where; *idam*—this; *kalevaram*—body; *aśeṣa*—unlimited; *rujām*—of diseases; *virohaḥ*—the place for generating; *nirvidyate*—become satiated; *na*—not; *tu*—but; *janaḥ*—people in general; *yat api*—although; *iti*—thus; *vidvān*—so-called learned philosophers, scientists and politicians; *kāma-analam*—the blazing fire of lusty desires; *madhu-lavaiḥ*—with drops of honey (happiness); *śamayan*—controlling; *durāpaiḥ*—very difficult to obtain.

TRANSLATION

In this material world, every living entity desires some future happiness, which is exactly like a mirage in the desert. Where is water in the desert, or, in other words, where is happiness in this material world? As for this body, what is its value? It is merely a source of various diseases. The so-called philosophers, scientists and politicians know this very well, but nonetheless they aspire for temporary happiness. Happiness is very difficult to obtain, but because they are unable to control their senses, they run after the so-called happiness of the material world and never come to the right conclusion.

PURPORT

There is a song in the Bengali language which states, "I constructed this home for happiness, but unfortunately there was a fire, and everything has now been burnt to ashes." This illustrates the nature of material happiness. Everyone knows it, but nonetheless one plans to hear or think something very pleasing. Unfortunately, all of one's plans are annihilated in due course of time. There were many politicians who planned empires, supremacy and control of the world, but in due time all their plans and empires—and even the politicians themselves—were vanquished. Everyone should take lessons from Prahlāda Mahārāja about how we are engaged in so-called temporary happiness through bodily exercises for sense enjoyment. All of us repeatedly make plans, which are all repeatedly frustrated. Therefore one should stop such planmaking.

As one cannot stop a blazing fire by constantly pouring ghee upon it, one cannot satisfy oneself by increasing plans for sense enjoyment. The blazing fire is *bhava-mahā-dāvāgni*, the forest fire of material existence. This forest fire occurs automatically, without endeavor. We want to be happy in the material world, but this will never be possible; we shall simply increase the blazing fire of desires. Our desires cannot be satisfied by illusory thoughts and plans; rather, we have to follow the instructions of Lord Kṛṣṇa: *sarva-dharmān parityajya mām ekaṁ śaraṇaṁ vraja.* Then we shall be happy. Otherwise, in the name of happiness, we shall continue to suffer miserable conditions.

TEXT 26

क्वाहं रजःप्रभव ईश तमोऽधिकेऽस्मिन्
जातः सुरेतरकुले क्व तवानुकम्पा ।
न ब्रह्मणो न तु भवस्य न वै रमाया
यन्मेऽर्पितः शिरसि पद्मकरः प्रसादः ॥२६॥

kvāhaṁ rajaḥ-prabhava īśa tamo 'dhike 'smin
jātaḥ suretara-kule kva tavānukampā
na brahmaṇo na tu bhavasya na vai ramāyā
yan me 'rpitaḥ śirasi padma-karaḥ prasādaḥ

kva—where; *aham*—I (am); *rajaḥ-prabhavaḥ*—being born in a body full of passion; *īśa*—O my Lord; *tamaḥ*—the mode of ignorance; *adhike*—surpassing in; *asmin*—in this; *jātaḥ*—born; *sura-itara-kule*—in a family of atheists or demons (who are subordinate to the devotees); *kva*—where; *tava*—Your; *anukampā*—causeless mercy; *na*—not; *brahmaṇaḥ*—of Lord Brahmā; *na*—not; *tu*—but; *bhavasya*—of Lord Śiva; *na*—nor; *vai*—even; *ramāyāḥ*—of the goddess of fortune; *yat*—which; *me*—of me; *arpitaḥ*—offered; *śirasi*—on the head; *padma-karaḥ*—lotus hand; *prasādaḥ*—the symbol of mercy.

TRANSLATION

O my Lord, O Supreme, because I was born in a family full of the hellish material qualities of passion and ignorance, what is my position? And what is to be said of Your causeless mercy, which was never offered even to Lord Brahmā, Lord Śiva or the goddess of fortune, Lakṣmī? You never put Your lotus hand upon their heads, but You have put it upon mine.

PURPORT

Prahlāda Mahārāja was surprised at the causeless mercy of the Supreme Lord, the Personality of Godhead, for although Prahlāda was born in a demoniac family and although the Lord had never before placed His lotus hand on the head of Brahmā, Śiva or the goddess of fortune, His constant companion, Lord Nṛsiṁhadeva kindly placed His hand on the head of Prahlāda. This is the meaning of causeless mercy. The causeless mercy of the Supreme Personality of Godhead may be bestowed upon anyone, regardless of his position in this material world. Everyone is eligible to worship the Supreme Lord, irrespective of his material position. This is confirmed in *Bhagavad-gītā* (14.26):

māṁ ca yo 'vyabhicāreṇa
bhakti yogena sevate
sa guṇān samatītyaitān
brahma-bhūyāya kalpate

"One who engages in full devotional service, who does not fall down in any circumstance, at once transcends the modes of material nature and thus comes to the level of Brahman." Anyone who engages in continuous devotional service to the Lord is situated in the spiritual world and has nothing to do with the material qualities (*sattva-guṇa, rajo-guṇa* and *tamo-guṇa*).

Because Prahlāda Mahārāja was situated on the spiritual platform, he had nothing to do with his body, which had been born of the modes of passion and ignorance. The symptoms of passion and ignorance are described in *Śrīmad-Bhāgavatam* (1.2.19) as lust and hankering (*tadā rajas tamo-bhāvāḥ kāma-lobhādayaś ca ye*). Prahlāda Mahārāja, being a great devotee, thought the body born of his father to be born of passion and ignorance, but because Prahlāda was fully engaged in the service of the Lord, his body did not belong to the material world. The pure Vaiṣṇava's body is spiritualized even in this life. For example, when iron is put into a fire it becomes red-hot and is no longer iron but fire. Similarly, the so-called material bodies of devotees who fully engage in the devotional service of the Lord, being constantly in the fire of spiritual life, have nothing to do with matter, but are spiritualized.

Śrīla Madhvācārya remarks that the goddess of fortune, the mother of the universe, could not get mercy similar to that which was offered to Prahlāda Mahārāja, for although the goddess of fortune is always a constant companion of the Supreme Lord, the Lord is more inclined to His devotees. In other words, devotional service is so great that when it is offered even by those born in low families, the Lord accepts it as being more valuable than the service offered by the goddess of fortune. Lord Brahmā, King Indra and the other demigods living in the upper planetary systems are situated in a different spirit of consciousness, and therefore they are sometimes troubled by demons, but a devotee, even if situated in the lower planets, enjoys life in Kṛṣṇa consciousness under any circumstances. *Parataḥ svataḥ karmataḥ:* as he acts himself, as he is instructed by others or as he performs his material activities, he enjoys life in every respect. In this regard, Madhvācārya quotes the following verses, which are mentioned in the *Brahma-tarka:*

śrī-brahma-brāhmīvīndrādi-
tri-katat strī-puru-ṣṭutāḥ
tad anye ca kramādeva
sadā muktau smṛtāv api

hari-bhaktau ca taj-jñāne
sukhe ca niyamena tu
parataḥ svataḥ karmato vā
na kathañcit tad anyathā

TEXT 27

नैषा परावरमतिर्भवतो ननु स्या-
जन्तोर्यथात्मसुहृदो जगतस्तथापि ।
संसेवया सुरतरोरिव ते प्रसादः
सेवानुरूपमुदयो न परावरत्वम् ॥२७॥

naiṣā parāvara-matir bhavato nanu syāj
jantor yathātma-suhṛdo jagatas tathāpi

saṁsevayā surataror iva te prasādaḥ
sevānurūpam udayo na parāvaratvam

na—not; *eṣā*—this; *para-avara*—of higher or lower; *matiḥ*—such discrimination; *bhavataḥ*—of Your Lordship; *nanu*—indeed; *syāt*—there can be; *jantoḥ*—of ordinary living entities; *yathā*—as; *ātma-suhṛdaḥ*—of one who is the friend; *jagataḥ*—of the whole material world; *tathāpi*—but still (there is such a demonstration of intimacy or difference); *saṁsevayā*—according to the degree of service rendered by the devotee; *surataroḥ iva*—like that of the desire tree in Vaikuṇṭhaloka (which offers fruits according to the desire of the devotee); *te*—Your; *prasādaḥ*—benediction or blessing; *sevā-anurūpam*—according to the category of service one renders to the Lord; *udayaḥ*—manifestation; *na*—not; *para-avaratvam*—discrimination due to higher or lower levels.

TRANSLATION

Unlike an ordinary living entity, my Lord, You do not discriminate between friends and enemies, the favorable and the unfavorable, because for You there is no conception of higher and lower. Nonetheless, You offer Your benedictions according to the level of one's service, exactly as a desire tree delivers fruits according to one's desires and makes no distinction between the lower and the higher.

PURPORT

In *Bhagavad-gītā* (4.11) the Lord clearly says, *ye yathā māṁ prapadyante tāṁs tathaiva bhajāmy aham:* "As one surrenders to Me, I reward him accordingly." As stated by Śrī Caitanya Mahāprabhu, *jīvera 'svarūpa' haya—kṛṣṇera 'nitya-dāsa':* every living being is an eternal servant of Kṛṣṇa. According to the service the living entity renders, he automatically receives benedictions from Kṛṣṇa, who does not make distinctions, thinking, "Here is a person in an intimate relationship with Me, and here is a person I dislike." Kṛṣṇa advises everyone to surrender to Him (*sarva-dharmān parityajya mām ekaṁ śaraṇaṁ vraja*). One's relationship with the Supreme Lord is in proportion to that surrender and the service one renders unto the Lord. Thus throughout the entire world the higher or lower positions of the living entities are selected by the living entities themselves. If one is inclined to dictate that the Lord grant something, one receives benedictions according to his desires. If one wants to be elevated to the higher planetary systems, the heavenly planets, he can be promoted to the place he desires, and if one wants to remain a hog or a pig on earth, the Lord fulfills that desire also. Therefore, one's position is determined by one's desires; the Lord is not responsible for the higher or lower grades of our existence. This is further explained quite definitely in *Bhagavad-gītā* (9.25) by the Lord Himself:

yānti deva-vratā devān
pitṝn yānti pitṛ-vratāḥ
bhūtāni yānti bhūtejyā
yānti mad-yājino 'pi mām

Some people want to be promoted to the heavenly planets, some want to be promoted to Pitṛloka, and some want to remain on earth, but if one is interested in returning home, back to Godhead, he can be promoted there also. According to the demands of a particular devotee, he receives a result by the grace of the Lord. The Lord does not discriminate, thinking, "Here is a person favorable to Me, and here is a person who is not favorable." Rather, He fulfills the desires of everyone. Therefore the *śāstras* enjoin:

akāmaḥ sarva-kāmo vā
mokṣa-kāma udāra-dhīḥ
tīvreṇa bhakti-yogena
yajeta puruṣaṁ param

"Whether one is without desire [the condition of the devotees], or is desirous of all fruitive results, or is after liberation, one should with all efforts try to worship the Supreme Personality of Godhead for complete perfection, culminating in Kṛṣṇa consciousness." (*Bhāg.* 2.3.10) According to one's position, whether as a devotee, a *karmī* or a *jñānī*, whatever one wants one can get if one fully engages in the service of the Lord.

TEXT 28

एवं जनं निपतितं प्रभवाहिकूपे
कामाभिकाममनु यः प्रपतन्प्रसङ्गात्।

कृत्वात्मसात् सुरर्षिणा भगवन् गृहीतः
सोऽहं कथं नु विसृजे तव भृत्यसेवाम् ॥ २८॥

evaṁ janaṁ nipatitaṁ prabhavāhi-kūpe
kāmābhikāmam anu yaḥ prapatan prasaṅgāt
kṛtvātmasāt surarṣiṇā bhagavan gṛhītaḥ
so 'haṁ kathaṁ nu visṛje tava bhṛtya-sevām

evam—thus; *janam*—people in general; *nipatitam*—fallen; *prabhava*—of material existence; *ahi-kūpe*—in a blind well full of snakes; *kāma-abhikāmam*—desiring the sense objects; *anu*—following; *yaḥ*—the person who; *prapatan*—falling down (in this condition); *prasaṅgāt*—because of bad association or increased association with material desires; *kṛtvā ātmasāt*—causing me (to acquire spiritual qualities like himself, Śrī Nārada); *sura-ṛṣiṇā*—by the great saintly person (Nārada); *bhagavan*—O my Lord; *gṛhītaḥ*—accepted; *saḥ*—that person; *aham*—I; *katham*—how; *nu*—indeed; *visṛje*—can give up; *tava*—Your; *bhṛtya-sevām*—the service of Your pure devotee.

TRANSLATION

My dear Lord, O Supreme Personality of Godhead, because of my association with material desires, one after another, I was gradually falling into a blind well full of snakes, following the general populace. But Your servant Nārada Muni kindly accepted me as his disciple and instructed me how to achieve this transcendental position. Therefore, my first duty is to serve him. How could I leave his service?

PURPORT

As will be seen in later verses, even though Prahlāda Mahārāja was directly offered all the benedictions he might have desired, he refused to accept such offerings from the Supreme Personality of Godhead. On the contrary, he asked the Lord to engage him in the service of His servant Nārada Muni. This is the symptom of a pure devotee. One should serve the spiritual master first. It is not that one should bypass the spiritual master and desire to serve the Supreme Lord. This is not the principle for a Vaiṣṇava. Narottama dāsa Ṭhākura says:

tāṅdera caraṇa sevi bhakta-sane vāsa
janame janame haya, ei abhilāṣa

One should not be anxious to offer direct service to the Lord. Śrī Caitanya Mahāprabhu advised that one become a servant of the servant of the servant of the Lord (*gopī-bhartuḥ pada-kamalayor dāsa-dāsānudāsaḥ*). This is the process for approaching the Supreme Lord. The first service should be rendered to the spiritual master so that by his mercy one can approach the Supreme Personality of Godhead to render service. While teaching Rūpa Gosvāmī, Śrī Caitanya Mahāprabhu said, *guru-kṛṣṇa-prasāde pāya bhakti-latā-bīja:* one can achieve the seed of devotional service by the mercy of the *guru,* the spiritual master, and then by the mercy of Kṛṣṇa. This is the secret of success. First one should try to please the spiritual master, and then one should attempt to please the Supreme Personality of Godhead. Viśvanātha Cakravartī Ṭhākura also says, *yasya prasādād bhagavat-prasādo.* One should not attempt to please the Supreme Personality of Godhead by concoction. One must first be prepared to serve the spiritual master, and when one is qualified he is automatically offered the platform of direct service to the Lord. Therefore Prahlāda Mahārāja proposed that he engage in the service of Nārada Muni. He never proposed that he engage directly in the service of the Lord. This is the right conclusion. Therefore he said, *so 'haṁ kathaṁ nu visṛje tava bhṛtya-sevām:* "How can I give up the service of my spiritual master, who has favored me in such a way that I am now able to see You face to face?" Prahlāda Mahārāja prayed to the Lord that he might continue to engage in the service of his spiritual master, Nārada Muni.

TEXT 29

मत्प्राणरक्षणमनन्त पितुर्वधश्च
मन्ये स्वभृत्यऋषिवाक्यमृतं विधातुम् ।
खड्गं प्रगृह्य यदवोचदसद्विधित्सु-
स्त्वामीश्वरो मदपरोऽवतु कं हरामि ॥२९॥

mat-prāṇa-rakṣaṇam ananta pitur vadhaś ca
manye sva-bhṛtya-ṛṣi-vākyam ṛtaṁ vidhātum

khaḍgaṁ pragṛhya yad avocad asad-vidhitsus
tvām īśvaro mad-aparo 'vatu kaṁ harāmi

mat-prāṇa-rakṣaṇam—saving my life; *ananta*—O unlimited one, reservoir of unlimited transcendental qualities; *pituḥ*—of my father; *vadhaḥ ca*—and killing; *manye*—I consider; *sva-bhṛtya*—of Your unalloyed servants; *ṛṣi-vākyam*—and the words of the great saint Nārada; *ṛtam*—true; *vidhātum*—to prove; *khaḍgam*—sword; *pragṛhya*—taking in hand; *yat*—since; *avocat*—my father said; *asat-vidhitsuḥ*—desiring to act very impiously; *tvām*—You; *īśvaraḥ*—any supreme controller; *mat-aparaḥ*—other than me; *avatu*—let him save; *kam*—your head; *harāmi*—I shall now separate.

TRANSLATION

My Lord, O unlimited reservoir of transcendental qualities, You have killed my father, Hiraṇyakaśipu, and saved me from his sword. He had said very angrily, "If there is any supreme controller other than me, let Him save you. I shall now sever your head from your body." Therefore I think that both in saving me and in killing him, You have acted just to prove true the words of Your devotee. There is no other cause.

PURPORT

In *Bhagavad-gītā* (9.29) the Lord says:

samo 'haṁ sarva-bhūteṣu
na me dveṣyo 'sti na priyaḥ
ye bhajanti tu māṁ bhaktyā
mayi te teṣu cāpy aham

The Supreme Personality of Godhead is undoubtedly equal to everyone. He has no friend and no enemy, but as one desires benefits from the Lord, the Lord is very pleased to award them. The lower and higher positions of different living entities are due to their desires, for the Lord, being equal to all, fulfills everyone's desires. The killing of Hiraṇyakaśipu and saving of Prahlāda Mahārāja also strictly followed this law of the supreme controller's activities. When Prahlāda's mother,

Hiraṇyakaśipu's wife, Kayādhu, was under the protection of Nārada, she prayed for the protection of her son from the enemy, and Nārada Muni gave assurance that Prahlāda Mahārāja would always be saved from the enemy's hands. Thus when Hiraṇyakaśipu was going to kill Prahlāda Mahārāja, the Lord saved Prahlāda to fulfill His promise in *Bhagavad-gītā* (*kaunteya pratijānīhi na me bhaktaḥ praṇaśyati*) and to prove true the words of Nārada. The Lord can fulfill many purposes through one action. Thus the killing of Hiraṇyakaśipu and the saving of Prahlāda were enacted simultaneously to prove the truthfulness of the Lord's devotee and the fidelity of the Lord Himself to His own purpose. The Lord acts only to satisfy the desires of His devotees; otherwise He has nothing to do. As confirmed in the Vedic language, *na tasya kāryaṁ karaṇaṁ ca vidyate:* the Lord has nothing to do personally, for everything is done through His different potencies (*parāsya śaktir vividhaiva śrūyate*). The Lord has multifarious energies, through which everything is done. Thus when He personally does something, it is only to satisfy His devotee. The Lord is known as *bhakta-vatsala* because He very much favors His devoted servant.

TEXT 30

एकस्त्वमेव जगदेतममुष्य यत् त्व-
माद्यन्तयोः पृथगवस्यसि मध्यतश्च ।
सृष्ट्वा गुणव्यतिकरं निजमाययेदं
नानेव तैरवसितस्तदनुप्रविष्टः ॥३०॥

ekas tvam eva jagad etam amuṣya yat tvam
ādy-antayoḥ pṛthag avasyasi madhyataś ca
sṛṣṭvā guṇa-vyatikaraṁ nija-māyayedaṁ
nāneva tair avasitas tad anupraviṣṭaḥ

ekaḥ—one; *tvam*—You; *eva*—only; *jagat*—the cosmic manifestation; *etam*—this; *amuṣya*—of that (the whole universe); *yat*—since; *tvam*—You; *ādi*—in the beginning; *antayoḥ*—at the end; *pṛthak*—separately; *avasyasi*—exist (as the cause); *madhyataḥ ca*—also in the middle (the duration between the beginning and end); *sṛṣṭvā*—creating; *guṇa-vyatikaram*—the transformation of the three modes of material nature;

nija-māyayā—by Your own external energy; *idam*—this; *nānā iva*—like many varieties; *taiḥ*—by them (the modes); *avasitaḥ*—experienced; *tat*—that; *anupraviṣṭaḥ*—entering into.

TRANSLATION

My dear Lord, You alone manifest Yourself as the entire cosmic manifestation, for You existed before the creation, You exist after the annihilation, and You are the maintainer between the beginning and the end. All this is done by Your external energy through actions and reactions of the three modes of material nature. Therefore whatever exists—externally and internally—is You alone.

PURPORT

As stated in the *Brahma-saṁhitā* (5.35):

eko 'py asau racayituṁ jagad-aṇḍa-koṭiṁ
yac-chaktir asti jagad-aṇḍa-cayā yad-antaḥ
aṇḍāntara-stha-paramāṇu-cayāntara-sthaṁ
govindam ādi-puruṣaṁ tam ahaṁ bhajāmi

"I worship the Personality of Godhead, Govinda, who, by one of His plenary portions, enters the existence of every universe and every atomic particle and thus unlimitedly manifests His infinite energy all over the material creation." To create this cosmic manifestation, Govinda, the Supreme Personality of Godhead, expands His external energy and thus enters everything in the universe, including the atomic particles. In this way He exists in the entire cosmic manifestation. Therefore the activities of the Supreme Personality of Godhead in maintaining His devotees are transcendental, not material. He exists in everything as the cause and effect, yet He is separate, existing beyond this cosmic manifestation. This is also confirmed in *Bhagavad-gītā* (9.4):

mayā tatam idaṁ sarvaṁ
jagad avyakta-mūrtinā
mat-sthāni sarva-bhūtāni
na cāhaṁ teṣv avasthitaḥ

The entire cosmic manifestation is but an expansion of the Lord's energy; everything rests in Him, yet He exists separately, beyond creation, maintenance and annihilation. The varieties of creation are performed by His external energy. Because the energy and energetic are one, everything is one (*sarvaṁ khalv idaṁ brahma*). Therefore without Kṛṣṇa, the Parabrahman, nothing can exist. The difference between the material and spiritual worlds is that His external energy is manifested in the material world whereas His spiritual energy exists in the spiritual world. Both energies, however, belong to the Supreme Lord, and therefore in a higher sense there is no exhibition of material energy because everything is spiritual energy. The energy in which the Lord's all-pervasiveness is not realized is called material. Otherwise, everything is spiritual. Therefore Prahlāda prays, *ekas tvam eva jagad etam:* "You are everything."

TEXT 31

त्वं वा इदं सदसदीश भवांस्ततोऽन्यो
माया यदात्मपरबुद्धिरियं ह्यपार्था ।
यद् यस्य जन्म निधनं स्थितिरीक्षणं च
तद् वैतदेव वसुकालवदष्टितर्वोः ॥३१॥

tvaṁ vā idaṁ sadasad īśa bhavāṁs tato 'nyo
māyā yad ātma-para-buddhir iyaṁ hy apārthā
yad yasya janma nidhanaṁ sthitir īkṣaṇaṁ ca
tad vaitad eva vasukālavad aṣṭi-tarvoḥ

tvam—You; *vā*—either; *idam*—the whole universe; *sat-asat*—consisting of cause and effect (You are the cause, and Your energy is the effect); *īśa*—O my Lord, the supreme controller; *bhavān*—Yourself; *tataḥ*—from the universe; *anyaḥ*—separately situated (the creation is made by the Lord, yet He remains separate from the creation); *māyā*—the energy that appears as a separate creation; *yat*—of which; *ātma-para-buddhiḥ*—the conception of one's own and another's; *iyam*—this; *hi*—indeed; *apārthā*—has no meaning (everything is Your Lordship, and therefore there is no hope for understanding "my" and "your"); *yat*—the substance from which; *yasya*—of which; *janma*—creation;

nidhanam—annihilation; *sthitiḥ*—maintenance; *īkṣaṇam*—manifestation; *ca*—and; *tat*—that; *vā*—or; *etat*—this; *eva*—certainly; *vasukāla-vat*—like the quality of being the earth and, beyond that, the subtle element of the earth (smell); *aṣṭi-tarvoḥ*—the seed (the cause) and the tree (the effect of the cause).

TRANSLATION

My dear Lord, O Supreme Personality of Godhead, the entire cosmic creation is caused by You, and the cosmic manifestation is an effect of Your energy. Although the entire cosmos is but You alone, You keep Yourself aloof from it. The conception of "mine and yours," is certainly a type of illusion [māyā] because everything is an emanation from You and is therefore not different from You. Indeed, the cosmic manifestation is nondifferent from You, and the annihilation is also caused by You. This relationship between Your Lordship and the cosmos is illustrated by the example of the seed and the tree, or the subtle cause and the gross manifestation.

PURPORT

In *Bhagavad-gītā* (7.10) the Lord says:

bījaṁ māṁ sarva-bhūtānāṁ
viddhi pārtha sanātanam

"O son of Pṛthā, know that I am the original seed of all existences." In the Vedic literature it is said, *īśāvāsyam idaṁ sarvam, yato vā imāni bhūtāni jāyante* and *sarvaṁ khalv idaṁ brahma.* All this Vedic information indicates that there is only one God and that there is nothing else but Him. The Māyāvādī philosophers explain this in their own way, but the Supreme Personality of Godhead asserts the truth that He is everything and yet is separate from everything. This is the philosophy of Śrī Caitanya Mahāprabhu, which is called *acintya-bhedābheda-tattva.* Everything is one, the Supreme Lord, yet everything is separate from the Lord. This is the understanding of oneness and difference.

The example given in this regard—*vasukālavad aṣṭi-tarvoḥ*—is very easy to understand. Everything exists in time, yet there are different phases of the time factor—present, past and future. Present, past and future are one. Every day we can experience the time factor as morning, noon and evening, and although morning is different from noon, which is different from evening, all of them taken together are one. The time factor is the energy of the Supreme Personality of Godhead, but the Lord is separate from the time factor. Everything is created, maintained and annihilated by time, but the Supreme Lord, the Personality of Godhead, has no beginning and no end. He is *nityaḥ śāśvataḥ*—eternal, permanent. Everything passes through time's phases of present, past and future, yet the Lord is always the same. Thus there is undoubtedly a difference between the Lord and the cosmic manifestation, but actually they are not different. Accepting them to be different is called *avidyā*, ignorance.

True oneness, however, is not equivalent to the conception of the Māyāvādīs. The true understanding is that the differences are manifested by the energy of the Supreme Personality of Godhead. The seed is manifested as a tree, which displays varieties in its trunk, branches, leaves, flowers and fruits. Śrīla Bhaktivinoda Ṭhākura has therefore sung, *keśava tuyā jagata vicitra:* "My dear Lord, Your creation is full of varieties." The varieties are one and at the same time different. This is the philosophy of *acintya-bhedābheda-tattva*. The conclusion given in *Brahma-saṁhitā* is this:

īśvaraḥ paramaḥ kṛṣṇaḥ
sac-cid-ānanda-vigrahaḥ
anādir ādir govindaḥ
sarva-kāraṇa-kāraṇam

"Kṛṣṇa, known as Govinda, is the supreme controller. He has an eternal, blissful, spiritual body. He is the origin of all. He has no other origin, for He is the prime cause of all causes." Because the Lord is the supreme cause, everything is one with Him, but when we consider varieties, we find that one thing is different from another.

We may conclude, therefore, that there is no difference between one thing and another, yet in varieties there are differences. In this regard, Madhvācārya gives an example concerning a tree and a tree in fire. Both trees are the same, but they look different because of the time factor. The time factor is under the control of the Supreme Lord, and therefore the Supreme Lord is different from time. An advanced devotee consequently does not distinguish between happiness and distress. As stated in *Śrīmad-Bhāgavatam* (10.14.8):

tat te 'nukampāṁ susamīkṣamāṇo
bhuñjāna evātma-kṛtaṁ vipākam

When a devotee is in a condition of so-called distress, he considers it a gift or blessing from the Supreme Personality of Godhead. When a devotee is always thus situated in Kṛṣṇa consciousness in any condition of life, he is described as *mukti-pade sa dāya-bhāk*, a perfect candidate for returning home, back to Godhead. The word *dāya-bhāk* means "inheritance." A son inherits the property of his father. Similarly, when the devotee is fully Kṛṣṇa conscious, undisturbed by dualities, he is sure that he will return home, back to Godhead, just as one inherits his father's property.

TEXT 32

न्यस्येदमात्मनि जगद् विलयाम्बुमध्ये
शेषेत्मना निजसुखानुभवो निरीहः ।
योगेन मीलितदृगात्मनिपीतनिद्र-
स्तुर्ये स्थितो न तु तमो न गुणांश्च युङ्क्षे ॥ ३२ ॥

nyasyedam ātmani jagad vilayāmbu-madhye
śeṣetmanā nija-sukhānubhavo nirīhaḥ
yogena mīlita-dṛg-ātma-nipīta-nidras
turye sthito na tu tamo na guṇāṁś ca yuṅkṣe

nyasya—throwing; *idam*—this; *ātmani*—in Your own self; *jagat*—cosmic manifestation created by You; *vilaya-ambu-madhye*—in the Causal Ocean, in which everything is preserved in a state of reserved energy; *śeṣe*—You act as if sleeping; *ātmanā*—by Yourself; *nija*—Your own personal; *sukha-anubhavaḥ*—experiencing the state of spiritual bliss; *nirīhaḥ*—appearing to be doing nothing; *yogena*—by the mystic power; *mīlita-dṛk*—the eyes appearing closed; *ātma*—by a manifestation of Yourself; *nipīta*—prevented; *nidraḥ*—whose sleeping; *turye*—in the transcendental stage; *sthitaḥ*—keeping (Yourself); *na*—not; *tu*—but; *tamaḥ*—the material condition of sleeping; *na*—nor; *guṇān*—the material modes; *ca*—and; *yuṅkṣe*—do You engage Yourself in.

TRANSLATION

O my Lord, O Supreme Personality of Godhead, after the annihilation the creative energy is kept in You, who appear to sleep with half-closed eyes. Actually, however, You do not sleep like an ordinary human being, for You are always in a transcendental stage, beyond the creation of the material world, and You always feel transcendental bliss. As Kāraṇodakaśāyī Viṣṇu, You thus remain in Your transcendental status, not touching material objects. Although You appear to sleep, this sleeping is distinct from sleeping in ignorance.

PURPORT

As explained very clearly in the *Brahma-saṁhitā* (5.47):

yaḥ kāraṇārṇava-jale bhajati sma yoga-
nidrām ananta-jagad-aṇḍa-sa-roma-kūpaḥ
ādhāra-śaktim avalambya parāṁ sva-mūrtiṁ
govindam ādi-puruṣaṁ tam ahaṁ bhajāmi

"I worship the primeval Lord Govinda, who lies down in the Causal Ocean in His plenary portion as Mahā-Viṣṇu, with all the universes generating from the pores of hair on His transcendental body, and who accepts the mystic slumber of eternity." The *ādi-puruṣa*, the original Supreme Personality of Godhead—Kṛṣṇa, Govinda—expands Himself as Mahā-Viṣṇu. After the annihilation of this cosmic manifestation, He keeps Himself in transcendental bliss. The word *yoga-nidrām* is used in reference to the Supreme Personality of Godhead. One should understand that this *nidrā*, or sleep, is not like our *nidrā* in the mode of ignorance. The Lord is always situated in transcendence. He is *sac-cid-*

ānanda—eternally in bliss—and thus He is not disturbed by sleep like ordinary human beings. It should be understood that the Supreme Personality of Godhead is in transcendental bliss in all stages. Śrīla Madhvācārya concisely states that the Lord is *turya-sthitaḥ*, always situated in transcendence. In transcendence there is no such thing as *jāgaraṇa-nidrā-suṣupti*—wakefulness, sleep and deep sleep.

The practice of *yoga* is similar to the *yoga-nidrā* of Mahā-Viṣṇu. *Yogīs* are advised to keep their eyes half closed, but this state is not at all one of sleep, although imitation *yogīs*, especially in the modern age, manifest their so-called *yoga* by sleeping. In the *śāstra*, *yoga* is described as *dhyānāvasthita*, a state of full meditation, but this is meditation upon the Supreme Personality of Godhead. *Dhyānāvasthita-tad-gatena manasā:* the mind should always be situated at the lotus feet of the Lord. *Yoga* practice does not mean sleeping. The mind should always be actively fixed at the lotus feet of the Lord. Then one's practice of *yoga* will be successful.

TEXT 33

तस्यैव ते वपुरिदं निजकालशक्त्या
सञ्चोदितप्रकृतिधर्मण आत्मगूढम् ।
अम्भस्यनन्तशयनाद् विरमत्समाधे-
र्नाभेरभूत् स्वकणिकावटवन्महाब्जम् ॥३३॥

tasyaiva te vapur idaṁ nija-kāla-śaktyā
sañcodita-prakṛti-dharmaṇa ātma-gūḍham
ambhasy ananta-śayanād viramat-samādher
nābher abhūt sva-kaṇikā-vaṭavan-mahābjam

tasya—of that Supreme Personality of Godhead; *eva*—certainly; *te*—of You; *vapuḥ*—the cosmic body; *idam*—this (universe); *nija-kāla-śaktyā*—by the potent time factor; *sañcodita*—agitated; *prakṛti-dharmaṇaḥ*—of Him, by whom the three *guṇas*, or qualities of material nature; *ātma-gūḍham*—dormant in Yourself; *ambhasi*—in the water known as the Causal Ocean; *ananta-śayanāt*—from the bed known as Ananta (another feature of Yourself); *viramat-samādheḥ*—having awakened from the *samādhi* (yogic trance); *nābheḥ*—from the navel; *abhūt*—appeared; *sva-kaṇikā*—from the seed; *vaṭa-vat*—like the great banyan tree; *mahā-abjam*—the great lotus of the worlds (has similarly grown).

TRANSLATION

This cosmic manifestation, the material world, is also Your body. This total lump of matter is agitated by Your potent energy known as kāla-śakti, and thus the three modes of material nature are manifested. You awaken from the bed of Śeṣa, Ananta, and from Your navel a small transcendental seed is generated. It is from this seed that the lotus flower of the gigantic universe is manifested, exactly as a banyan tree grows from a small seed.

PURPORT

The three different forms of Mahā-Viṣṇu—namely Kāraṇodakaśāyī Viṣṇu, Garbhodakaśāyī Viṣṇu and Kṣīrodakaśāyī Viṣṇu, who are the origin of creation and maintenance—are gradually being described. From Mahā-Viṣṇu, Garbhodakaśāyī Viṣṇu is generated, and from Garbhodakaśāyī Viṣṇu, Kṣīrodakaśāyī Viṣṇu gradually expands. Thus Mahā-Viṣṇu is the original cause of Garbhodakaśāyī Viṣṇu, and from Garbhodakaśāyī Viṣṇu comes the lotus flower from which Lord Brahmā is manifested. Thus the original cause of everything is Viṣṇu, and consequently the cosmic manifestation is not different from Viṣṇu. This is confirmed in *Bhagavad-gītā* (10.8), wherein Kṛṣṇa says, *ahaṁ sarvasya prabhavo mattaḥ sarvaṁ pravartate:* "I am the source of all spiritual and material worlds. Everything emanates from Me." Garbhodakaśāyī Viṣṇu is an expansion of Kāraṇodakaśāyī Viṣṇu, who is an expansion of Saṅkarṣaṇa. In this way, Kṛṣṇa is ultimately the cause of all causes (*sarva-kāraṇa-kāraṇam*). The conclusion is that both the material world and spiritual world are considered to be the body of the Supreme Lord. We can understand that the material body is caused by the spiritual body and is therefore an expansion of the spiritual body. Thus when one takes up spiritual activities, one's entire material body is spiritualized. Similarly, in this material world, when the Kṛṣṇa consciousness movement expands, the entire material world becomes spiritualized. As long as we do not realize this, we live in the material world, but when we are fully Kṛṣṇa conscious we live not in the material world but in the spiritual world.

TEXT 34

तत्सम्भवः कविरतोऽन्यदपश्यमान-
स्त्वां बीजमात्मनि ततं स बहिर्विचिन्त्य ।
नाविन्ददब्दशतमप्सु निमज्जमानो
जातेऽङ्कुरे कथमुहोपलभेत बीजम् ॥३४॥

tat-sambhavaḥ kavir ato 'nyad apaśyamānas
tvāṁ bījam ātmani tataṁ sa bahir vicintya
nāvindad abda-śatam apsu nimajjamāno
jāte 'ṅkure katham uhopalabheta bījam

tat-sambhavaḥ—who was generated from that lotus flower; *kaviḥ*—he who can understand the subtle cause of creation (Lord Brahmā); *ataḥ*—from that (lotus); *anyat*—anything else; *apaśyamānaḥ*—not able to see; *tvām*—Your Lordship; *bījam*—the cause of the lotus; *ātmani*—in himself; *tatam*—expanded; *saḥ*—he (Lord Brahmā); *bahiḥ vicintya*—considering to be external; *na*—not; *avindat*—understood (You); *abda-śatam*—for a hundred years according to the demigods;* *apsu*—in the water; *nimajjamānaḥ*—diving; *jāte aṅkure*—when the seed fructifies and is manifested as a creeper; *katham*—how; *uha*—O my Lord; *upalabheta*—one can perceive; *bījam*—the seed that has already fructified.

TRANSLATION

From that great lotus flower, Brahmā was generated, but Brahmā certainly could see nothing but the lotus. Therefore, thinking You to be outside, Lord Brahmā dove into the water and attempted to find the source of the lotus for one hundred years. He could find no trace of You, however, for when a seed fructifies, the original seed cannot be seen.

---

*One day for the demigods equals six of our months.

PURPORT

This is the description of the cosmic manifestation. The development of the cosmic manifestation is like the fructification of a seed. When cotton is transformed into thread, the cotton is no longer visible, and when the thread is woven into cloth, the thread is no longer visible. Similarly, it is perfectly correct that when the seed that had generated from the navel of Garbhodakaśāyī Viṣṇu became manifested as the cosmic creation, one could no longer understand where the cause of the cosmic manifestation is. Modern scientists have tried to explain the origin of creation by a chunk theory, but no one can explain how such a chunk might have burst. The Vedic literature, however, explains clearly that the total material energy was agitated by the three modes of material nature because of the glance of the Supreme Lord. In other words, in terms of the chunk theory, the bursting of the chunk was caused by the Supreme Personality of Godhead. Thus one must accept the supreme cause, Lord Viṣṇu, as the cause of all causes.

TEXT 35

स त्वात्मयोनिरतिविस्मित आश्रितोऽब्जं
कालेन तीव्रतपसा परिशुद्धभावः ।
त्वामात्मनीश भुवि गन्धमिवातिसूक्ष्मं
भूतेन्द्रियाशयमये विततं ददर्श ॥३५॥

sa tv ātma-yonir ativismita āśrito 'bjaṁ
kālena tīvra-tapasā pariśuddha-bhāvaḥ
tvām ātmanīśa bhuvi gandham ivātisūkṣmaṁ
bhūtendriyāśayamaye vitataṁ dadarśa

saḥ—he (Lord Brahmā); *tu*—but; *ātma-yoniḥ*—who is born without a mother (directly begotten by the father, Lord Viṣṇu); *ati-vismitaḥ*—very much surprised (not finding the source of his birth); *āśritaḥ*—situated on; *abjam*—the lotus; *kālena*—in due course of time; *tīvra-tapasā*—by severe austerities; *pariśuddha-bhāvaḥ*—being completely purified; *tvām*—You; *ātmani*—in his body and existence; *īśa*—O my Lord; *bhuvi*—within the earth; *gandham*—aroma; *iva*—like; *ati-*

sūkṣmam—very subtle; *bhūta-indriya*—composed of elements and senses; *āśaya-maye*—and that filled with desires (the mind); *vitatam*—spread out; *dadarśa*—found.

TRANSLATION

Lord Brahmā, who is celebrated as ātma-yoni, having been born without a mother, was struck with wonder. Thus he took shelter of the lotus flower, and when he had been purified after undergoing severe austerities for many hundreds of years, he could see that the cause of all causes, the Supreme Personality of Godhead, was spread throughout his own body and senses, just as aroma, although very subtle, is perceived in the earth.

PURPORT

Here the statement of self-realization *ahaṁ brahmāsmi,* which is interpreted by the Māyāvāda philosophy to mean "I am the Supreme Lord," is explained. The Supreme Lord is the original seed of everything (*janmādy asya yataḥ. ahaṁ sarvasya prabhavo mattaḥ sarvaṁ pravartate*). Thus the Supreme Lord extends everywhere, even throughout our bodies, because our bodies are made of material energy, which is the Lord's separated energy. One should realize that since the Supreme Lord spreads throughout one's body and since the individual soul is a part of the Supreme Lord, everything is Brahman (*sarvaṁ khalv idaṁ brahma*). This realization was achieved by Lord Brahmā after he was purified, and it is possible for everyone. When one is completely in knowledge of *ahaṁ brahmāsmi,* he thinks, "I am part of the Supreme Lord, my body is made of His material energy, and therefore I have no separate existence. Yet although the Supreme Lord is spread everywhere, He is different from me." This is the philosophy of *acintya-bhedābheda-tattva.* An example given in this regard is that of the aroma within the earth. In the earth there are aromas and colors, but one cannot see them. Actually we find that when flowers grow from the earth, they appear with different colors and aromas, which they have certainly gathered from the earth, although in the earth we cannot see them. Similarly, the Supreme Lord, by His different energies, spreads throughout one's body and soul, although we cannot see Him. An intelligent man, however, can see the Supreme Lord existing everywhere. *Aṇḍāntara-stha-paramāṇu-*

cayāntara-stham: the Lord is within the universe and within the atom by His different energies. This is the real vision of the Supreme Lord for the intelligent man. Brahmā, the first created being, became the most intelligent person by his *tapasya*, austerity, and thus he came to this realization. We must therefore take all knowledge from Brahmā, who became perfect by his *tapasya.*

TEXT 36

एवं सहस्रवदनाङ्घ्रिशिरःकरोरु-
नासाद्यकर्णनयनाभरणायुधाढ्यम् ।
मायामयं सदुपलक्षितसन्निवेशं
दृष्ट्वा महापुरुषमाप मुदं विरिञ्चः ॥३६॥

evaṁ sahasra-vadanāṅghri-śiraḥ-karoru-
nāsādya-karṇa-nayanābharaṇāyudhāḍhyam
māyāmayaṁ sad-upalakṣita-sanniveśaṁ
dṛṣṭvā mahā-puruṣam āpa mudaṁ viriñcaḥ

evam—in this way; *sahasra*—thousands and thousands; *vadana*—faces; *aṅghri*—feet; *śiraḥ*—heads; *kara*—hands; *uru*—thighs; *nāsa-ādya*—noses, etc.; *karṇa*—ears; *nayana*—eyes; *ābharaṇa*—varieties of ornaments; *āyudha*—varieties of weapons; *āḍhyam*—endowed with; *māyā-mayam*—all demonstrated by unlimited potency; *sat-upalakṣita*—appearing in different symptoms; *sanniveśam*—combined together; *dṛṣṭvā*—seeing; *mahā-puruṣam*—the Supreme Personality of Godhead; *āpa*—achieved; *mudam*—transcendental bliss; *viriñcaḥ*—Lord Brahmā.

TRANSLATION

Lord Brahmā could then see You possessing thousands and thousands of faces, feet, heads, hands, thighs, noses, ears and eyes. You were very nicely dressed, being decorated and bedecked with varieties of ornaments and weapons. Seeing You in the form of Lord Viṣṇu, Your symptoms and form being transcendental, Your legs extending from the lower planets, Lord Brahmā achieved transcendental bliss.

PURPORT

Lord Brahmā, being completely pure, could see the original form of the Lord as Viṣṇu, having many thousands of faces and forms. This process is called self-realization. Genuine self-realization consists not of perceiving the impersonal effulgence of the Lord, but seeing face to face the transcendental form of the Lord. As distinctly mentioned here, Lord Brahmā saw the Supreme Lord as *mahā-puruṣa*, the Supreme Personality of Godhead. Arjuna also saw Kṛṣṇa in this same way. Therefore he told the Lord, *paraṁ brahma paraṁ dhāma pavitraṁ paramaṁ bhavān puruṣaṁ śāśvataṁ divyam:* "You are the Supreme Brahman, the ultimate, the supreme abode and purifier, the Absolute Truth and the eternal divine person." The Lord is *parama-puruṣa*, the supreme form. *Puruṣaṁ śāśvatam:* He is everlastingly the supreme enjoyer. It is not that the impersonal Brahman assumes a form; on the contrary, the impersonal Brahman effulgence is an emanation from the supreme form of the Lord. Upon being purified, Brahmā could see the supreme form of the Lord. The impersonal Brahman cannot have heads, noses, ears, hands and legs. This is not possible, for these are attributes of the Lord's form.

The word *māyāmayam* means "spiritual knowledge." This is explained by Madhvācārya. *Māyāmayaṁ jñāna-svarūpam.* The word *māyāmayam*, describing the Lord's form, should not be taken to mean illusion. Rather, the Lord's form is factual, and seeing this form is the result of perfect knowledge. This is confirmed in *Bhagavad-gītā: bahūnāṁ janmanām ante jñānavān māṁ prapadyate.* The word *jñānavān* refers to one who is perfectly in knowledge. Such a person can see the Personality of Godhead, and therefore he surrenders unto the Lord. The Lord's being symptomized by a face, nose, ears and so on is eternal. Without such a form, no one can be blissful. The Lord, however, is *sac-cid-ānanda-vigraha*, as stated in the *śāstra* (*īśvaraḥ paramaḥ kṛṣṇaḥ sac-cid-ānanda-vigrahaḥ*). When one is in perfect transcendental bliss, he can see the Lord's supreme form (*vigraha*). In this regard, Śrīla Madhvācārya says:

gandhākhyā devatā yadvat
pṛthivīṁ vyāpya tiṣṭhati
evaṁ vyāptaṁ jagad viṣṇuṁ
brahmātma-sthaṁ dadarśa ha

Lord Brahmā saw that as aromas and colors spread throughout the earth, the Supreme Personality of Godhead pervades the cosmic manifestation in a subtle form.

TEXT 37

तस्मै भवान्हयशिरस्तनुवं हि बिभ्रद्
वेदद्रुहावतिबलौ मधुकैटभाख्यौ ।
हत्वानयच्छ्रुतिगणांश्च रजस्तमश्च
सत्त्वं तव प्रियतमां तनुमामनन्ति ॥३७॥

tasmai bhavān haya-śiras tanuvaṁ hi bibhrad
veda-druhāv atibalau madhu-kaiṭabhākhyau
hatvānayac chruti-gaṇāṁś ca rajas tamaś ca
sattvaṁ tava priyatamāṁ tanum āmananti

tasmai—unto Lord Brahmā; *bhavān*—Your Lordship; *haya-śiraḥ*—having the head and neck of a horse; *tanuvam*—the incarnation; *hi*—indeed; *bibhrat*—accepting; *veda-druhau*—two demons who were against the Vedic principles; *ati-balau*—extremely powerful; *madhu-kaiṭabha-ākhyau*—known as Madhu and Kaiṭabha; *hatvā*—killing; *anayat*—delivered; *śruti-gaṇān*—all the different *Vedas* (*Sāma*, *Yajur*, *Ṛg* and *Atharva*); *ca*—and; *rajaḥ tamaḥ ca*—by representing the modes of passion and ignorance; *sattvam*—pure transcendental goodness; *tava*—Your; *priya-tamām*—most dear; *tanum*—form (as Hayagrīva); *āmananti*—they honor.

TRANSLATION

My dear Lord, when You appeared as Hayagrīva, with the head of a horse, You killed two demons known as Madhu and Kaiṭabha, who were full of the modes of passion and ignorance. Then You delivered the Vedic knowledge to Lord Brahmā. For this reason, all the great saints accept Your forms as transcendental, untinged by material qualities.

PURPORT

The Supreme Personality of Godhead in His transcendental form is always ready to give protection to His devotees. As mentioned herein, the

Lord in the form of Hayagrīva killed two demons named Madhu and Kaiṭabha when they attacked Lord Brahmā. Modern demons think that there was no life in the beginning of creation, but from *Śrīmad-Bhāgavatam* we understand that the first living creature created by the Supreme Personality of Godhead was Lord Brahmā, who is full of Vedic understanding. Unfortunately, those entrusted with distributing Vedic knowledge, such as the devotees engaged in spreading Kṛṣṇa consciousness, may sometimes be attacked by demons, but they must rest assured that demoniac attacks will not be able to harm them, for the Lord is always prepared to give them protection. The *Vedas* provide the knowledge by which we can understand the Supreme Personality of Godhead (*vedaiś ca sarvair aham eva vedyaḥ*). The devotees of the Lord are always ready to spread knowledge by which one may understand the Lord through Kṛṣṇa consciousness, but the demons, being unable to understand the Supreme Lord, are full of ignorance and passion. Thus the Lord, whose form is transcendental, is always ready to kill the demons. By culturing the mode of goodness, one can understand the position of the transcendental Lord and how the Lord is always prepared to remove all obstacles on the path of understanding Him.

In summary, whenever the Lord incarnates, He appears in His original transcendental form. As the Lord says in *Bhagavad-gītā* (4.7):

yadā yadā hi dharmasya
glānir bhavati bhārata
abhyutthānam adharmasya
tadātmānaṁ sṛjāmy aham

"Whenever and wherever there is a decline in religious practice, O descendent of Bharata, and a predominant rise of irreligion—at that time I descend Myself." It is simply foolish to think of the Lord as being originally impersonal but accepting a material body when He appears as a personal incarnation. Whenever the Lord appears, He appears in His original transcendental form, which is spiritual and blissful. But unintelligent men, such as the Māyāvādīs, cannot understand the transcendental form of the Lord, and therefore the Lord chastises them by saying, *avajānanti māṁ mūḍhā mānuṣīṁ tanum āśritam:* "Fools deride

Me when I descend in the human form." Whenever the Lord appears, whether as a fish, a tortoise, a hog or any other form, one should understand that He maintains His transcendental position and that His only business, as stated here, is *hatvā*—to kill the demons. The Lord appears in order to protect the devotees and kill the demons (*paritrāṇāya sādhūnāṁ vināśāya ca duṣkṛtām*). Since the demons are always ready to oppose Vedic civilization, they are sure to be killed by the transcendental form of the Lord.

TEXT 38

इत्थं नृतिर्यगृषिदेवझषावतारै-
लोकान् विभावयसि हंसि जगत्प्रतीपान् ।
धर्मं महापुरुष पासि युगानुवृत्तं
छन्नः कलौ यदभवस्त्रियुगोऽथ स त्वम् ॥३८॥

itthaṁ nṛ-tiryag-ṛṣi-deva-jhaṣāvatārair
lokān vibhāvayasi haṁsi jagat pratīpān
dharmaṁ mahā-puruṣa pāsi yugānuvṛttaṁ
channaḥ kalau yad abhavas tri-yugo 'tha sa tvam

ittham—in this way; *nṛ*—like a human being (such as Lord Kṛṣṇa and Lord Rāmacandra); *tiryak*—like animals (such as the boar); *ṛṣi*—as a great saint (Paraśurāma); *deva*—as demigods; *jhaṣa*—as an aquatic (such as the fish and tortoise); *avatāraiḥ*—by such different incarnations; *lokān*—all the different planetary systems; *vibhāvayasi*—You protect; *haṁsi*—You (sometimes) kill; *jagat pratīpān*—persons who have simply created trouble in this world; *dharmam*—the principles of religion; *mahā-puruṣa*—O great personality; *pāsi*—You protect; *yuga-anuvṛttam*—according to the different millenniums; *channaḥ*—covered; *kalau*—in the age of Kali; *yat*—since; *abhavaḥ*—have been (and will be in the future); *tri-yugaḥ*—named Triyuga; *atha*—therefore; *saḥ*—the same personality; *tvam*—You.

TRANSLATION

In this way, my Lord, You appear in various incarnations as a human being, an animal, a great saint, a demigod, a fish or a

tortoise, thus maintaining the entire creation in different planetary systems and killing the demoniac principles. According to the age, O my Lord, You protect the principles of religion. In the age of Kali, however, You do not assert Yourself as the Supreme Personality of Godhead, and therefore You are known as Triyuga, or the Lord who appears in three yugas.

PURPORT

As the Lord appeared just to maintain Lord Brahmā from the attack of Madhu and Kaiṭabha, He also appeared to protect the great devotee Prahlāda Mahārāja. Similarly, Lord Caitanya appeared in order to protect the fallen souls of Kali-yuga. There are four *yugas*, or millenniums—Satya, Tretā, Dvāpara and Kali. In all the *yugas* but Kali-yuga, the Lord appears in various incarnations and asserts Himself as the Supreme Personality of Godhead, but although Lord Śrī Caitanya Mahāprabhu, who appears in Kali-yuga, is the Supreme Personality of Godhead, He never asserted Himself as such. On the contrary, whenever Śrī Caitanya Mahāprabhu was addressed as being as good as Kṛṣṇa, He blocked His ears with His hands, denying His identity with Kṛṣṇa, because He was playing the part of a devotee. Lord Caitanya knew that in Kali-yuga there would be many bogus incarnations pretending to be God, and therefore He avoided asserting Himself as the Supreme Personality of Godhead. Lord Caitanya Mahāprabhu is accepted as the Supreme Personality of Godhead, however, in many Vedic literatures, especially in *Śrīmad-Bhāgavatam* (11.5.32):

kṛṣṇa-varṇaṁ tviṣākṛṣṇaṁ
sāṅgopāṅgāstra-pārṣadam
yajñaiḥ saṅkīrtana-prāyair
yajanti hi sumedhasaḥ

In Kali-yuga, intelligent men worship the Supreme Personality of Godhead in the form of Śrī Caitanya Mahāprabhu, who is always accompanied by His associates such as Nityānanda, Advaita, Gadādhara and Śrīvāsa. The entire Kṛṣṇa consciousness movement is based on the principles of the *saṅkīrtana* movement inaugurated by Śrī Caitanya Mahāprabhu. Therefore one who tries to understand the Supreme Personality of Godhead through the medium of the *saṅkīrtana* movement knows everything perfectly. He is *sumedhas*, a person with substantial intelligence.

TEXT 39

नैतन्मनस्तव कथासु विकुण्ठनाथ
सम्प्रीयते दुरितदुष्टमसाधु तीव्रम् ।
कामातुरं हर्षशोकभयैषणार्तं
तस्मिन्कथं तव गतिं विमृशामि दीनः ॥३९॥

naitan manas tava kathāsu vikuṇṭha-nātha
samprīyate durita-duṣṭam asādhu tīvram
kāmāturaṁ harṣa-śoka-bhayaiṣaṇārtaṁ
tasmin kathaṁ tava gatiṁ vimṛśāmi dīnaḥ

na—certainly not; *etat*—this; *manaḥ*—mind; *tava*—Your; *kathāsu*—in transcendental topics; *vikuṇṭha-nātha*—O Lord of Vaikuṇṭha, where there is no anxiety; *samprīyate*—is pacified or interested in; *durita*—by sinful activities; *duṣṭam*—polluted; *asādhu*—dishonest; *tīvram*—very difficult to control; *kāma-āturam*—always full of different desires and lusty propensities; *harṣa-śoka*—sometimes by jubilation and sometimes by distress; *bhaya*—and sometimes by fear; *eṣaṇā*—and by desiring; *ārtam*—distressed; *tasmin*—in that mental status; *katham*—how; *tava*—Your; *gatim*—transcendental activities; *vimṛśāmi*—I shall consider and try to understand; *dīnaḥ*—who am most fallen and poor.

TRANSLATION

My dear Lord of the Vaikuṇṭha planets, where there is no anxiety, my mind is extremely sinful and lusty, being sometimes so-called happy and sometimes so-called distressed. My mind is full of lamentation and fear, and it always seeks more and more money. Thus it has become most polluted and is never satisfied in topics concerning You. I am therefore most fallen and poor. In such a status of life, how shall I be able to discuss Your activities?

PURPORT

Here Prahlāda Mahārāja represents himself as a common man, although he actually has nothing to do with this material world. Prahlāda is always situated in the Vaikuṇṭha planets of the spiritual world, but on behalf of the fallen souls he asks how, when his mind is always disturbed by material things, he can discuss the transcendental position of the Lord. The mind becomes sinful because we are always engaged in sinful activities. Anything not connected with Kṛṣṇa consciousness should be understood to be sinful. Indeed, Kṛṣṇa demands in *Bhagavad-gītā* (18.66):

sarva-dharmān parityajya
mām ekaṁ śaraṇaṁ vraja
ahaṁ tvāṁ sarva-pāpebhyo
mokṣayiṣyāmi mā śucaḥ

"Abandon all varieties of religion and just surrender unto Me. I shall deliver you from all sinful reaction. Do not fear." As soon as one surrenders unto the Supreme Personality of Godhead, Kṛṣṇa, Kṛṣṇa immediately relieves one of the reactions of sinful activities. Therefore one who is not surrendered to the lotus feet of the Lord should be understood to be sinful, foolish, degraded among men and bereft of all real knowledge because of atheistic propensities. This is confirmed in *Bhagavad-gītā* (7.15):

na māṁ duṣkṛtino mūḍhāḥ
pradyante narādhamāḥ
māyayāpahṛta-jñānā
āsuraṁ bhāvam āśritāḥ

Therefore, especially in this age of Kali, the mind must be cleansed, and this is possible only by the chanting of the Hare Kṛṣṇa *mahā-mantra. Ceto-darpaṇa-mārjanam.* In this age, the process of chanting the Hare Kṛṣṇa *mahā-mantra* is the only method by which to cleanse the sinful mind. When the mind is completely cleansed of all sinful reactions, one can then understand his duty in the human form of life. The Kṛṣṇa consciousness movement is meant to educate sinful men so that they may become pious simply by chanting the Hare Kṛṣṇa *mahā-mantra.*

harer nāma harer nāma
harer nāmaiva kevalam
kalau nāsty eva nāsty eva
nāsty eva gatir anyathā

To cleanse the heart so that one may become sober and wise in this age of Kali, there is no value to any method other than the chanting of the Hare Kṛṣṇa *mahā-mantra*. Prahlāda Mahārāja has confirmed this process in previous verses. *Tvad-vīrya-gāyana-mahāmṛta-magna-cittaḥ*. Prahlāda further confirms that if one's mind is always absorbed in thought of Kṛṣṇa, that very qualification will purify one and keep one purified always. To understand the Lord and His activities, one must free his mind from all contamination of the material world, and this one can achieve by simply chanting the Lord's holy name. Thus one becomes free from all material bondage.

TEXT 40

जिह्वैकतोऽच्युत विकर्षति मावितृप्ता
शिश्नोऽन्यतस्त्वगुदरं श्रवणं कुतश्चित् ।
घ्राणोऽन्यतश्चपलदृक् क्व च कर्मशक्ति-
र्बह्व्यः सपत्न्य इव गेहपतिं लुनन्ति ॥४०॥

jihvaikato 'cyuta vikarṣati māvitṛptā
śiśno 'nyatas tvag-udaraṁ śravaṇaṁ kutaścit
ghrāṇo 'nyataś capala-dṛk kva ca karma-śaktir
bahvyaḥ sapatnya iva geha-patiṁ lunanti

jihvā—the tongue; *ekataḥ*—to one side; *acyuta*—O my infallible Lord; *vikarṣati*—attracts; *mā*—me; *avitṛptā*—not being satisfied; *śiśnaḥ*—the genitals; *anyataḥ*—to another side; *tvak*—the skin (for touching a soft thing); *udaram*—the belly (for various types of food); *śravaṇam*—the ear (for hearing some sweet music); *kutaścit*—to some other side; *ghrāṇaḥ*—the nose (for smelling); *anyataḥ*—to still another side; *capala-dṛk*—the restless eyesight; *kva ca*—somewhere; *karma-śaktiḥ*—the active senses; *bahvyaḥ*—many; *sa-patnyaḥ*—co-wives; *iva*—like; *geha-patim*—a householder; *lunanti*—annihilate.

TRANSLATION

My dear Lord, O infallible one, my position is like that of a person who has many wives, all trying to attract him in their own way. For example, the tongue is attracted to palatable dishes, the genitals to sex with an attractive woman, and the sense of touch to contact with soft things. The belly, although filled, still wants to eat more, and the ear, not attempting to hear about You, is generally attracted to cinema songs. The sense of smell is attracted to yet another side, the restless eyes are attracted to scenes of sense gratification, and the active senses are attracted elsewhere. In this way I am certainly embarrassed.

PURPORT

The human form of life is meant for God realization, but this process, which begins with *śravaṇaṁ kīrtanaṁ viṣṇoḥ*—hearing and chanting of the holy name of the Lord—is disturbed as long as our senses are materially attracted. Therefore devotional service means purifying the senses. In the conditioned state our senses are covered by material sense gratification, and as long as one is not trained in purifying the senses, one cannot become a devotee. In our Kṛṣṇa consciousness movement, therefore, we advise from the very beginning that one restrict the activities of the senses, especially the tongue, which is described by Śrīla Bhaktivinoda Ṭhākura as most greedy and unconquerable. To stop this attraction of the tongue, one is authoritatively advised not to accept meat or similar uneatable things nor to allow the tongue to hanker to drink or smoke. Even the drinking of tea and coffee is not permitted. Similarly, the genitals must be restricted from illicit sex. Without such restraint of the senses, one cannot make advancement in Kṛṣṇa consciousness. The only method of controlling the senses is to chant and hear the holy name of the Lord; otherwise, one will always be disturbed, as a householder with more than one wife would be disturbed by them for sense gratification.

TEXT 41

एवं स्वकर्मपतितं भववैतरण्या-
मन्योन्यजन्ममरणाशनभीतभीतम् ।

पश्यञ्जनं स्वपरविग्रहवैरमैत्रं
हन्तेति पारचर पीपृहि मूढमद्य ॥४१॥

evaṁ sva-karma-patitaṁ bhava-vaitaraṇyām
anyonya-janma-maraṇāśana-bhīta-bhītam
paśyañ janaṁ sva-para-vigraha-vaira-maitraṁ
hanteti pāracara pīpṛhi mūḍham adya

evam—in this way; *sva-karma-patitam*—fallen because of the reactions of one's own material activities; *bhava*—compared to the world of nescience (birth, death, old age and disease); *vaitaraṇyām*—in the river known as Vaitaraṇī (which lies in front of the doorway of Yamarāja, the superintendant of death); *anyaḥ anya*—one after another; *janma*—birth; *maraṇa*—death; *āśana*—different types of eating; *bhīta-bhītam*—being exceedingly afraid; *paśyan*—seeing; *janam*—the living entity; *sva*—one's own; *para*—of others; *vigraha*—in the body; *vaira-maitram*—considering friendship and enmity; *hanta*—alas; *iti*—in this way; *pāracara*—O You, who are on the other side of the river of death; *pīpṛhi*—kindly save us all (from this dangerous condition); *mūḍham*—we are all foolish, bereft of spiritual knowledge; *adya*—today (because You are personally present here).

TRANSLATION

My dear Lord, You are always transcendentally situated on the other side of the river of death, but because of the reactions of our own activities, we are suffering on this side. Indeed, we have fallen into this river and are repeatedly suffering the pains of birth and death and eating horrible things. Now kindly look upon us—not only upon me but also upon all others who are suffering—and by Your causeless mercy and compassion, deliver us and maintain us.

PURPORT

Prahlāda Mahārāja, a pure Vaiṣṇava, prays to the Lord not only for himself but for all other suffering living entities. There are two classes of Vaiṣṇavas—the *bhajanānandīs* and *goṣṭhy-ānandīs*. The *bhajanānandīs* worship the Lord only for their own personal benefit, but the *goṣṭhy-ānandīs* try to elevate all others to Kṛṣṇa consciousness so that they may be saved. Fools who cannot perceive repeated birth and death and the other miseries of materialistic life cannot be sure of what will happen to them in their next birth. Indeed, these foolish, materially contaminated rascals have manufactured an irresponsible way of life that does not consider the next life. They do not know that according to one's own activities, one receives a body selected from 8,400,000 species. These rascals have been described in *Bhagavad-gītā* as *duṣkṛtino mūḍhāḥ.* Nondevotees, those who are not Kṛṣṇa conscious, must engage in sinful activities, and therefore they are *mūḍhas*—fools and rascals. They are such fools that they do not know what will happen to them in their next life. Although they see varieties of living creatures eating abominable things—pigs eating stool, crocodiles eating all kinds of flesh, and so on—they do not realize that they themselves, because of their practice of eating all kinds of nonsense in this life, will be destined to eat the most abominable things in their next life. A Vaiṣṇava is always afraid of such an abominable life, and to free himself from such horrible conditions, he engages himself in the devotional service of the Lord. The Lord is compassionate to them, and therefore He appears for their benefit.

yadā yadā hi dharmasya
glānir bhavati bhārata
abhyutthānam adharmasya
tadātmānaṁ sṛjāmy aham

"Whenever and wherever there is a decline in religious practice, O descendant of Bharata, and a predominant rise of irreligion—at that time I descend Myself." (Bg. 4.7) The Lord is always ready to help the fallen souls, but because they are fools and rascals, they do not take to Kṛṣṇa consciousness and abide by the instructions of Kṛṣṇa. Therefore although Śrī Caitanya Mahāprabhu is personally the Supreme Lord, Kṛṣṇa, He comes as a devotee to preach the Kṛṣṇa consciousness movement. *Yāre dekha, tāre kaha 'kṛṣṇa'-upadeśa.* One must therefore become a sincere servant of Kṛṣṇa. *Āmāra ājñāya guru hañā tāra' ei deśa* (Cc. *Madhya* 7.128). One should become a *guru* and spread Kṛṣṇa consciousness all over the world, simply by preaching the teachings of *Bhagavad-gītā.*

TEXT 42

को न्वत्र तेऽखिलगुरो भगवन्प्रयास
उत्तारणेऽस्य भवसम्भवलोपहेतोः ।
मूढेषु वै महदनुग्रह आर्तबन्धो
किं तेन ते प्रियजनाननुसेवतां नः ॥४२॥

ko nv atra te 'khila-guro bhagavan prayāsa
uttāraṇe 'sya bhava-sambhava-lopa-hetoḥ
mūḍheṣu vai mahad-anugraha ārta-bandho
kiṁ tena te priya-janān anusevatāṁ naḥ

kaḥ—what is that; *nu*—indeed; *atra*—in this matter; *te*—of Your Lordship; *akhila-guro*—O supreme spiritual master of the entire creation; *bhagavan*—O Supreme Lord, O Personality of Godhead; *prayāsaḥ*—endeavor; *uttāraṇe*—for the deliverance of these fallen souls; *asya*—of this; *bhava-sambhava*—of creation and maintenance; *lopa*—and of annihilation; *hetoḥ*—of the cause; *mūḍheṣu*—unto the foolish persons rotting in this material world; *vai*—indeed; *mahat-anugrahaḥ*—compassion by the Supreme; *ārta-bandho*—O friend of the suffering living entities; *kim*—what is the difficulty; *tena*—with that; *te*—of Your Lordship; *priya-janān*—the dear persons (devotees); *anusevatām*—of those always engaged in serving; *naḥ*—like us (who are so engaged).

TRANSLATION

O my Lord, O Supreme Personality of Godhead, original spiritual master of the entire world, what is the difficulty for You, who manage the affairs of the universe, in delivering the fallen souls engaged in Your devotional service? You are the friend of all suffering humanity, and for great personalities it is necessary to show mercy to the foolish. Therefore I think that You will show Your causeless mercy to persons like us, who engage in Your service.

PURPORT

Here the words *priya-janān anusevatāṁ naḥ* indicate that the Supreme Lord, the Supreme Personality of Godhead, is very favorable to devotees who act according to the instructions of His own pure devotee. In other words, one must become the servant of the servant of the servant of the Lord. If one wants to become the servant of the Lord directly, this is not as fruitful as engaging in the service of the Lord's servant. This is the direction of Śrī Caitanya Mahāprabhu, who shows us the way to become *gopī-bhartuḥ pada-kamalayor dāsa-dāsānudāsaḥ*. One should not be proud of becoming directly the servant of the Supreme Personality of Godhead. Rather, one must seek a pure devotee, a servant of the Lord, and engage oneself in the service of such a servant. The more one becomes the servant of the servant, the more one becomes perfect in devotional service. This is also the injunction of *Bhagavad-gītā: evaṁ paramparā-prāptam imaṁ rājarṣayo viduḥ*. One can understand the science of the Supreme Personality of Godhead simply by the *paramparā* system. In this regard, Śrīla Narottama dāsa Ṭhākura says, *tāṅdera caraṇa sevi bhakta-sane vāsa:* "Let me serve the lotus feet of the devotees of the Lord, and let me live with devotees." *Janame janame haya, ei abhilāṣa*. Following Narottama dāsa Ṭhākura, one should aspire to be a servant of the Lord's servant, life after life. Śrīla Bhaktivinoda Ṭhākura also sings, *tumi ta' ṭhākura, tomāra kukura, baliyā jānaha more:* "O my Lord, O Vaiṣṇava, please consider me your dog." One must become the dog of a Vaiṣṇava, a pure devotee, for a pure devotee can deliver Kṛṣṇa without difficulty. *Kṛṣṇa se tomāra, kṛṣṇa dite pāra*. Kṛṣṇa is the property of His pure devotee, and if we take shelter of a pure devotee, he can deliver Kṛṣṇa very easily. Prahlāda wants to engage in the service of a devotee, and therefore he prays to Kṛṣṇa, "My dear Lord, kindly give me the shelter of Your very dear devotee so that I may engage in his service and You may then be pleased." *Mad-bhakta-pūjābhyadhikā* (*Bhāg*. 11.19.21). The Lord says, "Engaging in the service of My devotee is better than trying to engage in My devotional service."

Another significant point in this verse is that by devotional service Prahlāda Mahārāja does not want to benefit alone. Rather, he prays to the Lord that all of us fallen souls in this material world may, by the grace of the Lord, engage in the service of His servant and thus be delivered. The grace of the Lord is not at all difficult for the Lord to bestow, and thus Prahlāda Mahārāja wants to save the whole world by spreading Kṛṣṇa consciousness.

TEXT 43

नैवोद्विजे पर दुरत्ययवैतरण्या-
स्त्वद्वीर्यगायनमहामृतमग्नचित्तः ।
शोचे ततो विमुखचेतस इन्द्रियार्थ-
मायासुखाय भरमुद्वहतो विमूढान् ॥४३॥

naivodvije para duratyaya-vaitaraṇyās
tvad-vīrya-gāyana-mahāmṛta-magna-cittaḥ
śoce tato vimukha-cetasa indriyārtha-
māyā-sukhāya bharam udvahato vimūḍhān

na—not; *eva*—certainly; *udvije*—I am disturbed or afraid; *para*—O Supreme; *duratyaya*—insurmountable or very difficult to cross; *vaitaraṇyāḥ*—of the Vaitaraṇī, the river of the material world; *tvat-vīrya*—of Your Lordship's glories and activities; *gāyana*—from chanting or distributing; *mahā-amṛta*—in the great ocean of nectarean spiritual bliss; *magna-cittaḥ*—whose consciousness is absorbed; *śoce*—I am simply lamenting; *tataḥ*—from that; *vimukha-cetasaḥ*—the fools and rascals who are bereft of Kṛṣṇa consciousness; *indriya-artha*—in sense gratification; *māyā-sukhāya*—for temporary, illusory happiness; *bharam*—the false burden or responsibility (of maintaining one's family, society and nation and elaborate arrangements for that purpose); *udvahataḥ*—who are lifting (by making grand plans for this arrangement); *vimūḍhān*—although all of them are nothing but fools and rascals (I am thinking of them also).

TRANSLATION

O best of the great personalities, I am not at all afraid of material existence, for wherever I stay I am fully absorbed in thoughts of Your glories and activities. My concern is only for the fools and rascals who are making elaborate plans for material happiness and maintaining their families, societies and countries. I am simply concerned with love for them.

PURPORT

Throughout the entire world, everyone is making big, big plans to adjust the miseries of the material world, and this is true at present, in the past and in the future. Nonetheless, although they make elaborate political, social and cultural plans, they have all been described herein as *vimūḍha*—fools. The material world has been described in *Bhagavad-gītā* as *duḥkhālayam aśāśvatam*—temporary and miserable—but these fools are trying to turn the material world into *sukhālayam*, a place of happiness, not knowing how everything acts by the arrangement of material nature, which works in her own way.

prakṛteḥ kriyamāṇāni
guṇaiḥ karmāṇi sarvaśaḥ
ahaṅkāra-vimūḍhātmā
kartāham iti manyate

"The bewildered spirit soul, under the influence of the three modes of material nature, thinks himself to be the doer of activities that are in actuality carried out by nature." (Bg. 3.27)

There is a plan for material nature, personally known as Durgā, to punish the demons. Although the *asuras*, the godless demons, struggle for existence, they are directly attacked by the goddess Durgā, who is well equipped with ten hands with different types of weapons to punish them. She is carried by her lion carrier, or the modes of passion and ignorance. Everyone struggles very hard to fight through the modes of passion and ignorance and conquer material nature, but at the end everyone is vanquished by nature's laws.

There is a river known as Vaitaraṇī between the material and spiritual worlds, and one must cross this river to reach the other side, or the spiritual world. This is an extremely difficult task. As the Lord says in *Bhagavad-gītā* (7.14), *daivī hy eṣā guṇamayī mama māyā duratyayā:* "This divine energy of Mine, consisting of the three modes of material nature, is difficult to overcome." The same word *duratyaya*, meaning "very difficult," is used here. Therefore one cannot surpass the stringent laws of material nature except by the mercy of the Supreme Lord. Nonetheless, although all materialists are baffled in their plans, they try again and again to become happy in this material world. Therefore they have been described as *vimūḍha*—first-class fools. As for Prahlāda Mahārāja, he was not at all unhappy, for although he was in the material world, he was full of Kṛṣṇa consciousness. Those who are Kṛṣṇa conscious, trying to serve the Lord, are not unhappy, whereas one who has no assets in Kṛṣṇa consciousness and is struggling for existence is not only foolish but extremely unhappy also. Prahlāda Mahārāja was happy and unhappy simultaneously. He felt happiness and transcendental bliss because of his being Kṛṣṇa conscious, yet he felt great unhappiness for the fools and rascals who make elaborate plans to be happy in this material world.

TEXT 44

प्रायेण देव मुनयः स्वविमुक्तिकामा
मौनं चरन्ति विजने न परार्थनिष्ठाः ।
नैतान्विहाय कृपणान्विमुमुक्ष एको
नान्यं त्वदस्य शरणं भ्रमतोऽनुपश्ये ॥४४॥

prāyeṇa deva munayaḥ sva-vimukti-kāmā
maunaṁ caranti vijane na parārtha-niṣṭhāḥ
naitān vihāya kṛpaṇān vimumukṣa eko
nānyaṁ tvad asya śaraṇaṁ bhramato 'nupaśye

prāyeṇa—generally, in almost all cases; *deva*—O my Lord; *munayaḥ*—the great saintly persons; *sva*—personal, own; *vimukti-kāmāḥ*—ambitious for liberation from this material world; *maunam*—silently; *caranti*—they wander (in places like the Himalayan forests, where they have no touch with the activities of the materialists); *vijane*—in solitary places; *na*—not; *para-artha-niṣṭhāḥ*—interested in working for others by giving them the benefit of the Kṛṣṇa consciousness movement, by enlightening them with Kṛṣṇa consciousness; *na*—not; *etān*—these; *vihāya*—leaving aside; *kṛpaṇān*—fools and rascals (engaged in materialistic activity who do not know the benefit of the human form of life); *vimumukṣe*—I desire to be liberated and to return home, back to Godhead; *ekaḥ*—alone; *na*—not; *anyam*—other; *tvat*—but for You; *asya*—of this; *śaraṇam*—shelter; *bhramataḥ*—of the living entity rotating and wandering throughout the material universes; *anupaśye*—do I see.

TRANSLATION

My dear Lord Nṛsiṁhadeva, I see that there are many saintly persons indeed, but they are interested only in their own deliverance. Not caring for the big cities and towns, they go to the Himalayas or the forest to meditate with vows of silence [mauna-vrata]. They are not interested in delivering others. As for me, however, I do not wish to be liberated alone, leaving aside all these poor fools and rascals. I know that without Kṛṣṇa consciousness, without taking shelter of Your lotus feet, one cannot be happy. Therefore I wish to bring them back to shelter at Your lotus feet.

PURPORT

This is the decision of the Vaiṣṇava, the pure devotee of the Lord. For himself he has no problems, even if he has to stay in this material world, because his only business is to remain in Kṛṣṇa consciousness. The Kṛṣṇa conscious person can go even to hell and still be happy. Therefore Prahlāda Mahārāja said, *naivodvije para duratyaya-vaitaraṇyāḥ:* "O best of the great personalities, I am not at all afraid of material existence." The pure devotee is never unhappy in any condition of life. This is confirmed in *Śrīmad-Bhāgavatam* (6.17.28):

nārāyaṇa-parāḥ sarve
na kutaścana bibhyati
svargāpavarga-narakeṣv
api tulyārtha-darśinaḥ

"Devotees solely engaged in the devotional service of the Supreme Personality of Godhead, Nārāyaṇa, never fear any condition of life. For them the heavenly planets, liberation and the hellish planets are all the same, for such devotees are interested only in the service of the Lord."

For a devotee, being situated in the heavenly planets and being in the hellish planets are equal, for a devotee lives neither in heaven nor in hell but with Kṛṣṇa in the spiritual world. The secret of success for the devotee is not understood by the *karmīs* and *jñānīs. Karmīs* therefore try to be happy by material adjustment, and *jñānīs* want to be happy by becoming one with the Supreme. The devotee has no such interest. He is not interested in so-called meditation in the Himalayas or the forest. Rather, his interest is in the busiest part of the world, where he teaches people Kṛṣṇa consciousness. The Kṛṣṇa consciousness movement was started for this purpose. We do not teach one to meditate in a secluded place just so that one may show that he has become very much advanced and may be proud of his so-called transcendental meditation, although he engages in all sorts of foolish materialistic activity. A Vaiṣṇava like Prahlāda Mahārāja is not interested in such a bluff of spiritual advancement. Rather, he is interested in enlightening people in Kṛṣṇa consciousness because that is the only way for them to become happy. Prahlāda Mahārāja says clearly, *nānyaṁ tvad asya śaraṇaṁ bhramato 'nupaśye:* "I know that without Kṛṣṇa consciousness, without taking shelter of Your lotus feet, one cannot be happy." One wanders within the universe, life after life, but by the grace of a devotee, a servant of Śrī Caitanya Mahāprabhu, one can get the clue to Kṛṣṇa consciousness and then not only become happy in this world but also return home, back to Godhead. That is the real target in life. The members of the Kṛṣṇa consciousness movement are not at all interested in so-called meditation in the Himalayas or the forest, where one will only make a show of meditation, nor are they interested in opening many schools for *yoga* and meditation in the cities. Rather, every member of the Kṛṣṇa consciousness movement is interested in going door to door to try to convince people about the teachings of *Bhagavad-gītā As It Is*, the teachings of Lord Caitanya. That is the purpose of the Hare Kṛṣṇa movement. The members of the Kṛṣṇa consciousness movement must be fully convinced that without Kṛṣṇa one cannot be happy. Thus the Kṛṣṇa conscious person avoids all kinds of pseudo spiritualists, transcendentalists, meditators, monists, philosophers and philanthropists.

TEXT 45

यन्मैथुनादि गृहमेधिसुखं हि तुच्छं
कण्डूयनेन करयोरिव दुःखदुःखम् ।
तृप्यन्ति नेह कृपणा बहुदुःखभाजः
कण्डूतिवन्मनसिजं विषहेत धीरः ॥४५॥

yan maithunādi-gṛhamedhi-sukhaṁ hi tucchaṁ
kaṇḍūyanena karayor iva duḥkha-duḥkham

tṛpyanti neha kṛpaṇā bahu-duḥkha-bhājaḥ
kaṇḍūtivan manasijaṁ viṣaheta dhīraḥ

yat—that which (is meant for material sense gratification); *maithuna-ādi*—represented by talking of sex, reading sexual literature or enjoying sex life (at home or outside, as in a club); *gṛhamedhi-sukham*—all types of material happiness based on attachment to family, society, friendship, etc.; *hi*—indeed; *tuccham*—insignificant; *kaṇḍūyanena*—with the itching; *karayoḥ*—of the two hands (to relieve the itching); *iva*—like; *duḥkha-duḥkham*—different types of unhappiness (into which one is put after such itching sense gratification); *tṛpyanti*—become satisfied; *na*—never; *iha*—in material sense gratification; *kṛpaṇāḥ*—the foolish persons; *bahu-duḥkha-bhājaḥ*—subjected to various types of material unhappiness; *kaṇḍūti-vat*—if one can learn from such itching; *manasi-jam*—which is simply a mental concoction (actually there is no happiness); *viṣaheta*—and tolerates (such itching); *dhīraḥ*—(he can become) a most perfect, sober person.

TRANSLATION

Sex life is compared to the rubbing of two hands to relieve an itch. Gṛhamedhis, so-called gṛhasthas who have no spiritual knowledge, think that this itching is the greatest platform of happiness, although actually it is a source of distress. The kṛpaṇas, the fools who are just the opposite of brāhmaṇas, are not satisfied by repeated sensuous enjoyment. Those who are dhīra, however, who are sober and who tolerate this itching, are not subjected to the sufferings of fools and rascals.

PURPORT

Materialists think that sexual indulgence is the greatest happiness in this material world, and therefore they make elaborate plans to satisfy their senses, especially the genitals. This is generally found everywhere, and specifically found in the Western world, where there are regular arrangements to satisfy sex life in different ways. Actually, however, this has not made anyone happy. Even the hippies, who have given up all the materialistic comforts of their fathers and grandfathers, cannot give up the sensational happiness of sex life. Such persons are described here as *kṛpaṇas*, misers. The human form of life is a great asset, for in this life one can fulfill the goal of existence. Unfortunately, however, because of a lack of education and culture, people are victimized by the false happiness of sex life. Prahlāda Mahārāja therefore advises one not to be misled by this civilization of sense gratification, and especially not by sex life. Rather, one should be sober, avoid sense gratification and be Kṛṣṇa conscious. The lusty person, who is compared to a foolish miser, never gets happiness by sense gratification. The influence of material nature is very difficult to surpass, but as stated by Kṛṣṇa in *Bhagavad-gītā* (7.14), *mām eva ye prapadyante, māyām etāṁ taranti te:* if one voluntarily submits to the lotus feet of Kṛṣṇa, he can be saved very easily.

In reference to the low-grade happiness of sex life, Yāmunācārya says in this connection:

yadāvadhi mama cetaḥ kṛṣṇa-padāravinde
nava-nava-rasa-dhāmanudyata rantum āsīt
tadāvadhi bata nārī-saṅgame smaryamāne
bhavati mukha-vikāraḥ suṣṭu niṣṭhīvanaṁ ca

"Since I have been engaged in the transcendental loving service of Kṛṣṇa, realizing ever-new pleasure in Him, whenever I think of sex pleasure, I spit at the thought, and my lips curl with distaste." Yāmunācārya had formerly been a great king who enjoyed sexual happiness in various ways, but since he later engaged himself in the service of the Lord, he enjoyed spiritual bliss and hated to think of sex life. If sexual thoughts came to him, he would spit with disgust.

TEXT 46

मौनव्रतश्रुततपोऽध्ययनस्वधर्म-
व्याख्यारहोजपसमाधय आपवर्ग्याः ।
प्रायः परं पुरुष ते त्वजितेन्द्रियाणां
वार्ता भवन्त्युत न वात्र तु दाम्भिकानाम् ॥४६॥

mauna-vrata-śruta-tapo-'dhyayana-sva-dharma-
vyākhyā-raho-japa-samādhaya āpavargyāḥ
prāyaḥ paraṁ puruṣa te tv ajitendriyāṇāṁ
vārtā bhavanty uta na vātra tu dāmbhikānām

mauna—silence; *vrata*—vows; *śruta*—Vedic knowledge; *tapaḥ*—austerity; *adhyayana*—study of scripture; *sva-dharma*—executing *varṇāśrama-dharma; vyākhyā*—explaining the *śāstras; rahaḥ*—living in a solitary place; *japa*—chanting or reciting *mantras; samādhayaḥ*—remaining in trance; *āpavargyāḥ*—these are ten types of activities for advancing on the path of liberation; *prāyaḥ*—generally; *param*—the only means; *puruṣa*—O my Lord; *te*—all of them; *tu*—but; *ajita-indriyāṇām*—of persons who cannot control the senses; *vārtāḥ*—means of living; *bhavanti*—are; *uta*—so it is said; *na*—not; *vā*—or; *atra*—in this connection; *tu*—but; *dāmbhikānām*—of persons who are falsely proud.

TRANSLATION

O Supreme Personality of Godhead, there are ten prescribed methods on the path to liberation—to remain silent, not to speak to anyone, to observe vows, to amass all kinds of Vedic knowledge, to undergo austerities, to study the Vedas and other Vedic literatures, to execute the duties of varṇāśrama-dharma, to explain the śāstras, to stay in a solitary place, to chant mantras silently, and to be absorbed in trance. These different methods for liberation are generally only a professional practice and means of livelihood for those who have not conquered their senses. Because such persons are falsely proud, these procedures may not be successful.

PURPORT

As stated in *Śrīmad-Bhāgavatam* (6.1.15):

kecit kevalayā bhaktyā
vāsudeva-parāyaṇāḥ
aghaṁ dhunvanti kārtsnyena
nīhāram iva bhāskaraḥ

"Only a rare person who has adopted complete, unalloyed devotional service to Kṛṣṇa can uproot the weeds of sinful actions with no possibility that they will revive. He can do this simply by discharging devotional service, just as the sun can immediately dissipate fog by its rays." The real purpose of human life is to attain liberation from material entanglement. Such liberation may be achieved by many methods (*tapasā brahmacaryeṇa śamena ca damena ca*), but all of them more or less depend on *tapasya*, austerity, which begins with celibacy. Śukadeva Gosvāmī says that those who are *vāsudeva-parāyaṇa*, who have fully surrendered to the lotus feet of Lord Vāsudeva, Kṛṣṇa, automatically achieve the results of *mauna* (silence), *vrata* (vows) and other such methods simply by discharging devotional service. In other words, these methods are not so powerful. If one takes to devotional serivce, all of them are very easily performed.

Mauna, for example, does not mean that one should just stop speaking. The tongue is meant for speaking, although sometimes, to make a big show, a person remains silent. There are many who observe silence some day in a week. Vaiṣṇavas, however, do not observe such silence. Silence means not speaking foolishly. Speakers at assemblies, conferences and meetings generally speak foolishly like toads. This is described by Śrīla Rūpa Gosvāmī as *vāco vegam.* One who wants to say something can show himself to be a big orator, but rather than go on speaking nonsense, better to remain silent. This method of silence, therefore, is recommended for persons very attached to speaking nonsense. One who is not a devotee must speak nonsensically because he does not have the power to speak about the glories of Kṛṣṇa. Thus whatever he says is influenced by the illusory energy and is compared to the croaking of a frog. One who speaks about the glories of the Lord, however, has no need to be silent. Caitanya Mahāprabhu recommends, *kīrtanīyaḥ sadā hariḥ:* one should go on chanting the glories of the Lord twenty-four hours a day. There is no question of becoming *mauna*, or silent.

The ten processes for liberation or improvement on the path of liberation are not meant for the devotees. *Kevalayā bhaktyā:* if one simply engages in devotional service to the Lord, all ten methods of liberation are automatically observed. Prahlāda Mahārāja's proposal is that such processes may be recommended for the *ajitendriya*, those who cannot conquer their senses. Devotees, however, have already conquered their senses. *Sarvopādhi-vinirmuktaṁ tat-paratvena nirmalam:* a devotee is already freed from material contamination. Śrīla Bhaktisiddhānta Sarasvatī Ṭhākura therefore said:

duṣṭa mana! tumi kisera vaiṣṇava? pratiṣṭhāra tare, nirjanera ghare,
tava harināma kevala kaitava

There are many who like to chant the Hare Kṛṣṇa *mantra* in a silent, solitary place, but if one is not interested in preaching, talking constantly to the nondevotees, the influence of the modes of nature is very difficult to surpass. Therefore unless one is extremely advanced in Kṛṣṇa consciousness, one should not imitate Haridāsa Ṭhākura, who had no other business than chanting the holy name always, twenty-four hours a day. Prahlāda Mahārāja does not condemn such a process; he accepts it, but without active service to the Lord, simply by such methods one generally cannot attain liberation. One cannot attain liberation simply by false pride.

TEXT 47

रूपे इमे सदसती तव वेदसृष्टे
बीजाङ्कुराविव न चान्यदरूपकस्य ।
युक्ताः समक्षमुभयत्र विचक्षन्ते त्वां
योगेन वह्निमिव दारुषु नान्यतः स्यात् ॥४७॥

rūpe ime sad-asatī tava veda-sṛṣṭe
bījāṅkurāv iva na cānyad arūpakasya
yuktāḥ samakṣam ubhayatra vicakṣante tvāṁ
yogena vahnim iva dāruṣu nānyataḥ syāt

rūpe—in the forms; *ime*—these two; *sat-asatī*—the cause and the effect; *tava*—Your; *veda-sṛṣṭe*—explained in the *Vedas; bīja-aṅkurau*—the seed and the sprout; *iva*—like; *na*—never; *ca*—also; *anyat*—any other; *arūpakasya*—of You, who possess no material form; *yuktāḥ*—those engaged in Your devotional service; *samakṣam*—before the very eyes; *ubhayatra*—in both ways (spiritually and materially); *vicakṣante*—can actually see; *tvām*—You; *yogena*—simply by the method of devotional service; *vahnim*—fire; *iva*—like; *dāruṣu*—in wood; *na*—not; *anyataḥ*—from any other means; *syāt*—it is possible.

TRANSLATION

By authorized Vedic knowledge one can see that the forms of cause and effect in the cosmic manifestation belong to the Supreme Personality of Godhead, for the cosmic manifestation is His energy. Both cause and effect are nothing but energies of the Lord. Therefore, O my Lord, just as a wise man, by considering cause and effect, can see how fire pervades wood, those engaged in devotional service understand how You are both the cause and effect.

PURPORT

As described in previous verses, many so-called students of spiritual understanding follow the ten different methods known as *mauna-vrata-śruta-tapo-'dhyayana-sva-dharma-vyākhyā-raho-japa-samādhayaḥ*. These may be very attractive, but by following such methods, one cannot actually understand the real cause and effect and the original cause of everything (*janmādy asya yataḥ*). The original source of everything is the Supreme Personality of Godhead Himself (*sarva-kāraṇa-kāraṇam*). This original source of everything is Kṛṣṇa, the supreme ruler. *Īśvaraḥ paramaḥ kṛṣṇaḥ sac-cid-ānanda-vigrahaḥ*. He has His eternal spiritual form. Indeed, He is the root of everything (*bījaṁ māṁ sarva-bhūtānām*). Whatever manifestations exist, their cause is the Supreme Personality of Godhead. This cannot be understood by so-called silence or by any other hodgepodge method. The supreme cause can be understood only by devotional service, as stated in *Bhagavad-gītā* (*bhaktyā mām abhijānāti*). Elsewhere in *Śrīmad-Bhāgavatam* (11.14.21), the Supreme Godhead personally says, *bhaktyāham ekayā grāhyaḥ:* one can understand the original cause of all causes, the Supreme Person, only by devotional service, not by show-bottle exhibitionism.

TEXT 48

त्वं वायुरग्निरवनिर्वियदम्बुमात्राः
प्राणेन्द्रियाणि हृदयं चिदनुग्रहश्च ।
सर्वं त्वमेव सगुणो विगुणश्च भूमन्
नान्यत् त्वदस्त्यपि मनोवचसा निरुक्तम् ॥४८॥

tvaṁ vāyur agnir avanir viyad ambu mātrāḥ
prāṇendriyāṇi hṛdayaṁ cid anugrahaś ca
sarvaṁ tvam eva saguṇo viguṇaś ca bhūman
nānyat tvad asty api mano-vacasā niruktam

tvam—You (are); *vāyuḥ*—air; *agniḥ*—fire; *avaniḥ*—earth; *viyat*—sky; *ambu*—water; *mātrāḥ*—the sense objects; *prāṇa*—the life airs; *indriyāṇi*—the senses; *hṛdayam*—the mind; *cit*—consciousness; *anugrahaḥ ca*—and false ego or the demigods; *sarvam*—everything; *tvam*—You; *eva*—only; *sa-guṇaḥ*—material nature with its three modes; *viguṇaḥ*—the spiritual spark and Supersoul, which are beyond material nature; *ca*—and; *bhūman*—O my great Lord; *na*—not; *anyat*—other; *tvat*—than You; *asti*—is; *api*—although; *manaḥ-vacasā*—by mind and words; *niruktam*—everything manifested.

TRANSLATION

O Supreme Lord, You are actually the air, the earth, fire, sky and water. You are the objects of sense perception, the life airs, the five senses, the mind, consciousness and false ego. Indeed, You are everything, subtle and gross. The material elements and anything expressed, either by the words or by the mind, are nothing but You.

PURPORT

This is the all-pervasive conception of the Supreme Personality of Godhead, which explains how He spreads everywhere and anywhere. *Sarvaṁ khalv idaṁ brahma:* everything is Brahman—the Supreme Brahman, Kṛṣṇa. Nothing exists without Him. As the Lord says in *Bhagavad-gītā* (9.4):

mayā tatam idaṁ sarvaṁ
jagad avyakta-mūrtinā
mat-sthāni sarva-bhūtāni
na cāhaṁ teṣv avasthitaḥ

"I exist everywhere, and everything exists in Me, yet I am not visible everywhere." The Lord can be visible only through devotional service.

Tatra tiṣṭhāmi nārada yatra gāyanti mad-bhaktāḥ: the Supreme Lord stays only where His devotees chant His glories.

TEXT 49

नैते गुणा न गुणिनो महदादयो ये
सर्वे मनःप्रभृतयः सहदेवमर्त्याः ।
आद्यन्तवन्त उरुगाय विदन्ति हि त्वा-
मेवं विमृश्य सुधियो विरमन्ति शब्दात्॥४९॥

naite guṇā na guṇino mahad-ādayo ye
sarve manaḥ prabhṛtayaḥ sahadeva-martyāḥ
ādy-antavanta urugāya vidanti hi tvām
evaṁ vimṛśya sudhiyo viramanti śabdāt

na—neither; *ete*—all these; *guṇāḥ*—three qualities of material nature; *na*—nor; *guṇinaḥ*—the predominating deities of the three modes of material nature (namely Lord Brahmā, the predominating deity of passion, and Lord Śiva, the predominating deity of ignorance); *mahat-ādayaḥ*—the five elements, the senses and the sense objects; *ye*—those which; *sarve*—all; *manaḥ*—the mind; *prabhṛtayaḥ*—and so on; *saha-deva-martyāḥ*—with the demigods and the mortal human beings; *ādi-anta-vantaḥ*—who all have a beginning and end; *urugāya*—O Supreme Lord, who are glorified by all saintly persons; *vidanti*—understand; *hi*—indeed; *tvām*—Your Lordship; *evam*—thus; *vimṛśya*—considering; *sudhiyaḥ*—all wise men; *viramanti*—cease; *śabdāt*—from studying or understanding the *Vedas.*

TRANSLATION

Neither the three modes of material nature [sattva-guṇa, rajo-guṇa and tamo-guṇa], nor the predominating deities controlling these three modes, nor the five gross elements, nor the mind, nor the demigods nor the human beings can understand Your Lordship, for they are all subjected to birth and annihilation. Considering this, the spiritually advanced have taken to devotional service. Such wise men hardly bother with Vedic study. Instead, they engage themselves in practical devotional service.

PURPORT

As stated in several places, *bhaktyā mām abhijānāti:* only by devotional service can the Supreme Lord be understood. The intelligent person, the devotee, does not bother much about the practices mentioned in text 46 (*mauna-vrata-śruta-tapo-'dhyayana-sva-dharma*). After understanding the Supreme Lord through devotional service, such devotees are no longer interested in studies of the *Vedas.* Indeed, this is confirmed in the *Vedas* also. The *Vedas* say, *kim arthā vayam adhyeṣyāmahe kim arthā vayam vakṣyāmahe.* What is the use of studying so many Vedic literatures? What is the use of explaining them in different ways? *Vayam vakṣyāmahe.* No one needs to study any more Vedic literatures, nor does anyone need to describe them by philosophical speculation. *Bhagavad-gītā* (2.52) also says:

yadā te moha-kalilaṁ
buddhir vyatitariṣyati
tadā gantāsi nirvedaṁ
śrotavyasya śrutasya ca

When one understands the Supreme Personality of Godhead by executing devotional service, one ceases the practice of studying the Vedic literature. Elsewhere it is said, *ārādhito yadi haris tapasā tataḥ kim.* If one can understand the Supreme Personality of Godhead and engage in His service, there is no more need of severe austerities, penances and so on. However, if after performing severe austerities and penances one does not understand the Supreme Personality of Godhead, such practices are useless.

TEXT 50

तत् तेऽर्हत्तम नमःस्तुतिकर्मपूजाः
कर्म स्मृतिश्चरणयोः श्रवणं कथायाम् ।
संसेवया त्वयि विनेति षडङ्गया किं
भक्तिं जनः परमहंसगतौ लभेत ॥५०॥

tat te 'rhattama namaḥ stuti-karma-pūjāḥ
karma smṛtiś caraṇayoḥ śravaṇaṁ kathāyām

saṁsevayā tvayi vineti ṣaḍ-aṅgayā kiṁ
bhaktiṁ janaḥ paramahaṁsa-gatau labheta

tat—therefore; *te*—unto You; *arhat-tama*—O supreme of all worshipable persons; *namaḥ*—respectful obeisances; *stuti-karma-pūjāḥ*—worshiping Your Lordship by offering prayers and other devotional activities; *karma*—activities being dedicated to You; *smṛtiḥ*—constant remembrance; *caraṇayoḥ*—of Your lotus feet; *śravaṇam*—always hearing; *kathāyām*—in topics (about You); *saṁsevayā*—such devotional service; *tvayi*—unto You; *vinā*—without; *iti*—thus; *ṣaṭ-aṅgayā*—having six different parts; *kim*—how; *bhaktim*—devotional service; *janaḥ*—a person; *paramahaṁsa-gatau*—obtainable by the *paramahaṁsa; labheta*—may attain.

TRANSLATION

Therefore, O Supreme Personality of Godhead, the best of all persons to whom prayers are offered, I offer my respectful obeisances unto You because without rendering six kinds of devotional service unto You—offering prayers, dedicating all the results of activities, worshiping You, working on Your behalf, always remembering Your lotus feet and hearing about Your glories—who can achieve that which is meant for the paramahaṁsas?

PURPORT

The *Vedas* enjoin: *nāyam ātmā pravacanena labhyo na medhayā na bahunā śrutena.* One cannot understand the Supreme Personality of Godhead simply by studying the *Vedas* and offering prayers. Only by the grace of the Supreme Lord can one understand Him. The process of understanding the Lord, therefore, is *bhakti.* Without *bhakti,* simply following the Vedic injunctions to understand the Absolute Truth will not be helpful at all. The process of *bhakti* is understood by the *paramahaṁsa,* one who has accepted the essence of everything. The results of *bhakti* are reserved for such a *paramahaṁsa,* and this stage cannot be obtained by any Vedic process other than devotional service. Other processes, such as *jñāna* and *yoga,* can be successful only when mixed with *bhakti.* When we speak of *jñāna-yoga, karma-yoga* and *dhyāna-yoga* the word *yoga* indicates *bhakti. Bhakti-yoga,* or *buddhi-yoga,* executed with intelligence and full knowledge, is the only successful method for going back home, back to Godhead. If one wants to be liberated from the pangs of material existence, he should take to devotional service for quick attainment of this goal.

TEXT 51

श्रीनारद उवाच
एतावद्वर्णितगुणो भक्त्या भक्तेन निर्गुणः ।
प्रह्रादं प्रणतं प्रीतो यतमन्युरभाषत ॥५१॥

śrī-nārada uvāca
etāvad varṇita-guṇo
bhaktyā bhaktena nirguṇaḥ
prahrādaṁ praṇataṁ prīto
yata-manyur abhāṣata

śrī-nāradaḥ uvāca—Śrī Nārada Muni said; *etāvat*—up to this; *varṇita*—described; *guṇaḥ*—transcendental qualities; *bhaktyā*—with devotion; *bhaktena*—by the devotee (Prahlāda Mahārāja); *nirguṇaḥ*—the transcendental Lord; *prahrādam*—unto Prahlāda Mahārāja; *praṇatam*—who was surrendered at the lotus feet of the Lord; *prītaḥ*—being pleased; *yata-manyuḥ*—controlling the anger; *abhāṣata*—began to speak (as follows).

TRANSLATION

The great saint Nārada said: Thus Lord Nṛsiṁhadeva was pacified by the devotee Prahlāda Mahārāja with prayers offered from the transcendental platform. The Lord gave up His anger, and being very kind to Prahlāda, who was offering prostrated obeisances, He spoke as follows.

PURPORT

The word *nirguṇa* is important. The Māyāvādī philosophers accept the Absolute Truth as *nirguṇa* or *nirākāra.* The word *nirguṇa* refers to one who possesses no material qualities. The Lord, being full of spiritual qualities, gave up all His anger and spoke to Prahlāda.

TEXT 52

श्रीभगवानुवाच
प्रह्राद भद्र भद्रं ते प्रीतोऽहं तेऽसुरोत्तम ।
वरं वृणीष्वाभिमतं कामपूरोऽस्म्यहं नृणाम् ॥५२॥

śrī-bhagavān uvāca
prahrāda bhadra bhadraṁ te
prīto 'haṁ te 'surottama
varaṁ vṛṇīṣvābhimataṁ
kāma-pūro 'smy ahaṁ nṛṇām

śrī-bhagavān uvāca—the Supreme Personality of Godhead said; *prahrāda*—O My dear Prahlāda; *bhadra*—you are so gentle; *bhadram*—all good fortune; *te*—unto you; *prītaḥ*—pleased; *aham*—I (am); *te*—unto You; *asura-uttama*—O best devotee in the family of *asuras* (atheists); *varam*—benediction; *vṛṇīṣva*—just ask (from Me); *abhimatam*—desired; *kāma-pūraḥ*—who fulfills everyone's desire; *asmi*—am; *aham*—I; *nṛṇām*—of all men.

TRANSLATION

The Supreme Personality of Godhead said: My dear Prahlāda, most gentle one, best of the family of the asuras, all good fortune unto you. I am very much pleased with you. It is My pastime to fulfill the desires of all living beings, and therefore you may ask from Me any benediction that you desire to be fulfilled.

PURPORT

The Supreme Personality of Godhead is known as *bhakta-vatsala*, the Supreme Personality who is very much affectionate to His devotees. It is not very extraordinary that the Lord offered His devotee all benedictions. The Supreme Personality of Godhead said in effect, "I fulfill the desires of everyone. Since you are My devotee, whatever you want for yourself will naturally be given, but if you pray for anyone else, that prayer also will be fulfilled." Thus if we approach the Supreme Lord or His devotee, or if we are blessed by a devotee, naturally we will automatically achieve the benedictions of the Supreme Lord. *Yasya prasādād bhagavat-*

prasādaḥ. Śrīla Viśvanātha Cakravartī Ṭhākura says that if one pleases the Vaiṣṇava spiritual master, all of one's desires will be fulfilled.

TEXT 53

मामप्रीणत आयुष्मन्दर्शनं दुर्लभं हि मे ।
दृष्ट्वा मां न पुनर्जन्तुरात्मानं तप्तुमर्हति ।।५३।।

mām aprīṇata āyuṣman
darśanaṁ durlabhaṁ hi me
dṛṣṭvā māṁ na punar jantur
ātmānaṁ taptum arhati

mām—Me; *aprīṇataḥ*—not pleasing; *āyuṣman*—O long-living Prahlāda; *darśanam*—seeing; *durlabham*—very rare; *hi*—indeed; *me*—of Me; *dṛṣṭvā*—after seeing; *mām*—Me; *na*—not; *punaḥ*—again; *jantuḥ*—the living entity; *ātmānam*—for himself; *taptum*—to lament; *arhati*—deserves.

TRANSLATION

My dear Prahlāda, may you live a long time. One cannot appreciate or understand Me without pleasing Me, but one who has seen or pleased Me has nothing more for which to lament for his own satisfaction.

PURPORT

One cannot be happy under any circumstances unless one pleases the Supreme Personality of Godhead, but one who has learned how to please the Supreme Lord need no longer lament for his material condition.

TEXT 54

प्रीणन्ति ह्यथ मां धीराः सर्वभावेन साधवः ।
श्रेयस्कामा महाभाग सर्वासामाशिषां पतिम् ।।५४।।

prīṇanti hy atha māṁ dhīrāḥ
sarva-bhāvena sādhavaḥ

śreyas-kāmā mahā-bhāga
sarvāsām āśiṣāṁ patim

prīṇanti—try to please; *hi*—indeed; *atha*—because of this; *mām*—Me; *dhīrāḥ*—those who are sober and most intelligent; *sarva-bhāvena*—in all respects, in different modes of devotional service; *sādhavaḥ*—persons who are very well behaved (perfect in all respects); *śreyas-kāmāḥ*—desiring the best benefit in life; *mahā-bhāga*—O you who are so fortunate; *sarvāsām*—of all; *āśiṣām*—kinds of benedictions; *patim*—the master (Me).

TRANSLATION

My dear Prahlāda, you are very fortunate. Please know from Me that those who are very wise and highly elevated try to please Me in all different modes of mellows, for I am the only person who can fulfill all the desires of everyone.

PURPORT

The words *dhīrāḥ sarva-bhāvena* do not mean "in whichever way you like." *Bhāva* is the preliminary condition of love of Godhead.

athāsaktis tato bhāvas
tataḥ premābhyudañcati
sādhakānām ayaṁ premṇaḥ
prādurbhāve bhavet kramaḥ
(*Bhakti-rasāmṛta-sindhu* 1.4.16)

The *bhāva* stage is the final division before one reaches love of Godhead. The word *sarva-bhāva* means that one can love the Supreme Personality of Godhead in different transcendental modes of mellows, beginning with *dāsya, sakhya, vātsalya* and *mādhurya.* In the *śānta* stage, one is on the border of loving service to the Lord. Pure love of Godhead begins from *dāsya* and develops to *sakhya, vātsalya* and then *mādhurya.* Still, in any of these five mellows one can render loving service to the Supreme Lord. Since our main business is to love the Supreme Personality of Godhead, one can render service from any of the above-mentioned platforms of love.

TEXT 55

श्रीनारद उवाच
एवं प्रलोभ्यमानोऽपि वरैर्लोकप्रलोभनैः ।
एकान्तित्वाद् भगवति नैच्छत् तानसुरोत्तमः ॥५५॥

śrī-nārada uvāca
evaṁ pralobhyamāno 'pi
varair loka-pralobhanaiḥ
ekāntitvād bhagavati
naicchat tān asurottamaḥ

śrī-nāradaḥ uvāca—the great saint Nārada said; *evam*—thus; *pralobhyamānaḥ*—being allured or induced; *api*—although; *varaiḥ*—by benedictions; *loka*—of the world; *pralobhanaiḥ*—by different kinds of allurements; *ekāntitvāt*—because of being solely surrendered; *bhagavati*—unto the Supreme Personality of Godhead; *na aicchat*—did not want; *tān*—those benedictions; *asura-uttamaḥ*—Prahlāda Mahārāja, the best of the family of *asuras.*

TRANSLATION

Nārada Muni said: Prahlāda Mahārāja was the best person in the family of asuras, who always aspire for material happiness. Nonetheless, although allured by the Supreme Personality of Godhead, who offered him all benedictions for material happiness, because of his unalloyed Kṛṣṇa consciousness he did not want to take any material benefit for sense gratification.

PURPORT

Pure devotees like Prahlāda Mahārāja and Dhruva Mahārāja do not aspire for any material benefit at any stage of devotional service. When the Lord was present before Dhruva Mahārāja, Dhruva did not want to take any material benefit from the Lord: *svāmin kṛtārtho 'smi varaṁ na yāce.* As a pure devotee, he could not ask the Lord for any material benefit. In this regard, Śrī Caitanya Mahāprabhu instructed us:

na dhanaṁ na janaṁ na sundarīṁ
kavitāṁ vā jagad-īśa kāmaye
mama janmani janmanīśvare
bhavatād bhaktir ahaitukī tvayi

"O my Lord, Jagadīśa, I do not pray for benedictions by which to achieve material wealth, popularity or beauty. My only desire is to serve You. Kindly engage me in the service of the servant of Your servant."

Thus end the Bhaktivedanta purports of the Seventh Canto, Ninth Chapter, of the Śrīmad-Bhāgavatam, *entitled "Prahlāda Pacifies Lord Nṛsiṁhadeva with Prayers."*

CHAPTER TEN

Prahlāda, the Best Among Exalted Devotees

This chapter describes how the Supreme Personality of Godhead Nṛsiṁhadeva disappeared, after pleasing Prahlāda Mahārāja. It also describes a benediction given by Lord Śiva.

Lord Nṛsiṁhadeva wanted to bestow benedictions upon Prahlāda Mahārāja, one after another, but Prahlāda Mahārāja, thinking them impediments on the path of spiritual progress, did not accept any of them. Instead, he fully surrendered at the Lord's lotus feet. He said: "If anyone engaged in the devotional service of the Lord prays for personal sense gratification, he cannot be called a pure devotee or even a devotee. He may be called only a merchant engaged in the business of give and take. Similarly, a master who wants to please his servant after taking service from him is also not a real master." Prahlāda Mahārāja, therefore, did not ask anything from the Supreme Personality of Godhead. Rather, he said that if the Lord wanted to give him a benediction, he wanted the Lord to assure him that he would never be induced to take any benedictions for the sake of material desires. Exchanges of devotional service for lusty desires are always very prominent. As soon as lusty desires awaken, one's senses, mind, life, soul, religious principles, patience, intelligence, shyness, beauty, strength, memory and truthfulness are all vanquished. One can render unalloyed devotional service only when there are no material desires in one's mind.

The Supreme Personality of Godhead was greatly pleased with Prahlāda Mahārāja for his unalloyed devotion, yet the Lord provided him one material benediction—that he would be perfectly happy in this world and live his next life in Vaikuṇṭha. The Lord gave him the benediction that he would be the king of this material world until the end of the *manvantara* millennium and that although in this material world, he would have the facility to hear the glories of the Lord and depend fully on the Lord, performing service to Him in uncontaminated *bhakti-yoga.*

The Lord advised Prahlāda to perform sacrifices through *bhakti-yoga*, for this is the duty of a king.

Prahlāda Mahārāja accepted whatever the Lord had offered him, and he prayed for the Lord to deliver his father. In response to this prayer, the Lord assured him that in the family of such a pure devotee as he, not only the devotee's father but his forefathers for twenty-one generations are liberated. The Lord also asked Prahlāda to perform the ritualistic ceremonies appropriate after his father's death.

Then Lord Brahmā, who was also present, offered many prayers to the Lord, expressing his obligation to the Lord for having offered benedictions to Prahlāda Mahārāja. The Lord advised Lord Brahmā not to offer benedictions to *asuras* as he had to Hiraṇyakaśipu, for such benedictions indulge them. Then Lord Nṛsiṁhadeva disappeared. On that day, Prahlāda Mahārāja was installed on the throne of the world by Lord Brahmā and Śukrācārya.

Thus Nārada Muni described the character of Prahlāda Mahārāja for Yudhiṣṭhira Mahārāja, and he further described the killing of Rāvaṇa by Lord Rāmacandra and the killing of Śiśupāla and Dantavakra in Dvāpara-yuga. Śiśupāla, of course, had merged into the existence of the Lord and thus achieved *sāyujya-mukti.* Nārada Muni praised Yudhiṣṭhira Mahārāja because the Supreme Lord, Kṛṣṇa, was the greatest well-wisher and friend of the Pāṇḍavas and almost always stayed in their house. Thus the fortune of the Pāṇḍavas was greater than that of Prahlāda Mahārāja.

Later, Nārada Muni described how the demon Maya Dānava constructed Tripura for the demons, who became very powerful and defeated the demigods. Because of this defeat, Lord Rudra, Śiva, dismantled Tripura; thus he became famous as Tripurāri. For this, Rudra is very much appreciated and worshiped by the demigods. This narration occurs at the end of the chapter.

TEXT 1

श्रीनारद उवाच

भक्तियोगस्य तत् सर्वमन्तरायतयार्भकः ।
मन्यमानो हृषीकेशं स्मयमान उवाच ह ॥ १ ॥

śrī-nārada uvāca
bhakti-yogasya tat sarvam
antarāyatayārbhakaḥ
manyamāno hṛṣīkeśaṁ
smayamāna uvāca ha

śrī-nāradaḥ uvāca—Nārada Muni said; *bhakti-yogasya*—of the principles of devotional service; *tat*—those (blessings or benedictions offered by Lord Nṛsiṁhadeva); *sarvam*—each and every one of them; *antarāyatayā*—because of being impediments (on the path of *bhakti-yoga*); *arbhakaḥ*—Prahlāda Mahārāja, although only a boy; *manyamānaḥ*—considering; *hṛṣīkeśam*—unto Lord Nṛsiṁhadeva; *smayamānaḥ*—smiling; *uvāca*—said; *ha*—in the past.

TRANSLATION

The saint Nārada Muni continued: Although Prahlāda Mahārāja was only a boy, when he heard the benedictions offered by Lord Nṛsiṁhadeva he considered them impediments on the path of devotional service. Thus he smiled very mildly and spoke as follows.

PURPORT

Material achievements are not the ultimate goal of devotional service. The ultimate goal of devotional service is love of Godhead. Therefore although Prahlāda Mahārāja, Dhruva Mahārāja, Ambarīṣa Mahārāja, Yudhiṣṭhira Mahārāja and many devotee kings were materially very opulent, they accepted their material opulence in the service of the Lord, not for their personal sense gratification. Of course, possessing material opulence is always fearful because under the influence of material opulence one may be misdirected from devotional service. Nonetheless, a pure devotee (*anyābhilāṣitā-śūnyam*) is never misdirected by material opulence. On the contrary, whatever he possesses he engages one hundred percent in the service of the Lord. When one is allured by material possessions, they are considered to be given by *māyā*, but when one uses material possessions fully for service, they are considered God's gifts, or facilities offered by Kṛṣṇa for enhancing one's devotional service.

TEXT 2

श्रीप्रह्राद उवाच
मा मां प्रलोभयोत्पत्त्या सक्तं कामेषु तैर्वरैः ।
तत्सङ्गभीतो निर्विण्णो मुमुक्षुस्त्वामुपाश्रितः ॥ २ ॥

śrī-prahrāda uvāca
mā māṁ pralobhayotpattyā
saktaṁ kāmeṣu tair varaiḥ
tat-saṅga-bhīto nirviṇṇo
mumukṣus tvām upāśritaḥ

śrī-prahrādaḥ uvāca—Prahlāda Mahārāja said (to the Supreme Personality of Godhead); *mā*—please do not; *mām*—me; *pralobhaya*—allure; *utpattyā*—because of my birth (in a demoniac family); *saktam*—(I am already) attached; *kāmeṣu*—to material enjoyment; *taiḥ*—by all those; *varaiḥ*—benedictions of material possessions; *tat-saṅga-bhītaḥ*—being afraid of such material association; *nirviṇṇaḥ*—completely detached from material desires; *mumukṣuḥ*—desiring to be liberated from material conditions of life; *tvām*—unto Your lotus feet; *upāśritaḥ*—I have taken shelter.

TRANSLATION

Prahlāda Mahārāja said: My dear Lord, O Supreme Personality of Godhead, because I was born in an atheistic family I am naturally attached to material enjoyment. Therefore, kindly do not tempt me with these illusions. I am very much afraid of material conditions, and I desire to be liberated from materialistic life. It is for this reason that I have taken shelter of Your lotus feet.

PURPORT

Materialistic life means attachment to the body and everything in relationship to the body. This attachment is based on lusty desires for sense gratification, specifically sexual enjoyment. *Kāmais tais tair hṛta-jñānāḥ:* when one is too attached to material enjoyment, he is bereft of all knowledge (*hṛta-jñānāḥ*). As stated in *Bhagavad-gītā*, those who are attached to material enjoyment are mostly inclined to worship the demigods to procure various material opulences. They are especially attached to worship of the goddess Durgā and Lord Śiva because this transcendental couple can offer their devotees all material opulence. Prahlāda Mahārāja, however, was detached from all material enjoyment. He therefore took shelter of the lotus feet of Lord Nṛsiṁhadeva, and not the feet of any demigod. It is to be understood that if one really wants release from this material world, from the threefold miseries and from *janma-mṛtyu-jarā-vyādhi* (birth, death, old age and disease), one must take shelter of the Supreme Personality of Godhead, for without the Supreme Personality of Godhead one cannot get release from materialistic life. Atheistic men are very much attached to material enjoyment. Therefore if they get some opportunity to achieve more and more material enjoyment, they take it. Prahlāda Mahārāja, however, was very careful in this regard. Although born of a materialistic father, because he was a devotee he had no material desires (*anyābhilāṣitā-śūnyam*).

TEXT 3

भृत्यलक्षणजिज्ञासुर्भक्तं कामेष्वचोदयत् ।
भवान् संसारबीजेषु हृदयग्रन्थिषु प्रभो ॥ ३ ॥

bhṛtya-lakṣaṇa-jijñāsur
bhaktaṁ kāmeṣv acodayat
bhavān saṁsāra-bījeṣu
hṛdaya-granthiṣu prabho

bhṛtya-lakṣaṇa-jijñāsuḥ—desiring to exhibit the symptoms of a pure devotee; *bhaktam*—the devotee; *kāmeṣu*—in the material world, where lusty desires predominate; *acodayat*—has sent; *bhavān*—Your Lordship; *saṁsāra-bījeṣu*—the root cause of being present in this material world; *hṛdaya-granthiṣu*—which (desire for material enjoyment) is in the cores of the hearts of all conditioned souls; *prabho*—O my worshipable Lord.

TRANSLATION

O my worshipable Lord, because the seed of lusty desires, which is the root cause of material existence, is within the core of

everyone's heart, You have sent me to this material world to exhibit the symptoms of a pure devotee.

PURPORT

Bhakti-rasāmṛta-sindhu has given considerable discussion about *nitya-siddha* and *sādhana-siddha* devotees. *Nitya-siddha* devotees come from Vaikuṇṭha to this material world to teach, by their personal example, how to become a devotee. The living entities in this material world can take lessons from such *nitya-siddha* devotees and thus become inclined to return home, back to Godhead. A *nitya-siddha* devotee comes from Vaikuṇṭha upon the order of the Supreme Personality of Godhead and shows by his example how to become a pure devotee (*anyābhilāṣitā-śūnyam*). In spite of coming to this material world, the *nitya-siddha* devotee is never attracted by the allurements of material enjoyment. A perfect example is Prahlāda Mahārāja, who was a *nitya-siddha,* a *mahā-bhāgavata* devotee. Although Prahlāda was born in the family of Hiraṇyakaśipu, an atheist, he was never attached to any kind of materialistic enjoyment. Desiring to exhibit the symptoms of a pure devotee, the Lord tried to induce Prahlāda Mahārāja to take material benedictions, but Prahlāda Mahārāja did not accept them. On the contrary, by his personal example he showed the symptoms of a pure devotee. In other words, the Lord Himself has no desire to send His pure devotee to this material world, nor does a devotee have any material purpose in coming. When the Lord Himself appears as an incarnation within this material world, He is not allured by the material atmosphere, and He has nothing to do with material activity, yet by His example He teaches the common man how to become a devotee. Similarly, a devotee who comes here in accordance with the order of the Supreme Lord shows by his personal behavior how to become a pure devotee. A pure devotee, therefore, is a practical example for all living entities, including Lord Brahmā.

TEXT 4

नान्यथा तेऽखिलगुरो घटेत करुणात्मनः ।
यस्त आशिष आशास्ते न स भृत्यः स वै वणिक् ॥४॥

nānyathā te 'khila-guro
ghaṭeta karuṇātmanaḥ
yas ta āśiṣa āśāste
na sa bhṛtyaḥ sa vai vaṇik

na—not; *anyathā*—otherwise; *te*—of You; *akhila-guro*—O supreme instructor of the entire creation; *ghaṭeta*—such a thing can happen; *karuṇā-ātmanaḥ*—the Supreme Person, who is extremely kind to His devotees; *yaḥ*—any person who; *te*—from You; *āśiṣaḥ*—material benefits; *āśāste*—desires (in exchange for serving You); *na*—not; *saḥ*—such a person; *bhṛtyaḥ*—a servitor; *saḥ*—such a person; *vai*—indeed; *vaṇik*—a merchant (who wants to get material profit from his business).

TRANSLATION

Otherwise, O my Lord, O supreme instructor of the entire world, You are so kind to Your devotee that You could not induce him to do something unbeneficial for him. On the other hand, one who desires some material benefit in exchange for devotional service cannot be Your pure devotee. Indeed, he is no better than a merchant who wants profit in exchange for service.

PURPORT

It is sometimes found that one comes to a devotee or a temple of the Lord just to get some material benefit. Such a person is described here as a mercantile man. *Bhagavad-gītā* speaks of *ārto jijñāsur arthārthī.* The word *ārta* refers to one who is physically distressed, and *arthārthī* refers to one in need of money. Such persons are forced to approach the Supreme Personality of Godhead for mitigation of their distress or to get some money by the benediction of the Lord. They have been described as *sukṛtī,* pious, because in their distress or need for money they have approached the Supreme Lord. Unless one is pious, one cannot approach the Supreme Personality of Godhead. However, although a pious man may receive some material benefit, one who is concerned with material benefits cannot be a pure devotee. When a pure devotee receives material opulences, this is not because of his pious activity but for the service of the Lord. When one engages in devotional service, one is automatically pious. Therefore, a pure devotee is *anyābhilāṣitā-śūnyam.* He has no desire for material profit, nor does the Lord induce him to try to profit materially. When a devotee needs something, the Supreme Personality of Godhead supplies it (*yoga-kṣemaṁ vahāmy aham*).

Sometimes materialists go to a temple to offer flowers and fruit to the Lord because they have learned from *Bhagavad-gītā* that if a devotee offers some flowers and fruits, the Lord accepts them. In *Bhagavad-gītā* (9.26) the Lord says:

patraṁ puṣpaṁ phalaṁ toyaṁ
yo me bhaktyā prayacchati
tad ahaṁ bhakty-upahṛtam
aśnāmi prayatātmanaḥ

"If one offers Me with love and devotion a leaf, a flower, fruit or water, I will accept it." Thus a man with a mercantile mentality thinks that if he can get some material benefit, like a large amount of money, simply by offering a little fruit and flower, this is good business. Such persons are not accepted as pure devotees. Because their desires are not purified, they are still mercantile men, even though they go to temples to make a show of being devotees. *Sarvopādhi-vinirmuktaṁ tat-paratvena nirmalam:* only when one is fully freed from material desires can one be purified, and only in that purified state can one serve the Lord. *Hṛṣīkena hṛṣīkeśa-sevanaṁ bhaktir ucyate.* This is the pure devotional platform.

TEXT 5

आशासानो न वै भृत्यः स्वामिन्याशिष आत्मनः ।
न स्वामी भृत्यतः स्वाम्यमिच्छन् यो राति चाशिषः ॥ ५ ॥

āśāsāno na vai bhṛtyaḥ
svāminy āśiṣa ātmanaḥ
na svāmī bhṛtyataḥ svāmyam
icchan yo rāti cāśiṣaḥ

āśāsānaḥ—a person who desires (in exchange for service); *na*—not; *vai*—indeed; *bhṛtyaḥ*—a qualified servant or pure devotee of the Lord;

svāmini—from the master; *āśiṣaḥ*—material benefit; *ātmanaḥ*—for personal sense gratification; *na*—nor; *svāmī*—the master; *bhṛtyataḥ*—from the servant; *svāmyam*—the prestigious position of being the master; *icchan*—desiring; *yaḥ*—any such master who; *rāti*—bestows; *ca*—also; *āśiṣaḥ*—material profit.

TRANSLATION

A servant who desires material profits from his master is certainly not a qualified servant or pure devotee. Similarly, a master who bestows benedictions upon his servant because of a desire to maintain a prestigious position as master is also not a pure master.

PURPORT

As stated in *Bhagavad-gītā* (7.20), *kāmais tais tair hṛta-jñānāḥ prapadyante 'nya-devatāḥ.* "Those whose minds are distorted by material desires surrender unto demigods." A demigod cannot become master, for the real master is the Supreme Personality of Godhead. The demigods, to keep their prestigious positions, bestow upon their worshipers whatever benedictions the worshipers want. For example, once it was found that an *asura* took a benediction from Lord Śiva by which the *asura* would be able to kill someone simply by placing his hands on that person's head. Such benedictions are possible to receive from the demigods. If one worships the Supreme Personality of Godhead, however, the Lord will never offer him such condemned benedictions. On the contrary, it is said in the *Śrīmad-Bhāgavatam* (10.88.8), *yasyāham anugṛhnāmi hariṣye tad-dhanaṁ śanaiḥ.* If one is too materialistic but at the same time wants to be a servant of the Supreme Lord, the Lord, because of His supreme compassion for the devotee, takes away all his material opulences and obliges him to be a pure devotee of the Lord. Prahlāda Mahārāja distinguishes between the pure devotee and the pure master. The Lord is the pure master, the supreme master, whereas an unalloyed devotee with no material motives is the pure servant. One who has materialistic motivations cannot become a servant, and one who unnecessarily bestows benedictions upon his servant to keep his own prestigious position is not a real master.

TEXT 6

अहं त्वकामस्त्वद्भक्तस्त्वं च स्वाम्यनपाश्रयः ।
नान्यथेहावयोरर्थो राजसेवकयोरिव ॥ ६ ॥

ahaṁ tv akāmas tvad-bhaktas
tvaṁ ca svāmy anapāśrayaḥ
nānyathehāvayor artho
rāja-sevakayor iva

aham—as far as I am concerned; *tu*—indeed; *akāmaḥ*—without material desire; *tvat-bhaktaḥ*—fully attached to You without motivation; *tvam ca*—Your Lordship also; *svāmī*—the real master; *anapāśrayaḥ*—without motivation (You do not become the master with motivation); *na*—not; *anyathā*—without being in such a relationship as master and servant; *iha*—here; *āvayoḥ*—our; *arthaḥ*—any motivation (the Lord is the pure master, and Prahlāda Mahārāja is the pure devotee with no materialistic motivation); *rāja*—of a king; *sevakayoḥ*—and the servitor; *iva*—like (just as a king exacts taxes for the benefit of the servant or the citizens pay taxes for the benefit of the king).

TRANSLATION

O my Lord, I am Your unmotivated servant, and You are my eternal master. There is no need of our being anything other than master and servant. You are naturally my master, and I am naturally Your servant. We have no other relationship.

PURPORT

Śrī Caitanya Mahāprabhu said, *jīvera 'svarūpa' haya—kṛṣṇera 'nitya-dāsa':* every living being is eternally a servant of the Supreme Lord, Kṛṣṇa. Lord Kṛṣṇa says in *Bhagavad-gītā* (5.29), *bhoktāraṁ yajña-tapasāṁ sarva-loka-maheśvaram:* "I am the proprietor of all planets, and I am the supreme enjoyer." This is the natural position of the Lord, and the natural position of the living being is to surrender unto Him (*sarva-dharmān parityajya mām ekaṁ śaraṇaṁ vraja*). If this relationship continues, then real happiness exists eternally between the master and servant. Unfortunately, when this eternal relationship is disturbed, the living entity wants to become separately happy and thinks that the master is his order supplier. In this way there cannot be happiness. Nor should the master cater to the desires of the servant. If he does, he is not the real master. The real master commands, "You must do this," and the real servant immediately obeys the order. Unless this relationship between the Supreme Lord and the subordinate living entity is established, there can be no real happiness. The living entity is *āśraya*, always subordinate, and the Supreme Personality of Godhead is *viṣaya*, the supreme objective, the goal of life. Unfortunate persons trapped in this material world do not know this. *Na te viduḥ svārtha-gatiṁ hi viṣṇum:* illusioned by the material energy, everyone in this material world is unaware that the only aim of life is to approach Lord Viṣṇu.

ārādhanānāṁ sarveṣāṁ
viṣṇor ārādhanaṁ param
tasmāt parataraṁ devi
tadīyānāṁ samarcanam

In the *Padma Purāṇa* Lord Śiva explains to his wife, Parvatī, the goddess Durgā, that the highest goal of life is to satisfy Lord Viṣṇu, who can be satisfied only when His servant is satisfied. Śrī Caitanya Mahāprabhu therefore teaches, *gopī-bhartuḥ pada-kamalayor dāsa-dāsānudāsaḥ.* One must become a servant of the servant. Prahlāda Mahārāja also prayed to Lord Nṛsiṁhadeva that he might be engaged as the servant of the Lord's servant. This is the prescribed method of devotional service. As soon as a devotee wants the Supreme Personality of Godhead to be his order supplier, the Lord immediately refuses to become the master of such a motivated devotee. In *Bhagavad-gītā* (4.11) the Lord says, *ye yathā māṁ prapadyante tāṁs tathaiva bhajāmy aham.* "As one surrenders unto Me, I reward him accordingly." Materialistic persons are generally inclined to material profits. As long as one continues in such an adulterated position, he does not receive the benefit of returning home, back to Godhead.

TEXT 7

यदि दास्यसि मे कामान् वरांस्त्वं वरदर्षभ ।
कामानां हृद्यसंरोहं भवतस्तु वृणे वरम् ॥ ७ ॥

yadi dāsyasi me kāmān
varāṁs tvaṁ varadarṣabha
kāmānāṁ hṛdy asaṁrohaṁ
bhavatas tu vṛṇe varam

yadi—if; *dāsyasi*—want to give; *me*—me; *kāmān*—anything desirable; *varān*—as Your benediction; *tvam*—You; *varada-ṛṣabha*—O Supreme Personality of Godhead, who can give any benediction; *kāmānām*—of all desires for material happiness; *hṛdi*—within the core of my heart; *asaṁroham*—no growth; *bhavataḥ*—from You; *tu*—then; *vṛṇe*—I pray for; *varam*—such a benediction.

TRANSLATION

O my Lord, best of the givers of benediction, if You at all want to bestow a desirable benediction upon me, then I pray from Your Lordship that within the core of my heart there be no material desires.

PURPORT

Lord Śrī Caitanya Mahāprabhu taught us how to pray for benedictions from the Lord. He said:

na dhanaṁ na janaṁ na sundarīṁ
kavitāṁ vā jagad-īśa kāmaye
mama janmani janmanīśvare
bhavatād bhaktir ahaitukī tvayi

"O my Lord, I do not want from You any amount of wealth, nor many followers, nor a beautiful wife, for these are all materialistic desires. But if I have to ask You for any benediction, I pray that in whatever forms of life I may take my birth, under any circumstances, I will not be bereft of Your transcendental devotional service." Devotees are always on the positive platform, in contrast to the Māyāvādīs, who want to make everything impersonal or void. One cannot remain void (*śūnyavādī*); rather, one must possess something. Therefore, the devotee, on the positive side, wants to possess something, and this possession is very nicely described by Prahlāda Mahārāja, who says, "If I must take some benediction from

You, I pray that within the core of my heart there may be no material desires." The desire to serve the Supreme Personality of Godhead is not at all material.

TEXT 8

इन्द्रियाणि मनः प्राण आत्मा धर्मो धृतिर्मतिः ।
ह्रीः श्रीस्तेजः स्मृतिः सत्यं यस्य नश्यन्ति जन्मना॥ ८ ॥

indriyāṇi manaḥ prāṇa
ātmā dharmo dhṛtir matiḥ
hrīḥ śrīs tejaḥ smṛtiḥ satyaṁ
yasya naśyanti janmanā

indriyāṇi—the senses; *manaḥ*—the mind; *prāṇaḥ*—the life air; *ātmā*—the body; *dharmaḥ*—religion; *dhṛtiḥ*—patience; *matiḥ*—intelligence; *hrīḥ*—shyness; *śrīḥ*—opulence; *tejaḥ*—strength; *smṛtiḥ*—memory; *satyam*—truthfulness; *yasya*—of which lusty desires; *naśyanti*—are vanquished; *janmanā*—from the very beginning of birth.

TRANSLATION

O my Lord, because of lusty desires from the very beginning of one's birth, the functions of one's senses, mind, life, body, religion, patience, intelligence, shyness, opulence, strength, memory and truthfulness are vanquished.

PURPORT

As stated in *Śrīmad-Bhāgavatam, kāmaṁ hṛd-rogam.* Materialistic life means that one is afflicted by a formidable disease called lusty desire. Liberation means freedom from lusty desires because it is only due to such desires that one must accept repeated birth and death. As long as one's lusty desires are unfulfilled, one must take birth after birth to fulfill them. Because of material desires, therefore, one performs various types of activities and receives various types of bodies with which to try to fulfill desires that are never satisfied. The only remedy is to take to devotional service, which begins when one is free from all material desires. *Anyābhilāṣitā-śūnyam. Anya-abhilāṣitā* means "material desire," and *śūnyam* means "free from." The spiritual soul has spiritual activities and spiritual desires, as described by Śrī Caitanya Mahāprabhu: *mama janmani janmanīśvare bhavatād bhaktir ahaitukī tvayi.* Unalloyed devotion to the service of the Lord is the only spiritual desire. To fulfill this spiritual desire, however, one must be free from all material desires. Desirelessness means freedom from material desires. This is described by Śrīla Rūpa Gosvāmī as *anyābhilāṣitā-śūnyam.* As soon as one has material desires, one loses his spiritual identity. Then all the paraphernalia of one's life, including one's senses, body, religion, patience and intelligence, are deviated from one's original Kṛṣṇa consciousness. As soon as one has material desires, one cannot properly use his senses, intelligence, mind and so on for the satisfaction of the Supreme Personality of Godhead. Māyāvādī philosophers want to become impersonal, senseless and mindless, but that is not possible. The living entity must be living, always existing with desires, ambitions and so on. These should be purified, however, so that one can desire spiritually and be spiritually ambitious, without material contamination. In every living entity these propensities exist because he is a living entity. When materially contaminated, however, one is put into the hands of material misery (*janma-mṛtyu-jarā-vyādhi*). If one wants to stop repeated birth and death, one must take to the devotional service of the Lord.

sarvopādhi-vinirmuktaṁ
tat-paratvena nirmalam
hṛṣīkeṇa hṛṣīkeśa-
sevanaṁ bhaktir ucyate

"Bhakti, or devotional service, means engaging all our senses in the service of the Lord, the Supreme Personality of Godhead, the master of all the senses. When the spirit soul renders service unto the Supreme, there are two side effects. One is freed from all material designations, and, simply by being employed in the service of the Lord, one's senses are purified."

TEXT 9

विमुञ्चति यदा कामान्मानवो मनसि स्थितान् ।
तर्ह्येव पुण्डरीकाक्ष भगवत्त्वाय कल्पते ॥ ९ ॥

vimuñcati yadā kāmān
mānavo manasi sthitān
tarhy eva puṇḍarīkākṣa
bhagavattvāya kalpate

vimuñcati—gives up; *yadā*—whenever; *kāmān*—all material desires; *mānavaḥ*—human society; *manasi*—within the mind; *sthitān*—situated; *tarhi*—at that time only; *eva*—indeed; *puṇḍarīka-akṣa*—O lotus-eyed Lord; *bhagavattvāya*—to be equally as opulent as the Lord; *kalpate*—becomes eligible.

TRANSLATION

O my Lord, when a human being is able to give up all the material desires in his mind, he becomes eligible to possess wealth and opulence like Yours.

PURPORT

Atheistic men sometimes criticize a devotee by saying, "If you do not want to take any benediction from the Lord and if the servant of the Lord is as opulent as the Lord Himself, why do you ask for the benediction of being engaged as the Lord's servant?" Śrīdhara Svāmī comments, *bhagavattvāya bhagavat-samān aiśvaryāya. Bhagavattva,* becoming as good as the Supreme Personality of Godhead, does not mean becoming one with Him or equal to Him, although in the spiritual world the servant is equally as opulent as the master. The servant of the Lord is engaged in the service of the Lord as a servant, friend, father, mother or conjugal lover, all of whom are equally as opulent as the Lord. This is *acintya-bhedābheda-tattva.* The master and servant are different yet equal in opulence. This is the meaning of simultaneous difference from the Supreme Lord and oneness with Him.

TEXT 10

ॐ नमो भगवते तुभ्यं पुरुषाय महात्मने ।
हरयेऽद्भुतसिंहाय ब्रह्मणे परमात्मने ॥१०॥

oṁ namo bhagavate tubhyaṁ
puruṣāya mahātmane

haraye 'dbhuta-siṁhāya
brahmaṇe paramātmane

oṁ—O my Lord, O Supreme Personality of Godhead; *namaḥ*—I offer my respectful obeisances; *bhagavate*—unto the Supreme Person; *tubhyam*—unto You; *puruṣāya*—unto the Supreme Person; *mahā-ātmane*—unto the Supreme Soul, or the Supersoul; *haraye*—unto the Lord, who vanquishes all the miseries of devotees; *adbhuta-siṁhāya*—unto Your wonderful lionlike form as Nṛsiṁhadeva; *brahmaṇe*—unto the Supreme Brahman; *parama-ātmane*—unto the Supreme Soul.

TRANSLATION

O my Lord, full of six opulences, O Supreme Person! O Supreme Soul, killer of all miseries! O Supreme Person in the form of a wonderful lion and man, let me offer my respectful obeisances unto You.

PURPORT

In the previous verse Prahlāda Mahārāja has explained that a devotee can achieve the platform of *bhagavattva*, being as good as the Supreme Person, but this does not mean that the devotee loses his position as a servant. A pure servant of the Lord, although as opulent as the Lord, is still meant to offer respectful obeisances to the Lord in service. Prahlāda Mahārāja was engaged in pacifying the Lord, and therefore he did not consider himself equal to the Lord. He defined his position as a servant and offered respectful obeisances unto the Lord.

TEXT 11

श्रीभगवानुवाच

नैकान्तिनो मे मयि जात्विहाशिष
आशासतेऽमुत्र च ये भवद्विधाः ।
तथापि मन्वन्तरमेतदत्र
दैत्येश्वराणामनुभुङ्क्ष्व भोगान् ॥११॥

śrī-bhagavān uvāca
naikāntino me mayi jātv ihāśiṣa
āśāsate 'mutra ca ye bhavad-vidhāḥ
tathāpi manvantaram etad atra
daityeśvarāṇām anubhuṅkṣva bhogān

śrī-bhagavān uvāca—the Supreme Personality of Godhead said; *na*—not; *ekāntinaḥ*—unalloyed, without desires except for the one desire for devotional service; *me*—from Me; *mayi*—unto Me; *jātu*—any time; *iha*—within this material world; *āśiṣaḥ*—benedictions; *āśāsate*—intent desire; *amutra*—in the next life; *ca*—and; *ye*—all such devotees who; *bhavat-vidhāḥ*—like you; *tathāpi*—still; *manvantaram*—the duration of time until the end of the life of one Manu; *etat*—this; *atra*—within this material world; *daitya-īśvarāṇām*—of the opulences of materialistic persons; *anubhuṅkṣva*—you can enjoy; *bhogān*—all material opulences.

TRANSLATION

The Supreme Personality of Godhead said: My dear Prahlāda, a devotee like you never desires any kind of material opulences, either in this life or in the next. Nonetheless, I order you to enjoy the opulences of the demons in this material world, acting as their king until the end of the duration of time occupied by Manu.

PURPORT

One Manu lives for a duration of time calculated to be an aggregate of seventy-one *yuga* cycles, each of which equals 4,300,000 years. Although atheistic men like to enjoy material opulences and they endeavor with great energy to build big residences, roads, cities and factories, unfortunately they cannot live more than eighty, ninety or at the utmost one hundred years. Although the materialist exerts so much energy to create a kingdom of hallucinations, he is unable to enjoy it for more than a few years. However, because Prahlāda Mahārāja was a devotee, the Lord allowed him to enjoy material opulence as the king of the materialists. Prahlāda Mahārāja had taken birth in the family of Hiraṇyakaśipu, who was the topmost materialist, and since Prahlāda was the bona fide heir of his father, the Supreme Lord allowed him to enjoy the kingdom created by his father for so many years that no materialist could calculate them. A devotee does not have to desire material opulence, but if he is a pure devotee, there is ample opportunity for him to enjoy material happiness also, without personal endeavor. Therefore, everyone is advised to take to devotional service under all circumstances. If one desires material opulence, he can also become a pure devotee, and his desires will be fulfilled. It is stated in *Śrīmad-Bhāgavatam* (2.3.10):

akāmaḥ sarva-kāmo vā
mokṣa-kāma udāra-dhīḥ
tīvreṇa bhakti-yogena
yajeta puruṣaṁ param

"Whether one desires everything or nothing, or whether he desires to merge into the existence of the Lord, he is intelligent only if he worships Lord Kṛṣṇa, the Supreme Personality of Godhead, by rendering transcendental loving service."

TEXT 12

कथा मदीया जुषमाणः प्रियास्त्व-
मावेश्य मामात्मनि सन्तमेकम् ।
सर्वेषु भूतेष्वधियज्ञमीशं
यजस्व योगेन च कर्म हिन्वन् ॥१२॥

kathā madīyā juṣamāṇaḥ priyās tvam
āveśya mām ātmani santam ekam
sarveṣu bhūteṣv adhiyajñam īśaṁ
yajasva yogena ca karma hinvan

kathāḥ—messages or instructions; *madīyāḥ*—given by Me; *juṣamāṇaḥ*—always hearing or contemplating; *priyāḥ*—extremely pleasing; *tvam*—yourself; *āveśya*—being fully absorbed in; *mām*—Me; *ātmani*—within the core of your heart; *santam*—existing; *ekam*—one (the same Supreme Soul); *sarveṣu*—in all; *bhūteṣu*—living entities; *adhiyajñam*—the enjoyer of all ritualistic ceremonies; *īśam*—the

Supreme Lord; *yajasva*—worship; *yogena*—by *bhakti-yoga,* devotional service; *ca*—also; *karma*—fruitive activities; *hinvan*—giving up.

TRANSLATION

It does not matter that you are in the material world. You should always, continuously, hear the instructions and messages given by Me and always be absorbed in thought of Me, for I am the Supersoul existing in the core of everyone's heart. Therefore, give up fruitive activities and worship Me.

PURPORT

When a devotee becomes materially very opulent, one should not think that he is enjoying the results of his fruitive activities. A devotee in this material world uses all material opulences for the service of the Lord because he is planning how to serve the Lord with these opulences, as advised by the Lord Himself. Whatever material opulence is within his possession he engages to expand the glories and service of the Lord. A devotee never performs any fruitive or ritualistic ceremony to enjoy the results of such *karma.* Rather, a devotee knows that *karma-kāṇḍa* is meant for the less intelligent man. Narottama dāsa Ṭhākura says in his *Prema-bhakti-candrikā, karma-kāṇḍa, jñāna-kāṇḍa, kevala viṣera bhāṇḍa:* both *karma-kāṇḍa* and *jñāna-kāṇḍa*—fruitive activities and speculation about the Supreme Lord—are like pots of poison. One who is attracted to *karma-kāṇḍa* and *jñāna-kāṇḍa* spoils his existence as a human being. Therefore a devotee is never interested in *karma-kāṇḍa* or *jñāna-kāṇḍa,* but is simply interested in favorable service to the Lord (*ānukūlyena kṛṣṇānuśīlanam*), or cultivation of spiritual activities in devotional service.

TEXT 13

भोगेन पुण्यं कुशलेन पापं
कलेवरं कालजवेन हित्वा ।
कीर्तिं विशुद्धां सुरलोकगीतां
विताय मामेष्यसि मुक्तबन्धः ॥१३॥

bhogena puṇyaṁ kuśalena pāpaṁ
kalevaraṁ kāla-javena hitvā
kīrtiṁ viśuddhāṁ sura-loka-gītāṁ
vitāya mām eṣyasi mukta-bandhaḥ

bhogena—by feelings of material happiness; *puṇyam*—pious activities or their results; *kuśalena*—by acting piously (devotional service is the best of all pious activities); *pāpam*—all kinds of reactions to impious activities; *kalevaram*—the material body; *kāla-javena*—by the most powerful time factor; *hitvā*—giving up; *kīrtim*—reputation; *viśuddhām*—transcendental or fully purified; *sura-loka-gītām*—praised even in the heavenly planets; *vitāya*—spreading all through the universe; *mām*—unto Me; *eṣyasi*—you will come back; *mukta-bandhaḥ*—being liberated from all bondage.

TRANSLATION

My dear Prahlāda, while you are in this material world you will exhaust all the reactions of pious activity by feeling happiness, and by acting piously you will neutralize impious activity. Because of the powerful time factor, you will give up your body, but the glories of your activities will be sung in the upper planetary systems, and being fully freed from all bondage, you will return home, back to Godhead.

PURPORT

Śrīla Viśvanātha Cakravartī Ṭhākura says: *evaṁ prahlādasyāṁśena sādhana-siddhatvaṁ nitya-siddhatvaṁ ca nāradādivaj jñeyam.* There are two classes of devotees—the *sādhana-siddha* and the *nitya-siddha.* Prahlāda Mahārāja is a mixed *siddha;* that is, he is perfect partly because of executing devotional service and partly because of eternal perfection. Thus he is compared to such devotees as Nārada. Formerly, Nārada Muni was the son of a maidservant, and therefore in his next birth he attained perfection (*sādhana-siddhi*) because of having executed devotional service. Yet he is also a *nitya-siddha* because he never forgets the Supreme Personality of Godhead.

The word *kuśalena* is very important. One should live in the material world very expertly. The material world is known as the world of duality because one sometimes has to act impiously and sometimes has to act piously. Although one does not want to act impiously, the world is so fashioned that there is always danger (*padaṁ padaṁ yad vipadām*). Thus even when performing devotional service a devotee has to create many enemies. Prahlāda Mahārāja himself had experience of this, for even his father became his enemy. A devotee should expertly manage to think always of the Supreme Lord so that the reactions of suffering cannot touch him. This is the expert management of *pāpa-puṇya*—pious and impious activities. An exalted devotee like Prahlāda Mahārāja is *jīvan-mukta;* he is liberated even in this very life in the material body.

TEXT 14

य एतत् कीर्तयेन्मह्यं त्वया गीतमिदं नरः ।
त्वां च मां च स्मरन्काले कर्मबन्धात् प्रमुच्यते ॥१४॥

ya etat kīrtayen mahyaṁ
tvayā gītam idaṁ naraḥ
tvāṁ ca māṁ ca smaran kāle
karma-bandhāt pramucyate

yaḥ—anyone who; *etat*—this activity; *kīrtayet*—chants; *mahyam*—unto Me; *tvayā*—by you; *gītam*—prayers offered; *idam*—this; *naraḥ*—human being; *tvām*—you; *ca*—as well as; *mām ca*—Me also; *smaran*—remembering; *kāle*—in due course of time; *karma-bandhāt*—from the bondage of material activities; *pramucyate*—becomes free.

TRANSLATION

One who always remembers your activities and My activities also, and who chants the prayers you have offered, becomes free, in due course of time, from the reactions of material activities.

PURPORT

Here it is stated that anyone who chants and hears about the activities of Prahlāda Mahārāja and, in relationship with Prahlāda's activities, the activities of Nṛsiṁhadeva, gradually becomes free from all the bondage of fruitive activities. As stated in *Bhagavad-gītā* (2.15, 2.56):

yaṁ hi na vyathayanty ete
puruṣaṁ puruṣarṣabha
sama-duḥkha-sukhaṁ dhīraṁ
so 'mṛtatvāya kalpate

"O best among men [Arjuna], the person who is not disturbed by happiness and distress and is steady in both is certainly eligible for liberation."

duḥkheṣv anudvigna-manāḥ
sukheṣu vigata-spṛhaḥ
vīta-rāga-bhaya-krodhaḥ
sthita-dhīr munir ucyate

"One who is not disturbed in spite of the threefold miseries, who is not elated when there is happiness, and who is free from attachment, fear and anger, is called a sage of steady mind." A devotee should not be aggrieved in an awkward position, nor should he feel extraordinarily happy in material opulence. This is the way of expert management of material life. Because a devotee knows how to manage expertly, he is called *jīvan-mukta.* As Rūpa Gosvāmī explains in *Bhakti-rasāmṛta-sindhu:*

īhā yasya harer dāsye
karmaṇā manasā girā
nikhilāsv apy avasthāsu
jīvan-muktaḥ sa ucyate

"A person acting in Kṛṣṇa consciousness (or, in other words, in the service of Kṛṣṇa) with his body, mind, intelligence and words is a liberated person even within this material world, although he may be engaged in many so-called material activities." Because of constantly engaging in devotional service, in any condition of life, a devotee is free from all material bondage.

bhaktiḥ punāti man-niṣṭhā
śva-pākān api sambhavāt

"Even one born in a family of meat-eaters is purified if he engages in devotional service." (*Bhāg.* 11.14.21) Śrīla Jīva Gosvāmī cites this verse in logically supporting that anyone who chants about the pure life and activities of Prahlāda Mahārāja is freed from the reactions of material activities.

TEXTS 15–17

श्रीप्रह्राद उवाच
वरं वरय एतत् ते वरदेशान्महेश्वर ।
यदनिन्दत् पिता मे त्वामविद्वांस्तेज ऐश्वरम् ॥१५॥
विद्धामर्षाशयः साक्षात् सर्वलोकगुरुं प्रभुम् ।
भ्रातृहेति मृषादृष्टिस्त्वद्भक्ते मयि चाघवान् ॥१६॥
तस्मात् पिता मे पूयेत दुरन्ताद् दुस्तरादघात् ।
पूतस्तेऽपाङ्गसंदृष्टस्तदा कृपणवत्सल ॥१७॥

śrī-prahrāda uvāca
varaṁ varaya etat te
varadeśān maheśvara
yad anindat pitā me
tvām avidvāṁs teja aiśvaram

viddhāmarṣāśayaḥ sākṣāt
sarva-loka-guruṁ prabhum
bhrātṛ-heti mṛṣā-dṛṣṭis
tvad-bhakte mayi cāghavān

tasmāt pitā me pūyeta
durantād dustarād aghāt
pūtas te 'pāṅga-saṁdṛṣṭas
tadā kṛpaṇa-vatsala

śrī-prahrādaḥ uvāca—Prahlāda Mahārāja said; *varam*—benediction; *varaye*—I pray; *etat*—this; *te*—from You; *varada-īśāt*—the Supreme Personality of Godhead, who offers benedictions even to such exalted demigods as Brahmā and Śiva; *mahā-īśvara*—O my Supreme Lord; *yat*—that; *anindat*—vilified; *pitā*—father; *me*—my; *tvām*—You; *avidvān*—without knowledge of; *tejaḥ*—strength; *aiśvaram*—supremacy;

viddha—being polluted; *amarṣa*—with anger; *āśayaḥ*—within the heart; *sākṣāt*—directly; *sarva-loka-gurum*—unto the supreme spiritual master of all living beings; *prabhum*—unto the supreme master; *bhrātṛ-hā*—the killer of his brother; *iti*—thus; *mṛṣā-dṛṣṭiḥ*—falsely envious because of a false conception; *tvat-bhakte*—unto Your devotee; *mayi*—unto me; *ca*—and; *agha-vān*—who committed heavily sinful activities; *tasmāt*—from that; *pitā*—father; *me*—my; *pūyeta*—may be purified; *durantāt*—very great; *dustarāt*—difficult to pass over; *aghāt*—from all sinful activities; *pūtaḥ*—(although he was) purified; *te*—of You; *apāṅga*—by the glance over him; *saṁdṛṣṭaḥ*—being looked at; *tadā*—at that time; *kṛpaṇa-vatsala*—O You who are merciful to the materialistic.

TRANSLATION

Prahlāda Mahārāja said: O Supreme Lord, because You are so merciful to the fallen souls, I ask You for only one benediction. I know that my father, at the time of his death, had already been purified by Your glance upon him, but because of his ignorance of Your beautiful power and supremacy, he was unnecessarily angry at You, falsely thinking that You were the killer of his brother. Thus he directly blasphemed Your Lordship, the spiritual master of all living beings, and committed heavily sinful activities directed against me, Your devotee. I wish that he be excused for these sinful activities.

PURPORT

Although Hiraṇyakaśipu was purified as soon as he came in contact with the Lord's lap and the Lord saw him, Prahlāda Mahārāja still wanted to hear from the Lord's own mouth that his father had been purified by the Lord's causeless mercy. Prahlāda Mahārāja offered this prayer to the Lord for the sake of his father. As a Vaiṣṇava son, despite all the inconveniences imposed upon him by his father, he could not forget his father's affection.

TEXT 18

श्रीभगवानुवाच

त्रिःसप्तभिः पिता पूतः पितृभिः सह तेऽनघ ।
यत् साधोऽस्य कुले जातो भवान्वै कुलपावनः ॥१८॥

śrī-bhagavān uvāca
triḥ-saptabhiḥ pitā pūtaḥ
pitṛbhiḥ saha te 'nagha
yat sādho 'sya kule jāto
bhavān vai kula-pāvanaḥ

śrī-bhagavān uvāca—the Supreme Personality of Godhead said; *triḥ-saptabhiḥ*—seven multiplied by three (that is to say, twenty-one); *pitā*—father; *pūtaḥ*—purified; *pitṛbhiḥ*—with your forefathers; *saha*—all together; *te*—your; *anagha*—O most sinless personality (Prahlāda Mahārāja); *yat*—because; *sādho*—O great saintly person; *asya*—of this person; *kule*—in the dynasty; *jātaḥ*—took birth; *bhavān*—you; *vai*—indeed; *kula-pāvanaḥ*—the purifier of the whole dynasty.

TRANSLATION

The Supreme Personality of Godhead said: My dear Prahlāda, O most pure, O great saintly person, your father has been purified, along with twenty-one forefathers in your family. Because you were born in this family, the entire dynasty has been purified.

PURPORT

The word *triḥ-saptabhiḥ* means seven multiplied by three. In one's family one can count back four or five generations—to one's great-grandfather or even one's great-grandfather's father—but since the Lord mentions twenty-one forefathers, this indicates that the benediction expands to other families also. Before the present family in which one has taken birth, one must have been born in other families. Thus when a Vaiṣṇava takes birth in a family, by the grace of the Lord he purifies not only that family but also the families of his previous births.

TEXT 19

यत्र यत्र च मद्भक्ताः प्रशान्ताः समदर्शिनः ।
साधवः समुदाचारास्ते पूयन्तेऽपि कीकटाः ॥१९॥

yatra yatra ca mad-bhaktāḥ
praśāntāḥ sama-darśinaḥ

sādhavaḥ samudācārās
te pūyante 'pi kīkaṭāḥ

yatra yatra—wherever and whenever; *ca*—also; *mat-bhaktāḥ*—My devotees; *praśāntāḥ*—extremely peaceful; *sama-darśinaḥ*—equipoised; *sādhavaḥ*—decorated with all good qualities; *samudācārāḥ*—equally magnanimous; *te*—all of them; *pūyante*—are purified; *api*—even; *kīkaṭāḥ*—a degraded country or the inhabitants of such a place.

TRANSLATION

Whenever and wherever there are peaceful, equipoised devotees who are well behaved and decorated with all good qualities, that place and the dynasties there, even if condemned, are purified.

PURPORT

Wherever exalted devotees stay, not only they and their dynasties but the entire country is purified.

TEXT 20

सर्वात्मना न हिंसन्ति भूतग्रामेषु किञ्चन ।
उच्चावचेषु दैत्येन्द्र मद्भावविगतस्पृहाः ॥२०॥

sarvātmanā na hiṁsanti
bhūta-grāmeṣu kiñcana
uccāvaceṣu daityendra
mad-bhāva-vigata-spṛhāḥ

sarva-ātmanā—in all respects, even in the modes of anger and jealousy; *na*—never; *hiṁsanti*—they are envious; *bhūta-grāmeṣu*—among all species of life; *kiñcana*—toward any one of them; *ucca-avaceṣu*—the lower and higher living entities; *daitya-indra*—O my dear Prahlāda, King of the Daityas; *mat-bhāva*—because of devotional service unto Me; *vigata*—given up; *spṛhāḥ*—all material modes of anger and greed.

TRANSLATION

My dear Prahlāda, King of the Daityas, because of being attached to devotional service to Me, My devotee does not distinguish between lower and higher living entities. In all respects, he is never jealous of anyone.

TEXT 21

भवन्ति पुरुषा लोके मद्भक्तास्त्वामनुव्रताः ।
भवान्मे खलु भक्तानां सर्वेषां प्रतिरूपधृक् ॥२१॥

bhavanti puruṣā loke
mad-bhaktās tvām anuvratāḥ
bhavān me khalu bhaktānāṁ
sarveṣāṁ pratirūpa-dhṛk

bhavanti—become; *puruṣāḥ*—persons; *loke*—in this world; *mat-bhaktāḥ*—My pure devotees; *tvām*—you; *anuvratāḥ*—following in your footsteps; *bhavān*—you; *me*—My; *khalu*—indeed; *bhaktānām*—of all devotees; *sarveṣām*—in different mellows; *pratirūpa-dhṛk*—tangible example.

TRANSLATION

Those who follow your example will naturally become My pure devotees. You are the best example of My devotee, and others should follow in your footsteps.

PURPORT

In this connection, Śrīla Madhvācārya quotes a verse from the *Skanda Purāṇa:*

ṛte tu tāttvikān devān
nāradādīṁs tathaiva ca
prahrādād uttamaḥ ko nu
viṣṇu-bhaktau jagat-traye

There are many, many devotees of the Supreme Personality of Godhead, and they have been enumerated in *Śrīmad-Bhāgavatam* (6.3.20) as follows:

svayambhūr nāradaḥ śambhuḥ
kumāraḥ kapilo manuḥ
prahlādo janako bhīṣmo
balir vaiyāsakir vayam

Of the twelve authorized devotees—Lord Brahmā, Nārada, Lord Śiva, Kapila, Manu and so on—Prahlāda Mahārāja is understood to be the best example.

TEXT 22

कुरु त्वं प्रेतकृत्यानि पितुः पूतस्य सर्वशः ।
मदङ्गस्पर्शनेनाङ्ग लोकान्यास्यति सुप्रजाः ॥२२॥

kuru tvaṁ preta-kṛtyāni
pituḥ pūtasya sarvaśaḥ
mad-aṅga-sparśanenāṅga
lokān yāsyati suprajāḥ

kuru—perform; *tvam*—you; *preta-kṛtyāni*—the ritualistic ceremony performed after death; *pituḥ*—of your father; *pūtasya*—already purified; *sarvaśaḥ*—in all respects; *mat-aṅga*—My body; *sparśanena*—by touching; *aṅga*—My dear child; *lokān*—to planets; *yāsyati*—he will be elevated; *su-prajāḥ*—to become a devotee-citizen.

TRANSLATION

My dear child, your father has already been purified just by the touch of My body at the time of his death. Nonetheless, the duty of a son is to perform the śrāddha ritualistic ceremony after his father's death so that his father may be promoted to a planetary system where he may become a good citizen and devotee.

PURPORT

In this regard, Śrīla Viśvanātha Cakravartī Ṭhākura says that although Hiraṇyakaśipu was already purified, he had to take birth on a higher planetary system to become a devotee again. Prahlāda Mahārāja was advised to perform the ritualistic ceremony as a matter of etiquette, for the Supreme Personality of Godhead under no circumstances wants to stop the regulative principles. Madhva Muni also instructs:

madhu-kaiṭabhau bhakty-abhāvā
dūrau bhagavato mṛtau
tama eva kramād āptau
bhaktyā ced yo hariṁ yayau

When the demons Madhu and Kaiṭabha were killed by the Supreme Personality of Godhead, their kinsmen also observed the ritualistic ceremonies so that these demons could return home, back to Godhead.

TEXT 23

पित्र्यं च स्थानमातिष्ठ यथोक्तं ब्रह्मवादिभिः ।
मय्यावेश्य मनस्तात कुरु कर्माणि मत्परः ॥२३॥

pitryaṁ ca sthānam ātiṣṭha
yathoktaṁ brahmavādibhiḥ
mayy āveśya manas tāta
kuru karmāṇi mat-paraḥ

pitryam—paternal; *ca*—also; *sthānam*—place, throne; *ātiṣṭha*—sit upon; *yathā-uktam*—as described; *brahmavādibhiḥ*—by the followers of Vedic civilization; *mayi*—unto Me; *āveśya*—being fully absorbed; *manaḥ*—the mind; *tāta*—My dear boy; *kuru*—just execute; *karmāṇi*—the regulative duties; *mat-paraḥ*—just for the sake of My work.

TRANSLATION

After performing the ritualistic ceremonies, take charge of your father's kingdom. Sit upon the throne and do not be disturbed by materialistic activities. Please keep your mind fixed upon Me. Without transgressing the injunctions of the Vedas, as a matter of formality you may perform your particular duties.

PURPORT

When one becomes a devotee, he no longer has any duty to the Vedic regulative principles. One has many duties to perform, but if one becomes fully devoted to the Lord, he no longer has any such obligations. As stated in *Śrīmad-Bhāgavatam* (11.5.41):

devarṣi-bhūtāpta-nṛṇāṁ pitṝṇāṁ
na kiṅkaro nāyam ṛṇī ca rājan
sarvātmanā yaḥ śaraṇaṁ śaraṇyaṁ
gato mukundaṁ parihṛtya kartam

One who has fully surrendered to the lotus feet of the Lord is no longer a debtor to his forefathers, the great sages, human society, the common man or any living entity.

The Supreme Personality of Godhead nonetheless advised Prahlāda Mahārāja to follow the regulative principles, for since he was going to be the king, others would follow his example. Thus Lord Nṛsiṁhadeva advised Prahlāda Mahārāja to engage in his political duties so that people would become the Lord's devotees.

yad yad ācarati śreṣṭhas
tat tad evetaro janaḥ
sa yat pramāṇaṁ kurute
lokas tad anuvartate

"Whatever action a great man performs, common men follow. And whatever standards he sets by exemplary acts, all the world pursues." (Bg. 3.21) One should not be attached to any materialistic activities, but a devotee may perform such activities as an example to show the common man that one should not deviate from the Vedic injunctions.

TEXT 24

श्रीनारद उवाच
प्रह्रादोऽपि तथा चक्रे पितुर्यत्साम्परायिकम् ।
यथाह भगवान् राजन्नभिषिक्तो द्विजातिभिः ॥२४॥

śrī-nārada uvāca
prahrādo 'pi tathā cakre
pitur yat sāmparāyikam
yathāha bhagavān rājann
abhiṣikto dvijātibhiḥ

śrī-nāradaḥ uvāca—Nārada Muni said; *prahrādaḥ*—Prahlāda Mahārāja; *api*—also; *tathā*—in that way; *cakre*—executed; *pituḥ*—of his father; *yat*—whatever; *sāmparāyikam*—ritualistic ceremonies performed after death; *yathā*—even as; *āha*—order; *bhagavān*—the Supreme Personality of Godhead; *rājan*—O King Yudhiṣṭhira; *abhiṣiktaḥ*—he was enthroned in the kingdom; *dvi-jātibhiḥ*—by the *brāhmaṇas* present.

TRANSLATION

Śrī Nārada Muni continued: Thus, as the Supreme Personality of Godhead ordered, Prahlāda Mahārāja performed the ritualistic ceremonies for his father. O King Yudhiṣṭhira, he was then enthroned in the kingdom of Hiraṇyakaśipu, as directed by the brāhmaṇas.

PURPORT

It is essential that society be divided into four groups of men—*brāhmaṇas*, *kṣatriyas*, *vaiśyas* and *śūdras*. Here we see that although Prahlāda was perfect in every respect, he nonetheless followed the instructions of the *brāhmaṇas* who performed the Vedic rituals. Therefore in society there must be a very intelligent class of leaders who are well versed in the Vedic knowledge so that they can guide the entire populace to follow the Vedic principles and thus gradually become most perfect and eligible to return home, back to Godhead.

TEXT 25

प्रसादसुमुखं दृष्ट्वा ब्रह्मा नरहरिं हरिम् ।
स्तुत्वा वाग्भिः पवित्राभिः प्राह देवादिभिर्वृतः ॥२५॥

prasāda-sumukhaṁ dṛṣṭvā
brahmā narahariṁ harim

stutvā vāgbhiḥ pavitrābhiḥ
prāha devādibhir vṛtaḥ

prasāda-sumukham—whose face was bright because the Supreme Lord was pleased; *dṛṣṭvā*—seeing this situation; *brahmā*—Lord Brahmā; *nara-harim*—unto Lord Nṛsiṁhadeva; *harim*—the Supreme Personality of Godhead; *stutvā*—offering prayers; *vāgbhiḥ*—by transcendental words; *pavitrābhiḥ*—without any material contamination; *prāha*—addressed (the Lord); *deva-ādibhiḥ*—by other demigods; *vṛtaḥ*—surrounded.

TRANSLATION

Lord Brahmā, surrounded by the other demigods, was bright-faced because the Lord was pleased. Thus he offered prayers to the Lord with transcendental words.

TEXT 26

श्रीब्रह्मोवाच
देवदेवाखिलाध्यक्ष भूतभावन पूर्वज ।
दिष्ट्या ते निहतः पापो लोकसन्तापनोऽसुरः ॥२६॥

śrī-brahmovāca
deva-devākhilādhyakṣa
bhūta-bhāvana pūrvaja
diṣṭyā te nihataḥ pāpo
loka-santāpano 'suraḥ

śrī-brahmā uvāca—Lord Brahmā said; *deva-deva*—O my Lord, Lord of all the demigods; *akhila-adhyakṣa*—owner of the whole universe; *bhūta-bhāvana*—O cause of all living entities; *pūrva-ja*—O original Personality of Godhead; *diṣṭyā*—by Your example or because of our good fortune; *te*—by You; *nihataḥ*—killed; *pāpaḥ*—most sinful; *loka-santāpanaḥ*—giving trouble to the entire universe; *asuraḥ*—the demon Hiraṇyakaśipu.

TRANSLATION

Lord Brahmā said: O Supreme Lord of all lords, proprietor of the entire universe, O benedictor of all living entities, O original

person [ādi-puruṣa], because of our good fortune You have now killed this sinful demon, who was giving trouble to the entire universe.

PURPORT

The word *pūrvaja* is described in *Bhagavad-gītā* (10.8): *ahaṁ sarvasya prabhavo mattaḥ sarvaṁ pravartate.* All the demigods, including Lord Brahmā, are manifested from the Supreme Personality of Godhead. Therefore the original person, the cause of all causes, is Govinda, the *ādi-puruṣam.*

TEXT 27

योऽसौ लब्धवरो मत्तो न वध्यो मम सृष्टिभिः ।
तपोयोगबलोन्नद्धः समस्तनिगमानहन् ॥२७॥

yo 'sau labdha-varo matto
na vadhyo mama sṛṣṭibhiḥ
tapo-yoga-balonnaddhaḥ
samasta-nigamān ahan

yaḥ—the person who; *asau*—he (Hiraṇyakaśipu); *labdha-varaḥ*—being given the extraordinary benediction; *mattaḥ*—from me; *na vadhyaḥ*—not to be killed; *mama sṛṣṭibhiḥ*—by any living being created by me; *tapaḥ-yoga-bala*—by austerity, mystic power and strength; *unnaddhaḥ*—thus being very proud; *samasta*—all; *nigamān*—Vedic injunctions; *ahan*—disregarded, transgressed.

TRANSLATION

This demon, Hiraṇyakaśipu, received from me the benediction that he would not be killed by any living being within my creation. With this assurance and with strength derived from austerities and mystic power, he became excessively proud and transgressed all the Vedic injunctions.

TEXT 28

दिष्ट्या तत्तनयः साधुर्महाभागवतोऽर्भकः ।
त्वया विमोचितो मृत्योर्दिष्ट्या त्वां समितोऽधुना ॥२८॥

diṣṭyā tat-tanayaḥ sādhur
mahā-bhāgavato 'rbhakaḥ
tvayā vimocito mṛtyor
diṣṭyā tvāṁ samito 'dhunā

diṣṭyā—by fortune; *tat-tanayaḥ*—his son; *sādhuḥ*—who is a great saintly person; *mahā-bhāgavataḥ*—a great and exalted devotee; *arbhakaḥ*—although a child; *tvayā*—by Your Lordship; *vimocitaḥ*—released; *mṛtyoḥ*—from the clutches of death; *diṣṭyā*—also by great fortune; *tvām samitaḥ*—perfectly under Your shelter; *adhunā*—now.

TRANSLATION

By great fortune, Hiraṇyakaśipu's son Prahlāda Mahārāja has now been released from death, for although he is a child, he is an exalted devotee. Now he is fully under the protection of Your lotus feet.

TEXT 29

एतद् वपुस्ते भगवन्ध्यायतः परमात्मनः ।
सर्वतो गोप्तृ संत्रासान्मृत्योरपि जिघांसतः ॥२९॥

etad vapus te bhagavan
dhyāyataḥ paramātmanaḥ
sarvato goptṛ santrāsān
mṛtyor api jighāṁsataḥ

etat—this; *vapuḥ*—body; *te*—Your; *bhagavan*—O Supreme Personality of Godhead; *dhyāyataḥ*—those who meditate upon; *parama-ātmanaḥ*—of the Supreme Person; *sarvataḥ*—from everywhere; *goptṛ*—the protector; *santrāsāt*—from all kinds of fear; *mṛtyoḥ api*—even from fear of death; *jighāṁsataḥ*—if one is envied by an enemy.

TRANSLATION

My dear Lord, O Supreme Personality of Godhead, You are the Supreme Soul. If one meditates upon Your transcendental body,

You naturally protect him from all sources of fear, even the imminent danger of death.

PURPORT

Everyone is sure to die, for no one is excused from the hands of death, which is but a feature of the Supreme Personality of Godhead (*mṛtyuḥ sarva-haraś cāham*). When one becomes a devotee, however, he is not destined to die according to a limited duration of life. Everyone has a limited duration of life, but a devotee's lifetime can be extended by the mercy of the Supreme Lord, who is able to nullify the results of one's *karma. Karmāṇi nirdahati kintu ca bhakti-bhājāṁ.* This is the statement of *Brahma-saṁhitā* (5.54). A devotee is not under the laws of *karma.* Therefore even a devotee's scheduled death can be avoided by the causeless mercy of the Supreme Lord. God protects the devotee even from the extreme danger of death.

TEXT 30

श्रीभगवानुवाच
मैवं विभोऽसुराणां ते प्रदेयः पद्मसम्भव ।
वरः क्रूरनिसर्गाणामहीनाममृतं यथा ॥३०॥

śrī-bhagavān uvāca
maivaṁ vibho 'surāṇāṁ te
pradeyaḥ padma-sambhava
varaḥ krūra-nisargāṇām
ahīnām amṛtaṁ yathā

śrī-bhagavān uvāca—the Supreme Personality of Godhead replied (to Brahmā); *mā*—do not; *evam*—thus; *vibho*—O great person; *asurāṇām*—unto the demons; *te*—by you; *pradeyaḥ*—bestow benedictions; *padma-sambhava*—O Lord Brahmā, born from the lotus flower; *varaḥ*—benediction; *krūra-nisargāṇām*—persons who are by nature very cruel and jealous; *ahīnām*—to snakes; *amṛtam*—nectar or milk; *yathā*—just as.

TRANSLATION

The Personality of Godhead replied: My dear Lord Brahmā, O great lord born from the lotus flower, just as it is dangerous to feed milk to a snake, so it is dangerous to give benedictions to demons, who are by nature ferocious and jealous. I warn you not to give such benedictions to any demon again.

TEXT 31

श्रीनारद उवाच

इत्युक्त्वा भगवान्राजंस्ततश्चान्तर्दधे हरिः ।
अदृश्यः सर्वभूतानां पूजितः परमेष्ठिना ॥३१॥

śrī-nārada uvāca
ity uktvā bhagavān rājaṁs
tataś cāntardadhe hariḥ
adṛśyaḥ sarva-bhūtānāṁ
pūjitaḥ parameṣṭhinā

śrī-nāradaḥ uvāca—Nārada Muni said; *iti uktvā*—saying this; *bhagavān*—the Supreme Personality of Godhead; *rājan*—O King Yudhiṣṭhira; *tataḥ*—from that place; *ca*—also; *antardadhe*—disappeared; *hariḥ*—the Lord; *adṛśyaḥ*—without being visible; *sarva-bhūtānām*—by all kinds of living entities; *pūjitaḥ*—being worshiped; *parameṣṭhinā*—by Lord Brahmā.

TRANSLATION

Nārada Muni continued: O King Yudhiṣṭhira, the Supreme Personality of Godhead, who is not visible to an ordinary human being, spoke in this way, instructing Lord Brahmā. Then, being worshiped by Brahmā, the Lord disappeared from that place.

TEXT 32

ततः सम्पूज्य शिरसा ववन्दे परमेष्ठिनम् ।
भवं प्रजापतीन्देवान्प्रह्लादो भगवत्कलाः ॥३२॥

tataḥ sampūjya śirasā
vavande parameṣṭhinam
bhavaṁ prajāpatīn devān
prahrādo bhagavat-kalāḥ

tataḥ—thereafter; *sampūjya*—worshiping; *śirasā*—by bowing the head; *vavande*—offered prayers; *parameṣṭhinam*—to Lord Brahmā; *bhavam*—to Lord Śiva; *prajāpatīn*—to the great demigods entrusted with increasing the population; *devān*—to all the great demigods; *prahrādaḥ*—Prahlāda Mahārāja; *bhagavat-kalāḥ*—influential parts of the Lord.

TRANSLATION

Prahlāda Mahārāja then worshiped and offered prayers to all the demigods, such as Brahmā, Śiva and the prajāpatis, who are all parts of the Lord.

TEXT 33

ततः काव्यादिभिः सार्धं मुनिभिः कमलासनः ।
दैत्यानां दानवानां च प्रह्लादमकरोत् पतिम् ॥३३॥

tataḥ kāvyādibhiḥ sārdhaṁ
munibhiḥ kamalāsanaḥ
daityānāṁ dānavānāṁ ca
prahrādam akarot patim

tataḥ—thereafter; *kāvya-ādibhiḥ*—with Śukrācārya and others; *sārdham*—and with; *munibhiḥ*—great saintly persons; *kamala-āsanaḥ*—Lord Brahmā; *daityānām*—of all the demons; *dānavānām*—of all the giants; *ca*—and; *prahrādam*—Prahlāda Mahārāja; *akarot*—created; *patim*—the master or king.

TRANSLATION

Thereafter, along with Śukrācārya and other great saints, Lord Brahmā, whose seat is on the lotus flower, made Prahlāda the king of all the demons and giants in the universe.

PURPORT

By the grace of Lord Nṛsiṁhadeva, Prahlāda Mahārāja became a greater king than his father, Hiraṇyakaśipu. Prahlāda's inauguration was performed by Lord Brahmā in the presence of other saintly persons and demigods.

TEXT 34

प्रतिनन्द्य ततो देवाः प्रयुज्य परमाशिषः ।
स्वधामानि ययू राजन्ब्रह्माद्याः प्रतिपूजिताः ॥३४॥

pratinandya tato devāḥ
prayujya paramāśiṣaḥ
sva-dhāmāni yayū rājan
brahmādyāḥ pratipūjitāḥ

pratinandya—congratulating; *tataḥ*—thereafter; *devāḥ*—all the demigods; *prayujya*—having offered; *parama-āśiṣaḥ*—exalted benedictions; *sva-dhāmāni*—to their respective abodes; *yayuḥ*—returned; *rājan*—O King Yudhiṣṭhira; *brahma-ādyāḥ*—all the demigods, headed by Lord Brahmā; *pratipūjitāḥ*—being thoroughly worshiped (by Prahlāda Mahārāja).

TRANSLATION

O King Yudhiṣṭhira, after all the demigods, headed by Lord Brahmā, were properly worshiped by Prahlāda Mahārāja, they offered Prahlāda their utmost benedictions and then returned to their respective abodes.

TEXT 35

एवं च पार्षदौ विष्णोः पुत्रत्वं प्रापितौ दितेः ।
हृदि स्थितेन हरिणा वैरभावेन तौ हतौ ॥३५॥

evaṁ ca pārṣadau viṣṇoḥ
putratvaṁ prāpitau diteḥ
hṛdi sthitena hariṇā
vaira-bhāvena tau hatau

evam—in this way; *ca*—also; *pārṣadau*—the two personal associates; *viṣṇoḥ*—of Lord Viṣṇu; *putratvam*—becoming the sons; *prāpitau*—having gotten; *diteḥ*—of Diti; *hṛdi*—within the core of the heart; *sthitena*—being situated; *hariṇā*—by the Supreme Lord; *vaira-bhāvena*—by conceiving as an enemy; *tau*—both of them; *hatau*—were killed.

TRANSLATION

Thus the two associates of Lord Viṣṇu who had become Hiraṇyākṣa and Hiraṇyakaśipu, the sons of Diti, were both killed. By illusion they had thought that the Supreme Lord, who is situated in everyone's heart, was their enemy.

PURPORT

The discourse concerning Lord Nṛsiṁhadeva and Prahlāda Mahārāja began when Mahārāja Yudhiṣṭhira asked Nārada how Śiśupāla had merged into the body of Kṛṣṇa. Śiśupāla and Dantavakra were the same Hiraṇyākṣa and Hiraṇyakaśipu. Here Nārada Muni is relating how in three different births the associates of Lord Viṣṇu were killed by Lord Viṣṇu Himself. First they were the demons Hiraṇyākṣa and Hiraṇyakaśipu.

TEXT 36

पुनश्च विप्रशापेन राक्षसौ तौ बभूवतुः ।
कुम्भकर्णदशग्रीवौ हतौ तौ रामविक्रमैः ॥३६॥

punaś ca vipra-śāpena
rākṣasau tau babhūvatuḥ
kumbhakarṇa-daśa-grīvau
hatau tau rāma-vikramaiḥ

punaḥ—again; *ca*—also; *vipra-śāpena*—being cursed by the *brāhmaṇas; rākṣasau*—the two Rākṣasas; *tau*—both of them; *babhūvatuḥ*—incarnated as; *kumbhakarṇa-daśa-grīvau*—known as Kumbhakarṇa and the ten-headed Rāvaṇa (in their next birth); *hatau*—they also were killed; *tau*—both of them; *rāma-vikramaiḥ*—by the extraordinary strength of Lord Rāmacandra.

TRANSLATION

Being cursed by the brāhmaṇas, the same two associates took birth again as Kumbhakarṇa and the ten-headed Rāvaṇa. These two Rākṣasas were killed by Lord Rāmacandra's extraordinary power.

TEXT 37

शयानौ युधि निर्भिन्नहृदयौ रामशायकैः ।
तच्चित्तौ जहतुर्देहं यथा प्राक्तनजन्मनि ॥३७॥

śayānau yudhi nirbhinna-
hṛdayau rāma-śāyakaiḥ
tac-cittau jahatur dehaṁ
yathā prāktana-janmani

śayānau—being laid down; *yudhi*—on the battlefield; *nirbhinna*—being pierced; *hṛdayau*—in the core of the heart; *rāma-śāyakaiḥ*—by the arrows of Lord Rāmacandra; *tat-cittau*—thinking or being conscious of Lord Rāmacandra; *jahatuḥ*—gave up; *deham*—body; *yathā*—even as; *prāktana-janmani*—in their previous births.

TRANSLATION

Pierced by the arrows of Lord Rāmacandra, both Kumbhakarṇa and Rāvaṇa lay on the ground and left their bodies, fully absorbed in thought of the Lord, just as they had in their previous births as Hiraṇyākṣa and Hiraṇyakaśipu.

TEXT 38

ताविहाथ पुनर्जातौ शिशुपालकरूषजौ ।
हरौ वैरानुबन्धेन पश्यतस्ते समीयतुः ॥३८॥

tāv ihātha punar jātau
śiśupāla-karūṣa-jau
harau vairānubandhena
paśyatas te samīyatuḥ

tau—both of them; *iha*—in this human society; *atha*—in this way; *punaḥ*—again; *jātau*—took their births; *śiśupāla*—Śiśupāla; *karūṣa-jau*—Dantavakra; *harau*—unto the Supreme Personality of Godhead; *vaira-anubandhena*—by the bondage of considering the Lord an enemy; *paśyataḥ*—were looking on; *te*—while you; *samīyatuḥ*—merged or went into the lotus feet of the Lord.

TRANSLATION

They both took birth again in human society as Śiśupāla and Dantavakra and continued in the same enmity toward the Lord. It is they who merged into the body of the Lord in your presence.

PURPORT

Vairānubandhena. Acting like the Lord's enemy is also beneficial for the living entity. *Kāmād dveṣād bhayāt snehād.* Whether in lusty desire, anger, fear or envy of the Lord, somehow or other, as recommended by Śrīla Rūpa Gosvāmī (*tasmāt kenāpy upāyena*), one should become attached to the Supreme Personality of Godhead and ultimately achieve the goal of returning home, back to Godhead. What, then, is to be said of one who is related to the Supreme Personality of Godhead as a servant, friend, father, mother or conjugal lover?

TEXT 39

एनः पूर्वकृतं यत् तद् राजानः कृष्णवैरिणः ।
जहुस्तेऽन्ते तदात्मानः कीटः पेशस्कृतो यथा ॥३९॥

enaḥ pūrva-kṛtaṁ yat tad
rājānaḥ kṛṣṇa-vairiṇaḥ
jahus te 'nte tad-ātmānaḥ
kīṭaḥ peśaskṛto yathā

enaḥ—this sinful activity (of blaspheming the Supreme Lord); *pūrva-kṛtam*—executed in previous births; *yat*—which; *tat*—that; *rājānaḥ*—kings; *kṛṣṇa-vairiṇaḥ*—always acting as enemies of Kṛṣṇa; *jahuḥ*—gave up; *te*—all of them; *ante*—at the time of death; *tat-ātmānaḥ*—attaining the same spiritual body and form; *kīṭaḥ*—a worm; *peśaskṛtaḥ*—(captured by) a black drone; *yathā*—just like.

TRANSLATION

Not only Śiśupāla and Dantavakra but also many, many other kings who acted as enemies of Kṛṣṇa attained salvation at the time of death. Because they thought of the Lord, they received spiritual bodies and forms the same as His, just as worms captured by a black drone obtain the same type of body as the drone.

PURPORT

The mystery of yogic meditation is explained here. Real *yogīs* always meditate on the form of Viṣṇu within their hearts. Consequently, at the time of death they give up their bodies while thinking of the form of Viṣṇu and thus attain Viṣṇuloka, Vaikuṇṭhaloka, where they receive bodily features the same as those of the Lord. From the Sixth Canto we have already learned that when the Viṣṇudūtas came from Vaikuṇṭha to deliver Ajāmila, they looked exactly like Viṣṇu, with four hands and the same features as Viṣṇu. Therefore, we may conclude that if one practices thinking of Viṣṇu and is fully absorbed in thinking of Him at the time of death, one returns home, back to Godhead. Even enemies of Kṛṣṇa who thought of Kṛṣṇa in fear (*bhaya*), such as King Kaṁsa, received bodies in a spiritual identity similar to that of the Lord.

TEXT 40

यथा यथा भगवतो भक्त्या परमयाभिदा ।
नृपाश्चैद्यादयः सात्म्यं हरेस्तच्चिन्तया ययुः ॥४०॥

yathā yathā bhagavato
bhaktyā paramayābhidā
nṛpāś caidyādayaḥ sātmyaṁ
hares tac-cintayā yayuḥ

yathā yathā—just as; *bhagavataḥ*—of the Supreme Personality of Godhead; *bhaktyā*—by devotional service; *paramayā*—supreme; *abhidā*—incessantly thinking of such activities; *nṛpāḥ*—kings; *caidya-*

ādayaḥ—Śiśupāla, Dantavakra and others; *sātmyam*—the same form; *hareḥ*—of the Supreme Personality of Godhead; *tat-cintayā*—by constantly thinking of Him; *yayuḥ*—returned home, back to Godhead.

TRANSLATION

By devotional service, pure devotees who incessantly think of the Supreme Personality of Godhead receive bodies similar to His. This is known as sārūpya-mukti. Although Śiśupāla, Dantavakra and other kings thought of Kṛṣṇa as an enemy, they also achieved the same result.

PURPORT

In *Caitanya-caritāmṛta*, in connection with Lord Caitanya's instructions to Sanātana Gosvāmī, it is explained that a devotee should externally execute his routine devotional service in a regular way but should always inwardly think of the particular mellow in which he is attracted to the service of the Lord. This constant thought of the Lord makes the devotee eligible to return home, back to Godhead. As stated in *Bhagavad-gītā* (4.9), *tyaktvā dehaṁ punar janma naiti mām eti:* after giving up his body, a devotee does not again receive a material body, but goes back to Godhead and receives a spiritual body resembling those of the Lord's eternal associates whose activities he followed. However the devotee likes to serve the Lord, he may constantly think of the Lord's associates—the cowherd boys, the *gopīs*, the Lord's father and mother, His servants and the trees, land, animals, plants and water in the Lord's abode. Because of constantly thinking of these features, one acquires a transcendental position. Kings like Śiśupāla, Dantavakra, Kaṁsa, Pauṇḍraka, Narakāsura and Śālva were all similarly delivered. This is confirmed by Madhvācārya:

pauṇḍrake narake caiva
śālve kaṁse ca rukmiṇi
āviṣṭās tu harer bhaktās
tad-bhaktyā harim āpire

Pauṇḍraka, Narakāsura, Śālva and Kaṁsa were all inimical toward the Supreme Personality of Godhead, but because all these kings constantly thought of Him, they achieved the same liberation—*sārūpya-mukti.* The *jñāna-bhakta,* the devotee who follows the path of *jñāna,* also attains the same destination. If even the enemies of the Lord achieve salvation by constantly thinking about the Lord, what is to be said of pure devotees who always engage in the Lord's service and who think of nothing but the Lord in every activity?

TEXT 41

आख्यातं सर्वमेतत्त ते यन्मां त्वं परिपृष्टवान् ।
दमघोषसुतादीनां हरेः सात्म्यमपि द्विषाम् ॥४१॥

ākhyātaṁ sarvam etat te
yan māṁ tvaṁ paripṛṣṭavān
damaghoṣa-sutādīnāṁ
hareḥ sātmyam api dviṣām

ākhyātam—described; *sarvam*—everything; *etat*—this; *te*—unto you; *yat*—whatever; *mām*—unto me; *tvam*—you; *paripṛṣṭavān*—inquired; *damaghoṣa-suta-ādīnām*—of the son of Damaghoṣa (Śiśupāla) and others; *hareḥ*—of the Lord; *sātmyam*—equal bodily features; *api*—even; *dviṣām*—although they were inimical.

TRANSLATION

Everything you asked me about how Śiśupāla and others attained salvation although they were inimical has now been explained to you by me.

TEXT 42

एषा ब्रह्मण्यदेवस्य कृष्णस्य च महात्मनः ।
अवतारकथा पुण्या वधो यत्रादिदैत्ययोः ॥४२॥

eṣā brahmaṇya-devasya
kṛṣṇasya ca mahātmanaḥ
avatāra-kathā puṇyā
vadho yatrādi-daityayoḥ

eṣā—all this; *brahmaṇya-devasya*—of the Supreme Personality of Godhead, who is worshiped by all *brāhmaṇas; kṛṣṇasya*—of Kṛṣṇa, the original Supreme Personality of Godhead; *ca*—also; *mahā-ātmanaḥ*—the Supersoul; *avatāra-kathā*—narrations about His incarnations; *puṇyā*—pious, purifying; *vadhaḥ*—killing; *yatra*—wherein; *ādi*—in the beginning of the millennium; *daityayoḥ*—of the demons (Hiraṇyākṣa and Hiraṇyakaśipu).

TRANSLATION

In this narration about Kṛṣṇa, the Supreme Personality of Godhead, various expansions or incarnations of the Lord have been described, and the killing of the two demons Hiraṇyākṣa and Hiraṇyakaśipu has also been described.

PURPORT

Avatāras, or incarnations, are expansions of the Supreme Personality of Godhead—Kṛṣṇa, Govinda.

advaitam acyutam anādim ananta-rūpam
ādyaṁ purāṇa-puruṣaṁ nava-yauvanaṁ ca
vedeṣu durlabham adurlabham ātma-bhaktau
govindam ādi-puruṣaṁ tam ahaṁ bhajāmi

"I worship the Supreme Personality of Godhead, Govinda, who is the original person—nondual, infallible, and without beginning. Although He expands into unlimited forms, He is still the original, and although He is the oldest person, He always appears as a fresh youth. Such eternal, blissful and all-knowing forms of the Lord cannot be understood by the academic wisdom of the *Vedas*, but they are always manifest to pure, unalloyed devotees." (*Brahma-saṁhitā* 5.33) The *Brahma-saṁhitā* describes the *avatāras*. Indeed, all the *avatāras* are described in the authentic scriptures. No one can become an *avatāra*, or incarnation, although this has become fashionable in the age of Kali. The *avatāras* are described in the authentic scriptures (*śāstras*), and therefore before one risks accepting a pretender as an *avatāra*, one should refer to the *śāstras*. The *śāstras* say everywhere that Kṛṣṇa is the original Personality of Godhead and that He has innumerable *avatāras*, or incarnations. Elsewhere in the *Brahma-saṁhitā* it is said, *rāmādi-mūrtiṣu kalā-niyamena tiṣṭhan:* Rāma, Nṛsiṁha, Varāha and many others are consecutive expansions of the Supreme Personality of Godhead. After Kṛṣṇa comes Balarāma, after Balarāma is Saṅkarṣaṇa, then Aniruddha, Pradyumna, Nārāyaṇa and then the *puruṣa-avatāras*—Mahā-Viṣṇu, Garbhodakaśāyī Viṣṇu and Kṣīrodakaśāyī Viṣṇu. All of them are *avatāras.*

One must hear about the *avatāras.* Narrations about such *avatāras* are called *avatāra-kathā,* the narrations of Kṛṣṇa's expansions. Hearing and chanting these narrations is completely pious. *Śṛṇvatāṁ sva-kathāḥ kṛṣṇaḥ puṇya-śravaṇa-kīrtanaḥ.* One who hears and chants can become *puṇya,* purified of material contamination.

Whenever there are references to the *avatāras,* religious principles are established, and demons who are against Kṛṣṇa are killed. The Kṛṣṇa consciousness movement is spreading all over the world with two aims—to establish Kṛṣṇa as the Supreme Personality of Godhead and to kill all the pretenders who falsely present themselves as *avatāras.* The preachers of the Kṛṣṇa consciousness movement must carry this conviction very carefully within their hearts and kill the demons who in many tactful ways vilify the Supreme Personality of Godhead, Kṛṣṇa. If we take shelter of Nṛsiṁhadeva and Prahlāda Mahārāja, it will be easier to kill the demons who are against Kṛṣṇa and to thus reestablish Kṛṣṇa's supremacy. *Kṛṣṇas tu bhagavān svayam:* Kṛṣṇa is the Supreme Lord, the original Lord. Prahlāda Mahārāja is our *guru,* and Kṛṣṇa is our worshipable God. As advised by Śrī Caitanya Mahāprabhu, *guru-kṛṣṇa-prasāde pāya bhakti-latā-bīja.* If we can be successful in getting the mercy of Prahlāda Mahārāja and also that of Nṛsiṁhadeva, then our Kṛṣṇa consciousness movement will be extremely successful.

The demon Hiraṇyakaśipu had so many ways to try to become God himself, but although Prahlāda Mahārāja was chastised and threatened in many ways, he rigidly refused to accept his powerful demoniac father as God. Following in the footsteps of Prahlāda Mahārāja, we should reject all the rascals who pretend to be God. We must accept Kṛṣṇa and His incarnations, and no one else.

TEXTS 43–44

प्रह्रादस्यानुचरितं महाभागवतस्य च ।
भक्तिर्ज्ञानं विरक्तिश्च याथार्थ्यं चास्य वै हरेः ॥४३॥

सर्गस्थित्यप्ययेशस्य गुणकर्मानुवर्णनम् ।
परावरेषां स्थानानां कालेन व्यत्ययो महान् ॥४४॥

prahrādasyānucaritaṁ
mahā-bhāgavatasya ca
bhaktir jñānaṁ viraktiś ca
yāthārthyaṁ cāsya vai hareḥ

sarga-sthity-apyayeśasya
guṇa-karmānuvarṇanam
parāvareṣāṁ sthānānāṁ
kālena vyatyayo mahān

prahrādasya—of Prahlāda Mahārāja; *anucaritam*—characteristics (understood by reading or describing his activities); *mahā-bhāgavatasya*—of the great and exalted devotee; *ca*—also; *bhaktiḥ*—devotional service unto the Supreme Personality of Godhead; *jñānam*—complete knowledge of the Transcendence (Brahman, Paramātmā and Bhagavān); *viraktiḥ*—renunciation of material existence; *ca*—also; *yāthārthyam*—just to understand each of them perfectly; *ca*—and; *asya*—of this; *vai*—indeed; *hareḥ*—always in reference to the Supreme Personality of Godhead; *sarga*—of creation; *sthiti*—maintenance; *apyaya*—and annihilation; *īśasya*—of the master (the Supreme Personality of Godhead); *guṇa*—of the transcendental qualities and opulences; *karma*—and activities; *anuvarṇanam*—description within the disciplic succession;* *para-avareṣām*—of different types of living entities known as demigods and demons; *sthānānām*—of the various planets or places to live; *kālena*—in due course of time; *vyatyayaḥ*—the annihilation of everything; *mahān*—although very great.

TRANSLATION

This narration describes the characteristics of the great and exalted devotee Prahlāda Mahārāja, his staunch devotional service,

---

*The word *anu* means "after." Authorized persons do not create anything; rather, they follow the previous *ācāryas.*

his perfect knowledge, and his perfect detachment from material contamination. It also describes the Supreme Personality of Godhead as the cause of creation, maintenance and annihilation. Prahlāda Mahārāja, in his prayers, has described the transcendental qualities of the Lord and has also described how the various abodes of the demigods and demons, regardless of how materially opulent, are destroyed by the mere direction of the Lord.

PURPORT

Śrīmad-Bhāgavatam is filled with descriptions of the characteristics of various devotees, with reference to the service of the Lord. This Vedic literature is called *Bhāgavatam* because it deals with the Supreme Personality of Godhead and His devotee. By studying *Śrīmad-Bhāgavatam* under the direction of the bona fide spiritual master, one can perfectly understand the science of Kṛṣṇa, the nature of the material and spiritual worlds, and the aim of life. *Śrīmad-Bhāgavatam amalaṁ purāṇam. Śrīmad-Bhāgavatam* is the spotless Vedic literature, as we have discussed in the beginning of *Śrīmad-Bhāgavatam.* Therefore, simply by understanding *Śrīmad-Bhāgavatam,* one can understand the science of the activities of the devotees, the activities of the demons, the permanent abode and the temporary abode. Through *Śrīmad-Bhāgavatam,* everything is perfectly known.

TEXT 45

धर्मो भागवतानां च भगवान्येन गम्यते ।
आख्यानेऽस्मिन्समाम्नातमाध्यात्मिकमशेषतः॥४५॥

dharmo bhāgavatānāṁ ca
bhagavān yena gamyate
ākhyāne 'smin samāmnātam
ādhyātmikam aśeṣataḥ

dharmaḥ—religious principles; *bhāgavatānām*—of the devotees; *ca*—and; *bhagavān*—the Supreme Personality of Godhead; *yena*—by which; *gamyate*—one can understand; *ākhyāne*—in the narration;

asmin—this; *samāmnātam*—is perfectly described; *ādhyātmikam*—transcendence; *aśeṣataḥ*—without reservations.

TRANSLATION

The principles of religion by which one can actually understand the Supreme Personality of Godhead are called bhāgavata-dharma. In this narration, therefore, which deals with these principles, actual transcendence is properly described.

PURPORT

Through the principles of religion, one can understand the Supreme Personality of Godhead, Brahman (the impersonal feature of the Supreme Lord) and Paramātmā (the localized aspect of the Lord). When one is well conversant with all these principles, he becomes a devotee and performs *bhāgavata-dharma*. Prahlāda Mahārāja, the spiritual master in the line of disciplic succession, advised that this *bhāgavata-dharma* be instructed to students from the very beginning of their education (*kaumāra ācaret prājño dharmān bhāgavatān iha*). To understand the science of the Supreme Personality of Godhead is the real purpose of education. *Śravaṇaṁ kīrtanaṁ viṣṇoḥ.* One must simply hear about and describe Lord Viṣṇu and His various incarnations. This narration concerning Prahlāda Mahārāja and Lord Nṛsiṁhadeva, therefore, has properly described spiritual, transcendental subjects.

TEXT 46

य एतत् पुण्यमाख्यानं विष्णोर्वीर्योपबृंहितम् ।
कीर्तयेच्छ्रद्धया श्रुत्वा कर्मपाशैर्विमुच्यते ॥४६॥

ya etat puṇyam ākhyānaṁ
viṣṇor vīryopabṛṁhitam
kīrtayec chraddhayā śrutvā
karma-pāśair vimucyate

yaḥ—anyone who; *etat*—this; *puṇyam*—pious; *ākhyānam*—narration; *viṣṇoḥ*—of Lord Viṣṇu; *vīrya*—the supreme power;

upabṛṁhitam—in which is described; *kīrtayet*—chants or repeats; *śraddhayā*—with great faith; *śrutvā*—after properly hearing (from the right source); *karma-pāśaiḥ*—from the bondage of fruitive activities; *vimucyate*—becomes liberated.

TRANSLATION

One who hears and chants this narration about the omnipotence of the Supreme Personality of Godhead, Viṣṇu, is certainly liberated from material bondage without fail.

TEXT 47

एतद् य आदिपुरुषस्य मृगेन्द्रलीलां
दैत्येन्द्रयूथपवधं प्रयतः पठेत ।
दैत्यात्मजस्य च सतां प्रवरस्य पुण्यं
श्रुत्वानुभावमकुतोभयमेति लोकम् ॥४७॥

etad ya ādi-puruṣasya mṛgendra-līlāṁ
daityendra-yūtha-pa-vadhaṁ prayataḥ paṭheta
daityātmajasya ca satāṁ pravarasya puṇyaṁ
śrutvānubhāvam akuto-bhayam eti lokam

etat—this narration; *yaḥ*—anyone who; *ādi-puruṣasya*—of the original Personality of Godhead; *mṛga-indra-līlām*—pastimes as a lion and human being combined; *daitya-indra*—of the King of the demons; *yūtha-pa*—as strong as an elephant; *vadham*—the killing; *prayataḥ*—with great attention; *paṭheta*—reads; *daitya-ātma-jasya*—of Prahlāda Mahārāja, the son of the demon; *ca*—also; *satām*—among elevated devotees; *pravarasya*—the best; *puṇyam*—pious; *śrutvā*—hearing; *anubhāvam*—the activities; *akutaḥ-bhayam*—where there is no fear anywhere or at any time; *eti*—reaches; *lokam*—the spiritual world.

TRANSLATION

Prahlāda Mahārāja was the best among exalted devotees. Anyone who with great attention hears this narration concerning the activities of Prahlāda Mahārāja, the killing of Hiraṇyakaśipu, and the

activities of the Supreme Personality of Godhead, Nṛsiṁhadeva, surely reaches the spiritual world, where there is no anxiety.

Thus end the Bhaktivedanta purports of the Seventh Canto, Tenth Chapter, First Part, of the Śrīmad-Bhāgavatam, *entitled "Prahlāda, the Best Among Exalted Devotees."*

CONTINUED IN THE NEXT VOLUME

Appendixes

The Author

His Divine Grace A. C. Bhaktivedanta Swami Prabhupāda appeared in this world in 1896 in Calcutta, India. He first met his spiritual master, Śrīla Bhaktisiddhānta Sarasvatī Gosvāmī, in Calcutta in 1922. Bhaktisiddhānta Sarasvatī, a prominent devotional scholar and the founder of sixty-four Gauḍīya Maṭhas (Vedic institutes), liked this educated young man and convinced him to dedicate his life to teaching Vedic knowledge. Śrīla Prabhupāda became his student, and eleven years later (1933) at Allahabad he became his formally initiated disciple.

At their first meeting, in 1922, Śrīla Bhaktisiddhānta Sarasvatī Ṭhākura requested Śrīla Prabhupāda to broadcast Vedic knowledge through the English language. In the years that followed, Śrīla Prabhupāda wrote a commentary on the *Bhagavad-gītā*, assisted the Gauḍīya Maṭha in its work and, in 1944, without assistance, started an English fortnightly magazine, edited it, typed the manuscripts and checked the galley proofs. He even distributed the individual copies freely and struggled to maintain the publication. Once begun, the magazine never stopped; it is now being continued by his disciples in the West.

Recognizing Śrīla Prabhupāda's philosophical learning and devotion, the Gauḍīya Vaiṣṇava Society honored him in 1947 with the title "Bhaktivedanta." In 1950, at the age of fifty-four, Śrīla Prabhupāda retired from married life, and four years later he adopted the *vānaprastha* (retired) order to devote more time to his studies and writing. Śrīla Prabhupāda traveled to the holy city of Vṛndāvana, where he lived in very humble circumstances in the historic medieval temple of Rādhā-Dāmodara. There he engaged for several years in deep study and writing. He accepted the renounced order of life (*sannyāsa*) in 1959. At Rādhā-Dāmodara, Śrīla Prabhupāda began work on his life's masterpiece: a multivolume translation and commentary on the eighteen thousand verse *Śrīmad-Bhāgavatam* (*Bhāgavata Purāṇa*). He also wrote *Easy Journey to Other Planets*.

After publishing three volumes of *Bhāgavatam*, Śrīla Prabhupāda came to the United States, in 1965, to fulfill the mission of his spiritual master. Since that time, His Divine Grace has written over forty volumes of authoritative translations, commentaries and summary studies of the philosophical and religious classics of India.

In 1965, when he first arrived by freighter in New York City, Śrīla Prabhupāda was practically penniless. It was after almost a year of great difficulty that he established the International Society for Krishna Consciousness in July of 1966. Under his careful guidance, the Society has grown within a decade to a worldwide confederation of almost one hundred *āśramas*, schools, temples, institutes and farm communities.

In 1968, Śrīla Prabhupāda created New Vṛndāvana, an experimental Vedic community in the hills of West Virginia. Inspired by the success of New Vṛndāvana, now a thriving farm community of more than one thousand acres, his students have since founded several similar communities in the United States and abroad.

In 1972, His Divine Grace introduced the Vedic system of primary and secondary education in the West by founding the Gurukula school in Dallas, Texas. The school began with 3 children in 1972, and by the beginning of 1975 the enrollment had grown to 150.

Śrīla Prabhupāda has also inspired the construction of a large international center at Śrīdhāma Māyāpur in West Bengal, India, which is also the site for a planned Institute of Vedic Studies. A similar project is the magnificent Kṛṣṇa-Balarāma Temple and International Guest House in Vṛndāvana, India. These are centers where Westerners can live to gain firsthand experience of Vedic culture.

Śrīla Prabhupāda's most significant contribution, however, is his books. Highly respected by the academic community for their authoritativeness, depth and clarity, they are used as standard textbooks in numerous college courses. His writings have been translated into eleven languages. The Bhaktivedanta Book Trust, established in 1972 exclusively to publish the works of His Divine Grace, has thus become the world's largest publisher of books in the field of Indian religion and philosophy. Its latest project is the publishing of Śrīla Prabhupāda's most recent work: a seventeen-volume translation and commentary—completed by Śrīla Prabhupāda in only eighteen months—on the Bengali religious classic *Śrī Caitanya-caritāmṛta.*

In the past ten years, in spite of his advanced age, Śrīla Prabhupāda has circled the globe twelve times on lecture tours that have taken him to six continents. In spite of such a vigorous schedule, Śrīla Prabhupāda continues to write prolifically. His writings constitute a veritable library of Vedic philosophy, religion, literature and culture.

References

The purports of *Śrīmad-Bhāgavatam* are all confirmed by standard Vedic authorities. The following authentic scriptures are specifically cited in this volume.

Glossary

A

Ācārya—a spiritual master who teaches by example.
Anubhāva—the bodily symptoms of ecstatic love for Kṛṣṇa.
Ārati—a ceremony for greeting the Lord with offerings of food, lamps, fans, flowers and incense.
Arcanā—the devotional practice of Deity worship.
Artha—economic development.
Āśrama—a spiritual order of life.
Asuras—atheistic demons.
Ātmā—the self (the body, the mind, or the soul).
Avatāra—a descent of the Supreme Lord.

B

Bhagavad-gītā—the basic directions for spiritual life spoken by the Lord Himself.
Bhāgavata-dharma—religious principles enunciated by the Supreme Lord.
Bhakta—a devotee.
Bhakti—pure devotional service to Lord Kṛṣṇa.
Bhakti-yoga—linking with the Supreme Lord in ecstatic devotional service.
Bhāva—the preliminary stage of ecstatic love of God.
Brahmacarya—celibate student life; the first order of Vedic spiritual life.
Brahman—the Absolute Truth; especially the impersonal aspect of the Absolute.
Brāhmaṇa—a person in the mode of goodness; first Vedic social order.

D

Dharma—eternal occupational duty; religious principles.

E

Ekādaśī—a special fast day for increased remembrance of Kṛṣṇa, which comes on the eleventh day of both the waxing and waning moon.

G

Goloka (Kṛṣṇaloka)—the highest spiritual planet, containing Kṛṣṇa's personal abodes, Dvārakā, Mathurā and Vṛndāvana.

Gopīs—Kṛṣṇa's cowherd girl friends who are His most confidential servitors.

Gṛhamedhis—materialistic householders.

Gṛhastha—regulated householder life; the second order of Vedic spiritual life.

Guru—a spiritual master or superior person.

H

Hare Kṛṣṇa mantra—*See: Mahā-mantra*

J

Jīva-tattva—the living entities, who are small parts of the Lord.

Jñāna—theoretical knowledge.

Jñānī—one who cultivates knowledge by empirical speculation.

K

Kali-yuga (Age of Kali)—the present age, which is characterized by quarrel. It is last in the cycle of four, and began five thousand years ago.

Kāma—lust.

Karatālas—hand cymbals used in *kīrtana.*

Karma—fruitive action, for which there is always reaction, good or bad.

Karma-kāṇḍa—a section of the *Vedas* concerning elevation to the heavenly planets.

Karmī—one who is satisfied with working hard for flickering sense gratification.

Kīrtana—chanting the glories of the Supreme Lord.

Kṛṣṇaloka—*See:* Goloka

Kṣatriyas—a warrior or administrator; the second Vedic social order.

L

Līlā—pastimes.

Līla-śakti—the energy of Kṛṣṇa which helps to enact His pastimes.

M

Mahā-bhāgavata—a pure devotee of the Lord.

Mahājana—the Lord's authorized devotee who by his teachings and behavior establishes the true purpose of religious principles.

Mahā-mantra—the great chanting for deliverance:
Hare Kṛṣṇa, Hare Kṛṣṇa, Kṛṣṇa Kṛṣṇa, Hare Hare/ Hare Rāma, Hare Rāma, Rāma Rāma, Hare Hare.

Mantra—a sound vibration that can deliver the mind from illusion.

Mathurā—Lord Kṛṣṇa's abode, surrounding Vṛndāvana, where He took birth and later returned to after performing His Vṛndāvana pastimes.

Māyā—(mā—not; *yā*—this), illusion; forgetfulness of one's relationship with Kṛṣṇa.

Māyāvādīs—impersonal philosophers who say that the Lord cannot have a transcendental body.

Mṛdaṅga—a clay drum used for congregational chanting.

P

Paramahaṁsa—the topmost class of devotees.

Paramātmā—the Supersoul, an expansion of the Supreme Lord situated in every living entity's heart and in every atom.

Paramparā—the chain of spiritual masters in disciplic succession.

Prasāda—food spiritualized by being offered to the Lord.

R

Rākṣasas—man-eating demons.

Ṛṣi—a great sage.

S

Sac-cid-ānanda-vigraha—the Lord's transcendental form, which is eternal, full of knowledge and bliss.

Sāṅkhya—the analytical study of matter and spirit.

Saṅkīrtana—public chanting of the names of God, the approved *yoga* process for this age.

Sannyāsa—renounced life; the fourth order of Vedic spiritual life.

Śāstras—revealed scriptures.

Śrāddha—ritualistic ceremony of offering oblations to one's deceased ancestors to free them from possible hellish conditions in their next lives.

Śravaṇaṁ kīrtanaṁ viṣṇoḥ—the devotional processes of hearing and chanting about Lord Viṣṇu.

Śūdra—a laborer; the fourth of the Vedic social orders.

Svāmī—one who controls his mind and senses; title of one in the renounced order of life.

T

Tantras—Vedic literatures consisting mostly of dialogues between Lord Śiva and Durgā.

Tapasya—austerity; accepting some voluntary inconvenience for a higher purpose.

Tilaka—auspicious clay marks that sanctify a devotee's body as a temple of the Lord.

V

Vaikuṇṭha—the spiritual world, where there is no anxiety.

Vaiṣṇava—a devotee of Lord Viṣṇu, or Kṛṣṇa.

Vaiśyas—farmers and merchants; the third Vedic social order.

Vānaprastha—one who has retired from family life; the third order of Vedic spiritual life.

Varṇas—the four occupational divisions of society: the intellectual class, the administrative class, the mercantile and agricultural class, and the laborer class.

Varṇāśrama—the Vedic social system of four social and four spiritual orders.

Vedas—the original revealed scriptures, first spoken by the Lord Himself.

Viṣṇu, Lord—Kṛṣṇa's first expansion for the creation and maintenance of the material universes.

Viṣṇudūtas—the messengers of Lord Viṣṇu who come to take perfected devotees back to the spiritual world at the time of death.

Vṛndāvana—Kṛṣṇa's personal abode, where He fully manifests His quality of sweetness.

Vyāsadeva—Kṛṣṇa's incarnation, at the end of Dvāpara-yuga, for compiling the *Vedas*.

Y

Yajña—sacrifice, work done for the satisfaction of Lord Viṣṇu.

Yamarāja—the demigod in charge of punishing sinful human beings after death.

Yoga-nidrā—the mystic slumber of Lord Viṣṇu.

Yogī—a transcendentalist who, in one way or another, is striving for union with the Supreme.

Yugas—ages in the life of a universe, occurring in a repeated cycle of four.

Sanskrit Pronunciation Guide

Vowels

अ a आ ā इ i ई ī उ u ऊ ū ऋ ṛ ॠ ṝ
ऌ ḷ ए e ऐ ai ओ o औ au

ं ṁ *(anusvāra)* ः ḥ *(visarga)*

Consonants

Gutturals:	क ka	ख kha	ग ga	घ gha	ङ ṅa
Palatals:	च ca	छ cha	ज ja	झ jha	ञ ña
Cerebrals:	ट ṭa	ठ ṭha	ड ḍa	ढ ḍha	ण ṇa
Dentals:	त ta	थ tha	द da	ध dha	न na
Labials:	प pa	फ pha	ब ba	भ bha	म ma
Semivowels:	य ya	र ra	ल la	व va	
Sibilants:	श śa	ष ṣa	स sa		
Aspirate:	ह ha	ऽ ' *(avagraha)* – the apostrophe			

The vowels above should be pronounced as follows:

a – like the *a* in org*a*n or the *u* in b*u*t.
ā – like the *a* in f*a*r but held twice as long as short *a*.
i – like the *i* in p*i*n.
ī – like the *i* in p*i*que but held twice as long as short *i*.
u – like the *u* in p*u*sh.
ū – like the *u* in r*u*le but held twice as long as short *u*.

ṛ – like the *ri* in *ri*m.
ṝ – like *ree* in *ree*d.
ḷ – like *l* followed by *ṛ* (*lṛ*).
e – like the *e* in th*e*y.
ai – like the *ai* in *ai*sle.
o – like the *o* in g*o*.
au – like the *ow* in h*ow*.
ṁ (*anusvāra*) – a resonant nasal like the *n* in the French word *bon*.
ḥ (*visarga*) – a final *h*-sound: *aḥ* is pronounced like *aha*; *iḥ* like *ihi*.

The consonants are pronounced as follows:

k – as in *k*ite
kh – as in Ec*kh*art
g – as in *g*ive
gh – as in di*g-h*ard
ṅ – as in si*ng*
c – as in *ch*air
ch – as in staun*ch-h*eart
j – as in *j*oy
jh – as in he*dgeh*og
ñ – as in ca*ny*on
ṭ – as in *t*ub
ṭh – as in ligh*t-h*eart
ḍ – as in *d*ove
ḍha – as in re*d-h*ot
ṇ – as r*na* (prepare to say the *r* and say *na*).

Cerebrals are pronounced with tongue to roof of mouth, but the following dentals are pronounced with tongue against teeth:

t – as in *t*ub but with tongue against teeth.
th – as in ligh*t-h*eart but with tongue against teeth.
d – as in *d*ove but with tongue against teeth.
dh – as in re*d-h*ot but with tongue against teeth.
n – as in *n*ut but with tongue between teeth.

p – as in *p*ine
ph – as in u*ph*ill (not *f*)
b – as in *b*ird
bh – as in ru*b-h*ard
m – as in *m*other
y – as in *y*es
r – as in *r*un
l – as in *l*ight
v – as in *v*ine
ś (palatal) – as in the *s* in the German word *sprechen*
ṣ (cerebral) – as the *sh* in *sh*ine
s – as in *s*un
h – as in *h*ome

There is no strong accentuation of syllables in Sanskrit, only a flowing of short and long (twice as long as the short) syllables.

Index of Sanskrit Verses

This index constitutes a complete listing of the first and third lines of each of the Sanskirt poetry verses and the first line of each Sanskrit prose verse of this volume of *Śrīmad-Bhāgavatam*, arranged in English alphabetical order. In the first column the Sanskrit transliteration is given, and in the second and third columns respectively the chapter-verse references and page number for each verse are to be found.

A

B

General Index

Numerals in boldface type indicate references to translations of the verses of *Śrīmad-Bhāgavatam.*

A

B

D

E

F

H

I

R

T